Plate 1 "The Resurrection" (1803–10?)

Blake's inscription in the bottom margin reads: "Christ died & was buried & arose again according to the Scriptures" (1 Corinthians 15:4).

Courtesy Fogg Art Museum, Harvard University, Bequest of Grenville L. Winthrop

The Imagination
of the
Resurrection:

The Poetic Continuity
of a Religious Motif
in Donne, Blake, and Yeats

Kathryn R. Kremen

Lewisburg
BUCKNELL UNIVERSITY PRESS

Associated University Presses, Inc.
Cranbury, New Jersey 08512

Library of Congress Cataloging in Publication Data

Kremen, Kathryn R   1943–
    The imagination of the resurrection.

    Bibliography: p.
    1. Jesus Christ in fiction, drama, poetry, etc. 2. Blake, William,
1757–1827. 3. Donne, John, 1573–1631. 4. Yeats, William Butler,
1865–1939.
I. Title.
PR508.J4K7   821′.0093   71-168812
ISBN 0-8387-7940-9

Printed in the United States of America

For my teachers,
most of all B.

Contents

7

Contents

Illustrations

13

Preface

My interest in the religious poems of Donne, Blake, and Yeats, especially of Blake, originates in an intuitive concern with the "perfect unity" of redemption. The subject involves, sometimes indirectly, a question about "continuity," particularly about the continuity of a religious reality with, and its divorce from, its poetic expression. While the resurrection motif begins as a religious doctrine—the revelation of God's mercy and the redemption of humanity—it becomes a possession of the romantic poets, a recreation of the imagination.

A word should be said about two assumptions underlying my choice of poets here. Within the tradition of English poetry, I have chosen the three great religious writers for whom, in differing ways, the resurrection is central. The inclusion of other authors (such as Milton) would add to, but not fundamentally change, my observations either about the relation between a religious doctrine and its poetic incorporation or about the process of secularization, when continuity becomes "conversion" from a realm which is grounded in divine authority and purpose to one which is determined solely by human means.

Besides the shared religious theme, there is a direct line of connectedness between Donne and Blake through their Protestant affiliation, and between Blake and Yeats through the latter's poetic affiliation with Blake as a spiritual authority.

First outlining the development and "meaning" of the resurrection, this study next shows 1) how Donne incorporates this doctrine in essentially traditional terms, 2) how Blake appropriates the motif as he expands it, by imaginatively defining it, while at the same time preserving its original redemptive essence, and 3) how Yeats's cyclic system secularizes, by subjectification, the desire for the resurrection, so that it is no longer attainable.

One of the book's arguments is that the sacred is not convertible into the secular. Accordingly, Yeats may appear at more of a loss in these religious matters than I think he is in terms of his own "self-begotten" aesthetic humanism. That Yeats's desire for "unity of being," for the perfectly proportioned human body and soul, is central to his work justifies including him with the two earlier poets, who hold this hope from a significantly different orientation. In discussing Yeats's work, I have consciously emphasized fundamental religious concerns, for this viewpoint clarifies the ways in which Yeats does not share the assumptions and implications of such belief, and some of the consequences of their disappearance. Further, in Yeats we can see the limits beyond which a traditional, Christian creed cannot continue without losing its previous theological meaning and sacramental authenticity.

Specifically, the ontological authority of religious language and symbolism directly derives from the revelation of a transcendent God. Without this prior certainty about the divine source of religious speech and without traditionally shared acceptance of its public forms, the poetic incorporation of a religious subject is not legitimated. When absolute theological authority disappears, the truth and reality of its symbolism are consequently lost. And when a religious symbol thus dies, its sacramental validity cannot be replaced by a secular one. A secular system cannot, with only its own resources, "reconvert" itself to a religious one, in which salvation is possible.

The revelation, then, of a transcendent God is central to humanity's "perfect unity" and eternal redemption. When the chief priests ask Jesus "By what authority doest thou these things? and who gave thee this authority?" he replies with a like question: "The baptism of John, whence was it? from heaven, or of men?" These are the two basic choices for the source, from God or from man, of our vision of reality.

> And they reasoned with themselves, saying, If we shall say from heaven; he will say unto us, Why did ye not then believe him? But if we shall say, Of men; we fear the people; for all hold John as a prophet. And they answered Jesus and said, We cannot tell. And he said unto them, neither tell I you by what authority I do these things
>
> (Matt. 21:23–27).

The divine origin and immortal power of Jesus' redemptive authority are definitively revealed in his Easter resurrection.

I am happy to acknowledge here my gratitude to the following persons who have kindly given of their intellectual labors. First,

I wish to thank Allen Grossman for his continuous generosity as a teacher, who knows the "burning fire of thought" and "spiritual gifts" of humanity, "in friendship & love," I honour. I am also grateful to Aileen Ward for her scrupulous reading of and comments on the Blake material; to Nathan Glatzer for looking over the Judaic material; to David Wiesen for his helping hand with Augustine; to James Preus for his good-willed guidance with Church history and the Protestant Reformation; to David Erdman for his precision with various particulars; and to Northrop Frye for his Blakean readings and writings; and to Sir Geoffrey Keynes for his editorial beneficence.

For the informative delight of looking at Blake's original manuscripts and pictures, I thank the Houghton Library and the Fogg Art Museum of Harvard University; the Museum of Fine Arts, Boston; the Alverthorpe Gallery; the Metropolitan Museum of Art; the Pierpont Morgan Library; and the Rare Book Division of the New York Public Library.

For the benefits of his earnest interest in the whole book and of his critical persuasions on the Yeats chapter, I thank Dr. James Carens, Editor of Bucknell University Press. And for her sympathetic copyediting of a voluminous manuscript, I thank Mrs. Mathilde Finch, Associate Editor, Associated University Presses.

K.R.K.

11 April 1971
Cambridge, Mass.

Acknowledgments

For permission to reproduce the illustrations in this book, the author is grateful to the following: to the Trustees of the British Museum for "The Ascension of the Dead"; to the Syndics of the Fitzwilliam Museum for permission to reproduce "The Third Temptation: The Tempter Foiled"; to the Fogg Art Museum, Harvard University, Bequest of Grenville L. Winthrop for "Christ Blessing" and "The Resurrection"; to the Harvard College Library for *Jerusalem* 76(D) and 99(D); to the Museum of Fine Arts, Boston, for "Ezekiel's Vision"; to the National Gallery of Art, Washington, D.C., Rosenwald Collection, for "The Dance of Albion, or Glad Day," "Queen Katherine's [Vision, or] Dream," "The Reunion of the Soul and the Body," and "A Vision of the Last Judgment"; to the Rare Book Division, The New York Public Library, Astor, Lenox, and Tilden Foundations for *Milton* 13(C) and 43(C); to the Pierpont Morgan Library for "The Sun at his Eastern Gate"; to The Tate Gallery, London, for "The Agony in the Garden," "Christ Blessing the Little Children," "Elohim Creating Adam," "The Four and Twenty Elders Casting their Crowns before the Divine Throne," and "The River of Life"; and to the Yale University Art Gallery for "Christ Appearing to the Apostles After the Resurrection."

For permission to quote from copyrighted material, the author wishes to thank the following:
A. and C. Black Ltd., for permission to quote from Archdeacon R. H. Charles, *Eschatology*, 1913.
The William Blake Trust, for permission to quote from William Blake, *Songs of Innocence and of Experience* (facsimile copy Z), edited by Geoffrey Keynes, 1967. Also for permission

to quote from Joseph Wicksteed, *William Blake's Jerusalem: A Commentary,* 1954.

The Clarendon Press, for permission to quote from William Blake, *Vala, or the Four Zoas,* edited by G. E. Bentley, Jr., 1963; from John Donne, *The Divine Poems,* edited by Helen Gardner, 1952; and from John Donne, *The Elegies, and The Songs and Sonnets,* edited by Helen Gardner, 1965.

Doubleday and Company, for permission to quote from William Blake, *The Poetry and Prose of William Blake,* edited by Harold Bloom and David Erdman, 1965. Also for permission to quote from St. Thomas Aquinas, *On the Truth of the Catholic Faith, Summa Contra Gentiles, Book Four: Salvation,* translated by Charles O'Neil, 1957.

Granada Publishing Limited, for permission to quote from *The Letters of W. B. Yeats,* edited by Michael Yeats and Alan Wade, 1954 (first published by Rupert Hart-Davis Ltd.).

The Johns Hopkins Press, for permission to quote from John Donne, *The Anniversaries,* edited by Frank Manley, 1963.

The Macmillan Company, for permission to quote from William Butler Yeats, *The Collected Plays of W. B. Yeats,* 1963; from William Butler Yeats, *Essays and Introductions,* 1961; from William Butler Yeats, *Explorations,* 1962; from William Butler Yeats, *Mythologies,* 1959; from William Butler Yeats, *The Variorum Edition of the Poems of W. B. Yeats,* edited by Peter Allt and Russell Alspach (second printing), 1965; and from William Butler Yeats, *A Vision* (1938 edition), 1961.

Oxford University Press, for permission to quote from William Blake, *Blake, Complete Writings with Variant Readings,* edited by Geoffrey Keynes, 1966; from *Documents of the Christian Church,* edited by Henry Bettenson, 1967; from Archdeacon R. H. Charles, *Lectures on the Apocalypse,* 1922 (for the British Academy).

Random House, for permission to quote from St. Augustine, *The City of God,* translated by Marcus Dods, 1950.

Schocken Books Inc., for permission to quote from Archdeacon R. H. Charles, *Eschatology,* 1913; reprinted 1963.

Charles Scribner's Sons, for permission to quote from Archdeacon R. H. Charles, *Critical and Exegetical Commentary on the Revelation of St. John.* 2 vols., 1920.

Society for Promoting Christian Knowledge, for permission to quote from Tertullian, *Treatise on the Resurrection* (*De Resurrectione Carnis*), edited and translated by Ernest Evans, 1960.

University of California Press, for permission to quote from John Donne, *Sermons,* edited by George Potter and Evelyn Simpson, 10 vols., 1953-62; originally published by the University of California Press; reprinted by permission of The Regents of the University of California.

The Westminster Press, for permission to quote from John Calvin, *Institutes of the Christian Religion,* vol. 2, translated by John Allen, edited by Benjamin B. Warfield. Published 1936 by the Presbyterian Board of Christian Education, Philadelphia, U.S.A.; and from John Calvin, *Theological Treatises,* vol. 22, The Library of Christian Classics, translated with introductions and notes by The Reverend J. K. S. Reid. Published in the United States by The Westminster Press, 1954. Used by permission. From *A Compend of Luther's Theology,* edited by Hugh Thomson Kerr, Jr. Copyright, 1953, by The Westminster Press. Used by permission.

M. B. Yeats and The Macmillan Company, for permission to quote from William Butler Yeats, *The Collected Plays of W. B. Yeats,* 1963; from William Butler Yeats, *Essays and Introductions,* 1961; from William Butler Yeats, *Explorations,* 1962; from William Butler Yeats, *Mythologies,* 1959; from William Butler Yeats, *The Variorum Edition of the Poems of W. B. Yeats,* edited by Peter Allt and Russell Alspach, (second printing), 1965; and from William Butler Yeats, *A Vision* (1938 edition), 1961.

Introduction:
In the Beginning

This study of the resurrection motif first outlines its Biblical origins and development and explores what constitutes the religious doctrine of the resurrection. While I have tried to be complete in locating all pertinent examples, my text emphasizes those instances which are both representative and recurrent.

An overview shows the central features of the resurrection. Essentially, the resurrection represents an image of complete and perfect unity—of man and God, of the real and the ideal, of body and soul, of the individual and the collective, of present and future, of time and eternity, of subject and object, of man's beginning and end. As man and God are hypostatically united in the incarnated Jesus, so all saved men will be joined with the Godhead in the heavenly "great marriage." In new Jerusalem all desire is fulfilled in simultaneous blessing and happiness. The mortal body and soul are reunited and transfigured in their spiritual body, as Paul defines it in 1 Corinthians: "It is sown a natural body; it is raised a spiritual body" (15:44). In the communion of saints individual identity is preserved and yet is also coterminous with the communal identity. As implied in the fourth Gospel and as developed in Protestant soteriology, the first resurrection of the spirit with Jesus Christ in the present time assures the last resurrection of body and soul in the future end of time. This transfiguration of human time (*chronos*) into divine time (*kairos*) prefigures eternity's subsuming all time in heaven. The resurrection includes a union of subject and object, of that which knows and that which is known: "For it ["the sight of God"] is both the object, and the wit," as Donne writes in the "Second Anniversary." In the final beatific vision, man shall see all fully and will know himself, others, and God, as he is now fully known by God: the kingdom of God "will bring to light the hidden things of darkness, and will make manifest the counsels of the hearts" (1 Cor. 4:5). Finally, the resurrection unites man's beginning and his end.

This harmony can be understood both in theological and psychological terms: as man was first made by God, so he will return to Him in the end; and as in some prior state of himself, man was holy and whole (without "sin" and without conflict), so in the end he will return to this unity of the self. In the beginning, according to Blake, are the Four Zoas:

> Four Mighty Ones are in every Man;
>   a Perfect Unity
> Cannot Exist but from the Universal
>   Brotherhood of Eden,
> The Universal Man, to Whom be Glory Evermore. . . .
> [Sing] His fall into Division and
>   his Resurrection to Unity. . . .

And in the end in *Jerusalem* "every Man stood Fourfold; each Four Faces had . . . revealing the lineaments of Man,/ Driving outward the Body of Death in an Eternal Death & Resurrection . . . rejoicing in Unity."

These unions comprise the resurrection's "meaning." I now ask "What does it mean to believe in the resurrection?"; that is, "What does it mean to believe?" An answer involves a consideration of the relation between belief and what is believed in. This affirmation ("I believe in. . . .") is the form repeated in the creeds, and it is the grammar of religious faith. In Hebrews Paul defines this phenomenon: "Now faith is the substance of things hoped for, the evidence [or, conviction] of things not seen" (11:1). To believe in, to have faith in the resurrection, then, is to hope for the resurrection; *"et expecto resurrectionem mortuorum et vitam venturi saeculi,"* as celebrated (and sung) in the Mass.

What is the origin of this hoped-for assurance? We can observe, first, that the origin and root meaning of "believe" is "to hold dear" and, second, that both "belief" and "love" come from the same Indo-germanic root, *leubh*. We believe in that which we love. The content of this belief may be expressed as that which is "wanted," both in the sense of "desired" and "lacked." To say with the creeds "I believe in the resurrection is to express a desire and hope for the eternal and complete realization of perfect unity, as Jesus prays: "And the glory which thou [God] gavest me I have given them, that they may be one, even as we are one: I in them, and thou in me, that they may be made perfect in one" (John 17:22-23).

Two possible interpretations of belief in the resurrection are, I think, alternate ways of locating its origin—either as the revelation of a merciful God or as the creation of man's mind. As a revelation of divinity, John's apocalyptic vision symbolizes the Word's subsuming and transforming the world. From a theological viewpoint, the Word is Christ, the only incarnation of the divine *Logos;* from an aesthetic viewpoint, the word is literature, an expression of man's mind.

For Blake, and for the author, the Word is Jesus-the- imagination, "the Divine Humanity." Uniting man and God, the imagination is the "Poetic Genius, which is the Lord" and from which both art and religion arise: "The Jewish & Christian Testaments are An original derivation from the Poetic Genius. . . . So all Religions . . . have one source. The true Man is the source, he being the Poetic Genius." What is finally re-created, revealed, and realized is the human image divine; the eternal body and spirit of this true and real resurrected man ever expand "in the Bosom of God, the Human Imagination."

"What is now proved was once only imagin'd," and "the Hebrew Bible and Gospel of Jesus are . . . Eternal Vision or Imagination of All that Exists," "Really & Unchangeably." Likewise, I believe that art and religion have the same source— the eternal imagination, which, as Jesus Christ, mysteriously unites man and God; the human image (or, imagination) divine manifests itself in poetry and theology which share the desire for and belief in the resurrection to complete and perfect unity: "I know of no other Christianity and of no other Gospel than the Divine Arts of Imagination, Imagination, the real & Eternal World . . . in which we shall live in our Eternal or Imaginative Bodies. . . ."

"Everything possible to be believ'd is an image of truth," said Blake. This book will study 1) the continuity of the resurrection as it is dogmatized in the collective language of theology and 2) its conversion as it is secularized in the individual language of modern poetry. When conventional religion loses its acceptance by the poet, as in the case of Yeats, traditional eschatology reappears as privately conceived versions of last things. This poetic appropriation presumes that, nonetheless, the same belief and desire—the same truth of human expectations—informs the mind. As Blake maintains: "We do not want either Greek or Roman Models if we are but just and true to our own [Human] Imaginations, those Worlds of Eternity in which we shall live for ever in Jesus our Lord" and "which is the Divine Vision & Fruition."

The Imagination
of the
Resurrection

"What is the Divine Spirit? is the Holy Ghost any other than an Intellectual Fountain? . . . What are the Treasures of Heaven. . . ? What are all the gifts of the Gospel: are they not all Mental Gifts? . . . . Let every Christian, as much as in him lies, engage himself openly & publically before all the world in some Mental pursuit for the Building up of Jerusalem." William Blake, *Jerusalem*, Plate 77.

1

The Origins and Development
of the Resurrection Doctrine

Old Testament Eschatology

Resurrection is the rising from the dead to life. For Christians, Jesus Christ's Easter resurrection provides the definitive pattern and efficient cause of the general resurrection of all men: the saved are resurrected in the reunited body and soul to new Jerusalem in heaven. The resurrection is central to Christian eschatology because it reveals the mystery of creation and redemption.[1] Before considering the Christian doctrine of the resurrection, we will begin with its development in the Old Testament and inter-testamental Apocrypha and Pseudepigrapha. I will emphasize those characteristic elements and examples which recurringly constitute the resurrection motif.

In Old Testament eschatology the resurrection first appears as the hope for individual immortality—in Jeremiah 31:31–34, Ezekiel 18:4-9, Job, and Psalms 49 and 78. Of these examples, Job is the *locus classicus* in the Old Testament of the individual's blessed preservation after death. Job asks "If a man die, shall he live again?" (14:14). His answer to himself appears to affirm a resurrection of the body:

> For I know that my redeemer liveth, and that he shall stand at the latter day upon the earth: And though after my skin worms destroy this body, yet in my flesh shall I see God: Whom I shall see for myself, and mine eyes shall behold, and not another (19:25–27).

In spite of the textual problem[2] (primarily in the literal meaning of "redeemer"), this passage conventionally serves as the chief

Old Testament example of the individual's bodily resurrection.

The first basic component of the resurrection motif is the righteous individual's immortality. To this is added the prophetic concept of the Messianic kingdom, the other basic component. In Old Testament eschatology this communal form eventually subsumes its initial individual prototype. Old Testament eschatology of the nation prophesies future national blessedness as a regenerated community which fulfills the divine will; this reformed and ideal society of eternal duration on earth is known as the Messianic kingdom, though the emphasis belongs on the concept of a theocratic kingdom rather than on the Messiah (in contrast to Christian doctrine). By the first century B.C., however, the hope of a resurrection again divides into its original components before their final reunion in Christianity. Because the common good of Israel as God's chosen people is of first importance in Old Testament belief,

> the Messianic kingdom was a more fundamental article of their faith than that of a blessed future life of the individual. Hence when these doctrines were fused together, the doctrine of the resurrection, which was the direct outcome of their fusion, soon displaced that of the individual immortality of the righteous. . . . Thus the resurrection, . . . conceived in its essence, marks the entrance of the individual after death into the divine life of the community, the synthesis of the individual and the common good.[3]

Before the exile (586 B.C.) first Isaiah (1-40) is the only prophet to foretell this Messianic kingdom. During the exile, expectation of the Messianic kingdom predominates,[4] while after the exile, eschatologies of the nation and the individual become more interdependent because the destruction of the state of Israel leads to joining the future of the individual with that of the whole nation. Second Isaiah (40-55) elaborates this prophecy of rebuilding Jerusalem.

In Isaiah 45–66 first appears the announcement of a new heaven and new earth, in which the Messianic Jerusalem is born, and this concept recurs in Jubilees 1:29; 4:26; and 23:26–28; in 2 Peter 3:13; and in Revelation 21:1:

> For, behold, I [God] create new heaven and a new earth: and the former shall not be remembered, nor come into mind. But be ye glad and rejoice for ever in that which I create: for, behold, I create Jerusalem a-rejoicing, and her people a joy. And I shall rejoice in Jerusalem, and joy in my people: and the voice of weeping shall be heard no more in her, nor the voice of crying (65:17–19).

While this passage prefigures John's final apocalyptic vision (Rev. 21:1-4), it is more accurate to interpret Isaiah 65 as a prophecy of earthly reformation, rather than as an apocalyptic complete destruction and transformation. Accordingly, the "new heavens and new earth" which God creates should be interpreted as a renewed heaven and earth. There is still natural generation, men still build and inhabit houses and plant vineyards; though death still exists, "mine elect shall long enjoy the work of their hands" (65:22), and the life of the righteous is full. In Isaiah 66 the prophet speaks of the genesis of this earthly Jerusalem and further distinguishes it from the heavenly new Jerusalem of Revelation. John's metaphor suggests instantaneous and final consummation—"And I saw the holy city, new Jerusalem, coming down out of heaven from God, prepared as a bride adorned for her husband"—whereas Isaiah's metaphor first suggests the prolonged labour of natural birth: "Shall the earth be made to bring forth in one day? Shall a nation be born at once?" And after this birth of the blessed earthly Jerusalem, the prophet continues the maternal metaphor in which the righteous are lovingly sustained: "As one whom his mother comforts, so I will comfort you; and ye shall be comforted in Jerusalem" (66:8 and 13).

The last two chapters of Isaiah describe the unity of the blessed individual and community:

> For as the new heavens and the new earth, which I will make, shall remain before me, saith the Lord, so shall your seed and your name remain. And it shall come to pass that from one new moon to another, shall all flesh come to worship before me, saith the Lord (66:22–23).

The final chapters of Isaiah thus begin the synthesis of the eschatology of the righteous individual with that of the whole nation. The future life of the righteous is not alone as an individual, but among the community of a new-born and blessed Jerusalem.

During the exile (586 B.C.) Old Testament eschatology emphasizes Israel's restoration to Jerusalem and the advent of the Messianic kingdom. This national renewal depends on individual ethical reformation, and this mutual relation between the fate of the state and of the individual constitutes the characteristic teaching of Old Testament prophecy. Considering the immediate destiny of Israel as a nation on earth, Old Testament prophecy deals minimally with life after death and primarily with moral reformation in this life.

However, another element of Old Testament eschatology developed when the Jews were almost constantly oppressed, between 200 and 100 B.C.: the prediction of the apocalypse. This addition became an essential part of intertestamental and New Testament expectations of the resurrection.

Whereas the prophetic speaker is concerned with ameliorating existing moral and social ills and emphasizes the necessity of man's acting positively to effect this improvement, the apocalyptic speaker is primarily concerned with an imminent and catastrophic end to this world and a future blessed after-life in a newly created heavenly city. While the prophetic and apocalyptic speakers are similar in their finally expecting a blessed life, wherein God's covenant with man is renewed, they differ, initially, in the location, in time, space, and human accessibility, of this desired end.[5]

In contrast to the prophetic possibility of rectifying one's moral state and returning to God, the apocalyptic message ignores this imperative. The apocalyptic speaker predicts an imminent and irreversible end, since creation has grown old and degenerate. Because the apocalyptic ignores the significance of individual and communal struggle toward paths of righteousness and believes that the end of all history is "at hand," it is ahistorical.

This basic contrast between the prophetic cry "It is never too late" and the apocalyptic shudder "The end has come" affects the kind and scope of predictions made by the two speakers. Assuming that it is no longer possible to improve (morally and socially), and that consequently the end of this world is upon us, the apocalyptic speaker envisions the creation of a new earth and new heaven. Related to, if not arising out of, extreme social discontent and viewed as a promise of divine compensation for present affliction,[6] apocalyptic predictions exaggerate both penultimate horrors and the glorious world they shall end in. While the prophetic speaker assumes an individual moral and social responsibility for the community which has turned away from God and his covenant, the apocalyptic speaker preempts the possibility of effective moral or social improvement and describes the imminent end. Because the two voices are speaking with radically different attitudes toward world history and toward the individual in relation to history, their visions and styles differ accordingly. The apocalyptic speaks of an imagined situation in which, as later in Blake, mind subsumes time and history, i.e., in which word subsumes world.

In 168 B.C. Judaism was declared illegal by Antiochus IV (Epiphanes), and between 168 and 164 B.C. the political and religious oppression of the Jews was at its height. Prophetic renewal of the nation was now conceived of as no longer possible.[7] Accordingly, Daniel (168–165 B.C.) presents an apocalyptic vision of the destruction of the present evil kingdoms and a glorious future Messianic kingdom with no successors:

> But the judgment shall sit, and they shall take away his dominion [that of the wicked king], to consume and destroy it unto the end. And the kingdom and dominion, and the greatness of the kingdom under the whole heaven, shall be given to the people of the saints of the most High, whose kingdom is an everlasting kingdom and all dominions shall serve and obey him (7 : 25–26).

In contrast to the prophetic speaker, the apocalyptic deals with the totality of world history and portrays the Messianic kingdom of the righteous at the end of time and not in the immediate future on earth, as one finds in Jeremiah, Ezekiel, and Isaiah.[8]

Daniel's last vision ends with a resurrection of an indeterminate portion of Israel, and this version—of partial resurrection of both the good and evil—is here first clearly taught:[9]

> And many of them that sleep in the dust of the earth shall awake, some to everlasting life, and some to shame and everlasting contempt. And they that be wise shall shine as the brightness of the firmament; and they that turn many to righteousness as the stars for ever and ever (12 : 2–3).

Although this passage speaks of a resurrection and judgment of some of the dead and, for the first time, both righteous and wicked, it is an incomplete or abbreviated presentation of the concept.

Thus far, the development of Old Testament eschatologies of the individual and of the nation have been outlined. Whereas before the exile the future life of the individual and the nation were separate, from 586 B.C. on they mutually influence each other:

> This mutual interaction, however, does not lead to any true synthesis till the close of the third century or the early decades of the second, when they are both seen to be the two complementary sides of a religious system, that subsumes and does justice to the essential claims of both. Thus, when the doctrine of the blessed immortality of the faithful is connected with that of the coming Messianic kingdom, *the separate eschatologies of the individual and of the nation issue finally in their*

synthesis: the righteous individual, no less than the righteous nation, will participate in the Messianic kingdom, for the righteous dead of Israel will rise to share therein.[10]

As discussed in Jeremiah, Ezekiel, and Isaiah, the Messianic kingdom is morally contingent upon prophetic regeneration of the soul to righteousness and is thus an individual and communal return to God, through the restored covenant, on earth. In addition, the passages (Job 19:25-27, Isaiah 26:1-19, and Daniel 12:2-3) which speak of the rising again of the dead and the restoration of the righteous to God and to the reformed community constitute the Old Testament conception of the resurrection.

Intertestamental Eschatologies

In intertestamental eschatologies, expectations of the resurrection proliferate,[11] with two major effects: 1) preserving the characteristic Old Testament ethical content, individual desirability, and communal necessity of the event, while 2) varying the forms of the resurrection. They are at last gathered together in Paul's teaching in 1 Corinthians.

In the books of the Apocrypha and Pseudepigrapha of the Old Testament[12] written in the second century B.C. there are five versions of the resurrection: 1) in the bodies and souls of some righteous and some wicked Israelites to the eternal Messianic kingdom on earth (as in Daniel 12 and Testaments of the Twelve Patriarchs); 2) in the bodies and souls of all the righteous and some wicked to the eternal Messianic kingdom on earth (1 Enoch 6-36 and Testaments of the Twelve Patriarchs); 3) in the body of only and all righteous Israelites to the earthly Messianic kingdom (2 Maccabees 7:11, 22-29, and 33-38; 14:15 and 46); 4) in the souls only of the righteous to blessed immortality (Book of Jubilees 23:30-31); and 5) in the bodies of all righteous Israelites and none of the wicked; their earthly bodies are subsequently changed into "spiritual" bodies, which live in a spiritual kingdom (1 Enoch 83-90:20, 28-30, and 38-39).

As the present historical situation worsens, the hope for future resurrection becomes more prevalent and varied. This compensatory relation—that present oppression leads to projecting or imagining recompense in the future—recurs as a distinctive feature of eschatological predictions.

Eschatology of the second century B.C. continues to hold that the righteous individual and the righteous nation shall be joined in the eternal Messianic kingdom. As the above fifth version of the resurrection suggests, there is also an incipient change in conception whereby the resurrection involves not only the reanimation of the righteous individual and nation but also their subsequent transformation from the physical to the "spiritual" body and heavenly kingdom. This separation of the earthly, no matter how praiseworthy, from the heavenly reflects the growing dualism of the second century B.C.; in the following century, an eternal Messianic kingdom on earth becomes inconceivable. Accordingly, the intertestamental writers of the first century B.C. more closely anticipate the New Testament concept of the resurrection to the heavenly city of God.

There are two versions of the resurrection in the Apocrypha and Pseudepigrapha of the first century B.C. Both, found in 1 Enoch, a composite work, emphasize the spirituality of the righteous only who rise. In 1 Enoch 91-104 the Messianic kingdom is, for the first time, conceived of as existing for a limited time only; accordingly, the destiny of the righteous is postponed and fulfilled at the close of the temporal Messianic kingdom when the souls only of the righteous arise to blessed immortality (104:1-5). Two other, though less explicit, examples of this version, wherein the righteous souls alone are raised, appear in the first century B.C.—1) in the Psalms of Solomon 3:16, 13:9, 14:7, and 15:15; and 2) in Wisdom of Solomon 1-10, especially 3:1, 4:7, 5:16, and 8:20.

The other version of the resurrection in the first century B.C. occurs in 1 Enoch 37-71, which teaches 1) that there will be a resurrection of all the dead in body and soul to judgment, 2) that the bodies of all the righteous will be changed to and clothed in a "spiritual" body of glory and light and will be of an angelic nature, and 3) that they will arise to an eternal Messianic kingdom on a new earth.[13]

At the end of the first century B.C., the resurrection is conceived of essentially as a spiritual phenomenon for the righteous; the expectation of an eternal Messianic kingdom on earth has virtually vanished and been displaced by the hope for an eternal heavenly spiritual kingdom. In this century this growing dualism between the present on earth and the future in heaven continues and therein attains its final development. Sometimes, however, the actual duration of the Messianic kingdom is defined and accepted as a period of one thousand years, the Millennium.[14]

In the first century A.D. the separation widens between 1) the fate of the individual and the nation and 2) the present earth and the future heaven. Accordingly, hope for the blessed future community of the Messianic kingdom declines while hope for the transcendence of the righteous ascends. Both Alexandrian and Palestinian Judaism continue to emphasize the spiritual content of the resurrection, though they differ in their "psychologies" and accordingly differ in their understandings of the resurrection.

The Alexandrians hold 1) that matter is eternal and essentially evil, hence there can be no blessed resurrection of the flesh; 2) that the ethical nature of the soul before it enters the body is apparently predetermined; and 3) that at death, souls enter into their final state, hence there is no intermediate abode and no last judgment. Accordingly, Alexandrian writers teach that the spirits of the righteous are resurrected to heaven immediately after death. Philo, the chief Alexandrian Jew, holds that there is no resurrection of the body, for the body is the polluted prison of the soul.[15] Likewise, 2 Enoch, or the Book of the Secrets of Enoch, holds that there is no resurrection of the body; instead, the risen righteous will have a heavenly body composed of and clothed in the glory of the Lord (22:8). Finally, throughout 4 Maccabees, a book more philosophic than apocalyptic, there is no resurrection of the body but only a blessed immortality of the soul.

In Palestinian Judaism there are two major versions of the resurrection, the second of which is contemporary with and similar to the New Testament teaching. The first, in the Assumption of Moses, speaks of a resurrection of the spirit of the righteous only after the last judgment, and there is no resurrection of the body (10). The second, and more important version, occurring in 2 Baruch and 4 Ezra, holds that there is a resurrection of the body of all mankind and that the earthly body is subsequently transformed into a "spiritual" body.

Second Baruch, or the Syriac Apocalypse of Baruch, is a composite work (written in the last half of the first century by orthodox Jews) and is a fair representation of the Judaism against which the Pauline doctrine was directed.[16] Second Baruch 49-52 treats the nature of the resurrected body, which will be restored and raised in its exact earthly form (1, 2). After judgment, however, the defective physical bodies of the righteous will be transformed into glorious "spiritual" bodies of the "splendour of angels":

They shall behold the world which is now
    invisible to them,
And they shall behold the time which is
    now hidden from them:
And time shall no longer change them.
For in the heights of that world shall they
    dwell,
And they shall be made like unto the angels,
And be made equal to the stars,
And they shall be changed into every form
    they desire,
From beauty to loveliness,
From light into the splendour of glory
                    (51:8-16).

Fourth Ezra, a composite work, also teaches the same concept of the resurrection of the earthly body and its later change into a "spiritual" body. Adapting the Old Testament prophetic concept of the Messianic kingdom and anticipating the "first resurrection" into the Millennium (Rev. 20:5), 4 Ezra teaches that there will be a partial first resurrection of Old Testament heroes when the Messiah appears. Following the Messianic kingdom of indeterminate length, there will be the general resurrection of all mankind in body and soul to the last judgment. The righteous, changed into spiritual form, will dwell in an incorruptible "paradise of delight" lit with "only the splendour of the brightness of the Most High" (7:36 and 42).

These Judaic versions of the resurrection are contemporaneous with New Testament writings, though basic theological differences of course affect the provenance and content of the doctrine. Paul's teaching in 1 Corinthians is not so much an innovation as it is a spiritualization, through Jesus Christ, of a concept already current among Pharasaic Jews.

Before considering New Testament eschatology, where the future fate of the saved individual and that of the saved nation are again, and finally, joined in the Christian doctrine of the resurrection, a brief recapitulation shows the development toward this synthesis. In Old Testament eschatology before the exile, hope for individual immortality first develops and then hope for the whole nation's preservation follows. Whereas these two components remain separate before 586 B.C., after the exile, they are first tentatively and roughly joined toward the end of the fourth century B.C. in the concept of the resurrection taught in Isaiah 26 and in the second century B.C. in Daniel 12. By the end of the second century B.C., however, this initial combination of both halves of the resurrection motif divides into its separate components: hope for the blessed immortality of both the righteous individual and the whole nation remains separated until its final synthesis in Christianity. Moreover, by the first century B.C., hope for the Old Testament eternal Messianic kingdom is abandoned, and consequently the various versions of the resurrection motif emphasize the remaining hope for transcendent spiritual immortality. Further, the proper home for the righteous is no longer conceived of as ever appearing on earth, but rather heaven itself becomes the hoped-for eternal abode. In the context of the Old Testament and the Apocrypha and Pseudepigrapha, the New Testament assimilates and further develops earlier, Judaic concepts.

New Testament Eschatology of the Synoptic Gospels

The determinate event of New Testament eschatology is Jesus' Easter resurrection, the definitive promise and realization of man's redemption. In the Old Testament, hope for a resurrection derives from 1) the renewal of God's covenant and 2) the compensatory phenomenon of projecting well-being into the future if it is denied in the present. Whereas these Old Testament expectations are either in the past or the future, respectively, in the New Testament the resurrection has occurred in a precise historical moment in the present; the cross expresses the accomplished intersection of time and eternity and the empty sepulchre expresses the accomplished transmutation of time into eternity. In New Testament eschatology the resurrection is anticipated in the future because it definitively occurred in the past, on Easter.

The eschatology of the synoptic Gospels begins with the kingdom of God (Matt. 25), the eternal spiritual community of the righteous wherein the divine will is realized; though this kingdom can begin on earth, it is consummated in heaven (Matt. 21: 28 and Luke 11: 20 and 17: 2-21). Accordingly, Christian eschatology includes the events which precede the advent of the kingdom of heaven, namely the *parousia,* or second coming, the last judgment, and the resurrection and total consummation.[17] Following Jesus' own teaching, as recorded in Matthew 10: 2 and

16:28, in Luke 9:27, and in Mark 14:62, the *parousia* was to take place within the current generation, and with it, the immediate advent of the kingdom of heaven. In later apocalyptic literature both expectations are indefinitely postponed.

After the second coming follows the last judgment of all men (living and dead) by Jesus Christ, according to works (Matt. 16:27, 13:41–43, and 22:11–14). Finally comes the consummation of the kingdom of heaven and the resurrection of all the righteous (living and formerly dead) to eternal life, wherein the good of the individual and of the community are joined.[18] This kingdom is of a heavenly and not an earthly character; hence, those who arise "are equal unto the angels" (Luke 20:36, Matt. 22:30, and Mark 12:25) and are free from the world of natural generation. As we have seen, this New Testament concept of final resurrection to a transformed spiritual body originates and derives from previous religious (Judaic) writings, in 1 Enoch 37-190, the Syriac Apocalypse of (2) Baruch 51, and 4 Ezra 7.

In the fourth Gospel, according to John the three last events are conceived of as occurring twice in time. Thus the *parousia* occurs 1) as a present spiritual event (14:18-19, 10:14, 12:26, 14:20-23, and 17:23 and 26) whereby man communes with Christ, and 2) as a future historical event, at the end of time, soon to be fulfilled (21:22). Likewise, judgment in John has a twofold significance, as 1) present and internal and 2) future and external. The first depends on man's attitude toward and acceptance of Christ (3:17-21 and 9:39). Present judgment is thus self-determined, and hence John teaches

God sent not his Son into the world to condemn the world; but that the world through him might be saved. He that believeth on him is not condemned: but he that believeth not is condemned already, because he hath not believed in the name of the only begotten Son of God (3:17–18).

Further, this present judgment of belief determines the last judgment:

Verily, verily, I say unto you, He that heareth my word, and believeth on him that sent me, hath everlasting life, and shall not come into condemnation but is passed from death unto life. Verily, verily, I say unto you, The hour is coming, and now is, that they that hear shall live. (5:24–25).

Finally, the Johannine resurrection is also conceived of in two temporal parts—begun in the present through belief in Christ and consummated in the future in communal and eternal life in the kingdom of heaven (5:25). This belief "now" is fulfilled on the last day, for "every one which seeth the Son and believeth on him, may have everlasting life: and I will raise him up at the last day" (6:40). The source of this belief is beautifully expressed in Jesus' definitive teaching of self-identification:

> I am the resurrection, and the life: he that believeth in me, though he were dead, yet shall he live: And whosoever liveth and believeth in me shall never die (11:25–26).

The spiritual resurrection begun on earth is fully realized in the faithful's transformation into the divine likeness in God's heavenly kingdom: "when he shall appear, we shall be like him; for we shall see him as he is" (1 John 3:2).

Paul's Eschatology

Although there are other New Testament teachings about the resurrection,[19] Paul's writings most fully elucidate the Christian principle of man's transfiguration from the mortal "natural body" to the immortal "spiritual body." The development of his eschatology moves from a legalistic view[20] to emphasizing the spiritual kingdom of heaven and culminates in I Corinthians. Though Paul does not here emphasize imminent evil (as in 1 and 2 Thess.), he does expect the second coming within his lifetime (1 Cor. 4:5, 7:29, 11:26, and 15:51-52). Again Christ's return will be glorious (1 Cor. 1:7) and commence the last judgment (1 Cor. 1:8, 4:4-5, 5:5) according to works (1 Cor. 4:4, and 6:9-10); later, however, Paul predicates judgment upon faith and belief in Christ.[21] In contrast to the eschatology of John, of Revelation, and of Paul's later writings, in 1 Corinthians Paul does not teach that there will be a first spiritual resurrection to a temporary Messianic or Millennial period between the *parousia* and last judgment.

Christ's glorious resurrection is not only the foundation of salvation in the New Testament, but also the definitive cause and effective pattern of man's resurrection, as Paul emphasizes: "As God hath both raised up the Lord, and will also raise us up by his own power" (1 Cor. 6:14).[22] Paul's teaching involves God's definitively raising Jesus from the dead—"if there be no resurrection of the dead, then is Christ not risen; and if Christ be not risen, then our preaching is vain, and your faith is also vain. . . . And if Christ be not raised, your faith is vain; ye are yet in your sins. . . . For as in Adam all die, even so in Christ shall all be made alive" (15:13-14, 17, and 22). The *Jerusalem Bible* interprets this relation as preaching the "foundation of faith" in Christ's resurrection:

> Christ's resurrection, of which the apostles are witnesses . . . is the decisive proof . . . of the future resurrection of all . . . not only heralding but causing the resurrection of all Christians.[23]

Paul's "Corinthian" emphasis on the necessity of faith in Christ —in his glorious Easter resurrection which causes the general resurrection—becomes more pronounced in his subsequent writings and in those of the Church fathers.

The Risen "Spiritual Body": The Pneumatikon

Just as Christ was gloriously raised from the dead in a spiritual body by God, so will all faithful be resurrected from death to everlasting life. This principle of divine correspondence generates both man's belief and the "kind of body" resurrected:

> So also is the resurrection of the dead. It is sown in corruption; it is raised in incorruption: It is sown in dishonour; it is raised in glory: it is sown in weakness; it is raised in power: It is sown a natural body; it is raised a spiritual body (1 Cor. 15:42–44).

In order to understand this fundamental Pauline conception, his special use of body, soul, and spirit must be distinguished, for

> Le dualisme πνεομα –σαρε est une des grandes antithèses de la littérature Paulienne. . . . cette classification paulienne est basée sur une conception trichotomiste de la nature humaine; d'après laquelle l'homme serait constitué d'une partie inférieure comprenant le corps et l'âme (σωμα, φυχη) et d'une partie supérieure, le πνευμα. Il faut remarquer en outre que cette séparation nette entre la φυχη, désignant la partie animale de l'homme, et le πνεμμα, indiquant le germe divin, ne se rencontre pas avant l'ère chrétienne.[24]

Returning to the tripartate division of Genesis 2:7, Paul speaks of the physical body, the *psychikon,* as the natural, mortal, and

corrupt form of life in man: "In Paul, as in the O.T., *psyche*
(Hebr. *nepsh*) is what gives life to animals, to the human body
[as flesh]. . . . Something that is alive because it has a *psyche*
giving it merely natural life [is] subject to decay and corruption."[25] In 1 Corinthians 2:14 Paul defines the "unspiritual man"
(who "does not receive the gifts of the Spirit of God") as
"psychikos, man left to his own natural resources."[26] Moreover,
as a function of only the physical body (the *psychikon*), the soul
is mortal and perishes with it: "flesh and blood cannot inherit
the kingdom of God; neither doth corruption inherit incorruption" (1 Cor. 15:50). Whereas the soul, *psyche,* is a portion of
the mortal body and confined to this natural life, the spirit,
pneuma, partakes of the immortal, the divine, and the saved.

Paul uses "spirit" in three ways: as 1) the "higher nature of
man as an intellectual and moral being, and 2) the immaterial
personality of man as surviving death" and 3) in 1 Corinthians
14:14-15 and 15:42-54 as "that part of man's immaterial nature which is capable of direct communication with the Spirit
. . . [and] as it is recreated by God."[27] In 1 Corinthians 15:44
Paul radically contrasts the mortal body and soul, the *psychikon,*
with the immortal spiritual body, the *pneumatikon.* With the infusion of *pneuma,* which begins as a gift of the Spirit (1 Cor.
2:14 and Rom. 5:5 and 10:8-13) and which is completed after
death in the resurrection of the spiritual body, "human life is
divinised."[28]

Speaking of this divine transfiguration to the immortal, incorruptible, and glorious *pneumatikon* completed on the last day,
Paul proclaims,

> Behold, I shew you a mystery; We shall not all sleep, but we shall all
> be changed, in a moment, in the twinkling of an eye, at the last trump:
> for the trumpet shall sound, and the dead shall be raised incorruptible,
> and we shall be changed. For this corruptible must put on incorruption,
> and this mortal must put on immortality. So when this corruptible shall
> have put on incorruption, and this mortal shall have put on immortality,
> then shall be brought to pass the saying that is written, Death is swal-
> lowed up in victory. O death, where is thy sting? O grave, where is thy
> victory? (1 Cor. 15:50–55).

Christ's Easter resurrection from the dead to divine life is the
definitive cause and efficient pattern, for all those who believe
and live in the spirit of Christ, of man's resurrection to the
spiritual body.

Though they belong to the same individual, these psychical and spiritual bodies cannot exist together simultaneously, for "the existence of one [the *pneumatikon*] depends on the death of the other [the *psychikon*]."[29] Baptism signifies an absolute exchange whereby life according to the flesh gives way to life according to the Spirit, as Paul teaches in Romans 8:9–11. While psychical man must die, spiritual man will be raised like Christ in a transfigured, glorious, pneumatic body. This complete change, then, implies that the radical differential is whether the *psyche* or the *pneuma* inhabits the body. Deliverance, therefore, consists in the transfiguration of the mortal, corruptible flesh to the immortal, incorruptible spiritual body.

Given that Paul's doctrine of the resurrection, definitively preached in 1 Corinthians, involves the radical transfiguration of the Christian from the *psychikon* to the *pneumatikon* through faith and baptism into the life of Christ's spirit, one can see both its distant ancestors in Old Testament and intertestamental eschatologies and how Paul's Christian doctrine differs from previous versions of the resurrection. Though there are varying Old Testament conceptions of a resurrection to blessed immortality, Judaic eschatology emphasizes the Messianic kingdom on earth. In the Apocrypha and Pseudepigrapha, however, occur versions of the resurrection which emphasize the transformation of the mortal body to its final spiritual content and which are thus closer to Paul's precepts. As discussed, those apocalyptic writers of the Jewish faith who teach that the resurrected earthly body will be finally transformed into a "spiritual" body are 1 Enoch 82–90 in the second century B.C., 1 Enoch 37–71 in the first century B.C., and the Syriac Apocalypse of (2) Baruch 49–52 and 4 Ezra in the first century A.D. Paul's preaching significantly differs, however, in his emphasis on the Christian's spiritual transfiguration first on earth through belief in Christ and in baptism, and subsequently fulfilled in the resurrection in the spiritual body to the community of Christians in the heavenly kingdom of God.

Pauline Sacramental Participation

Having elaborated Paul's teaching of the transfiguration of the resurrection, as defined by Jesus Christ on Easter and completed (for the saved) on the last day, we will now explore its "incorporation" in present history through the sacraments. In Romans Paul emphasizes that faith assures salvation and that baptism is the ceremony of Christian belief in the individual's new life "through" the risen Jesus (Rom. 5:1-11, 6:1-11, and 8:1-13). Underlying each of these precepts is the Pauline belief in achieving a "spiritual resurrection" through love of Christ in this life which preludes the final bodily resurrection after the last judgment: "Therefore being justified by faith, we have peace with God through our Lord Jesus Christ: by whom also we have access by faith into this grace wherein we stand, and rejoice in the hope of the glory of God" (Rom. 5:1-2). Moving from the last day to the present one, baptism, the sacramental ceremony of faith, is based on and imitates the transfiguration completed in the final resurrection:

> Know ye not, that so many of us as were baptized into Jesus Christ were baptized into his death? Therefore we are buried with him by baptism into death: that like as Christ was raised up from the dead by the glory of the Father, even so we also should walk in newness of life. For if we have been planted together in the likeness of his death, we shall be also in the likeness of his resurrection (Rom. 6:2-5).

Through this spiritual resurrection, celebrated in baptism, the believer is incorporated into the resurrected body of Christ:

> But ye are not in the flesh, but in the Spirit, if so be that the Spirit of God dwell in you. Now if any man have not the Spirit of Christ, he is none of his. And if Christ be in you, the body is dead because of sin; but the Spirit is life because of righteousness. But if the Spirit of him that raised up Jesus from the dead dwell in you, he that raised up Christ from the dead shall also quicken your mortal bodies by his Spirit that dwelleth in you (Rom. 8:9-11).

Accordingly, in his later writings, Paul speaks of eschatological reality as already existing.[30]

In Colossians Paul preaches that on earth the faithful already live with the risen Christ, individually through baptism and collectively in the Church (3:1-4). At the second coming the redeemed body which will be finally resurrected is both the single, transfigured body of the faithful individual, and the Church, the collective body and community of Christians. As the earthly "image of the unseen God," an incarnation of the divine, who gives man redemption through "forgiveness of sins," Christ is the head of the Church, his collective body.[31]

In Ephesians Paul emphasizes that because of God's gift of

grace, man believes in Christ and through this faith he is saved. Speaking of this redemption, Paul implies that this first "spiritual" resurrection has already been realized through the believer's new life in Christ (2:4–6); and it continues "till we all come in the unity of the faith, and of the knowledge of the Son of God, unto a perfect man, unto the measure of the stature of the fulness of Christ. . . . For we are members of his body, of his flesh, and of his bones" (4:13 and 5:30).

In conclusion, then, Paul teaches that man's resurrection through God's gift of grace and faith in Jesus Christ, whereby the baptized Christian is transfigured from a mortal and corruptible *psychikon* to an immortal and incorruptible *pneumatikon* on the last day, is caused and informed by Jesus' Easter resurrection.

Revelation

The last Biblical apocalyptic work, the Book of Revelation of Jesus Christ to John of Patmos, written by a "Jewish Christian" about A.D. 93, primarily portrays the last things: the *parousia,* Messianic kingdom, the "first resurrection" to the Millennium, the catastrophic destruction of this world, the general resurrection and last judgment, and the creation of a new heaven and new earth wherein the saved will rise and dwell eternally with God in the heavenly city, new Jerusalem. Like the earlier Jewish apocalyptic writings, which are the literary ancestors of this book, and in contrast to the eschatology of the gospels, Revelation arises from John's vision—"of all the things that he saw" in heaven (1:2); accordingly, the book reveals this vision's contents instead of directly preaching a way of salvation.

Like Daniel and many of the intertestamental apocalyptic writings, Revelation was written in response to present affliction and projects into the future the ideal which is desired but not yet realized.[32] The interpretation of Revelation which is most suggestive in the context of this study understands John's vision as a revelation of the divine imagination; at this point, however, we will consider Revelation primarily in relation to the eschatology of previous apocalyptic writings.

Instead of invoking prophetic reformation, the apocalyptic speaker envisions imminent destruction as the necessary prelude to complete transformation. John of Patmos's eschatology begins with natural disturbances followed by the turbulent reign of the Antichrist, and it ends with the resurrection of the saved to the new heaven and city of God. Christ's second coming, which follows these natural disasters (14), gives way first to resulting cosmic warfare (16) in which the Antichrist and his allies, the false prophets, are annihilated and an Angel binds the Beast, "the Dragon, that old serpent, which is the Devil, and Satan" (20:2) and casts him into the pit of fire for one thousand years.

Then follows the Millennium in which only the dead martyrs are raised in the "first resurrection" to "be priests of God and of Christ" (20:6) and reign in the temporary Messianic kingdom for one thousand years. At the beginning of the first century, this concept first appears in 2 Enoch 32–33 and in 4 Ezra, as previously mentioned. This idea occurs first in Jewish, and not Christian, eschatology.

Aside from its origin in Jewish apocalyptic writings, there are two contrasting Christian interpretations of the first resurrection. First, considering John's probable meaning in the context of other apocalyptic writings, Archdeacon Charles concludes that Revelation 20:4–6

> must not be construed in a purely spiritual sense and taken to mean a death to sin and a new birth into righteousness. The earliest expounders of the Apocalypse, such as Justin Martyr, Tertullian, Irenaeus, Hippolytus, and Victorinius, quite rightly take the words in a literal sense of an actual reign of Christ with the glorified martyrs on earth. The spiritualizing method, which emanated from Alexandria, put an end to all trustworthy exegesis of the Apocalypse. . . . The context itself is wholly against taking the words in a spiritual sense; for (a) this resurrection is obviously the guerdon of martyrdom and begins *not with the beginning of the Christian life but after its close.* (b) As Alford rightly urges: "no legitimate treatment of it (i.e., the text itself) will extort what is known as the spiritual interpretation now in fashion."[33]

Though a literal interpretation of the first resurrection, as Charles points out, was widespread in the early Church, there later develops a second and sacramental ("spiritualized") interpretation: "according to Augustine and those who follow him, the 'reign of 1000 years' is to be reckoned from Christ's resurrection, and the 'first resurrection' is baptism. . . ."[34] When the content of this first resurrection is interpreted as spiritual, as we shall find in Augustine and Donne, the first resurrection, to the Millennium in this world, assures us a part in the second resurrection, to heaven in the new world to come. While the early Church

Fathers (until Augustine) understand the "first resurrection" in its literal sense, Augustine and later commentators transpose it to its sacramental meaning as a spiritual resurrection, celebrated in baptism and commemorated in the Eucharist.

To return to Revelation in the context of its historical conception, the differences between the Jerusalem of the Millennium, a version of the Old Testament Messianic kingdom, and the new Jerusalem of the apocalypse are crucial and arise from the differences between an earthly and heavenly and between a natural and a supernatural existence. If Old Testament eschatology emphasizes a first resurrection to the earthly Messianic kingdom, New Testament eschatology and Christian doctrine celebrate the last resurrection to the heavenly kingdom of God.

Leading to this final promised end, there follows a gradual degeneration of human and physical nature, culminating at the end of one thousand years by the second loosening of Satan from his prison (20:7). Consequently, the battle of Gog and Magog continues until the end of the world of evil, when everything is consumed by the purifying fire which comes "down from God out of heaven" (20:9).

The three concluding phases of the apocalyptic pattern are the resurrection of all men to the last judgment, the creation of a new heaven and new earth, and the final resurrection of the saved to God's new Jerusalem. Thus, as Augustine and Donne will do, one can speak of three resurrections: 1) the first resurrection of the righteous believers into the Millennium; as discussed, there are two interpretations of this event—a) literally as the actual reign of Christ on earth with the martyrs, as Revelation apparently intended, or b) spiritually as a present resurrection, whose source is faith in the risen Christ, whose sacrament is baptism, and whose form is the *pneumatikon* (Rom. 6:1–10 and 1 Cor. 15:44); 2) the second and general resurrection of all men, in body and soul, to the last judgment; and 3) the final resurrection of the saved to the holy city of God, new Jerusalem, wherein the raised live eternally in their transfigured form as an immortal, incorruptible spiritual body.[35]

After the "first resurrection" follows, in the Revelation narrative, the last judgment, the final moral determination and "reparation."[36] As part of the process of divine transformation, the old heaven and earth pass away and a new heaven and new earth are created whereby the whole of creation is freed from the dominance of corruption, renewed, and transformed by the glory

of God (21:1). Those saved are raised to the heavenly new
Jerusalem, the "holy city" of God, where they dwell for eternity (21:2).

According to Charles's scholarship in editing Revelation,
John's vision of new Jerusalem immediately follows the last
judgment; the restored, and unjumbled, original order of the
complete description reads:

> And he that sat upon the throne said,
> The former things have passed away;
> Behold I make all things new.
>
> And I saw a new heaven and a new earth;
> For the first heaven and the first earth
>   had passed away;
> And there was no more sea.
>
> And the holy city, New Jerusalem, I saw
> Coming down out of heaven from God,
> Made ready as a bride adorned for her husband.
> And I heard a great voice from the throne
>   saying,
>
> Behold the tabernacle of God is with men,
> And he shall dwell with them,
> And they shall be his people,
> And he shall be their God.
>
> And God shall wipe away every tear from
>   their eyes,
> And death shall be no more,
> Neither shall there be mourning nor crying
>   nor pain anymore,
> Neither shall there be any more curse.
>
> And the throne of God and the Lamb shall
>   be in it,
> And his servants shall serve him,
> And they shall see his face,
> And his name shall be on their foreheads.
>
> And there shall be no more night,

And they shall have no need of lamp or
     light of sun,
For the Lord God shall cause (his face)
     to shine upon them:
And they shall reign for ever and ever.[37]

Whether or not one edits the description to a single passage, it
is clear that the divine omnipresence and immanence in new
Jerusalem consummate the blessedness of the resurrected. John's
vision combines the preexilic hopes for the immortality of the
individual with the postexilic and intertestamental hope for immortality of the nation, so that the resurrected compose and
share the communal blessedness of the city of God. Joined in
worship and joy, the community of the resurrected everywhere
see God face to face (22:4), for "the city had no need of sun,
neither of the moon, to shine in it: for the glory of God did lighten
it" (21:23). Moreover, this immanent and "unmediated" vision is eternal, since "there shall be no night there; and they
need no candle, neither light of the sun; for the Lord God
giveth them light: and they shall reign for ever and ever"
(22:5).

New Jerusalem's symbolic significance should be observed: in
the heavenly Jerusalem, the ideal kingdom of God becomes
real. Revelation completes the Biblical narrative in more than a
chronological or historical sense: structurally and anagogically,
apocalyptic predictions provide a harmony between beginnings
and endings[38] by imagining the desired fulfillment of human
existence, completed in salvation in the holy city of God. As a
revelation of divinity, John's vision—which "bore record of the
word of God, and of the testimony of Jesus Christ, and all
things that he saw. . . . I was in the Spirit on the Lord's day,
and heard behind me a great voice, as of a trumpet" (1:2 and
10)—symbolizes the Word's subsuming and transfiguring the
world:

> I looked, and, behold a door was opened in heaven; and the first voice
> which I heard was as it were of a trumpet talking with me; which
> said, Come up hither, and I will show thee things which must be here-
> after (4:1).

From a theological viewpoint, the Word is Jesus Christ, "full
of grace and truth" (John 1:14), while from a Blakean viewpoint, the word is the imagination.

In the Old Testament the resurrection motif originates as a preexilic hope for personal immortality and as a postexilic hope for communal (national) preservation; in both cases, suffering is relieved by projecting a presently denied and desired condition into the future. Aside from other variations, the crucial difference between Old and New Testament doctrines of the resurrection involves how one conceives of Jesus—as a human prophet or as God's only son and annointed Messiah. For Christians, his Easter resurrection from the dead is the definitive cause and model of God's gift of redemption to man. Henceforth, Christian belief and eschatological expectation are founded on this historically real and unique redemptive event, which reveals the mystery of man's salvation. In contrast to Jewish soteriology, which looks to the future for the Messiah's first coming, the Christian looks back to ("remembers") Jesus' resurrection as definitively establishing the coming eschatological reality, begun in the past (on Easter) and to be completed in the future (on the last day). In terms of the Savior's relation to history, the Old and New Testaments thus differ. However, in terms of an anagogic, or universal symbolic meaning, Biblical eschatologies share, I think, a source in man's eternal and infinite desire for redemption and bespeaking and embodying divine unity, because "the Word was with God and the Word was God" (John 1:1).

Post-Apostolic Eschatology

In this section we shall study the major patristic interpretations of the resurrection as it becomes dogmatized as essential to Christian belief; the Nicene "credo" ends "Et expecto resurrectionem mortuorum et vitam venturi saeculi."

In post-Apostolic Christianity the *parousia* is no longer expected immediately but "soon." However, the expectation of the resurrection continues independently and it becomes a fundamental belief in salvation in the coming glorious kingdom. Belief in the resurrection of the body from the dead and its reunion with the soul is central to Christian faith in the second century—both 1) as a doctrine of the early Church and 2) as an assertion of Christianity in direct opposition to Hellenistic views of immortality.[39]

Rejecting the entire Christian eschatology, especially the second coming of Christ and the resurrection of the body, Gnosticism holds that salvation exclusively involves the spirit and means its deliverance from corporality. Basilides, Valentius, and Maricon, major Gnostics, teach that God delivers only the souls, not the bodies of the believers. Warning against this heresy, Justin, for example, says " 'If you have fallen in with some who are called Christians . . . and who say that there is no resurrection of the dead, but that their souls, when they die, are taken to heaven; do not imagine that they are Christians.' "[40] In direct contrast to Gnosticism, then, Christian doctrine differs by maintaining that because of Christ's resurrection, there will be a resurrection of the body (in the flesh, from the dead) and soul as among the Apologists (A.D. 150-180).[41]

Both the Christian importance of the resurrection and its defiant unacceptability by the pagans is narrated in Eusebius's *History of the Church* (c. 325); in the section on "Gallic martyrs of Verus's reign" (presumably that of Marcus Aurelius, A.D. 177) there is a long, detailed description of their sufferings. The cause of their tortured martyrdoms is only "being Christian," that is, specifically believing in the resurrection, from the dead, of Jesus, in body and soul; this transfiguration of the natural to the supernatural was anathema to the pagan instinct:

> Thus the martyrs' bodies, after six days' exposure to every kind of insult and to the open sky, were finally burnt to ashes and swept by these wicked men into the Rhone which flows near by, that not even a trace of them might be seen on the earth again. And this they did as if they could defeat God and rob the dead of their rebirth [Matt. 19:28], "in order," they said, "that they may have no hope of resurrection—the belief that has led them to bring into this country a new foreign cult and treat torture with contempt, going willingly and cheerfully to their death. Now let's see if they'll rise again, and if their god can help them and save them from our hands [Dan. 3:15]."[42]

Irenaeus: Five Books Against Heresies

The chief of the anti-Gnostic fathers is Irenaeus, whose eschatological teachings constitute the accepted beliefs of the Church at that time. Irenaeus's major writings on the resurrection (of Jesus and man) occur in the *Five Books Against Heresies,* written at the end of the second century. Herein this basic Christian doctrine is expounded as an essential article of Christian belief and in opposition to Gnostic views of immortality.

Before discussing man's resurrected body, however, Irenaeus's "psychology" should be understood.

Like Paul, Irenaeus speaks of man as a tripartite being composed of body (flesh), soul, and spirit; the flesh is mortal and corruptible and likewise the incorporeal soul, the breath of life, infused into natural man, is subject to time and death of the body: if "the spirit is wanting to the soul [and body, together the *psychikon*], such an one is truly an Animal Man, and as being left carnal, will be imperfect."[43] In contrast to these corruptible and mortal components, the spirit, the divine *pneuma*, renders man perfect and immortal:

> But when this Spirit, mingled with the soul, is united to that which God formed; then by the effusion of the Spirit the spiritual and perfect Man is made: and this is he who was made after the image and likeness of God. . . . Now what cause in the world had he to ask for these three, i.e., soul, body, and spirit, entire and perfect perseverence to the coming Lord, except that he knew that the restoration and union of all three was their only salvation, and that the same for them all? . . . Perfect then are they, who both have the Spirit of God remaining in them, and have kept their souls and bodies without reproach (V, vi, 1).

Describing the relations between these three parts, Irenaeus explains that the "perfect Man consists: of Flesh, Soul, and Spirit" (V, ix, 1). Such a man whose body and soul are thus purified and mastered is "no more carnal but spiritual because of his participation in the Spirit" (V, ix, 2).

Speaking further of this distinction between the *psychikon* and *pneumatikon*, Irenaeus teaches that the faithful man can begin this transfiguration on earth as it will be fulfilled in heaven. Irenaeus describes what Augustine and Donne will call the "first resurrection" on earth, though he does not use this exact Augustinian term: God's Spirit

> therefore so abiding in us, makes us already spiritual. *For you,* saith he, [Rom. 8: 9] *are not in the flesh, but in the Spirit: if indeed the Spirit of God dwelleth in you:* And this takes place, *not by our losing the flesh, but by our partaking of the Spirit.* . . . Those then who have the earnest ["a portion of that honour which is promised to us by God"] of the Spirit, and serve not the lusts of the flesh, but submit themselves to the Spirit, and walk reasonable in all things: the Apostle rightly calleth Spiritual because the Spirit of God dwelleth in them. But incorporeal spirits will not be spiritual men; rather our substance, i.e., *the combination of soul and flesh, receiving the Spirit of God, maketh up the full spiritual man* (V, viii, 1–2; italics mine).

Participation in and possession of the Spirit of God not only transfigure mortal man (of flesh and soul) into the spiritual body but also represent the way to redemption, for "without the Spirit of God, we cannot be saved" (V, ix, 3).

Further, both teaching against Gnostic heresies and following Paul's emphasis on the incarnation and resurrection, Irenaeus insists on Christ's glorious resurrection from the dead in a spiritual body as the cause and model of man's resurrection. Irenaeus expands the Pauline doctrine of 1 Corinthians 15 as the major source of this central belief: "as in Adam we all die as being merely animal [*psychikon*], so in Christ we may live, as being spiritual—putting off, not the form in which God moulded us, but the lusts of the flesh,—and receiving the Holy Ghost [Spirit]" (V, xi, 3). This present possession of the Holy Spirit and consequent transfiguration into an incorruptible spiritual body begins on earth. Christ's resurrection is the "pledge of our own": the faithful are "awaiting the resurrection; afterwards receiving back their bodies, and rising again entirely, i.e., bodily, as the Lord Himself arose, so they will come into the Vision of God" (V, xxxi, 2).

On the last day there will be a general resurrection of all men in their same earthly body and soul to judgment (II, xxxiii, 5 and V, xiii, 1); the saved will be raised to heaven in their *pneumatikon* to complete their salvation:

> For then shall death be truly overcome, when the flesh which is holden by it shall have gone out from under its sway. . . . What then is the body of humility, which the Lord will transfigure to be conformed to the body of His glory? Plainly, the body which is flesh: the same which is humbled by falling to earth. And the transformation of it is, that being mortal and corruptible, not of its own substance, but through the Lord's working, His power of winning immortality for the mortal, and for the corrupt incorruption (V, xiii, 3).

Speaking of the glory of the risen, Irenaeus stresses individual bliss:

> What will it be, when rising again, we shall see Him face to face? When all the members shall most abundantly utter the hymn of exultation, glorifying Him who will have raised them from the dead, and given them eternal life? . . . What will be the effect of the entire grace of the Spirit, which God shall give unto men? It will render us like unto Him, and perfect us, by the will of the Father; for it will make man to be after the image and likeness of God (V, viii, 1).

Irenaeus ends his *Five Books Against Heresies* with this final description of Christian faith in the bodily resurrection of the just and their transfiguration to an immortal *pneumatikon* in heaven[44] where they "shall be made according to the Image and Likeness of GOD" (V, xxxvi, 3).

Tertullian: De Resurrectione Carnis

Tertullian is the next Church Father to write specifically and extensively about the resurrection (from the dead) in the body. Like Irenaeus, Tertullian defends the three fundamental dogmas of the early Church—belief in God, in Jesus' incarnation, and in his resurrection from the dead in the body—as the true Catholic faith and against heretics; the titles of Tertullian's works indicate his repeated affirmation of these basic doctrines. His *Treatise on the Resurrection* (*De Resurrectione Carnis,* written 208-11), which continues and completes his *De Carne Christe,* teaches that on the last day God will raise the bodies, souls, and spirits of the living and the dead to the last judgment; following this general resurrection, the faithful, each as a whole man composed of body and soul—both transfigured by the addition of the divine spirit, will ascend to the kingdom of God.

Tertullian's argument in the *Resurrection Treatise* begins by asserting the doctrine's definitive importance: "The resurrection of the dead is the Christian man's confidence. By believing it, we are what we claim to be."[45] Following Genesis, Paul, and Irenaeus, Tertullian holds that man is made of body, soul, and spirit; against the Hellenistic heretics, Tertullian maintains that the soul is not divine, that it is of a corporeal nature, and that the soul is conceived, born, and lives together with the body;[46] likewise, when the flesh is raised from the dead, so is the soul, for

> no soul can ever obtain salvation unless while it is in the flesh it has become a believer. To such a degree is the flesh the pivot of salvation, since by it the soul becomes linked with God, it is the flesh which makes possible the soul's election by God. (8)

While both body and soul partake of salvation in the resurrection, however, the determining agent of redemption is the spirit, the divine substance.

Explaining Paul's distinction between the *psychikon* and

pneumatikon in 1 Corinthians, Tertullian, it seems to me, changes
the Apostle's view slightly by teaching that the relation between
body, soul, and spirit is additive, rather than substitutive.[47]
Following Paul, Tertullian first says that man "is both the soul-
informed body when it is sown, and the spirit-informed when it
is wakened up," i.e., "corpus animale cum seminatur, et spiritale
cum suscitatur" (53). "As therefore the flesh is first a soul-
informed body when it receives the soul, so also it is afterwards
a spirit-informed body when it clothes itself with a spirit" (53).
This "afterwards" suggests the addition of the spirit to the soul
and body, rather than the substitution of spirit for soul in the
transfiguration to the *pneumatikon*. By faith can "the flesh even
now have the Spirit" (53), though this present infusion of the
spirit will be fulfilled at the final resurrection: "in due course
it will become, through the fullness of the Spirit, a spirit-informed body besides [the soul-informed body], and in that
fullness it is raised up again" (53; and 50, 51, and 56). This
passage, and others like it, suggests that the acquisition of the
spirit is additive for Tertullian, rather than substitutive, as it is
for Paul.

Tertullian is primarily concerned with the final resurrection
of the body; hence he does not discuss a first (spiritual) resurrection on earth, except briefly to mention its possibility and
primarily to see it as further evidence of the last corporeal resurrection (25). Christ's resurrection, which conquered death, is the
source of man's salvation, fulfilled in the resurrected body: "For
if *as in Adam all die, even so in Christ shall all be made alive,*
they will live in Christ in the flesh" (48; see also 44 and 47).
The saved arise in the body (flesh and blood) and soul, and
ascend to heaven in a transfigured body, composed of flesh, soul,
and spirit, which is immortal and incorruptible:

> And so all flesh and blood, without distinction, do rise again in their
> proper quality, but those to whom it appertains to approach the kingdom
> of God will, before they are able to attain it, have to clothe them-
> selves with that principle of incorruptibility and immortality without
> which they cannot approach to the kingdom of God (50; see also 42
> and 51).

On 1 Corinthians 15:51-52, Tertullian comments that the flesh
and soul, which are mortal and corruptible, will not be destroyed,
but changed—transformed into an incorruptible and immortal

heavenly body (42, 55, and 56) ; all discomfort, injuries, natural processes, and death itself will have vanished from body and soul, and they will be blessed with *"everlasting joy,"* as Isaiah prophesied (58 and 61-62).

Tertullian ends his *Resurrection Treatise* with "the Lord's pronouncement" that after the resurrection men *"will be,* he says, *like angels"* (62), though not the same as angels because still men. Affirming the final home and integrity of the body, soul, and spirit, Tertullian teaches that they will all be resurrected to heaven and there eternally live joyously praising God.

Discussing the importance of Irenaeus's and Tertullian's writings on the resurrection, which affirm, against the Gnostics and other heretics, the Church belief in the raising of the spiritual body of the faithful, Harnack points out that Christian belief in this doctrine was now fixed and transferred to the general creed, along with related doctrines; the bodily ascension of Christ into heaven and the consequent resurrection of all flesh were now unquestionably and irrevocably accepted.[48]

Thus the Apostles' Creed[49] ends with "I believe in the Holy Spirit, the holy Catholic Church, and communion of saints, the resurrection of the body, and life everlasting." Likewise the creeds of the fourth century hold the same belief. The Nicene Creed (325), produced at the first ecumenical council, includes Christ's resurrection, though it does not specifically teach man's bodily resurrection. The two other major creeds which follow, however, do specifically teach the bodily resurrection of the faithful. The Niceno--Constantinopolitan Creed (381) ends with "we expect the resurrection of the dead and the life of the world to come." The long form of the Creed of Epiphanius (c. 374) includes a section of belief "in the resurrection of the dead, in the last judgment of souls with their bodies, in the kingdom of heaven and in life everlasting." Though the creedal language may vary, the doctrine remains the same:

A general conclusion from the documents of the Church teaching is that there will be a resurrection, that it will be for all men, and that all men will arise with the same bodies they now have. It is to this resurrection that the Church from the very beginning has been the believing witness. It can be said quite definitively that there is hardly any truth of Christian revelation that is so openly and clearly taught by the Fathers and Christian writers as the resurrection of the body. Indeed, it is the very keystone of Christianity, mirroring as it does, the Resurrection of the Lord.[50]

St. Augustine: *The* Enchiridion

In the *Enchiridion,* the *City of God,* and the Easter-season sermons, Augustine deals extensively with the resurrection. Since it was written to provide a summary of his thought on the essential teaching of Christianity, we will first consider the *Enchiridion.* Augustine begins his discussion of this doctrine with the fact and nature of salvation in the resurrection (LXXXIV-XCII) and concludes with its causes (XCIII-CXIII). Christ's bodily resurrection from the dead to eternal life is the model for man's: "that the bodies of all men . . . shall be raised again, no Christian ought to have the shadow of a doubt."[51] After briefly overcoming problematic and doubtful cases (abortive conceptions, monstrous births, and decayed or deformed bodies), Augustine considers the risen body and explains this final condition of perfection and happiness in terms of Paul's "psychology":

> their bodies have been called spiritual, though undoubtedly they shall be bodies and not spirits. For just as now the body is called *animate,* though it is a body, and not a soul [anima], so then the body shall be called spiritual, though it shall be a body, not a spirit. . . . as far as regards the substance, even then it shall be flesh. For even after the resurrection the body of Christ was called flesh. The Apostle says: "It is sown a natural body; it is raised a spiritual body;" because so perfect shall then be the harmony between flesh and spirit, . . . that no part of our nature shall be in discord with another; but as we shall be free from enemies without, so we shall not have ourselves for enemies within (XCI).

As this passage indicates, Augustine follows Irenaeus's and Tertullian's—that of the early Catholic Church—interpretation of the Pauline "spiritual body." Like John, Augustine conceives of the resurrection as occurring twice in time; it is first begun in the sacrament of baptism, commemorated in the Eucharist, and then completed on the last day with the ascension to heaven, where the saved "shall live truly and happily in eternal life" (CXI), which is a gift of God's grace.[52]

Augustine's "Psychology": Pneuma *and* Psyche *as* Spiritus

Before treating Augustine's elaboration of the spiritual resurrection in the *City of God,* his use of "spirit" should be clarified. As discussed, Paul distinguishes between the corruptible and mortal soul (*psyche*), associated with the natural body of flesh, and the incorruptible and immortal divine spirit (*pneuma*). Irenaeus and Tertullian, respectively, preserve the tripartite distinction, though Tertullian teaches that there will be a resurrection of the whole threefold man (body, soul, and the added spirit); Irenaeus, like Paul, emphasizes the believer's transfiguration by substituting the body and spirit (the *pneumatikon*) for the body and soul (the *psychikon*). However, unlike his predecessors, Augustine speaks of the spirit (*pneuma, spiritus*) as including the formerly distinct soul (*psyche, anima*). Further, from Augustine's usages, it is apparent that the two words, soul and spirit, can be used synonymously: Augustine incorporates the meanings of the Greek *pneuma* and *psyche* into the Latin *spiritus*.

Augustine, however, uses *spiritus* in three ways: "La première signification du terme *spiritus* se rapporte donc à l'essence de la divinité."[53] Augustine's second use of *spiritus* is new because it combines the formerly distinct elements of the mortal soul and the immortal spirit. Though Augustine distinguishes "dans l'homme *spiritus, anima,* et *corpus,* . . . [il] admet également le caractère spirituel de l'anima."[54] Third,

> Le terme spiritus désigne également, dans la langue de saint Augustin, une faculté au moyen de laquelle l'homme peut se représenter le monde exterieur. . . . la *visio spiritalis* accompagne nécessairement la *visio corporalis,* à tel point que, sans cette *visio spiritalis,* il n'y a pas de perception possible. [55]

After this excursion on Augustine's peculiar *spiritus,* we can return to his discussions of the resurrection, particularly of the first, or spiritual, resurrection, in the *City of God*.

St. Augustine: The City of God

In *The City of God* (written 413-426) most of Augustine's discussion of eschatology occurs in Books XX-XXII, though in Book XIII he also treats the resurrection of the flesh. Speaking of the Christian view of the promised end, and in opposition to Platonists, who believe in immortality only of the soul, Augustine explains and affirms Paul's teaching:

> remember what has been promised by Him who deceives no man, and who gave them security for the safekeeping even of the hairs of their

head, they [the departed saints] with a longing patience wait in hope of the resurrection of their bodies. . . . For as, when the spirit serves the flesh, it is fitly called carnal, so, when the flesh serves the spirit, it will justly be called spiritual. Not that it is converted into spirit as some fancy from the words "It is sown in corruption, it is raised in incorruption;" but because it is subject to the spirit with a perfect and marvelous readiness of obedience, and responds in all things to the will that has entered on immortality—all reluctance, all corruption, and all slowness removed. For the body will not only be better than it was here in its best estate of health, but it will surpass the bodies of our first parents ere they sinned.[56]

In Book XXII Augustine continues to explain the resurrected spiritual body, which, though "yet real flesh," will no longer be subject to natural weaknesses because informed by the supernatural: "And so they will be spiritual not because they cease to be bodies, but because they shall subsist by the quickening spirit" (XIII, 22).

When Augustine considers "what we are to understand by the animal and spiritual body" in Book XIII, chapters 23 and 24, unlike earlier commentators he conceives of the soul's (*psyche, anima*) acquiring the spirit (*pneuma, spiritus*). Accordingly, like Tertullian, Augustine views the transfiguration as additive, rather than substitutive. Following Romans 8:10-11 and 1 Corinthians 15:21-22, he makes the traditional Christian analogy of the animal body and soul which are made alive in Christ: when informed by the spirit "man will then be not earthly but heavenly—not because his body will not be that very body which was made of earth, but because by its heavenly endowment, and this by not losing its nature, but by changing its quality" (XIII, 23). In Christ it "afterwards [be]comes the spiritual body, which already is worn in anticipation by Christ as our head, and will be worn by His members in the resurrection of the dead" (XIII, 23). Augustine emphasizes the crucial principle of change in the resurrection from the animal to the spiritual through partaking of the heavenly body of Christ (XIII, 23); retaining the tripartite view of man like Tertullian, Augustine, however, conceives of the transfiguration as the addition of the spirit to the body and soul of the faithful Christian.

Returning to last things at the conclusion of *The City of God*, Augustine discusses Revelation; of particular interest is his sacramental interpretation of the first and second resurrections (XX, 6). Beginning with the Gospel of John, Augustine also conceives of the resurrection as occurring twice in time: 1) the resurrection of the soul, which he calls the "first and spiritual resurrection" (XX, 6), begins on earth with "hearing" the Word of God and thus believing in Christ and "preserves us from coming into the second death (XX, 6); 2) "the other, the second [resurrection], which is of the body, not of the soul and which by the last judgment shall dismiss some into the second death, others into that life which has no death" (XX, 6) is thus the final resurrection of the faithful to the city of God.

This first resurrection, which is now, determines man's future, "for in this first resurrection none have a part save those who shall be eternally blessed" (XX, 6), though all participate in the general resurrection (of body and soul) to judgment. Commenting on the judgment of all and only those who have heard and believed in (the Word of) Christ and thus have "a part in the first resurrection, by which a transition from death to life is made in this present time" (XX, 6) and on all those who have not, Augustine thus interprets John 5 : 28-29:

> "but they that have done evil unto the resurrection of judgment," *i.e.,* of damnation. He therefore who would not be damned in the second resurrection, let him rise in the first. For "the hour is coming, and now is, when the dead shall hear the voice of the Son of God; and they [all and only] that hear shall live," *i.e.,* shall not come unto damnation, which is called the second death; into which death, after the second or bodily resurrection, they shall be hurled who do not rise into the first or spiritual resurrection (XX, 6).

Preceding and determining the last judgment and resurrection, "there are two regenerations . . . the one according to faith, and which takes place in this present life by means of baptism; the other according to the flesh, and which shall be accomplished in its incorruption and immortality by means of the great and final judgment" (XX, 6). Accordingly, the regeneration through faith constitutes "the first, or spiritual, resurrection, which has place in this life," whereas the regeneration of the flesh occurs on the last day as the final resurrection (XX, 6).

Moreover, Augustine continues this temporal distinction, implied in John but not previously developed, when interpreting Revelation 20 : 5-6. Augustine does not view literally this "first resurrection" of the saints who reign with Christ for one thousand years (the Millennium); instead he considers it sacramentally. Unlike the last resurrection, Augustine teaches that this first is not of the body and soul, but only of the soul, "for certainly it was in the inner and not the outer man that those had risen again to whom he [Paul] says 'If ye have risen with Christ, mind the things that are above'" (XX, 10). Following the distinction between the first, or spiritual, and the second, and bodily, resurrections, elaborated earlier, Augustine here applies it to Revelation 20:5-6. He understands the "priests of God and Christ, [who] shall reign with Him a thousand years" non-literally: "as we are all believers Christians on account of the mystical chrism, so we are all priests because they are members of the one Priest" (XX, 10). This sacramental interpretation reiterates Augustine's preaching that the first resurrection, which alone assures the second, is spiritual and results only from God's gift of grace to "hear" and believe in the Word of Christ.

Continuing to comment on Revelation, Augustine speaks of the glorious change throughout the universe after the last judgment, with God's creation of the new heaven and new earth:

And by this universal conflagration the qualities of the corruptible bodies shall utterly perish, and our substance shall receive such qualities as shall, by a wonderful transmutation harmonize with our immortal bodies so that as the world itself is renewed to some better thing, it is fitly accommodated to men, themselves renewed in their flesh to some better thing (XX, 16).

In Book XXII Augustine elaborates on this "better thing"; not only will there be no bodily loss, but also a restoration of man's physical prime after and because of Christ's model: "the meaning of the [resurrection of the body] is that all shall rise neither beyond nor under youth, but in that vigour and age to which we know that Christ had arrived . . . the bloom of youth at the age of thirty" (XXII, 15). There shall be no infirmity of mind or body. Though men and women will retain their sexual differences, they "shall remain adapted not to the old uses, but to a new beauty, which, so far from provoking lust, now extinct, shall excite praise to the wisdom and clemency of God" (XXII, 17). There will be no marriages, and "they shall be equal to the angels in immortality and happiness" (XXII, 17).

Augustine seems to delight in contemplating the resurrected body and repeats and elaborates his descriptions of it. Characteristic of this tendency,[57] he holds "that all bodily blemishes which mar human beauty in this life should be removed in the resurrection, the natural substance of the body remaining, but the quality and quantity of it being altered so as to produce beauty"

(XXII, 19, and XXII, 24). The "proportions of the various parts of the body" will be preserved, "for all bodily beauty consists in the proportion of the parts, together with a certain agreeableness of colour" (XXII, 19).

Besides this individual bodily perfection, the resurrected will compose the collective Christian body and share in the "endless glory of the Church" in the new Jerusalem, where " 'God shall wipe all tears from their eyes' " in their blissful communal blessedness (XX, 17). Explaining the means of this continuous and unmediated vision of the divine, of which Revelation 21-22 also speaks, Augustine elucidates that

> wherever we shall look with those spiritual eyes of our future bodies, we shall then, too, by means of bodily substances behold God, though a spirit, ruling all things. . . . God will be so known to us, and shall be so much before us, that we shall see Him by the Spirit in ourselves, in one another, in Himself, in the new heavens and the new earth, in every created thing which shall then exist; and also by the body we shall see Him in every body which the keen vision of the eye of the spiritual body shall reach (XXII, 29).[58]

Finally Augustine ends with the "eternal felicity of the city of God and of the perpetual Sabbath" (XXII, 30). This great and everlasting happiness involves two forms of unity: 1) of body and soul—"one thing is certain, the body shall forthwith be wherever the spirit wills, and the spirit shall will nothing which is unbecoming to either the spirit or to the body" (XXII, 30); and 2) of what is desired with what is—"each shall receive this further gift of contentment to desire no more than he has" (XXII, 30). With desire fulfilled, the resurrected shall live in "an eighth and eternal day, consecrated by the resurrection of Christ, and pre-figuring the eternal repose not only of the spirit, but also of the body. There we shall rest and see, see and love, love and praise. This is what shall be in the end without end" (XXII, 30).

St. Augustine: Easter Sermons

In his Easter-season sermons Augustine preaches the same doctrine of the resurrection, the "distinctive belief of Christians": "our faith has been established in the resurrection of Christ. Pagans, wicked people, and Jews believed in the Passion of Christ, Christians alone believe in His resurrection . . . [which] points to the happiness of the life to come."[59]

Briefly, Augustine emphasizes the following traditional aspects of the resurrection: that Christ's glorious Easter resurrection is the paradigm of the resurrection of the righteous in a spiritual body (240, 242, 274, 356, 360-61, 379, 388-89, 394, and 406); that there will be a general resurrection of all men in body and soul to judgment (321 and 401); that the saved will rise to a new life in an immortal spiritual body (205, 221, 231, 240, 252, 262, 266-67, and 270-71); that they will enjoy a happy and blessed eternal life (163, 209, 217, and 388); that nothing is hidden among men (295-96); and that the resurrected will enjoy a blessed fellowship with God and Christ (209), whom they will always see face to face (354).

Speaking of the risen spiritual body, Augustine explains its name:

> Why, then, is it called a spiritual body, my dearly beloved, except because it will obey the direction of the spirit? Nothing in yourself will be at variance with yourself, nothing in yourself will rebel against yourself. . . . Those conflicts [between body and mind] will not exist there [in the kingdom of God], wherever you will have wished to be, there you will be; but you will not depart from God. Wherever you will have gone, you will possess your God. You will always be with Him in whom your happiness consists (271).

Once out of their natural and corruptible bodies and transfigured to their immortal spiritual bodies, the resurrected shall sing the joyous "Alleuja" to God. In this chorus and song "the utmost harmony of those giving praise exists there where there is tranquil rejoicing among those singing, where no law in the members opposes the law of the mind, where there is no conflict of desire" (357). The kingdom of God, the new Jerusalem, represents the personal and communal unity of blessedness.

The Post-Nicene Creeds

After Augustine the next major statement of the resurrection doctrine occurs in the Athanasian Creed, an authoritative source of Catholic belief, probably written in the fifth or sixth century. At Christ's second coming all men are to arise with their own bodies, and they are to give an account of their lives. Those who have done good deeds will go to everlasting life.

In the Creed of the Eleventh Council of Toledo of 675, there is a longer assertion of the resurrection of the earthly body:

according to the model of our Head, we profess that there is a true bodily resurrection of all the dead. And we do not believe that we shall rise in a body of air or in any different kind of body (as some have foolishly thought); but we shall rise in this very body in which we now live and are and move. . . . By this faith we truly believe in the resurrection of the dead, and we look forward to the joys of the world to come.

In the next six centuries, the resurrection doctrine remains the same and

by the time of the Lateran Council IV (1215) the developed teaching of the Christian tradition regarding the resurrection of the body received definitive formulation in its essential elements; that is, that there will be a resurrection, and that all men will rise with the same bodies they now possess.[60]

The relevant proclamation of the Lateran Council IV is that at the *parousia* and last judgment "all will arise with their own bodies which they now have so that they may receive according to their works, whether good or bad; . . . the good eternal glory with Christ." Likewise, the second Council of Lyon (1274) holds that "on the day of judgment all men appear before the judgment seat of Christ with their own bodies to give an account of their deeds."

St. Thomas: Summa Contra Gentiles, IV: Salvation *and* Summa Theologica

St. Thomas Aquinas discusses the resurrection primarily in the *Summa Theologica* and in the *Summa Contra Gentiles, Book IV: Salvation.* In the *Summa Theologica,* before discussing eschatology, Thomas begins with Christ's resurrection, the source of the faithful man's: "Now our Head lives and will live eternally in body and soul. Therefore men who are His members will live in body and soul; and consequently there needs must be a resurrection of the body."[61] And further, "it is a necessary tenet of the faith to believe that there will be a resurrection of the dead."[62]

Though Thomas speaks of both soul and spirit, it should be

noted that the "spiritualization" of the soul, begun in Augustine, and continued in the creeds, is now complete to the extent that in his discussion of the resurrection doctrine Thomas does not differentiate spirit from soul and uses them synonymously. Body and soul receive their reward or punishment together (*SCG*, IV, 96) and together the soul and body of the saved share in the final beatitude.

Like Augustine, Thomas distinguishes between a first and second resurrection, though he does not elaborate the distinction so fully as Augustine and even appears less certain of it:

> Moreover, our Lord promises both resurrections, for He says: "Amen, amen, I say unto you that the hour cometh and now is when the dead shall hear the voice of the Son of God and they that hear shall live." And this seems to pertain to the spiritual resurrection of souls, which even then was beginning to be completed, when some were clinging to Christ in faith. But later, it is the bodily resurrection He expresses (*SCG,* IV, 79).

Interpreting Revelation 20, Thomas follows Augustine's sacramental understanding of the first resurrection, confirmed by baptism and commemorated in the Eucharist, and does not view the Millennium literally:

> Now, the saying of the Apocalypse (22.2) about "the thousand years" and "the first resurrection of the martyrs" must be understood of that first resurrection of souls from their sins, of which the Apostle says: "Arise from the dead and Christ shall enlighten thee" (Eph. 5:14). And by the thousand years one understands the whole time of the Church in which the martyrs as well as other saints reign with Christ, both in the present Church which is called the kingdom of God, and also as far as souls are concerned—in the heavenly country (*SCG,* IV, 83).

In connection with the possibility of this first, spiritual, resurrection on earth, the soul is judged immediately after separation from the body in death (*SCG,* IV, 91). On the last day, all men "in the selfsame body will rise again" (*ST,* XX, 157; *SCG,* IV, 79) from the dead and be reunited with the soul, both of which will receive the last judgment (*ST,* XX, 123-25; *SCG,* IV, 79).

Speaking of the final resurrection to heaven, Thomas explains that

> The necessity of holding the resurrection arises from this,—that man may obtain the last end for which he was made; for this cannot be accomplished in this life, nor in a life of the separated soul, . . . lest it appear to be made without purpose, it is necessary for the selfsame soul

being united to the selfsame body. For otherwise there would be no resurrection properly speaking if the man were not reformed. (*ST,* XX, 162).

No longer natural, but being supernatural, "among the risen there will be no use of food or sexual love" (*SCG,* IV, 83); "although the bodies of the risen are to be the same in species as our bodies now, they will have a different disposition" (*SCG,* IV, 85). Thus describing the risen spiritual body, Thomas notes that the body will be transfigured and will "glow with resplendent soul" (*ST,* XX, 248-49; and *SCG,* IV, 85-86). This resurrected, transfigured body will be immortal and incorruptible, as Paul predicts in 1 Corinthians xv, and will live in heaven "united to God by vision" (*SCG,* IV, 87).[63]

Elaborating the "quality of the glorified body," Thomas explains that it is unified in complete accord with the soul:

> Moreover, the soul which will enjoy the divine vision, united to its ultimate end will in all matters experience the fulfillment of desire. And since it is out of the soul's desire that the body is moved, the consequence will be the body's utter obedience to the spirit's slightest wish (*SCG,* IV, 86).

This description is reminiscent of Augustine's elaborations of fulfilled desire in heaven and "preminiscent" of Yeats's longing for a similar unity between body and soul, "for when one has what suffices him, he seeks nothing beyond it. But whoever is happy has what suffices him in the true beatitude; otherwise his desire would not be fulfilled" (*SCG,* IV, 92). And man's "ultimate beatitude" consists of the everlasting and face-to-face vision of God (*ST,* XXI, 73; *SCG,* IV, 91 and 92). For the Church Fathers, the resurrection is the eternal and complete fulfillment of all desire and blessed unity of man in God.

Protestant Eschatology: Luther

The Creed of the Council of Trent (1564) includes the traditional "hope for the resurrection of the dead and the life of the world to come." During and after the Protestant Reformation, the resurrection doctrine does not substantially change, although there arise more individual interpretations of the "meaning" of this fundamental Christian belief.

While Luther's main didactic concern is with this life rather than with an afterlife, his eschatology does not differ significantly from previous (Catholic) doctrine. His stress on leading a good Christian earthly life reflects the Protestant emphasis on judgment and on the preceding, correlative question "How shall I be saved?" As suggested, this present concern with future salvation is also important in Paul and Augustine, Luther's spiritual ancestors. Luther's treatises are characterized by his expounding on the necessary right and sanctity of each individual Christian to live and believe according to his own interpretation of Scripture.[64]

Following Augustine, Luther emphasizes God's gift of grace and salvation in the person of Jesus Christ. For Luther, faith in the Son has its source in the individual (as opposed to any external institution). The individual's personal relation to God through his incarnated Son receives Luther's primary attention, which concerns the human accessibility to salvation.

Luther's apotheosis of the Word exemplifies both his Christ-oriented belief and the Protestant sanctity of man's direct relation to Jesus:

> In the Word alone does God work in the hearts of men: "The Word alone is the vehicle of Grace." Therefore man should hear the Word and meditate upon what he has heard. . . . Only in this [verbal] form can we apprehend Christ: "He is of no benefit to thee and thou canst not know anything about him, unless *God put him into words,* that thou mayest hear and thus learn to know him."[65]

Speaking of this distinctive Lutheran emphasis on the *Logos,* the divine creator whose spoken Word to man is the incarnated Jesus, Harnack holds that his "greatest service" is "above all the recognition of the inseparableness of the Spirit and the word. . . . Rightly did he contend that Christ himself works through the Word."[66]

Thus, for example, the Confession of Augsberg (1550), the first of Lutheran "symbolical statements," teaches that

> without the Holy Spirit it [the human will] has no power of accomplishing the righteousness of God, or spiritual righteousness "because animal man does not perceive the things which belong to the spirit of God": but these came into being in our hearts when the Holy Spirit is conceived through the Word.[67]

Given God's grace, the Christian has faith in Christ, the means of his justification, through the possession of the Holy Spirit, who is "conceived through the Word."

"Luther's Catechism" explains this individual reception of God's Word now as it applies to man's final fate. In Protestant soteriology the connection between the continuity and the conclusion of history is direct. The Third Article of the Sanctification states the meaning of the creedal belief in "the Holy Ghost, a holy Christian Church, the Communion of Saints, the forgiveness of sins, the resurrection of the body, and life everlasting":

> I believe that I cannot of my own understanding and strength believe in or come to Jesus Christ my Lord, but that the Holy Ghost has called me by the Gospel, and illuminated me with His gifts, and sanctified and preserved me in the true faith, just as He calls, gathers together, illuminates, sanctifies, and preserves in Jesus Christ all Christendom throughout the earth in the one true faith; in which Christendom he daily bestows abundantly on me and all true believers forgiveness of sins; and on the last day He will awaken me and all the dead and will give to me and all that believe in Christ eternal life.[68]

Characteristically, Luther teaches that the final resurrection of body and soul, after the last judgment, to heaven directly depends on the first resurrection of the spirit on earth:

> If we are, at the last day, to rise bodily, in our flesh and blood, to eternal life, we must have had a previous spiritual resurrection here on earth. Paul's words in Romans 8: 11 are: "But if the Spirit of him that raised up Jesus from the dead dwelleth in you, he that raised up Christ Jesus from the dead shall give life also to your mortal bodies through his Spirit that dwelleth in you." In other words: God having quickened, justified, and saved you spiritually, he will not forget the body, the building or tabernacle of the living spirit; the spirit being in this life risen from sin and death, the tabernacle, or the corruptible flesh-and-blood garment, must also be raised; it must emerge from the dust of the earth, since it is the dwelling-place of the saved and risen spirit, that the two may be re-united unto life eternal.[69]

In opposition to Catholic dogma, Luther and the Protestants deny purgatory and hold that even the saints await the reunion of the body and soul which are judged on the last day before their final resurrection to heaven.[70]

On the last day Luther affirms that "we who are true Christians shall have everlasting joy, peace, and salvation." Again, following 1 Corinthians 15, Luther teaches that in the final resurrection the righteous man rises a *pneumatikon,* immortal, incorruptible, and full of "nothing but charming and joyful aspects of promised life," which "will be an eternal day. Upon the instant of its appearing, every heart and all things will stand revealed."[71] As part of his primary concern with salvation's arising from man's life here and now, Luther wrote extensive commentaries on Paul, but only a "Preface" to Revelation, of which he was not fond; yet in his commentary on Galatians, for example, Luther affirms the beatitude of the resurrection in the kingdom of God.[72]

With characteristic straightforwardness, Luther gives his reasons for writing little on Revelation: he holds "it to be neither apostolic nor prophetic. . . . There is one sufficient reason for me not to think highly of it,—Christ is not taught or known in it. . . . Therefore I stick to the books which give me Christ, clearly and purely."[73] Luther's preaching that each Christian should now act to receive salvation is not because, like Paul, he expects the imminent *parousia;* rather, it is because he affirms the individual's freedom and responsibility to hear God's Word in his own following of Jesus Christ. Whereas the early Church Fathers interpret Revelation literally, and whereas Augustine interprets it sacramentally, it seems to me that Luther interprets Revelation allegorically. No doubt because of the controversy with Rome and Catholicism, Luther sees the Antichrist as the Pope who persecutes the faithful German Protestants. But this allegorizing of much of the text may also result from and reflect 1) Luther's insistence on the importance of the individual's personal relation to Scripture and 2) his apotheosis of the Word, Jesus Christ, as the only mediator between man and God.

Protestant Eschatology: Calvin

In his discussions of the resurrection, Calvin does not question the doctrine and therefore does not emphasize it as did earlier theologians, who established and defended it against unbelievers. In the Reformation the resurrection doctrine is accepted without dispute, and accordingly it is not repeatedly "proved" as in post-Apostolic and early Church writings. Instead, Protestants characteristically emphasize the immediate problem of attaining salvation, and the criteria of judgment. In regard to the sacraments and the resurrection, Protestant soteriology is more open to individual and symbolic interpretations.

Calvin's eschatology resembles both Catholic and Lutheran teaching. Beginning with Paul (1 Corinthians 15), Calvin also holds "that we shall rise, because Christ has risen."[74] Further, the agent of Christ's resurrection, the Spirit of the Father, is also accessible to the faithful in this life, though Calvin does not stress this first, spiritual resurrection: "He was raised by the power of the Spirit, who is given to us also for the purpose of quickening us" (*Instit.*, III, xxv, iii, II). Of the first resurrection in Revelation 20: 4-6, however, Calvin says only that "the term of one thousand years there mentioned refers not to the eternal blessedness of the Church, but to the various agitations which awaited the Church in its militant state upon earth" (*Instit.*, III, xxv, v, II).

Luther, having reduced the essential sacraments to two—baptism and the Eucharist—takes them literally; in contrast, Calvin, extending the Word, views the sacraments symbolically. In Book IV of the *Institutes* Calvin thus defines a sacrament:

> An external symbol by which the Lord attests in our own consciences his promises of good-will towards us to sustain the inferiority of our faith. . . . A testimony of God's grace to us confirmed by an external sign, with our answering witness of piety towards him.[75]

Explaining this symbolic form, in baptism, Calvin writes of the "ministry of Word and Sacrament" that

> There is no more need for this [Christ's actual physical presence] than in Baptism, in order that we may be true members of the body of Christ, the body of Christ itself should descend from heaven into the water or under the water or stand not far from the water. Similarly there is no need for the descent of the body in such literal sense, for us to be made partakers of the whole of Christ; we believe that enough of the power of the Spirit of the Lord, who proceeds from the Father and the Son, is in us, for in Baptism to be made members of his body, which yet is and remains in heaven, he nourishes us more and more through his secret and most efficacious power and virtue.[76]

Though Calvin significantly changes the formal substance of the sacrament from the literal to the symbolic,[77] he does not alter its purpose.

Summarizing the importance of the Eucharist, Calvin's catechism teaches that "the resurrection of the body is there [in the Lord's Supper] confirmed to us, as by a given pledge, since the body itself shares in the symbol of life" (*Theol. Treats.*, 138). Like baptism, the Eucharist is patterned on the resurrection.[78]

While the final promise of the resurrection remains unchanged, the Protestant Reformation alters its relation to the present in that the historical event is no longer conceived of as literally imminent but as symbolically conferred and present throughout time.

Before discussing Calvin's eschatology, we must briefly consider the problem of the state of the soul after death.[79] Whereas Luther rejects purgatory, Calvin attacks a consequence of this Catholic doctrine by substituting the doctrine of psychopannychism for that of purgatory. This doctrine, held by Calvin, includes the possibility of the unconscious sleep of the soul after death (psychosomnolence) or the death of the soul with the body (thnetopsychism). While not teaching the "mortalist heresy" portion of psychopannychism, Calvin believes in "a natural persistence of the soul after death. Calvin thought of the afterlife as a *watchful* wake of the righteous soul in an unspecified realm, blissfully anticipating the resurrection of its body and the final judgment of both the elect and the reprobate."[80] On the last day, however, all, both the living and dead, will rise in body and soul in the general resurrection to judgment.

Calvin dismisses the "monstrous error of those who think that souls will not resume the bodies which at present belong to them" (*Instit.*, III, xxv, vii, II); and he then affirms the Pauline distinction between the form and content of the resurrected body. Whereas the faithful man still lives in his bodily form and substance, its "quality" is transfigured by the infusion of the Spirit:

> we shall rise again in the same bodies we now have, as to the substance, but that the quality will be different; just as the very body of Christ which had been offered as a sacrifice was raised again, but with such new and superior qualities, as it had been altogether different (*Instit.*, III, xxv, viii, II).

In the "Catechism of the Church of Geneva" Calvin elaborates on the three "manifold benefits" of Christ's resurrection which "are given to the saved":

> For by it righteousness is obtained for us (Rom. 4:24); it is a sure pledge of our future immortality (I Cor. 15); and even now by its virtue we are raised to newness of life that we may obey God's will by pure and holy living (Rom. 6:4) (*Theol. Treats.*, 100).

Here Calvin implies the doctrine of the first resurrection, though he does not distinguish it as a separate and preceding event, as do Augustine and Luther. Instead, Calvin includes the first, or spiritual, resurrection, which assures the final resurrection, in his doctrine of predestination, the principal, and arbitrary, sign of salvation in Calvinism.

After the last judgment, the elect rise to heaven; Calvin reminds accordingly, "let us always reflect on eternal felicity as the end of the resurrection" (*Instit.*, III, xxv, x, II). This is the promised beatitude.[81] Unlike Augustine, Calvin does not dwell on the final resurrection, but he does conclude the *Institutes* with this last description: "Since the children of God will want nothing of all its vast and incorruptible abundance, but will be like the angels of God, whose freedom from all animal necessities is the symbol of eternal blessedness" (*Instit.*, III, xxv, xi, II). While Calvin develops Protestant individualism primarily in his doctrine of predestination, Luther preaches a more benign form of personal responsibility, reiterating John, in speaking of man's directly and personally hearing the Word of God in Jesus Christ.

"Last Things"

In chapter 1 this study of the origins and development of the resurrection doctrine concerns what the resurrection involves, which I shall now recapitulate.

In the Old Testament, hope for a redemptive future shifts from the prophetic to the apocalyptic viewpoint as social oppression increases. Instead of preaching personal and communal renewal, realized in the Messianic kingdom on earth, Daniel clearly presents a more radical picture of future survival—the apocalyptic vision of the imminent catastrophic destruction of this old world and the creation of a new heaven and new earth wherein both the righteous individual and community will live eternally in God's blessed kingdom. The apocalyptic speaker appears when existing life is felt to be so unbearable—"tragedy wrought to its uttermost"—that it cannot continue without total destruction and radical re-creation.

To understand the "last things" in Christian eschatology, it is helpful to ask the following questions: 1) What is the cause of the resurrection; why does it occur? 2) How, by what means, by what mode, does it occur? 3) To whom does it occur; who participates? 4) At what time, when, does it occur? 5) What ceremonies or rituals are associated with the resurrection? 6) What are the contents and result of the resurrection?

Traditionally, this "catechism" would be completed thus. Because God is omnipotent and inscrutable, the reason for the resurrection must remain unknown to man, except that it is the crucial instance of God's merciful love whereby the mystery of creation and of man's redemption are revealed. The mode of redemption is God's gift of grace, primarily manifest as faith in Jesus Christ, as the only son of God and the only means of salvation.

Christian theology conceives of the resurrection as occurring potentially twice in time: while it can be begun in the present on earth in the first, or spiritual, resurrection, it is consummated on the last day in heaven, in the final resurrection of body and soul to the city of God; for Augustine (and Donne) this first resurrection assures the final resurrection. Participation involves 1) on earth, the rising of the faithful soul from sin to salvation by means of God's gift of grace, with which man's will to repent may simultaneously coexist and cooperate; and 2) on the last day, the rising of the dead bodies, the reunion of each with the soul, and the resurrection to heaven in the *pneumatikon,* the spiritual body. The resurrection is the model for two Christian sacraments. Christ's Easter resurrection is celebrated and participated in through baptism, and it is commemorated through the Eucharist. Fundamentally, Jesus Christ's Easter resurrection is the earthly manifestation of the divine cause of man's salvation, which is consummated following the last judgment in the final resurrection of body and soul to God in heaven. The content of this final resurrection is eternal beautitude and blessing in the city of God.

We can now observe the following distinctive features which characterize the religious content of the resurrection: 1) immortality in the new Jerusalem in the new heaven and new earth of both the righteous (Old Testament) or faithful (New Testament) nation and individual in his reunited and transfigured body and soul, the spiritual body; 2) unceasing and unmediated vision of God; 3) eternal beatitude and blessing; and 4) constant fulfillment of all desire. The resurrection represents the complete and eternal realization of man's proper and ideal condition.

NOTES: CHAPTER 1

1. See "Resurrection," *Catholic Encyclopedia,* ed. Charles Herberman (New York: Encyclopedia Press Inc., 1911), 12:792.
2. All quotations of the Bible are from the King James translation, unless other-

wise stated. The exact text and literal meaning of this passage, however, are disputed. See *Anchor Job,* ed. and trans. Marvin Pope (New York: Doubleday Anchor, 1965), pp. 129 and 134–35.

3. R. H. Charles, *Eschatology* (New York: Schocken Books, 1963), pp. 79–80; hereafter abbreviated as *Eschat.* The author wishes to express her thankful indebtedness to Archdeacon Charles's scholarly, lucid, and most helpful studies of the doctrines of future life in the Biblical period.

4. See Jer. 3:13 and 19–25, and 19:10–14; and Ezek. 11:17–21, and 36:25–32. Continuing Jeremiah's emphasis on individual moral renewal, which leads to communal restoration, Ezekiel prophesies that to the scattered house of Israel, God, out of his mercy "will give them one heart, and I will put a new spirit within you" (11:19) and that He will restore Israel to its own land, where the Messianic kingdom will be established.

5. See Martin Buber, *Pointing the Way,* trans. Maurice Friedman (New York: Harper and Row, 1963), pp. 194, 197, and 203.

6. See Norman Cohn, *The Pursuit of the Millennium* (London: Secker and Warburg, 1962), p. 3; hereafter abbreviated as *Pursuit.*

7. See *ibid.,* pp. 3–4. See also Neville Clark, *Interpreting the Resurrection* (Philadelphia: Westminster Press, 1967), pp. 3–4, 21–22, and 28–29.

8. See Hans Lietzmann, *Beginnings of the Christian Church,* trans. Bertram Woolf (New York: Charles Scribner's Sons, 1949), p. 25.

9. The book of Joel also introduces an apocalyptic speaker and world judgment, though both are rather ungracefully presented. However, beginning with Joel (about 400 B.C.) the prophetic gives way to the apocalyptic speaker.

10. Charles, *Eschat.,* pp. 129–30.

11. The intertestamental *Apocrypha and Pseudepigrapha of the Old Testament* are the uncanonized books written by unknown, spurious, or pseudonymous authors in the period of history between the Old Testament and the events recorded in the New Testament (about 200 B.C. to A.D. 50). These books were not written in Hebrew and not counted as "genuine" by the Jews; at the Protestant Reformation, they were excluded from the Sacred Canon.

12. R. H. Charles has edited the standard English edition of these works, which I have used: *The Apocrypha and Pseudepigrapha of the Old Testament,* ed. and trans. R. H. Charles (Oxford: Oxford University Press, 1963), 2 vols.; hereafter abbreviated as *Apoc. and Pseud.*

13. See 1 Enoch 46:2–4; 48:2; 41:1; 51:4; 54:6; 48:9–10; 72:12; 53:3–5; 54:1–2; 65:5; and 62:15–16; 17:12; 4 Ezra 2:45; 2 Cor. 5:3–4; and Rev. 3:4–5 and 18; 4:4; 6:11; 7:9 and 13–14.

14. See 2 Enoch 32–33 and 4 Ezra 6:28–29. Attainment of this temporal kingdom is spoken of as the "first resurrection" in Rev. 20:5.

15. See Erwin Goodenough, *By Light, Light; The Mystic Gospel of Hellenistic Judaism* (New Haven: Yale University Press, 1935), p. 316.

16. For a good discussion of 2 Bar. in relation to Christian writings of the same period, see Charles, *Apoc. and Pseud.,* 2:470–80.

17. In the synoptic gospels there are two different accounts of the manner of the *parousia:* that the second coming will be by surprise (Mark 12:33–36; Matt. 24:37–44; 25:1–12; and Luke 21:35–40) or that it will be indicated by unmistakable signs. Although the manner of the second coming was to be unexpected and sudden, it was to be preceded by certain, albeit indefinite, signs, primarily persecution of the faithful.

18. Matt. 21:23-33 and Mark 12:18-27 teach that there is a resurrection of only the righteous whereas Luke 20: 27-40 teaches that there is a general resurrection of "those who are accounted worthy" (20:35); because of the last judgment, in both versions, it is therefore only the righteous who will partake of the kingdom of God. Further, the wicked are cast down to torment (Matt. 5:29-30; 10:28; and Mark 9:43-48).

19. See James 1:12 and 2:5; Heb. 9:5, 10, and 14; 1 Pet. 1:3-5; 4:6; and 5:4; and 2 Pet. 3:13.

20. See 1 and 2 Thess. for the *parousia:* 1 Thess. 1:10; 2:19; 3:13; 4:15-16; and 5:23; 2 Thess. 1:7 and 2; for judgment day, 1 Thess. 4:6; 5:3; 2 Thess. 1:6-9; and 2:3, 8, and 10; for the resurrection, 1 Thess. 2:12; and 4:16-17; and 2 Thess. 1:5.

21. See 2 Cor. 3:6; Gal. 2:16 and 20; 3:11 and 24; 5:6; Eph. 1:7; 2:8; 4:23-24; Phil. 3:9-11; Col. 2:12; 2 Thess. 1-2; 1 Tim., 1:4-6; and Heb. 11:1-3.

22. See Clark, *Interpreting the Resurrection,* p. 44; see also Adolf Harnack, *History of Dogma,* trans. Neil Buchanan (London: Williams and Nougate, 1894), 1, 85-86, 94-95, and 158; hereafter abbreviated as *Hist. Dogma;* and Oscar Cullman, "Immortality of the Soul," in *Immortality and Resurrection,* ed. Krister Stendahl (New York: Macmillan, 1965), pp. 11, 20, 28-29, and 33; hereafter abbreviated as *Immort. and Resur.*

23. *Jerusalem Bible* (New York: Doubleday and Co., 1966), New Testament, p. 309; hereafter abbreviated *J.B.,* N.T. See also Arthur D. Nock, *St. Paul* (New York: Harper and Row, 1963), pp. 189-90; and Clark, *Interpreting the Resurrection,* pp. 72, 79, and 99.

24. G. Verbeke, *L'évolution de la Doctrine du Pneuma* (Paris: Desclée de Brouwer, 1945), pp. 399-402; hereafter abbreviated as *L'évolution.*

25. *J.B.,* N.T., p. 309.

26. *Ibid.,* p. 295.

27. Charles, *Eschat.,* pp. 470 and 472.

28. *J.B.,* N.T., p. 309. See also Lietzmann, *Beginnings of the Christian Church,* pp. 119 and 127; and Verbeke, *L'évolution,* p. 399.

29. Charles, *Eschat.,* p. 542. This description also applies to Yeats's conception of the reversed symbiotic relation between God and/or the Daimon and man, as observed in *A Vision,* and this duality will be explored in chapter 4. See also Clark, *Interpreting the Resurrection,* pp. 69, 77, and 97-98; and Cullman, "Immortality of the Soul," in *Immort. and Resur.,* pp. 23-27, 35-36, and 53.

30. For further commentary on Paul's teaching on baptism, see *J.B.,* N.T. pp. 277-79 and 347; Verbeke, *L'évolution,* p. 400; and Nock, *St. Paul,* pp. 178-79, 194-95, and 214.

31. Thus Christ is the creative head of all that exists naturally and of all that exists supernaturally through having been saved by him. Chapter 3 will discuss Blake's Jesus as the supreme creative, unifying, and redemptive figure.

32. See Cohn, *Pursuit,* p. 7.

33. R. H. Charles, *Critical and Exegetical Commentary on the Revelation of S. John* (New York: Charles Scribner's Sons, 1920), 2:184-85; hereafter abbreviated as *Crit. and Exig. Comment.*

34. *J.B.,* N.T., p. 449. See also Austin Ferrer, *A Rebirth of Images* (Boston: Beacon Press, 1963), p. 291.

35. Trying to clarify Rev. 20:12-13, Charles further explains that

This stanza [13] betrays in its present form a hopeless confusion of thought, which can only be due to a deliberate change of the text. . . . The general sense would be: all souls together with their bodies . . . are given up by Hades for judgment before the great white throne. . . . Body and soul would thus be reunited. . . . Only the righteous are to possess bodies, *i.e.*, spiritual bodies. . . . Our text thus, like the Pauline epistles, teaches a resurrection of persons (the "dead" so called), not a resurrection of dead bodies even though in company with souls. The personality of the righteous is complete—the soul clothed with a spiritual body (*Crit. and Exig. Comment.*, 2:194–96; see also 197–99).

36. Whereas God judges the dead "according to their works" (Rev. 20:13), Christ judges the living (Rev. 17:11–21 and 20:7–10). Paul sometimes ascribes the final judgment to God (Rom. 14:10) and sometimes to Christ (2 Cor. 5:10). The wicked are cast into the lake of fire and condemned to the second death (Rev. 20:15), which represents the failure to attain eternal life and thus is the death of the soul as well as of the body.

37. R. H. Charles, *Lectures on the Apocalypse* (Oxford: Oxford University Press, 1922), p. 20.

38. See Frank Kermode, *The Sense of an Ending* (New York: Oxford University Press, 1967), pp. 6–7 and 30.

39. See Harnack, *Hist. Dogma,* 1:169 and 240–61, and 2:10–11; *ibid., Outlines of the History of Dogma,* trans. E. E. Mitchell (Boston: Beacon Press, 1957), p. 81, hereafter abbreviated as *Outlines;* Reinhold Seeberg, *Textbook of the History of Doctrines* (Grand Rapids: Baker Book House, 1952), 1:134, hereafter abbreviated as *Textbook;* and Harry Wolfson, "Immortality and Resurrection in the Philosophy of the Church Fathers," in *Immort. and Resur.*, pp. 57, 63, and 69–74.

40. Anders Nygren, *Agape and Eros,* trans. Philip Watson (London: S.P.C.K. 1953), p. 281; see also *ibid.*, p. 313, and Harnack, *Hist. Dogma,* 1:272.

41. See Seeberg, *Textbook,* 1:117; see also Harnack, *Hist. Dogma,* 1:331; Wolfson, "Immortality and Resurrection in the Philosophy of the Church Fathers," in *Immort. and Resur.,* pp. 51–54, 63–65, 69–70, and 77; and J. N. D. Kelly, *Early Christian Creeds* (New York: Longmans Green, 1955), pp. 164 and 196.

42. Eusebius, *The History of the Church from Christ to Constantine,* trans. G. A. Williamson (Baltimore: Penguin Books, 1965), p. 203.

43. Irenaeus, *Five Books Against Heresies,* trans. John Keble (London: n.p., 1872), V, vii, 1, 463 and V, xi, 1, 461; hereafter abbreviated as *Ag. Her.,* with references to book, chapter, and section numbers included in text in parenthesis.

44. In another description of this divine transformation of the faithful in heaven Irenaeus says of the last day, "Now when this fashion has passed away, and man is made young again, and hath become ripe for incorruption, so as never more to be susceptible of decay and age, there shall be the new Heaven and the new earth; in them, being new, shall man abide always new, and in communion with God." (V, xxxvi, 1; see also V, ix, 1–4; V, x, 1–4; V, xii, 2–3; and V, xiii, 1–3).

45. Tertullian, *Treatise on the Resurrection,* trans. Ernest Evans (London: S.P.C.K, 1960), ¶ 1; hereafter abbreviated as *Treat. Resur.;* references to paragraph numbers will be included in text in parenthesis.

46. See Tertullian, *Treat. Resur.,* ¶ 7 and *De Anima,* ¶ 27; also Nygren, *Agape and Eros,* p. 338. Further, because "the whole of the soul's living belongs to the flesh," for "apart from it [the flesh] it [the soul] does not exist" (*Treat. Resur.,* ¶ 7 and ¶ 15). Yet Evans notes that the soul does not die, though what happens to the soul after the death of the body and before the resurrection is not clear; see Evans's note, *Treat. Resur.,* pp. 323–24.

47. See the preceding section on "the Risen Spiritual Body: The *Pneumatikon.*"

48. See Harnack, *Hist. Dogma,* 2:29; see also Nygren, *Agape and Eros,* p. 156.

49. Though not written by the Apostles, the creed is a faithful summary of the beliefs taught from the beginning of the Church; see Jesuit Fathers of St. Mary's College, eds., *The Church Teaches* (St. Louis: Herder, 1955) p. 1; the quotations from the Nicene Creed and the Creed of Epiphanius are from *ibid.,* pp. 3 and 4.

50. *New Catholic Encyclopedia* (New York: McGraw Hill, 1967), 5:425-26; see also Kelly, *Early Christian Creeds,* p. 156.

51. Augustine, *Enchiridion,* trans. J. F. Shaw (New York: Henry Regnery Co., 1966), chap. LXXXIV; hereafter abbreviated as *Enchir.* References to chapter numbers will be included in text in parenthesis.

52. See also *Enchir.,* XIX–XX and XXVIII; and Augustine, "On Grace and Free Will" in *Basic Writings of S. Augustine,* ed. and trans. Whitney Oates (New York: Random House, Inc., 1948), 1:748–49 and 755.

53. Verbeke, *L'évolution,* p. 492.

54. *Ibid.,* p. 498. Applied to man, *spiritus* "présente une signification analogue à celle qui caracterise la spiritualité divine. Il s'agit, ici encore, de la simplicité et de l'invisibilité de l'âme, bien qu'elles ne soient pas aussi absolues dans le principe vital de l'homme qu'en Dieu" (*ibid.,* p. 504).

55. *Ibid.,* pp. 501-2.

56. Augustine, *City of God,* trans. Marcus Dods (New York: Random House, Inc., 1950), Bk. XIII, chap. 20; hereafter abbreviated as *CG.* References to book and chapter numbers will be included in text in parenthesis.

57. Augustine's descriptions of the beauty and perfection of the resurrected body recall Yeats's "perfectly proportioned human body" of the fifteenth phase; see *CG,* XXII, 19 and 24.

58. See Rev. 21:23, and 22:3-4 for examples.

59. Augustine, *Sermons on the Liturgical Seasons,* trans. Sister Mary Muldowney (New York: Fathers of the Church, 1955), p. 255; hereafter abbreviated as *Sermons.* References to page numbers of this edition will be included in text in parenthesis.

60. *New Catholic Encyclopedia,* 5:426. The creedal quotations are from *The Church Teaches:* of the Eleventh Council of Toledo, p. 346; of the Lateran Council IV, p. 347; and of the second Council of Lyon, p. 349. See also Harnack, *Hist. Dogma,* 3:164–65.

61. Thomas Aquinas, *Summa Theologica,* trans. Fathers of the English Dominican Province (London: T. Baker Ltd., 1927), 20:120; hereafter abbreviated as *ST.* References to volume and page numbers of this edition will be included in text in parenthesis.

62. Thomas Aquinas, *Summa Contra Gentiles, Book IV: Salvation,* trans. Charles O'Neil (New York: Doubleday and Co., 1957), p. 79. Hereafter abbreviated as *SCG, IV.* References to chapter number will be included in text in parenthesis.

63. Blake uses similar language, but with his own meaning, to teach a similar expectation, as will be discussed in chapter 3.

64. See James Hastings, *Encyclopedia of Religion and Ethics* (New York: Charles Scribner's Sons, 1908–26), 8:201; Harnack, *Outlines,* p. 547; R. H. Bainton, *Reformation in the 16th Century* (Boston: Beacon Press, 1952), pp. 24, 32–33, and 68; and George Williams, *The Radical Reformation* (Philadelphia: Westminster Press, 1962), p. 822.

65. Seeberg, *Textbook,* 2:279; see also Harnack, *Outlines,* pp. 548, 553, and 562; and Henry Bettenson, ed., *Documents of the Christian Church* 2nd ed. (New York: Oxford University Press, 1963), p. 189; hereafter abbreviated as *Documents.*

66. Harnack, *Outlines,* p. 562; see also Seeberg, *Textbook,* 2:179.

67. Martin Luther, "Confession of Ausberg, X, viii, Free Choice," in *Documents,* p. 211.

68. *Ibid.,* pp. 205-6.

69. Martin Luther, *A Compend of Luther's Theology,* ed. Hugh Kerr (Philadelphia: United Lutheran Publication House, 1953), p. 239; hereafter abbreviated as *Compend.*

70. See Luther, *Compend,* pp. 122 and 242; see also Luther, "Luther's 95 Theses," no 29 in *Documents,* p. 187; and Williams, *Radical Reformation,* pp. 682-83.

71. Luther, *Compend,* pp. 244, 239, and 247.

72. In the life to come we shall no more have need of faith (1 Cor. 13:12). For then we shall not see through a glass darkly (as we do now) but we shall see face to face: that is to say, there shall be a most glorious brightness of the eternal majesty, in which we shall see God even as he is. There shall be a true and a perfect knowledge and love of God, a perfect light of reason and a good will (Luther, *Compend,* p. 248).

73. Martin Luther, *Works of Martin Luther,* trans. H. E. Jacobs (Philadelphia: Westminster Press, 1915-32), 6:488-89.

74. John Calvin, *Institutes of the Christian Religion,* trans. John Allen (Philadelphia: Westminster Press, n.d.), III, xxv, vii, II; hereafter abbreviated as *Instit.* References to book, chapter, section, and paragraph number will be included in text in parenthesis.

75. Bettenson, *Documents,* p. 214.

76. John Calvin, *Theological Treatises,* trans. J. Reid (Philadelphia: Westminster Press, n.d.), 22:174-75; hereafter abbreviated as *Theol. Treats.* and references to page number of this edition will be included in text in parenthesis.

77. See "Catechism of the Church of Geneva," *Theol. Treats.,* p. 134. In a discussion of religious language, Tillich distinguishes between "religious signs, [which] do not participate in any way in the reality and power of that to which they point," and "religious symbols, [which] although they are not the same as that which they symbolize, participate in its power and meaning" (Paul Tillich, *Theology of Culture* (New York: Oxford University Press, 1959), p. 54). In terms of Luther's and Calvin's differing interpretations of the sacraments, Tillich would call Luther's "the genuinely symbolic," whereas Calvin's, like Zwingli's, holds that "they are only signs pointing to a story of the past" (*ibid.,* p. 65). Such a distinction suggests the process of secularization in which the immanent substance of an event or concept is replaced by the external form traditionally associated with it. Once the substance, or that in which a symbol participates, is altered or lost, the "meaning and power" therein pointed to are changed. Hence religious symbols, as Tillich here defines them, must "die" in the face of change. Religious signs, conversely, can alter because they are external pointers to a reality of which they are not part (see *ibid.,* p. 58). We will explore this process of secularization, and its results, in the study of Yeats, in chap. 4 below.

78. The Eucharist is
as a mirror in which we contemplate our Lord Jesus Christ crucified to abolish our faults and offenses, and raised to deliver us from corruption and death and restoring us to a heavenly immortality. Here, then, is the peculiar consolation we receive from the Supper, that it directs and conducts us to the Cross of Jesus Christ and to his resurrection in order to assure us that, whatever inequity

there may be in us, the Lord does not cease to regard and accept us as righteous . . . yet he does not cease to fill us with all felicity. ("Treatise on the Lord's Supper" *Theol. Treats,* p. 145).

79. At the Council of Florence in 1439 the Roman Church "imposed upon the Greek Church a belief that had been current in the West, namely the belief in Purgatory with the presumption that the souls of the dead are conscious and are therefore capable of pain and joy even prior to the resurrection of their bodies" (Williams, *Radical Reformation,* p. 21). Through the influence of natural theology, Catholic dogma, which taught that the soul was immortal, was thus "much closer to Platonic philosophy than the Bible" (*ibid.,* p. 23).

80. *Ibid.,* pp. 21 and 582.

81. Yet as any intimation of that happiness must kindle in us a fervour of desire, let us chiefly dwell on this reflection—If God, an inexhaustible fountain, contains within himself a plentitude of all blessings, nothing beyond him can ever be desired by those who aspire to the supreme good, and a perfection of happiness (*Instit.,* III, xxv, x, II).

2

The First Resurrection in Donne's Religious Prose and Poetry: The Whole "World's Contracted Thus"

Donne's Protestant Preaching

Of the Church Fathers, Augustine appears most concerned with the relation between the first and last resurrection; he is the initial theologian to treat the last resurrection, to heaven, in terms of the first resurrection of the spirit, or soul, on earth. Though Augustine holds that, in the end, man's salvation is a gift of God's grace, his particular discussion of the resurrection doctrine suggests a concern with a correlative question: How shall I be saved? Catholic eschatology is oriented toward man's eternal fate after the last judgment, while Protestant eschatology seems to remain within this world a while longer because it is oriented toward how man must act before the *dies irae,* as Luther and Donne preach.

If the number of citations of another theologian in Donne's sermons indicates an affinity, it is not surprising that he refers to Augustine most often.[1] Although Augustine holds that God's grace is the only necessary gift of salvation, in his treatment of the resurrection, he is typically concerned with the first, spiritual, resurrection on earth, which assures the last, bodily, resurrection to heaven. And Donne is likewise concerned with this relation between the present life and the afterlife: to resolve this matter with the assurance of grace constitutes the characteristic subject of many sermons and forms the distinctive drama of much of his religious poetry. And in both, he bears witness to the Protestant preoccupation with judgment by "contracting" (joining and focusing) the last day to the present moment of penitence.

The doctrine of the resurrection is not questioned in Anglican dogma, for Christ's Easter resurrection is the definitive cause and model of man's: "The first is our patterne, Christ Jesus: He is risen, therefore we shall" (*Ser.,* 8:101 and 219; and 3: 112-13, 4:346 and 356, 7:371). Donne's treatment of the resurrection reiterates its immediate "relevance":

> To beleeve his [Christ's] Resurrection, is the proper character of a Christian: *for the first stone of the Christian faith, was laid in this article of the Resurrection;* In the Resurrection onley was the first promise performed, *Ipse conteret,* He shall bruise the Serpents head, for in this, he triumphed over Death, and Hell, too; And the last stone of our faith, is laid in the same article too, that is, the day of Judgement; and of a day of Judgement God hath given an assurance unto all men (saies S. Paul at Athens) *In that he hath raised Christ Jesus from the dead.* In this Christ makes up his circle; in this he is truly *Alpha and Omega. His comming in Paradise is a promise; his comming to judgement in the clouds, are tied together in the Resurrection. And therefore all the Gospel, all our preaching, is contracted to the one text, To beare witnesse of the Resurrection* (*Ser.,* 4:355, 6:64 and 78–79, 7:100–101, and 8:355).

This passage locates Donne's distinctive bearing witness to the Christian past and future in the present resurrection.

Donne's Enumerations of the Resurrection

Because Donne connects salvation in the present and afterlife, he distinguishes four resurrections: 1) that from natural calamities; 2) the first, or spiritual resurrection on earth from sin to grace; 3) the general resurrection of all men, living and dead, in body and soul on the last day to judgment; and 4) the final resurrection of the saved in body and soul to the kingdom of God.[2] His usual terminology, however, absorbs the natural into the spiritual resurrection. Accordingly, the three resurrections Donne considers are 1) the spiritual resurrection from sin to grace on earth; 2) the general resurrection of all men in body and soul from the grave to the last judgment; and 3) the final resurrection of the saved, in the transfigured body and soul, to heaven. Accounting for this arrangement, Donne explains

> But this first Resurrection, which is but from temporal calamities, doth

so little concerne a true and established Christian . . . as that, as though this first resurrection were no resurrection, not to be numbered among the resurrections, *S. John* calls that which we call the second, which is from sin, the first resurrection: *Blessed and holy is he, who hath part in the first resurrection*. And by this resurrection, Christ implies, when he saies, *Verely, verely, I say unto you, the houre is comming, and now is, when the dead shall heare the voyce of the Son of God; and they that heare shall live*. That is, by the voyce of the word of life, the Gospell of repentance, they shall have a spiritual resurrection to a new life (*Ser.,* 4:58–59).[3]

Of these three resurrections which Donne enumerates, the most important, following Christ's resurrection, is the first, spiritual, resurrection because on it depends the final, bodily, resurrection to heaven:

> whosoever hath this second [the spiritual resurrection] hath an infallible seale of the third resurrection, too, to a fulnesse of glory in body, as well as in soule (*Ser.,* 4:60).

Donne transfers the Christian's concern with salvation from the last to the present day in the first resurrection of the spirit from sin to grace on earth through repentance.

Donne's eschatology begins, essentially, with the first resurrection of the spirit, which assures the last resurrection. However, he does not explicitly define the cause of the first, except insofar as it arises from and includes God's grace. Unlike Augustine, who consistently teaches that the gift of grace is the *sine qua non* of salvation, Donne struggles with the possibility of attaining grace through the simultaneous cooperation of divine and human wills. Accordingly, in his sermons he at times speaks of God's grace as the only determinant of the first (and hence also of the last) resurrection, while at other times he seems to suggest that man can work to facilitate, it not attain, his own salvation. This ambiguity occurs, for example, in this typical description of the first resurrection: "By the pure word of God, delivered and applied by his publique Ordinance, by Hearing and Beleeving, and Practising, under the Seales of the Church and Sacraments, is your first resurrection from sin, by grace, accomplished" (*Ser.,* 4:72).

Though in his sermon on Revelation 20:6 Donne begins to elaborate the meaning of the first resurrection following Augustine, he ends with a "more particular appropriation to every person": "This is the first resurrection, in the first acceptation, a resurrection from persecution, a peaceable enjoying of the Gospell: And in a second, it is a resurrection from sin. . . . So *S. Augustine* takes his place" (*Ser.*, 6:68). Then asking how "God affords us this first resurrection," Donne answers that

> death is the Divorce of body and soule; Resurrection is the Re-union of body and soule; And in this spiritual death, and resurrection, which we consider now, and which is all determined in the soule itself, Grace is the soule of the soule, and so the departing of Grace, is the death, and the returning of grace is the resurrection of this sinfull soule. But how? (*Ser.*, 6:72).

Again replying:

> To the resurrection of the soule, there is an ordinary way, too, The Church. . . . God hath provided a resurrection for both deaths, but first for the first; This is the first Resurrection, Reconciliation to God, and the returning of the Soule of our soule, Grace, in his Church, by his Word, and his seales there (*Ser.*, 6:72–73).

Though "every repentance is not a resurrection," man's labours result in attaining possible salvation: "so labour thou to finde these endowments, in thy soule here, if thou beest come to this first Resurrection" (*Ser.*, 6:73).[4]

Divine and Human Cooperation: the First Resurrection of Repentance

As will be elaborated, the distinctive drama of Donne's divine poems turns on this very point of proper penance:[5] "Yet grace, if thou repent, thou canst not lacke;/ But who shall give thee that grace to beginne?"[6] Donne's attempts to resolve this question—in the first, spiritual, resurrection—inspire his particular Christian eloquence.

Characteristically, Donne would predicate this "return" and resurrection upon individual will (alone). Preaching on John 5:28-29, Donne thus describes how the first, spiritual, resurrection can be accomplished "by ordinary meanes, by Preaching, and Sacraments, and it shall be accomplished ever day . . . by hearing to come to repentance, and so to such a resurrection" (*Ser.*, 6:264). He then confronts the relation between the necessity of rising to judgment on the last day and the possibility of rising to salvation in the present:

In both resurrections, That in the Church, now, by Grace, And that in the Grave hereafter, by Power, it is said, *They shall heare him.* They shall which seems to imply necessity, though not a coaction; But that necessity, not of equal force, not equally irresistible in both; In the Grace, *They shall;* Though they be dead, and senseless as the dust (for they are dust itselfe) though they bring no concurrence, no co-operation, *They shall heare,* that is, They shall not chuse but heare. In the other resurrection, which is, in the Church, by Grace, in God's ordinance, *They shall heare too,* that is, There shall be a voice uttered so, as that they may heare, *if they will,* but not whether they will or no, as in the other case, in the grave (*Ser.,* 6:276; last italics mine).

Donne's contrast between necessary and volitional rising suggests that whereas rising to judgment is not voluntary ("They shall not chuse") but mandatory, rising in the first, spiritual resurrection is voluntary through the willed and shared "concurrence and co-operation" of the divine and human wills. Thus Donne concludes this sermon by affirming the reward of this willed simultaneity:

And assure yourselfe, that that God that loves you to perfect his own works, when you shall lie dead in your graces, will give you that Resurrection to life which he hath promised to all them that do good, and will extend to all them, who having done evil, yet truly repent the evil they have done (*Ser.,* 6:279).

In a sermon on 1 Corinthians 15:29 Donne reiterates the importance of the soul's own redemptive activity: "This then is our first Resurrection, for the duty that belongs to the soule, That the soule doe at all times think upon God, and at some times thinke upon nothing but him" (*Ser.,* 7:105). Protestant theology (as suggested in Luther) transfers the concern with salvation from the last to the present day. Further, as Donne is particularly sensible of, *"it is impossible to separate the consideration of the Resurrection, from the consideration of the Judgement"* (*Ser.,* 6:277; italics mine).

Donne's characteristic combination and transference of eschatological events, which "contracts" traditional "last things" to the individual's present day, is explicitly treated at the end of this Easter sermon:

He that rises to this Judgement of recollecting, and of *judging himselfe,* shall rise with a chearfulnesse, and stand with a confidence, when Christ Jesus shall come in the second . . . *he shall make his possession of this first resurrection his title and his evidence to the second* (*Ser.,* 7:117; italics mine).

On the other hand, in the last lines of this sermon, Donne, though less strongly than Augustine, implies that grace is the *sine qua non* of any resurrection.[7] Donne expresses an eschatological concern in his sermons by joining the Protestant dependence of the last on the first resurrection with the immediacy of individual judgment in the present.

Although he usually abstains from doctrinal controversies, in an Easter sermon of 1626 Donne is occupied with the controversy on the matter of prayers for the dead and the doctrine of purgatory.[8] Here he not only directly rejects Roman dogma on the subject, but also emphasizes the present and individual responsibility for the state of one's soul. Interpreting 1 Corinthians 15:29, Donne argues that "the Fathers did not intend any such building upon that foundation, not a Purgatory, which should be a place of torment, upon those prayers for the dead" (*Ser.*, 7:181). Rather, "our true Purgatory," preaches Donne, is found within the individual, in a "wanton, froward, and impatient soule" (*Ser.*, 7:184); hence, Anglicans' concern should be for the state of their own soul now (*Ser.*, 7:188-214).

Like the Roman Catholics, however, Donne believes the soul is immortal, albeit through divine sustenance rather than inherently: "And for the Immortality of the Soule, It is safelier said to be immortal, by preservation, then immortal by nature; That God keeps it from dying, then, that it cannot dye" (*Ser.*, 2:201).[9] In the same sermon on Psalm 89:48 Donne affirms that with the death of the body, the soul receives its last judgment and that of the righteous is immediately rewarded with ascension to heaven:

> Now, a Resurrection of the Soule, seemes an improper, an impertinent, an improbable, an impossible form of speech; for, Resurrection implies death, and the soule does not dye in her passage to Heaven . . . the soule hath a Resurrection, not from death, but from the deprivation of her former state; that state, which she was made for, and is ever enclined to. But that is the last Resurrection, and so the soule hath part even in that last Resurrection (*Ser.*, 6:74–75, and 2:210).

"The Better Resurrection"

On the last day there is a reunion of all bodies (dead and alive) with their souls as they rise to final judgment; this event is accepted in both Roman and Anglican dogma as assumed

(*Ser.,* 4:62), rather than disputed. However, characteristically transferring the eschatological drama from the last to the present day, Donne compares the reunion of each man's body and soul on the final day with that of the righteous in this life:

> The soule and body concurred to the making of a sinner, the body and soule must concur to the making of a Saint. So it is in the last Resurrection, so it is in the first . . . in a natural death, there is a *casus in separationem.* The man, the person falls into a separation, a divorce of body and soul; and so the resurrection of this fall is by the Re-union, the soule and the body are re-united at the last day (*Ser.,* 7:103).[10]

Preaching on Job 19:26 during Easter season, Donne, like previous theologians, interprets this passage literally (in spite of the textual ambiguity of idiom) and emphatically says of it:

> but *after all this* [bodily destruction], *Ego,* I, I that speak now, and shall not speak then, silenced in the grave, I that see now, and shall not see then, *ego videbo,* I shall see (I shall have a new *faculty*), *videbo Deum,* I shall see God (I shall have a new *object*), and *In carne,* I shall see him in the *flesh* (I shall have a new *organ,* and a new *medium*) and, *In carne mea,* that flesh shall be *my flesh* (I shall have a new *propriety* in that flesh) this flesh which I have now, is not *mine,* but the wormes; but that flesh shall be so mine, as I shall never *devest it more,* but *In my flesh I shall see God for ever* (*Ser.,* 3:92).[11]

As Donne's eloquent development of the text bespeaks, the resurrection of the body primarily involves an improvement in "seeing," whereby man and God are joined in the divine vision: "The [general] Resurrection is common to all; the Prerogative lies not in the Rising, but in the rising to the fruition of the sight of God" (*Ser.,* 3:107).[12]

At the end of the sermon Donne reiterates how individual and communal immortality are attained in the resurrection. While joining the collective body of Christ, thus forming the Communion of Saints, the individual also retains his own body:

> But, in heaven, it is *Caro mea, My flesh,* my soul's flesh, my Saviour's flesh. As my heart is assimilated to my flesh, and made one flesh with it; as my soul is assimilated to my God, and *made partaker of the divine nature* and *Idem Spiritus, the same Spirit with it;* so, there my flesh shall be assimilated to the flesh of my Saviour, and made the same flesh with him too. *Verbum caro factum, ut caro resurgeret;* therefore the Word was made flesh, and therefore God was made man, that the union might exalt the flesh of man to the right hand of God. . . . But when after all this, when *after my skinne worms shall destroy this body,* I

shall see God, I shall see him in my flesh, which shall be mine as inseparably (in the *effect,* though not in the *manner*) as the *Hypostaticall Union* of God and man, in Christ, makes our nature and the Godhead one person in him. My flesh shall no more be none of mine; then Christ shall not be man, as well as God (*Ser.,* 3:112–13).

This divine union—which preserves the individual by completing him in the "great marriage"—is the model not only for heavenly perfection but also for its earthly prefiguration, as we shall see in Donne's love poems.

Since Donne's sermons comment only on 1 Corinthians 15:26, 29, and 50, that on 1 Corinthians 15:50 is the most contextually pertinent to Paul's distinction in 1 Corinthians 15:40-45 between the mortal, corruptible "natural body" and that to which it is raised, the immortal, incorruptible "spiritual body." Whereas the sinful flesh cannot inherit the kingdom of God, the purified body of the first, spiritual resurrection on earth can and will inherit the heavenly kingdom; traditionally, this transfiguration begun on earth (celebrated in baptism) is consummated in heaven:

Flesh and bloud, when it is conformed to the flesh and bloud of Christ now *glorified,* and made like his [body] by our *resurrection,* may inherit the kingdome of God, in heaven. Yea flesh and bloud being conformed to Christ by the *sanctification* of the *holy Ghost,* here, in this world, may inherite the kingdome of God, here upon earth . . . for *our present possession of the kingdome of God here,* our *corrupt* flesh must be purged by *Sanctification* here, for the future kingdome, our natural *Corruptiblenesse* must be purged by *glorification* there (*Ser.,* 3:116–17).

Donne hesitates to give too detailed a description of this transfigured body because "till our Resurrection, we cannot know clearly, we should not speak boldly, of the glory of the Saints of God, nor of our blessed endowments in that state" (*Ser.,* 3:122). Here and elsewhere,[13] however, he does rest assured that Jesus Christ's risen body causes and represents the final form of the saved, as he affirms in his last sermon, "Death's Duel":

Now this which is so singularly peculiar to him [Christ], that *his flesh should not see corruption,* at his *second coming,* his coming to Judgement, shall extend to all that are then alive, their flesh shall *not see corruption,* because (as the Apostle saies, and saies as a secret, as a mystery, *behold I shew you a mystery*) we shall not all sleepe (that is, not continue in the state of the dead in the grave), *but we shall all be changed* (*Ser.,* 10:283).

The eschatology of Donne's sermons usually concerns the transfiguration from the mortal, corruptible *psychikon* to the immortal, incorruptible *pneumatikon* as it is begun in this life rather than completed in the afterlife of the final resurrection. But he also speaks of the cosmic transformation of the apocalypse, in which "new creation" "the whole frame and course of nature is changed" (*Ser.,* 9:203, 1:164, 8:233-35). The "Communion of Saints" is likewise accepted, repeated, but not greatly detailed in Donne's sermons; a relevant and eloquent example, however, of this belief occurs in the Easter-day sermon of 1627 on Hebrews 11:35 and "the better Resurrection." While the righteous members of the Church on earth "already" form "a holy communion of saints," later, when all is restored eternally in heaven, it will be better, as Donne assures:

> This is the faith that sustaines me, when I lose by the death of others, or when I suffer in misery my selfe, That the dead, and we, are all now one Church, and at the resurrection, shall be all one Quire. . . . They that rise then, shall see death no more, for it is (sayes our Texte) *A better Resurrection* (*Ser.,* 7:384).[14]

Later in this sermon Donne eloquently speaks of the ineffable "better Resurrection," which I quote for its representative and beautiful expression:

> Beloved, there is nothing so little in heaven, as that we can expresse it; But if wee could tell you the fulnesse of a soul there, what that fulnesse is, the infinitenesse of that glory there, how far that infinitenesse goes; the Eternity of that happinesse there, how long that happinesse lasts; if we could make you know all this, yet this *Better Resurrection* is a heaping, even of that Fulnesse, and an enlarging, even of that Infinitenesse, and an extension, even of that eternity of happinesse; For, all these, this Fulnesse, this Infinitenesse, this Eternity are in all the Resurrections of the Righteous, and this is a *better Resurrection;* We may almost say, it is something more than Heaven; for, all that have any Resurrection to life, have all heaven; And something more, more than God, for, all that have any Resurrection to life, have all God; and yet these shall have a *better Resurrection.* Amourous soule, ambitious soule, covetous soule, voluptuous soule, what wouldest thou have in heaven? What doth thy holy amourousnesse, thy holy covetousnesse, thy holy ambition, and voluptuousnesse most carry thy desire upon? Call it what thou wilt; think it what thou canst; think it something that thou canst not think; and all this thou shalt have, if thou have any Resurrection unto life; and yet there is a *Better Resurrection* (*Ser.,* 7:389–90).

This "better resurrection" is fulfilled in the unmediated vision of God, a Pauline promise of epiphany (1 Cor. 13:12) on which Donne preached on Easter day 1628. Of this perfect sight and sight of perfection, Donne says

> It ["the sight of God, the knowledge of God"] is not called a better sight, nor a better knowledge, but there is no other sight, no other knowledge proposed, or mentioned, or intimated, or imagined but this; All other sight is blindnesse, all other knowledge is ignorance. . . . But in heaven, our sight is face to face. And our knowledge is *to know, as we are knowne* (*Ser.,* 8:220).

Further, "it shall be a knowledge so like his knowledge, as it shall produce a love, like his love, and we shall love him, as he loves us" (*Ser.,* 8:235). To see God intuitively is to know and thereby to love the divine. And finally, this seeing, this knowing, and this loving God are to possess the divine:

> And as this seeing and this knowing of God crownes all other joyes, and glories, even in heaven, so this very crown is crowned; There growes from this a higher glory, which is, *participes erimus Divinae naturas* (words, of which *Luther* sayes, that both Testaments afford none equal to them) *That we shall be made partakers of the Divine nature;* Immortal as the Father, Righteous as the Son, and full of comfort as the Holy Ghost (*Ser.,* 8:236, and 9:373).

In an earlier sermon Donne describes these "endowments of the blessed"—"*Visio, Dilectio, Fruitio,* The sight of God, the love of God, and the fruition, the injoying, the possessing of God" (*Ser.,* 4:87).[15]

In a sermon on Revelation 7:9, having attested to the "infinite extensions, infinite durations of infinite glory," Donne gives to the congregation the task of meditation on the heavenly Jerusalem:

> Go in, beloved, and raise your own contemplations, to a height worthy of this glory; and chide me for so lame an expressing of so perfect a state, and when the abundant spirit of God hath given you, and me, and all, a real expressing of it, by making us all actual possessors of that Kingdome (*Ser.,* 6:167).

The Erotic Resurrection of the Body

The resurrection motif informs much of Donne's best and most representative poetry. This chapter will now attempt to illuminate the relation between sexual and spiritual experiences in terms of the continuity of this motif in Donne's "profane" and "sacred" poetry.[16] Many of Donne's secular love poems concern sexual experience, and his particular "turning to the body" contributes a new subject "fit for verse" to English lyric poetry. In the Elegy "To his Mistris Going to Bed," for example, Donne uses religious language to hasten his mistress "in[to] this hallow'd temple, this soft bed":

> Off with that girdle, like heavens zone
> > glistening
> But a farre fairer world encompassing. . . .
> How blest am I in this discovering thee.
> To enter in these bonds is to be free,
> Then where my hand is set my seal shall be.
> > Full nakedness, all joyes are due to thee.
> As soules unbodied, bodies uncloth'd must bee
> To taste whole joyes.

What legitimates Donne's distinctive joining sexual and religious experiences?

Erich Auerbach's concept of *figura* describes the principle by which Donne "interinanimates" religious and sexual experience. Seen in figural relation, the eschatological and the erotic incorporate each other:

> Figural interpretation establishes a connection between two events or persons, the first of which signifies not only itself but also the second, while the second encompasses or fulfills the first. The two poles of the figure are separate in time, but both, being real events, or figures, are within time, within the stream of historical life.

In the context of Donne's poetry, the two temporal events are the resurrection of the body in sexual experience (the first event begun in the past), which prefigures the resurrection of the soul (the first, or spiritual resurrection), the second event which both preserves and encompasses the first. From this figural relation of the two historical events, there arises one future, last event:

> yet both, looked at in this way, have something provisional and incomplete about them; they point to one another, and both point to something in the future, something still to come, which will be the actual, real, and definitive event.[17]

This future definitive event, twice partially prefigured in each past event, is the final resurrection of the body and soul to the heavenly union with the Trinity.

We may now observe the following relation between Donne's secular and religious poems. The erotic songs and sonnets present the resurrection of the body in the sexual union of man and woman, while the penitential divine poems portray the resurrection of the soul in the spiritual union of man and Christ; both events take place in history, and their relation is figural. The resurrection of the body prefigures the resurrection of the soul, which preserves and completes it by assuring the final resurrection, of body and soul, to heaven. Further, while each temporal event reflects the other, together they also adumbrate the final definitive event—the resurrection of body and soul to eternal union with the Trinity. Finally, the relation between the two present events and the third future event, which they both "point to," is anamnetic; that is, the temporal event "re-presents" an eternal event which has already occurred *sub specie aeternitatis,* but which remains to be realized *sub specie temporis.*

Anamnesis joins *kairos* (divine time, which is eternal) with *chronos* (human time, which is linear); the figural events in history "point to" and are consummated by the definitive event in eternity. This final, future fulfillment establishes temporal accord between beginnings and endings.[18] While the present earthly resurrections of body and soul prefigure this future heavenly resurrection, they also commemorate its past occurrence in Jesus Christ's Easter resurrection.

Traditional eschatology sanctions Donne's "interinanimating" sexual and spiritual love 1) because the relation between these resurrections of body and soul is figural and 2) because, taken together in anamnesis, they "re-present" the temporal adumbration of an eternal event. Just as man's resurrections in body and soul on earth both foreshadow each other and their future definitive realization, so also they celebrate and anticipate the divine resurrection—the eternal, hypostatical union of man's body and soul with the Godhead in heaven, as Donne preaches:

But, in heaven, it is *Caro mea, My flesh,* my souls flesh, my Saviour's flesh. As my meat is assimilated to my flesh, and made one flesh with it; as my soul is assimilated to my God, and *made partaker of the divine nature,* and *Idem Spiritus, the same Spirit with it;* so, there my flesh shall be assimilated to the flesh of my Saviour, and made the same flesh with him too. *Verbum caro factum, ut caro resurgeret;* Therefore God was made man, that that union might exalt the flesh of man to the right hand of God. . . . And *God shall quicken your mortall bodies, by his Spirit that dwelleth in you.* But this is not in consummation, in full accomplishment, till this resurrection, when it shall be *Caro mea, my flesh,* so, as that nothing can draw it from the allegiance of my God, . . . I shall see him in my flesh, which shall be mine as inseparably (in the *effect,* though not in the *manner*) as the *Hypostaticall Union* of God and man, in Christ, makes our nature and the Godhead one person in him (*Ser.,* 3 : 112–13).

In this and other passages, the theology of Donne's sermons provides doctrinal endorsement of this characteristic reflection of future eternity in the present moment through anamnesis, which we find in the figural relation between the secular and religious poems. Expanding John's conception of the resurrection as occurring twice in time—first in resurrection of the spirit, or soul, "now" on earth, and second in the resurrection of the dead in body and soul on the last day to heaven—both Augustine and Donne incorporate the present and first resurrection with the future and "last things." Donne's religious verse is primarily concerned with attaining this resurrection of the soul now on earth; accordingly, it dramatizes his struggle to repent, which reflects the simultaneous cooperation of divine and human wills and thereby assures redemption. Donne's secular verse is immediately concerned with the resurrection of the body now on earth; accordingly, it describes his experience of sexual love, which "re-presents" the redemption of the flesh (as the early Fathers insist will be preserved).

Further, as the present and temporal celebration of a past and future eternal event, the resurrection is enacted on earth as well as in heaven; it is a rising of both body and soul here and hereafter. From a psychological and theological viewpoint, the resurrection represents an ideal condition of complete unity in which all desire is satisfied momentarily on earth as a *figura* and "remembrancer" of heaven. Traditional eschatology sanctions the earthly configuration of union in sexual love as an anamnetic type of heavenly consummation. The temporal resurrection of the body in sexual experience both forms the present "pattern" of divine love "above" and yet, at the same time, originates from and is authenticated by Jesus' resurrection of body and soul on Easter, collectively consummated in the "great marriage" of Christ with the saved on the last day. The sexual union of man and woman on earth is the temporal and secular image which prefigures and commemorates the eternal and religious event which sanctions and fulfills it—the hypostatical union in body and soul of man and the Godhead in heaven.

Donne Contrasted with Shakespeare and Marvell

Donne's distinctive development of this religious relation between the erotic and the eschatological contrasts with the secular perspective in Shakespeare's sonnets. In sonnets 129, 144, 146, and 151 we find the collocation of sexual and Christian love, but Shakespeare speaks of them as opposite and mutually exclusive whereas Donne treats them as complementary and mutually inclusive. One basic reason for this difference (which will reappear in Blake and Yeats) arises from and illustrates part of the difference between a religious and secular viewpoint. In sonnet 129, for example, sexual, spiritual, and artistic desires —the expenses of spirit—are, at best, only momentarily satisfied—"a bliss in proof, and proved, a very woe"; further, their fulfillment betrays their promise: "a joy proposed," and, "proved, a very woe." Here, consummation (in the three forms of "spirit") is but a transitory heaven which leads to and quite literally end in hell ("to shun the heaven that leads men to this hell").[19]

Similarly, in sonnet 144 Shakespeare portrays an opposition between his two temporal loves, "of comfort and despair," in terms of the two final Christian alternatives, i.e., between the hope of salvation and the fear of damnation. Though the result of this conflict is not known (l. 13), the sonnet ends with a purgatorial image of sexual love wherein the bad angel fires (infects with venereal disease) the good angel into hell.

In sonnet 146 the "débat" between body and soul constitutes the same opposition between the physical and spiritual; it takes place with the "sense of an ending" and the ending of sense. Since body and soul exist only in a mutually destructive exchange— "then, soul, live upon thy servant's [the body's] loss"—"thy body's end," or death, becomes the life of the soul: "Buy terms divine in selling hours of dross."

While the content of Shakespeare's sonnet 146 resembles that of Donne's holy sonnet "Death, be not proud," the context of this final defiance of death significantly differs. It is unclear, i.e., unexplained, in Shakespeare's poem why "and Death once dead, there's no more dying then"; hopefully, death is denied by "buy[ing] terms divine," although I find no reason either within the sonnet, or in any Shakespearean sonnet, positively to affirm this Christian belief.[20] Briefly to substantiate this contrast, we can look ahead to the difference at the end of Donne's holy sonnet "Death, be not proud," where he emphasizes not only the natural finality in the fact of death ("there's no more dying then") but also the Christian certainty of immortal life for the saved: "one short sleep past, wee wake eternally." From a religious, in contrast to a secular, viewpoint, death is neither absolute nor without memorial.

The fourth and last example of Shakespeare's opposite, natural, perspective of the relation between physical and spiritual love will return us to Donne's religious treatment of this subject. Dealing with the first and last facts of natural life, birth and death, Shakespeare's sonnet 151 views these postlapsarian phenomena from a secular perspective. Again, in the separation and opposition between body and soul (ll. 5-8), the body ascends ("rising"); further, like the unfaithful relation between poet and mistress (ll. 3-6), the gross body also "betrays" the gentle soul. Though love may give birth to an ethical "conscience," this awareness belongs to a sexual and not a spiritual consciousness (ll. 13-14). Accordingly, the direction of movement is only physical and inevitably downward; the poet is like the first Adam ("whose dear love"—costly indeed—is Eve), the image of the fall to sin and death, and not like the last Adam, the image of his resurrection to salvation and eternal life. The sonnet concludes by "embracing" only the first act of the Christian narrative and thereby presents a secular position; betraying the soul, the body is aware only of its own ascendency, which is here sexual and temporary, so that man returns downward and unredeemed. Excluding or reversing the traditional Christian pattern of the resurrection, Shakespeare presents only the Adamic movement of sexuality: "I rise and fall."

The fullness of Donne's eschatological expectations also contrasts with Marvell's view of "love's body" after death. In "To his Coy Mistress" Marvell begins and ends with a secular view of time, as *chronos,* i.e., as linear and limited to natural life:

> Had we but World enough and Time
> This Coyness Lady were no crime. . . .
> My vegetable Love should grow
> Vaster than Empires, and more slow.[21]

Further, he expects no supernatural life, made possible for the faithful through Christ's slaying death and rising to immortal life.

Accordingly, Marvell speaks of love as confined to the time-bound world:

> But at my back I alwaies hear
> Time's winged Charriot hurrying near:
> And yonder all before us lye
> Desarts of Vast Eternity.

As the metaphor indicates, Marvell here views eternity as a "vast" "desart" of "dust" and "ashes" to which man returns after death. Because man is only mortal and corruptible, in the Pauline "natural body," and because he is not raised an immortal and incorruptible "spiritual body" here or hereafter, his future is vacant and without resurrection to divine union: "The Grave's a fine and private place,/ But none I think do there embrace."

In direct contrast with Shakespeare's and Marvell's natural perspective, Donne's eschatological expectations are fully supernatural: "We dye and rise the same, and prove/ Mysterious by this love," for

> Only our love hath no decay;
> This no tomorrow hath, nor yesterday,
> Running it never runs from us away,
> But truly keepes his first, last,
>   everlasting day.[22]

Taking the "little" "pretty roomes" built in sonnets as an "everywhere" of the poet's world, we can return to Donne's, where the above contrasts will help distinguish how Donne incorporates the eschatological into the erotic through Christian figura and anamnesis. In his songs and sonnets Donne insists on the union of two bodies and two souls into one body joined with one soul while each remains both individuated and shared: "Let us possess one [or, our] world, each hath one, and is one."[23]

Moreover, the results of this physical and spiritual union, or "marriage," illuminate the distinction between Donne's and Shakespeare's views of love. As J. B. Leishman has shown, Shakespeare and Donne do share one similar attitude on this subject: that love defies time.[24] But, whereas Shakespeare's "marriage of true minds" endures "even to the edge of doom," i.e., until the apocalyptic destruction of this fallen world, Donne's "marriage" lives eternally in the "good-morrow": "If our two loves be one, or, thou and I/ Love so alike, that none doe slacken, none can die." Whereas Shakespeare's "two loves" are "of comfort and despair" (sonnet 144), Donne's "two loves" are of man and woman and man and Christ; and, seen in figural relation, they are "one." Thus, as suggested, this difference between Shakespeare and Donne arises from Donne's essentially religious view of sexual love: the resurrection in soul and body to heavenly union with the Trinity sanctions both sacred and profane love relationships.

In the context of the wholly-holy union of the lovers recurring in the erotic poems, the theological model for this sexual union which subsumes and also preserves the individual identity of body and soul is the relation between the faithful Christian and Christ: the first resurrections of the body and soul on earth prefigure and "remember" the reunion of body and soul and their last resurrection to heaven and eternal hypostatical union with the Godhead.

Donne's Theology and Poetry of "Marriage"

Revelation is, not surprisingly, one of Donne's favorite Biblical books,[25] and two of his marriage sermons deal also with the "great marriage" (of Rev. 19:9 and 21:1-2); this collocation elucidates the sacred pattern of the profane love poems. Donne's theology of "marriage" views the temporal union of man and woman as both anticipating and "remembering" the eternal union of God in man; as a type of "incarnation," human marriage prefigures the resurrection to divine marriage. Accordingly, "marriage" defines the three major Christian relations between body and soul which unite the human and divine: "God having thus maried soule and body in one man, and man [the human body] and God [the divine Spirit], in one Christ, he marries this Christ [the world's soul] to the Church [the collective body]" (*Ser.*, 6:155).

Preaching at the wedding of Mistress Margaret Washington (on 30 May 1621), Donne ends by thus reminding that the present marriage of a man and a woman in soul and body on earth is patterned after and consummated by the eternal marriage of the resurrected Christian in body and soul with Christ in heaven. In a passage which recalls "The Second Anniversary," Donne elaborates on this essential temporal difference:

> for the eternity is a great part of that marriage. Consider then how poor and needy thing, all the riches of this world, how flat and tasteless a thing, all the pleasures of this world, how pallid, faint and dilute a thing, all the honours of this world are, when the very Treasure, our Joy, and glory of heaven it self were unperfect, if it were not eternall, and my marriage shall be soe, In aeternum, for ever (*Ser.,* 3:254).

While the "true" human marriage endures "even to the edge of doom," the divine marriage of body and soul with Christ lasts "without interruption, or diminution, or change of affections" forever in eternity (Ser., 3:255).

In a later marriage sermon preached at the wedding of the Earl of Bridgewater's daughter (on 19 November 1627) on Matthew 22:30, Donne compares and distinguishes earthly marriage and heavenly marriage so

> that they may all make this union of Mariage a *Type,* or a *remembrancer of their union with God in Heaven . . . that our admission to the Mariage here, may be our invitation to the Marriage Supper of the Lamb there.* (*Ser.,* 8:96; continuous italics mine).

With these typical pronouncements on marriage, both of a man and a woman *sub specie temporis* and between the faithful and Christ *sub specie aeternitatis,* the divine figure in Donne's tapestry of human love in the erotic poems can be seen. That human love originates from and "remembers" the divine love of the Christian and Christ sanctions Donne's "contracting" (metaphoric transferring or "metaphysical conceit") sexual with spiritual love, consummated in the final heavenly resurrection and "great marriage."

Before discussing Donne's erotic love poems, we can ask: how shall a writer express a religious belief in poetic language, i.e., what are the philosophic and linguistic relations between Donne's theology and poetry? In "The Relique" and "Upon the Sydneyan Psalme Translations" Donne confronts this problem of naming the unnameable, and the former ends with the literal difficulty of relating "what miracles we harmlesse lovers wrought": "But now alas,/ All measure, and all language, I shoulde passe,/ Should I tell what a miracle she was." Yet, of course, Donne did write his love poems, which do tell what miracles he wrought.

What is the provenance of Donne's recurring and distinctive image of love's wholeness-holiness?

I suggest that the Christian doctrine of the resurrection not only sanctions Donne's incorporating the erotic into the eschatological in anamnetic relation, but also gives him "metaphors for poetry." That is, because, as a traditional religious symbol, the resurrection "represents" final reality, it permits "contracting," or transferring, the image of the as-yet-unconsummated last day into known experience and language of the present reality so that the eternal intersects the temporal. This "transfiguration" is not an "expense" but an "expanse" ("like gold to ayrey thinesse beate") of spirit which preserves and enhances the validity of the religious and erotic experiences so "married."

"Valediction: Forbidding Mourning"

The erotic motif of the resurrection follows Donne's eschatological model, and in a "Valediction: Forbidding Mourning" the underlying analogy compares the separation of an individual's body and soul at death with that of the lovers' separation of bodies and soul because of a journey.[26] As virtuous men need not fear death, so the "super-earthly" lovers need not fear separation, since their refined love includes the physical and the spiritual. Unlike that of the "dull sublunary lovers," the soul of their love is not made of sense but of a more enduring and intangible substance, "that our selves know not what it is."

Donne's affinity for words, especially for verbs, dealing with joining together ("marrying"), bespeaks his recurring concern for relations of unity.[27] As earlier observed, the pattern for this, and other love unions, sexual and spiritual, is the "hypostaticall union" of God and man; and this theological model legitimates erotic experiences and poetic expressions of unity. Because their love is a "true marriage," it is "inter-assured of the mind"; the couple are mutually and mentally certain of their love, given and returned. In "Valediction" the cause of the inter-assuredness is the union of their souls which renders their love invulnerable (unlike that of the "dull sublunary lovers"):

> Our two soules therefore, which are one,
> Though I must goe, endure not yet
> A breach, but an expansion
> Like gold to ayrey thinesse beate.

While Donne here insists on the refined and golden unity of these lovers' souls so that they are always spiritually together, in the next stanza he elaborates how they also preserve their individuality in this union: "If they be two, they are two so/ As stiffe twin compasses are two."

Though thus far the poem argues that the union of the two souls defines and refines their "marriage," the last two stanzas represent this primary relation of spiritual love in sexual form. If the twin feet of the compass are their souls joined in the center (i.e., at the top), the circle they draw is one of sexual union "and makes me end, where I begunne." Because the "super-earthly" lovers are first united spiritually, their love never suffers death or breach or diminution. Similarly in "The Good-morrow" to these "waking soules" Donne argues that "whatever dyes was not mixt equally;/ If our two loves be one, or thou and I/ Love so alike, that none doe slacken, none can die." Following and expressing this spiritual union, the lovers then (in the last three stanzas) join in sexual union. The contextual pattern for this erotic progression is eschatological. As the final resurrection of body and soul to heaven depends on this initial resurrection of the spirit on earth, so their spiritual love sanctions and leads to sexual union. Further, this human "marriage" on earth antici-pates and celebrates the "great marriage" in heaven.

"The Extasie"

In "The Extasie" following the same argument, Donne elab-orates this figural relation of the lovers' bodies and souls. While much of the commentary on this poem disputes its Platonic ele-ments,[28] we shall consider the theological model which generates the "Extasie" and which the erotic experience commemorates. Donne's proposing the proper relation (in the earthly body and soul) between the lovers here both imitates and adumbrates the relation (in the heavenly body and soul) between Christ and his Bride hereafter.

To reflect this distinctive relation which transfers theological into erotic images, Donne uses two new words in the "Extasie" —"sepulchrall" and "interinanimates."[29] Of the first—"And whil'st our soules negotiate there,/ Wee like sepulchrall statues lay,"—I suggest that the ground for comparing the lovers to "sepulchrall statues" resides primarily in the metaphor under-lying the poem's argument (to which Donne's new usage points):

as "sepuchrall statues" can be associated with the final rising of
the dead body and its reunion with the soul, so these lovers
imitate and prefigure on earth the resurrection to heaven. While
such an interpretation is not "proveable," I think Panofsky's
observations in *Tomb Sculpture* support this reading of the
"sepulchrall" ambiance:

> [The greater flexibility of the *demi-gisant* form appeared] in England,
> in such a way that the privilege of facing eternity in a state of moderate
> wakefulness was reserved to the husband while his lady—placed as was
> fairly usual in British tombs, on a lower level—had to be satisfied with
> perpetual recumbency. Much more important, however, is the fact that
> the reclining but activated effigy could be interpreted, depending on
> whether the occupant of the tomb was thought of as dead or still alive,
> either as *the portrayal of a person rising from the grave* . . . or as *the
> portrayal of a person giving up his ghost to God.*[30]

The following stanzas (6-12) elaborate the definition of the
lovers' spiritual relation. "So by love refin'd," they speak the
same language of the soul, and their shared spiritual ecstasy reveals and "tells us what we love." Their mode of understanding
is analogous, I feel, to the traditional Christian mode of knowing
God in heaven, as Donne describes it, for example, in the "Second Anniversary": "Onely who haue enioyd/ The sight of God,
in fulnesse, can thinke it;/ For it is both the obiect and the wit."[31]
Ecstasy involves obtaining knowledge of the divine directly and
intuitively, without discursive reason; and it includes the use of
the transfigured senses, especially of seeing (as Blake reminds,
"thro' the eye"), as Paul describes in 1 Corinthians 13:12, as
Augustine describes in the *City of God*, Book XXII, and as
Donne preaches in his Easter sermon of 1628, on this passage
of 1 Corinthians:

> prepare you to see him then [in heaven] in his Essence. . . . It is not
> called a better sight, nor a better knowledge, but there is no other sight,
> no other knowledge proposed, mentioned, or intimated, or imagined but
> this: All other sight is blindnesse, all other knowledge is ignorance. . . .
> But in heaven, our sight is *face to face,* And our knowledge is *to know,
> as we are knowne* (*Ser.,* 8:220).

Earthly ecstasy imitates and adumbrates intuitive sight and
knowledge in heaven.

Further, the results of this divine sight resemble that which
the lovers see (ll. 31-32):

> And it shall be a knowledge so like his knowledge, as it shall produce a

love, like his love, and we shall love him, as he loves us. . . . And as this seeing, and this knowing of God crownes all other joys, and glories, even in heaven, so this very crown is crowned. There growes from this a higher glory, which is . . . That we shall be made partakers of the Divine nature (*Ser.,* 8:236).

The final paragraph from this sermon returns from contemplating this heavenly ecstasy to its earthly practice: "Only that man that loves God, hath the art of love himself" (*Ser.,* 8:236). This image and this art appear throughout Donne's love poems, and they confirm the figural relation between divine and human love. The definitive model for human love between man and woman is divine love between man and God.

In the "Extasie" the content (what they "containe") of these model earthly lovers is "not sexe," though after their initial spiritual union, they express their love in sexual form. But first their souls join to engender a new, single soul which combines and preserves the individuality of each separate soul: "Love, these mixt soules, doth mixe again,/ And makes both one, each this and that." While these lines may express a "Neo-Platonic commonplace,"[32] they also describe Donne's characteristic Christian image of the united lovers, whose sexual union represents secular "incarnation" (*Ser.,* 6:155).

Donne's Easter sermon of 1626 (on 1 Corinthians 15:20) ends with his interpretation of the first and last resurrections, the second part of which bears directly on our discussion of the "Extasie" (while the first part pertains to his religious poetry, to be discussed shortly):

> He that rises to this judgment of recollecting, and of judging himselfe, shall rise with a chearfulnesse, and stand with a confidence, when Christ shall come in the second: [the last judgment at the *parousia*] And, *Quando exacturus est in secundo, quod dedit in primo* [Augustine], when Christ shall call for an account, in that second judgment, how he hath husbanded those graces, which he gave him; for the first, he shall make his possession of this first resurrection, his title, and his evidence to the second . . . [when] body and soule [shall be] so united, as if both were one spirit in itselfe, and God so united to both, as thou shalt be the same spirit with God (*Ser.,* 7:117).

This theological image of the final union between the resurrected man's body and soul with God sanctions and informs Donne's poetic image of the lovers' union in the "Extasie."[33]

Further describing the new soul which arises from the union of each lover's soul, Donne coins the second new word in the

"Extasie"—"interinanimates." Both Donne's predilection for making new words to describe his lovers and this verb's meaning suggest his characteristic concern for mutual relations, especially for unions of love on earth and in heaven and their connection:

> When love, with one another so
> Interinanimates two soules,
> That abler soule, which thence doth flow.
> Defects of lonelinesse controules.
>
> Wee then, who are this new soule, know,
> Of what we are compos'd, and made,
> For, th'Atomies of which we grow,
> Are soules, whom no change can invade.

These lines are glossed by a lovely description from an early sermon which applies to love's "interinanimation":

> Love is a Possessory Affection; it delivers over him that loves into the possession of that that he loves; it is a transmutory Affection; it changes him that loves into the very nature of that that he loves, and he is nothing else (*Ser.*, 1: 184–85).

This union and transmutation "repairs" the lovers, who, as Blake reminds, became defective when separated in the fall (in the "wars of Eden divided into male and female"). Just as the first resurrection assures "wounded" man's reunion of body and soul, so this spiritual "interinanimation" pairs (joins) and thereby repairs (mends) them, in body and soul. As in "Valediction," the poem's development suggests an initial spiritual union which then enhances a sexual union; this order imitates the conventional Christian pattern of redemption, as Donne preaches in his sermons.

The last seven stanzas of the "Extasie" return to the "repaired" lovers, now joined in body and soul, who imitate and adumbrate the relation between the resurrected and Christ, as the conclusion of this sermon on Job 19: 26 bespeaks:

> We shall see the Humanity of Christ with our bodily eyes, then glorified; but that flesh, though glorifyed, cannot make us see God better, nor clearer, then the soul alone hath done, all the time, from our death to our resurrection . . . such a gladnesse shall my soul have, that this flesh, (which shall no longer be her prison, nor her tempter, but her friend, her companion, her wife) that this flesh, that is, I, in the re-union and redintegration of both parts, shall see God (*Ser.*, 3: 112).

While here "love's mysteries in soules doe grow,/ But yet the body is his booke," hereafter these "mysteries" are traditionally revealed when body and soul are joined with Christ:

> But, in heaven, it is *Caro mea, My flesh,* my soul's flesh, my Saviour's flesh, . . . as my soul is assimilated to my flesh, and made one flesh with it, as my soul is assimilated to my God, and made partaker of the divine nature, and *Idem Spiritus, the same spirit* with it, so, there my flesh shall be assimilated to the flesh of my Saviour, and made the same flesh with him too. . . . I shall see God, I shall see him in my flesh, which shall be mine as inseparably (in the *effect,* though not in the *manner*), as the *Hypostaticall Union* of God, and man, in Christ, makes our nature and the Godhead one person in him. My flesh shall no more be none of mine, then Christ shall not be man, as well as God (*Ser.,* 3:112–13).

This final union is the eschatological source of the erotic pattern of the "Extasie." The eternal hypostatical union of God and man in body and soul in heaven sanctions the temporal sexual union of man and woman on earth, which prefigures and "remembers" the resurrection to new Jerusalem.

"The Sunne Rising"

While the "Extasie" ends with the "small change" when the spiritual lovers go to enjoy their bodies, "The Sunne Rising" presents the "morning after," and I will deal briefly with its language and argument.[34] "The Sunne Rising" is a brilliant example of Donne's witty defiance of time and the world through an apotheosis of sexual love "in that the world's contracted thus"—into the lovers' bed. If one reads the poem in the Ovidian tradition, which it echoes, the excessive claims, especially in stanza three, are proper and successful; but if one considers the poem's language within the Christian tradition, then I think that Donne's religious pronouncements add to the "meaning," success, and enjoyment of the poem. Here, as in the "Anniversaries," we must ask "who is the lady?"; and in both poems I think we must answer that she has a historical and secular (*sub specie temporis*) as well as an ahistorical and theological (*sub specie aeternitatis*) identity.

Adding a religious perspective illuminates a reading of "Sunne Rising," as Helen Gardner's helpful note on another use of "the rags of time" (repeated here in l. 10) will show:

We begin with that which is elder than our beginning, and shall over-
live our end, The mercy of God. . . . The names of the first and last
derogate from it, for the first and last are but the ragges of time, and his
mercy hath no relation to time, no limitation in time, it is not first, nor
last, but eternal, everlasting.[35]

First, in content, this passage speaks of the Christian principle of
figural fulfillment that we have observed. Second, in the context
of "Sunne Rising," this passage suggests a relation between the
concepts of time from a religious and sexual viewpoint. As was
discussed briefly in Shakespeare's sonnets, both the priest and
lover scorn time, albeit for different reasons. Now, in "Sunne
Rising," Donne is, at least covertly, playing with the similarities
and differences between an ecclesiastical and a sexual defiance of
time and worldy goods.

Characteristically, Donne's gesture throughout "Sunne Rising" moves centripetally toward an image of sexual unification:
"All here in one bed lay." Yet, we must ask what Donne means
by "all" and who the beloved lady he speaks of is. Here again
figural interpretation completes the identity and meaning of the
separate individual parts. Not denying the literal, historical
actuality of the woman, I think that we must add that as the
earthly, sexual bride, she is also a figura of the heavenly, hypostatical bride. Further, because human love anticipates and remembers divine love, the effect of these analogous, but different,
loves is similar; each lover possesses the other and a better world
than the material, natural world both scorn:

> She is all States, and all Princes, I,
>   Nothing else is.
> Princes doe but play us; compar'd to this,
>   All honor's mimique; All wealth alchimie.

From a Christian viewpoint, Christ, the principle of creation, is
everything and the natural world nothing;[36] whereas from a
romantic viewpoint, the beloved is all.

While in this poem Donne clearly enjoys the erotic embodiment of the whole world, this temporal, earthly resurrection of
the body prefigures and celebrates the eternal, heavenly resurrection of the body and soul: "Thou sunne art halfe as happy as
wee,/ In that the world's contracted thus." Though there is no
question that these suggestive and festive lines function, at least
partially, in an Ovidian context, I think that their "meaning" is

completed by a Christian understanding of their figural relation. In thus "contracting" the natural world, Donne images the earthly, sexual bride as a figural and anamnetic type of the heavenly, hypostatical bride "contracted" in the supernatural "great marriage."

"The Canonization"

This discussion of the figural anamnetic relation between the eschatological and erotic in Donne's secular poems concludes with "The Canonization"; it emphatically speaks of natural (physical love) experience in supernatural (religious) language: "For Godsake hold your tongue, and let me love." This combination—the "marriage" of the sexual and spiritual—not only contributes a new subject—the resurrection of the body—"fit for verse," but also generates most of Donne's best poetry, which his sermons elucidate. The "Canonization's" central image is of resurrection, and here again the dying and rising are the sexual mode of the religious motif. This underlying metaphor transfers the eschatological to the erotic while it preserves and enhances (literally "elevates") the individual validity of both.

Donne's initial invocation can refer to and join both kinds of experience: "For Godsake . . . let me love." Turning from the exaggerated external opposition to his love, the lover's self-definition (beginning with stanza three) comprises the erotic "doctrine" of the poem. The images form a progression 1) from the small, separate, and natural to the large, unified, and supernatural and 2) from what is consumed and dies to what is reborn the same and finally better. Though dramatically this pseudo-spontaneous list of alternatives befits the lover's impassioned self-defense, which mocks the interfering world, his arrangement of these choices is more important to his argument. Through this imagistic development the lover shows 1) that he and his beloved do not harm anyone else because, in typically Donnean fashion, they are one world to each other (and hence preclude or possess all other worlds); and moreover, 2) that these lovers are a necessary and exemplary model for the very world which wrongly scorns them. The basis for each claim, which determines the structure of imagery in stanza three, is religious: that finally the spiritual lovers' sexual union forms the present (*sub specie temporis*) "pattern" of the past and future (*sub specie aeterni-*

tatis) central event of redemption, Christ's resurrection; their human union, in soul and body, thus prefigures and "remembers" the divine union.

Let us now attend to Donne's development of this underlying metaphor which joins the erotic with the eschatological at the center (stanzas three and four) of the "Canonization." Both the flye (butterfly or moth) and the taper to which it is attracted die at their own cost and choice without regeneration. The image of each lover's containing the "eagle and the Dove" 1) expands that of the winged moth and prepares for the Phoenix and 2) introduces the male-female contrast resolved by the androgynous Phoenix and then by sexual union. Since the eagle and the Dove so joined signify typical masculine and feminine traits, there is also a progression toward unity and perfection, traditionally consummated in the resurrection. If we consider the Phoenix's miraculously arising from flames and ashes, both the act and the context are conventional apocalyptic motifs, and this pattern adds a specifically religious ambiance to the regenerations. The lovers' sexual consummation appropriately climaxes the imagistic argument of this central stanza: "Wee can dye by it, if not live by love, and prove,/ Mysterious by this love."

From both a secular and a religious viewpoint, this rising the same is "mysterious," but for different reasons; whereas a hostile interfering Petrarchan viewpoint (of stanzas one and two) cannot understand or accept the lovers' complete union and sexual fulfillment, a religious viewpoint considers dying and rising the same as divinely "mysterious" because not fully known (and revealed) and "realized" until the "second coming" on the last day:[37] "Behold, I shew you a mystery; We shall not sleep [in the grave], but we shall all be changed" (1 Cor. 15:51). Here, however, Donne incorporates this future, eternal eschatological event into the present, temporal erotic event because the sexual resurrection of the body prefigures and "re-presents" the final resurrection of the dead body and soul.

After enacting this "miracle," in the telling of it, Donne reflexively finds it a source of poetic perpetuation (in stanza four). If they are love's martyrs, they will also be love's saints, immortalized in verse: "And by these hymnes, all shall approve/ Us *Canoniz'd* for Love." The last stanza substantiates this claim of canonization by turning back to the world which initially scorned them but which now invokes the "reverend" and archetypal earthly lovers who have risen ("above") to the elevated terrestrial paradise; accordingly, the future, fallen world addresses this prelapsarian Adam and Eve as "You, to whom love as peace, that now is rage" because they have returned to the peaceful love of Eden, which passeth lapsarian understanding of love ("that now is rage"). Again, to use the figural principle, these "canonized" lovers are New Testament embodiments of the resurrection who thus complete the Old Testament Adam and Eve, who enacted the fall.[38]

Though the textual variant—"extract" or "contract" (in l. 40)—in the penultimate image suggests an alchemical metaphor, the lovers' transmutation of the "whole worlds soule," extracted or contracted, is both physical and spiritual; i.e., having "died" in sexual love and yet mysteriously risen "above," they are the "patterne" of love both human and divine, for the "whole worlds soule" is Christ,[39] whom they "contract" or "marry."[40] This miracle the canonized lovers wrought, and the theological model for Donne's joining ("marrying") the eschatological with the erotic is the present (*sub specie temporis*) resurrection of body and soul in sexual union as the earthly "patterne" which prefigures and "celebrates" the past and future (*sub specie aeternitatis*) resurrection of body and soul to the hypostatical union of man and the Godhead.

The First, or Spiritual, Resurrection in the Divine Poems

While the resurrection motif informs Donne's secular poems as the resurrection of the body in sexual love of man and woman which anticipates and commemorates the divine union of man and God in heaven, in the divine poems Donne portrays the first resurrection of the soul in spiritual love and union with God. Taken together, Donne's "profane" and "sacred" poems concerning the resurrection share a figural, anamnetic relation.[41] While in the "Extasie" Donne proposes that "Loves mysteries in soules doe grow,/ But yet the body is his booke," in the divine poems he "restores" "with a new verse the ancient rhyme. Redeem/ The time, Redeem/ The unread vision in the higher dream."[42]

This redemptive imperative applies to Donne's treatment of the resurrection in the divine poems in that the first, or spiritual resurrection, must be realized *sub specie temporis* (on earth in *chronos*) in order to be fulfilled *sub specie aeternitatis* (in heaven in *kairos*):

> He that rises to this Judgement of recollecting, and of *judging himselfe,* shall rise with a chearfulnesse, and stand with a confidence, when Christ Jesus shall come in the second . . . *he shall make his possession of this first resurrection his title and his evidence to the second* (*Ser.,* 7:117; italics mine).

While in the songs and sonnets Donne "contracts" his present erection as prefiguring and celebrating the final resurrection, in the divine poems he "contracts" his first, or spiritual, resurrection as assuring the last resurrection of body and soul. Accordingly, in the divine poems Donne emphasizes proper penance ("judging himselfe") and dramatizes the doctrine of the resurrection (preached in his sermons) from a traditional and personal perspective.

Donne's prime concern in the divine poems is with the doctrine of the first, or spiritual, resurrection through the simultaneous cooperation of God's grace and man's penance, which assures his final resurrection. Whereas in the songs and sonnets Donne speaks of eschatological expectation as the figural model for erotic experience, in the divine poems he reverses this pattern to speak of man's present spiritual relation with God as sexual. Further, whether Donne portrays his relation with God in spiritual or sexual terms, his most important concern in the divine poems remains proper penance and the resulting first resurrection of the soul.

In the holy sonnet "Batter my heart," for example, Donne informs a traditional religious doctrine (penance through God's gift of grace) with a sexual content (ravishment); in a sermon Donne provides the ecclesiastical basis for this metaphor: "Repentance, is an everlasting Divorce from our beloved Sin, and an everlasting Marriage and superinduction of our ever-living God" (*Ser.,* 7:163). Donne's sexual metaphor for religious experience in this sonnet coincides with and supports the intensity of his invocation for divine sustenance. Not only does Donne appeal to the Christian Trinity (" three-person'd God") but, to triple the strength of his plea, he invests each member of the Trinity with the conventional attributes of the others and thus in effect invokes a nine-personed God.[43] The underlying metaphor which generates this triple plea is clear: sexual union is the temporal pattern of the eternal union with the Trinity.

In the second and third quatrains Donne draws on the Biblical convention wherein the formerly righteous community which has turned from God's to evil ways is spoken of as a "beseiged city" and as an adulterous woman who have broken the divine covenant and betrayed God's love; in Revelation these Old Testaments types climax in "Babylon, the mother of harlots and earth's abominations."[44] Donne's plea for personal salvation combines the Old Testament prophetic imperative of individual and communal renewal with the New Testament apocalyptic imperative of complete transformation, the Christian image of redemption: "make me new."

Donne incorporates these traditional images in the underlying metaphor which generates the sonnet's religious invocation: the first resurrection ("That I may rise") as sexual union with God:

> Take mee to you, imprison mee, for I
> Except you'enthrall mee, never shall be free,
> Nor ever chaste, except you ravish mee.

What may appear paradoxical in expression (freedom through enthrallment and chastity through ravishment) is traditional in Christian conception: after the final resurrection to heaven,

I shall see all the beauty, and all the glory of all the saints of God, and love them all, and know that the Lamb loves them too, without jealousie, on his part, to theirs, or mine, and so be maried *in aeternum,* for ever, without interruption, or diminution, or change of affections. . . . Christ himself shall no longer [be] a Mediator, an Intercessor, an Advocate, and yet shall continue a Husband to my soul for ever . . . [and] this very body which cannot choose but die, shall live, and live as long as that God of life that made it . . . this secular mariage [is] a type of the spirituall, and the spirituall an earnest of that eternall [great marriage of the Lamb] (*Ser.,* 3:254–55).

Earthly marriage—1) of man and woman in body and soul and 2) of man and God in spirit, the first resurrection—prefigures and is consummated in the heavenly "great marriage."

Whereas the songs and sonnets present this divine union as the temporal sexual union which anticipates and "remembers" this eternal hypostatical union, the divine poems present this divine marriage as the first resurrection of the soul to God, which assures the final resurrection. In both groups of poems, as in the "Anniversaries," Donne's central concern is traditionally Christian in its proper penance and resulting final resurrection to a complete and eternal beatitude—both individual and communal.

"Showe me deare Christ, thy Spouse"

The holy sonnet "Batter my heart" dramatizes Donne's plea for divine love returned through God's gift of grace—"Yet dearly I love you, and would be lov'd faine"—in terms of a personal, spiritual marriage with God. And the holy sonnet "Show me deare Christ, thy spouse" expands the marriage metaphor from the individual to the communal configuration. Though Donne most frequently treats his own personal salvation in the divine poems, he also presents the collective form of redemption, completed in the "communion of saints." In light of Gardner's scholarly "Interpretation of Donne's Sonnet on the Church," this discussion will emphasize Donne's answer to " 'What is the mark of the Church of Christ?' ": " 'Unity and Godly love.' "[45]

In a sermon on Revelation 7:9 Donne first speaks of the multiplicity of the heavenly dwelling and of the *"sociablenesse, the communciablenesse* of God":

> He loves holy meetings, he loves the *communion of Saints,* the *houshold of the faithfull.* . . . [New Jerusalem] is a *city,* a *kingdome,* not onely a house, but a house that hath *many mansions* in it: still it is a *plurall* thing, consisting of *many:* and very good *grammarians* amongst the *Hebrews,* have thought, and said, that the very *name,* by which God notifies himself to the world, in the very beginning of *Genesis,* which is *Elohim,* as it is a *plurall* word there, so it hath no *singular:* they say we cannot name God but *plurally;* so sociable, so communciable, so extensive, so derivative of himself, is God, and so manifold are the beames, and the emanations that flow out from him (*Ser.,* 6:152).

But while the content of God's kingdom is plural, its form is unified and singular:

> Beyond all this, God having maried soule and body in one man, and man and God in one Christ, he marries this Christ to the Church . . . God hast made to the consummation of this Marriage, between Christ and the Church (*Ser.,* 6:155).

Just as Noah's Ark was "a Type and figure of the Church," so the earthly Church should be a type and figure of the heavenly Church.

This figural principle which interprets *chronos* as preserved and fulfilled by *kairos,* structures Donne's invocations in "show me deare Christ, thy spouse so bright and cleare." The Christian image of the marriage of Christ with the collective body of Christians, the Church, informs the underlying metaphor:

> Betray kind husband thy spouse to our sights,
> And let myne amorous soule court thy mild Dove,
> Who is most trew, and pleasing to thee, then
> When she is embrac'd and open to most men.

Paradoxically elaborating the view of the Church as Christ's bride (deriving from Rev. 21 : 2-4), Donne is certain of figural fulfillment.[46]

These introductory meditations on last things illuminate Donne's distinctive dramatization of them. Donne "contracts" Christian expectations of the last day into the present moment. In the sermons this immediateness results in his emphasizing the first, or spiritual, resurrection on earth from sin to salvation through God's gift of grace; in the divine poems this view provides numerous occasions for enacting this present drama of penance. Donne's religious poems portray this Christian doctrine preached in his sermons; his poetic and theological sensibilities are unified in "the amourousnesse of an harmonious Soule" in properly loving the Godhead: "Thou lov'st not, till from loving more, thou free/ My Soule: who ever gives, takes libertie."[47]

"*Hymne to God, my God, in my Sicknesse*"

This healing union of body and soul through present penitential labor is the reflexive subject of "Hyme to God, my God, in my Sicknesse"; its temporal "instrumentation" occurs in the first, or spiritual, resurrection on earth:

> Since I am comming to that Holy roome,
> Where, with thy Quire of Saints for evermore,
> I shall be made thy Musique; As I come
> I tune the Instrument here at the dore,
> And what I must doe then, thinke now before.

The Biblical origin of these lines, Revelation 4 (especially verse 8, announced in Isaiah 6:2-3), envisions the eternal glorious praises and union of the heavenly host with God, as Donne assures "That the dead, and we, are now all in one Church, and at the resurrection, shall be all in one Quire."[48] The present spiritual resurrection, which Donne seeks in the "Hymne to God, my God" (and in the other divine poems concerning penance) assures the future possession of that kingdom of God.

This "Hymne's" underlying metaphor argues that the present spiritual resurrection assures the future resurrection of body and soul; stanza three geographically describes the unity which traditionally results:

> I joy, that in these straits, I see my West;
> . . . As West and East
>   In all flatt Maps (and I am one) are one,
>   So death doth touch the Resurrection.[49]

With this hope of the last resurrection, the last two stanzas apply the figural principle in basically traditional terms:[50]

> Looke Lord, and finde both *Adams* met in me;
>   As the first *Adams* sweat surrounds my face,
>   May the last *Adams* blood my soule embrace.

Elaborating this potential identity, the last stanza joins Donne's present vocation with his future fulfillment:

> And as to others soules I preach'd thy word,
>   Be this my Text, my Sermon to mine owne,
>   Therfore that he may raise the Lord throws down.

In the above lines "this" refers to Donne's sick body, which is the physical text, a type of Biblical "incarnation" from which he reads understanding of the divine. The sermon resulting from this text, he preaches "to mine owne" soul, the earthly participant in the first, or spiritual, resurrection. In this "hymne" Donne speaks of his present sickness as physical death and of his future health as the spiritual resurrection.[51]

While the resurrection depends on God's sustenance,[52] this "hymne" bespeaks Donne's particular and recurrent concern for present human cooperation with the divine. The theology of the poem's conclusion implies that if Donne's sermon (this poem) to his own soul on this text (his sick body) is acceptable, then the Lord will raise him; Donne emphasizes this causal relation in the last lines: "Be this my Text, my Sermon to mine owne,/ Therfore that he may raise the Lord throws down."

"At the round earth's imagin'd corners, blow"

Donne's imagination is characteristically attracted to last things, and his interpretation of the resurrection doctrine reflects this "contracting" the last day into the present moment, specifically in expanding John and Augustine and teaching that the first, or spiritual, resurrection on earth assures the last resurrection, of body and soul, to heaven. Thus, as Donne preaches, "it is impossible to separate the consideration of the Resurrection, from the consideration of the Judgement" (*Ser.*, 6:277); and further, the first judgment is the self-judgment of Christian penance.[53] The apocalyptic sonnet "At the round earth's imagin'd corners, blow" dramatizes not only Donne's eschatological imagination, but also his personal, urgent *agon* of proper penance.

The theology of "At the round earths imagin'd corners" is traditional, except for varying, by delaying, the saved soul's resurrection to the beatific vision from the hours of death until after the general last judgment.[54] In lines 9-14 of this sonnet, however, the reason (so far as it is poetically discernible) for this postponement derives from and emphasizes Donne's personal and presently sinful condition:

> But let them sleepe, Lord, and mee mourne a space,
> For, if above all these, my sinnes abound,
> 'Tis late to aske abundance of thy grace,

If Donne deviates from his usual view of the state of the soul after death, it is dramatically and theologically "justified" here since he would delay God's last judgment in order to pass favourable first judgment upon himself by repenting of his sins: "Teach mee how to repent; for that's as good/ As if thou hadst seal'd my pardon, with thy blood."

The model of salvation implied in these lines typifies Donne's particular interpretation of traditional theology. While Donne recognizes God's grace as the necessary and sufficient cause of redemption, he also believes that salvation arises from the simultaneous cooperation of divine and human wills; thus, his will to repent would be *"as good/ As if"* (italics mine) God had already pardoned him through grace. In effect, to the Gospel of divine forgiveness of sins, Donne adds man's own penitence.

"Goodfriday, 1613. Riding Westward"

This individual and immediate concern with humanly enacting divine forgiveness of sins adds to the last judgment by God the first judgment by the self in each man; and the result of this self-judgment is repentance, which gives rise to the first, or spiritual, resurrection, which, finally, assures the last resurrection to heaven. This causal relation supports Donne's Protestant view that it is impossible to consider the resurrection without first considering judgment (*Ser.*, 6 : 277). "Goodfriday, 1613. Riding Westward" portrays the *passio* of proper penance which "repairs" (mends and repatriates) man by restoring the divine image within him.

The title—"Goodfriday, 1613. Riding Westward"—concerns the intersection, literally on the cross, of the eternal (*kairos*) with the temporal (*chronos*); the poem's subject is man's proper relation to the *passio* of Christ's incarnation, culminated in the crucifixion. The cross portrays the spiritual tension Donne experiences on Good Friday: "I am carryed towards the West/ This day, when my Soules forme bends toward the East." Continuing the metaphor of man as microcosm whose body and soul form a round map, Donne meditates on how he may come to the East, i.e., to Christ, for "the name of Christ is *Oriens, the East*."[55] Though this metaphor begins in literal terms—"there I should see a Sunne, by rising set,/ And by that setting endlesse day beget"—it is transferred from the natural, East, to the supernatural, Christ. While Good Friday is the devotional occasion to feel and thereby share Christ's suffering, a sinful nature almost prevents (Donne's) confronting and participating in Christ's *passio*." "Yet dare I almost be glad, I do not see/ That spectacle of too much weight for mee."

But, as Donne realizes,

> Though these things [Christ's merciful ransom],
>   as I ride, be from mine eye,

> They are present yet unto my memory,
> For that looks toward them; and thou look'st
>   towards mee,
> O Saviour, as thou hang'st upon the tree;

Here Donne's devotional task is to unite the memorial image of a past event (Christ's crucifixion on Good Friday) with its temporal (re-)occurrence in himself through his capacity to enter into Christ's *passio:* "I'll turne my backe to thee, but to receive/ Corrections, till thy mercies bid thee leave." Donne combines the initial and traditional penitential image of Christ, as the supernatural sun—"O think mee worth thine anger, punish mee,/ Burne off my rusts, and my deformity"—with the apocalyptic pattern of divine transfiguration—"Restore thine Image, so much, by thy Grace,/ That thou may'st know mee, and I'll turne my face."

While the cause of this desired "making new" is traditional—by God's grace, man is redeemed—Donne develops the Son-sun metaphor to include his own simultaneous cooperation: 1) by riding westward, toward the setting sun, Donne continually exposes his "rusts" to the Son-sun that he may penitentially "burne [them] off";[56] and 2) by both the direction (west) and effect (repentance) of his "pilgrimmage," Donne finally arrives in the East (since in a round map west becomes east and man's soul is a sphere) with Christ, the risen Son-sun. Through penitentially participating in Christ's *passio,* Donne turns and returns his own face toward his Image. And this divine "restoration"—the incarnation and knowledge of God in man—culminates in the first, or spiritual, resurrection.

The Resurrection in the "Anniversaries"

Taken together as a complementary pair, the "First and Second Anniversary" contemplate the death of this world and the resurrection to heaven.[57] While this progression follows the traditional Christian apocalyptic pattern, Donne's particular imaging of this *imitatio dei* differs from conventional treatments. "Goodfriday, 1613" concerns the same religious problem: how to "restore" fallen man to the divine image and to "repair" (mend and repatriate) man with God. Whereas in "Goodfriday" the model of repentance and the pattern of devotion is Jesus'

Good Friday *passio,* in the "Anniversaries" Donne's "restoration" involves not a traditional, public, but an individual, private, image of the soul's proper likeness to God—"the idea of a woman," on which Donne meditates and whom he imitates.

The first, or spiritual, resurrection is both the theological subject and poetic act of the "Anniversaries"; that is, by contemplating its future ecstasy, "till meditation master all its parts," Donne's soul rises to that desired condition of blessedness, of which Elizabeth Drury is "now partaker, and a part" ("I Anniv.," l. 434). In the "Anniversaries" Donne incorporates the eschatological into the symbolic, for

> through the realization of his soul's loss he has regained the wisdom that orients him toward God, and the entire poem surges upward toward eternal life. It is as a concrete image of that Wisdom, its direct emotional apprehension, that the mysterious figure of woman at the center of the poem is best understood. She is in herself both the object and the wit: the realization as well as the means to realize it, for the only way to understand the *Anniversaries* is intuitively, through symbolic understanding.[58]

Religious symbols, as Tillich explains, "are directed toward the infinite which they symbolize *and* toward the finite through which they symbolize it. . . . They open the divine for the human and the human for the divine."[59]

The "Anniversaries" are memorial celebrations 1) of the historical Elizabeth Drury, whose "vntimely death" and associated "fraility and decay of the whole world" are the subject of the "First Anniversary" and 2), and most importantly, of symbolic woman, whose Christian form is the soul, or spirit, and whose exemplary identity is to keep "by diligent deuotion/ God's Image, in such reparation,/ Within her heart" ("II Anniv.," ll. 455-57). As a religious symbol, Elizabeth Drury is the temporal example of this divine pattern, as Jesus is its eternal incarnation. As God's betrothed ("II Anniv.," ll. 461-62), it is "shee whom we celebrate" ("II Anniv.," l. 448) in the "Anniversaries."

They are sacramental poems which commemorate 1) the sacred event of Elizabeth Drury's resurrection to heaven and 2) the religious occasion for Donne's spiritual resurrection, the subject of the "Second Anniversary." The poem's personal, religious drama is the soul's recognition and possession of its proper likeness to God. The "Second Anniversary" is a "meditation" on that ideal love of perfection which joins man with

God, in the spiritual resurrection here and in the bodily resurrection hereafter.

Much of the difficulty and success of the "Anniversaries" arises from Donne's changing the "vntimely death" to the "religious death" of Elizabeth Drury; to understand this metamorphosis, we must consider the "identity" of the mysterious "shee" in the poems. In public, theological vocabulary, "shee" is an image of the soul of the whole world (*anima mundi*), Christ,[60] while in private, psychological vocabulary, "shee" is analogous to the soul of collective man (*anima hominis*):

> [the] "Idea of a Woman" in man [is] the image of his own soul, his own deepest reality. It is a universal symbol of otherness in man, either of desire, the completion of one's androgynous self, as in the Platonic myth, or of strange intuitive knowledge otherwise unavailable to him.[61]

Donne's awareness and possession of this intuitive self-knowledge structures the "Anniversaries" as they present the decay of the fallen world and the soul's rising to the heavenly kingdom.

The "First Anniversary":
The Soul's Lament in the Fallen World

As an anatomy, or general satire, of "the fraility and the decay of this whole world," the "First Anniversary" describes, most importantly, the cause of this decay.[62] Commemorating Elizabeth Drury, Donne sees her "vntimely death" as spiritually tantamount to the death of the world:

> Then tongues, the soule being gone, the losse
>   deplore.
> But though it be too late to succor thee,
> Sicke world, yea dead, yea putrified, since shee
> Thy'ntrinsique Balme, and thy preseruatiue,
> Can neuer be renew'd, thou neuer liue, . . .
> Her death hath taught vs dearely, that thou
>   [the world] art
> Corrupt and mortall in thy purest part
> ("I Anniv.," ll. 54-62).

Analyzing the "worlds infirmities," Donne proceeds with this "dissectione," or anatomy, of this fallen world, in a series of five sections which indicate the world's loss of her "riche soule."[63]

Not only is the whole world sick, "but this is worse, that thou are speechelesse growne," i.e., unable to utter the Word and hence unable to know one's proper identity: "Thou hast forgot thy name, thou hadst, thou was/ Nothing but she." ("I Anniv.," ll. 31-32). Traditionally, Christ is a source of divine wisdom, necessary to knowing and speaking one's Christian identity;[64] and as an image of the whole world's soul, "shee" symbolizes Christ, whom the individual soul seeks and with whom it would be united.

In the meantime, on this "widowed earth," until the *parousia,* Donne reminds of the present Christian compensation: We

> Will yearely celebrate thy second birth,
> That is, thy death. For though the soule of man
> Be got when man is made, 'tis borne but than
> When man doth die. . . .
> From her example, and her vertue, if you
> In reuerence to her, doe thinke it due,
> That no one should her prayses thus reherse,
> As a matter fit for Chronicle, not verse,
> Vouchsafe to call to minde that God did make
> A last, and lastingst peece a song ("I Anniv.,"
>   ll. 450-62).

It is this everlasting, heavenly chorus of which "shee's now a part both of the Quire and Song" ("I Anniv.," l. 10 and Rev. 4 and 21).

While the theme of the "First Anniversary" is the soul's lament for the loss of wisdom, the provenance of the "Second Anniversary" is the soul's own seeking that which it most loves— the essential joy in the full, eternal sight of God.[65] The significance of this "progress" extends to the canon of Donne's divine poems, of which the "Anniversaries" are the most extensive single effort and the most complete. Whereas the eschatological meditations of the six holy sonnets, "La Corona" (of 1609), are incomplete because they lack a treatment of this heavenly beatitude, the" Anniversaries" do encompass this promised end. That Donne finds such completion in these poems is related, I feel, to their symbolic subject and structure.

In the "Second Anniversary" the essential joy of the final resurrection to heaven is represented as directly depending on the soul's first resurrection on earth. While this subject is conventional conceptually, Donne's development of it expands the traditional manner and model of this first resurrection. That is, Donne's "sacramental" meditation sanctifies a secular figure, so that the object of his devotion here is not Jesus Christ *per se* but rather the Christian salvation that the risen Elizabeth Drury now partakes of and symbolizes.

The "Second Anniversary": The Resurrection to Heaven

"By occasion of the religious death of Mistris Elizabeth Drury," the "Second Anniversary" "of the progress of the soule," contemplates the future "exaltation" of the resurrected —"that blessed state" which Elizabeth Drury now enjoys and which Donne in the poem "aspires to see."[66] The "Second Anniversary" develops five related motifs—1) the knowledge that this rotten world is "fragmentary rubbidge" (ll. 49 and 82-83); 2) the soul's insatiate thirst for the *parousia* (ll. 44-45) and last resurrection (ll. 60-65); 3) death as the soul's groom, its enfranchisement, and third birth (ll. 85, 179-80, and 214-15); 4) the mysterious "shee" as an image of the *anima mundi,* Christ (ll. 72, 245-46, 455-57, 507-8, and 524); and 5) the essential, eternal joy of God's world to come (ll. 441, 469-70, and 491-96).

Of these, the "idea" of Elizabeth Drury as the ideal woman (the soul who is Christ's bride) is most original and important because it represents the "transfiguration" of a historical personage as a religious symbol. Accordingly, the poet acts as a priest-prophet whose words confer the blessing of the first resurrection: "These Hymnes thy issue, may encrease so long,/ As till Gods great Venite change the song" ("II Anniv.," ll. 43-44).

Until that time, Donne's soul "forget[s] this rotten world" ("II Anniv.," l. 49) and looks upward to the risen "shee" "whose happy state it will congratulate," i.e., joy with "because shee was the forme ["in the Aristotelian-Scholastic sense of soul, that which gives life, movement, and individuality to the body"[67]] that made it liue" ("II Anniv.," l. 72). As this soul, she is also "to whose person Paradise adhear'd" ("II Anniv.," l. 77). This divine representation and Donne's aspiration thereto constitute the soul's upward transmutation—"her exaltation in the next [life]"—the poem's subject.

The "religious death" of the mortal, corruptible body is but the occasion of the virtuous soul's enfranchisement, wherein "thou hast thy expansion now and libertee" ("II Anniv.," l. 180) in the heavenly marriage; in it death is groom and mother: "For when our soule enioyes this her third birth,/ (Creation gaue her one, a second, grace,)/ Heauen is neare, and present to her face" ("II Anniv.," ll. 214-16). This "third birth" is *"Per Resurrectionem"* (*Ser.,* 6:135) and the gestation of the spiritual body is here characterized by the beauty of mortal unity (hereafter immortal):

> Shee, of whose soule, if we may say,
>   t'was Gold,
> Her body was th'Electrum, and did hold
> Many degrees of that; we vnderstood
> Her by her sight, her pure and eloquent blood
> Spoke in her cheekes, and so distinckly wrought,
> That one might almost say, her bodie thought
>   ("II Anniv.," ll. 241-46).[68]

The source of this healing union of body and soul is her keeping "by diligent deuotion,/ Gods Image, in such reparation,/ Within her heart, that . . . was here/ Betrothed to God, and now is married there" ("II Anniv.," ll. 455-57 and 461-62). We remember that in Donne's Protestant theology, the first resurrection of the spirit here assures the last resurrection of body and soul in the "great marriage" in heaven.[69]

As he is wont to do in the sermons, and as he refrains from doing in the other divine poems, whose drama more often concerns penance and judgment, Donne here elaborates on the essential, eternal joys of the resurrection to heaven:

> Onely in Heauen ioies strength is neuer spent;
> And accidentall things are permanent.
> Ioy of a soules arriuall neere decaies;
> For that soule euer ioyes, and euer staies.
> Ioy that their last great Consummation
> Approches in the resurrection;
> When earthly bodies more celestiall
> Shalbe, then Angels were, for they could fall;
> This kind of ioy doth euery day admit
> Degrees of grouth, but none of loosing it
>   ("II Anniv.," ll. 507-10).

The doctrine of this description of the risen, spiritual body, of course, derives from I Corinthians xv, 40-47, and Donne (not unlike Augustine) himself joys in its realization, when

> Shee, who by making full perfection grow,
> Peeces a Circle, and still keepes it so,
> Long'd for, and longing for it, to heauen is gone,
> Where shee receiues, and giues addition
>   ("II Anniv.," ll. 507-10).

The "Second Anniversary" concludes by invoking the "Immortal Maid," with both "lawes of poetry" and religion ("II Anniv.," ll. 514-16), for "thou shouldest for life, and death, a patterne bee" ("II Anniv.," l. 524). The content of this eternal pattern is the soul's proper likeness to God, begun in the first, or spiritual, resurrection on earth and completed in the final, bodily, resurrection to heaven. As Elizabeth Drury is the model of religious virtue on earth, the idea of this holy woman symbolizes Donne's own spiritual resurrection, herein represented: "Thou art the Proclamation, and I ame/ The Trumpet, at whose voice the people came" ("II Anniv.," ll. 527-28).

In contrast, for example, to Donne's postponement in the apocalyptic holy sonnet "At the round earths imagin'd corners, blow," here he advances to judgment with certainty. And this assurance arises, I think, from his contemplation herein of the coming resurrection: "Returne not, my soule, from this extasee,/ And meditation of what thou shalt bee" ("II Anniv.," ll. 321-22). In such union of the knower and the known,[70] the resurrected share God's absolute unity:

> . . . Onely who haue enioyd
> The sight of God, in fulnesse, can thinke it;
> For it is both the object, and the wit.
> This is essentiall ioye, where neither hee
> Can suffer Diminution, nor wee;
> Tis such a full, and such a filling good
>   ("II Anniv.," ll. 440-45).

"Shee whom we celebrate, is gone before" and symbolizes the soul's direct, intuitive knowledge of God's presence—on earth as man's spiritual likeness to the divine and in heaven as participating in that wisdom and joy of the final resurrection.

Conclusions

One illustration of the unity among Donne's major writings—the sermons and religious prose, the elegies, songs, and sonnets, the divine poems, and the "Anniversaries"—is his distinctive incorporation throughout of the resurrection doctrine, a primary concern of the preacher, poet, and lover. In the sermons Donne emphasizes the direct relation between the present first resurrection of the soul, from sin to grace, and the final resurrection of the body to heaven on the last day; this spiritual resurrection is also a first judgment as man's will simultaneously cooperates with God's grace in proper penance.

In the songs and sonnets Donne presents the resurrection of the body in sexual love as a prefiguration and "remembrancer" of the "hypostaticall union" of man and God in Christ in heaven, which sanctions this figural incorporation of the eschatological into the erotic. Besides generating his best "secular" love poems, this divine "patterne of your [sexual] love" provides a new subject fit for English verse.

While the temporal configuration of the eternal pattern in the "secular" poems is this resurrection of the body, in the divine poems its present example is the first resurrection of the soul, which assures the final resurrection of body and soul. Characteristically, Donne "contracts" (joins and presents-in-miniature) the last day to the present one, in both erotic and religious experiences. The particular drama of the divine poems, however, portrays the *agon* of proper penance, through which simultaneous cooperation of God's grace and man's will he attains salvation.

In the "Anniversaries" the "religious death" of Elizabeth Drury occasions Donne's sacramental meditations on the soul's proper likeness to God, to which he aspires; "shee" symbolizes the resurrected soul's divine perfection, the theological subject and poetic act represented in the "Second Anniversary." Celebrating and imagining this historical, private event of her resurrection, Donne portrays his own first, spiritual, resurrection.

"A Metaphorical God"

In the *Devotions upon Emergent Occasions* Donne "expostulates" the relation between literal and metaphorical expressions of the divine, a subject which also concerns this study:

My God, my God, thou art a direct God, may I not say a literal God, a God that wouldst be understood literally and according to the plain sense of all that thou sayest? but thou art also (Lord, I intend it to thy glory, and let no profane misinterpreter abuse it to thy diminution), thou art a figurative, a metaphorical God too; a God in whose words there is such a height of figures, such voyages, such peregrinations to fetch remote and precious metaphors, such extensions, such spreadings, such curtains of allegories, such third heavens of hyperboles, so harmonious elocutions, so retired and so reserved expressions, so commanding persuasions, so persuading commandments, such sinews even in thy milk, and such things in thy words, as all profane authors seem of the seed of the serpent that creeps, thou art the Dove that flies. . . . *Neither art thou thus a figurative, a metaphorical God in thy word only, but in thy works too. The style of thy works, the phrase of thine actions, is metaphorical.* The institution of thy whole worship in the old law was a continual allegory; types and figures overspread all, and figures flowed into figures, and poured themselves out into farther figures; circumcision carried a figure of baptism, and baptism carries a figure of that purity which we shall have in perfection in the new Jerusalem. Neither didst thou speak and work in this language only in the time of thy prophets; but since thou spokest in thy Son it is so too. How often, how much more often, doth thy Son call himself a way, and a light, and a gate, and a vine, and bread, than the Son of God, or of man? *How much oftener doth he exhibit a metaphorical Christ, than a real, a literal?*[71]

As implied in the above discussion of the "Anniversaries," we must consider the relation between the metaphorical and literal exhibitions of the divine. In this passage Donne holds that the figurative expressions of the divinity originate from a real and literal Godhead. This prior ontological authority recurs variously throughout Donne's work and legitimates his incorporation of the resurrection doctrine, as shown. As the principal sacraments, baptism and the Eucharist, are founded on and modeled after Jesus Christ's resurrection, so symbolic poetry whose substance is religious, as in the "Anniversaries," depends on divine teleology for its reality, power, and meaning.[72] In observing how Blake exhibits Jesus Christ as "the Human Imagination" we shall see how religious language preserves its original validity while combining its transcendent (Godly) and immanent (sacramental) elements in Blake's "Divine Analogy."

NOTES: CHAPTER 2

1. See, for example, Charles Coffin, "Donne's Divinity," *Kenyon Review* 16 (1954):298.

2. John Donne, *Sermons*, ed. George Potter and Evelyn Simpson (Berkeley: University of California Press, 1953-62), 10:346 and "Appendix A," 376-86.

Hereafter abbreviated as *Ser.;* references to volume and page numbers will be included in text in parenthesis.

3. Preaching on 1 Cor. 15:26 Donne outlines a threefold resurrection: "First, a Resurrection from dejections and calamities of this world, a Temporary Resurrection; Secondly, the Resurrection from sin, a Spiritual Resurrection; and then a Resurrection from the grave, a final Resurrection" (*Ser.*, 4:56–57 and 359).

4. In a later sermon Donne adds the fourth and final "consideration" of the resurrection:

And these foure considerations of the words [of Rev. 20:6]; a Resurrection from persecution, by deliverance; a Resurrection from sin by grace; A Resurrection from tentation to sin, by the way of death, to the glory of heaven; and all these, in the first Resurrection, in him that is the roote of all, Christ Jesus (*Ser.*, 6:64).

5. Echoing the Old Testament prophets, Donne again speaks of the first resurrection as the "returning of the soule to him [God]" (*Ser.*, 6:75).

6. John Donne, *Divine Poems,* ed. Helen Gardner (Oxford: Clarendon Press, 1966), Holy Sonnet "Oh, my blacke Soule!", p. 7. Hereafter abbreviated as *DP;* all citations of these poems are from this edition unless otherwise stated.

7. But when he establishes the last and everlasting world in the last Resurrection, he shall admit such a number, as that none of us who are here now, none that is, or that shall be, upon the face of the earth, shall be denied in that Resurrection, if he have truly felt this [his body and soul united in one spirit with God]; for Grace accepted, is the infallible earnest of Glory (*Ser.*, 7:117; see also 7:189; 4:71–72, and 76–77).

8. Potter and Simpson, "Introduction," *Ser.,* 7:14. Though Anglican dogma was undecided about the state of the soul after death and before the general resurrection (see Gardner, "Introduction," *DP*, pp. xliii–xliv; and Herbert Thorndike, "Commentary on 'Prayer for the Dead'" in Henry Bettenson, ed. *Documents of the Christian Church* (New York: Oxford University Press, 1963), pp. 310–11), they generally agree, in opposition to Roman dogma, that the soul did not go to Purgatory. See John Cosin, Bishop of Durham, on "Differences" and "Agreements" between Anglicans and Romans, in *Documents,* pp. 303–6, especially "Differences, no. 8" and "Agreements, nos. 2 and 9." See also William Wake, from "A Discourse on Purgatory, V, That the Doctrine of Purgatory is contrary to Scripture, Antiquity, and Reason," in Paul More and Frank Cross, eds., *Anglicanism* (Milwaukee: Morehouse Publishing Co., 1953), pp. 339–42.

9. See also Gardner, "Introduction," *DP,* pp. xliii–xliv; Potter and Simpson, "Introduction," *Ser.,* 2:27; and Donne, "Hymne to God, My God, in my Sicknesse," "Verse Letter to Countess Bedford": "For bodies shall from death redeemed bee,/ Soules but preserved, not naturally free"; and *Ser.,* 6:64 and 74.

10. See also *Ser.,* "Introduction," 1:85; 1:285; 2:204; 3:103; 6:71; and 10:338; and John Donne, *Devotions Upon Emergent Occasions* (Ann Arbor: University of Michigan Press, 1965), p. 128; hereafter abbreviated *Devotions.*

11. See also *Ser.,* 3:109–10; 3:57–62; and 4:76–77.

12. See also *Ser.,* 4:87, and 8:220.

13. See *Ser.,* 3:93, 108, 110, 113–14; 4:61, 64, 74, 83, and 356–57; 6:73; 7, 93; 8:97, 355, and 364.

14. This sermon is appropriate gloss for the occasion of the "First Anniversary"; other references to the "communion of saints" occur in *Ser.* 3:91, 121; 4, 84; 5:96; 6:152; 8:229; and 10:64.

15. See also *Ser.* 4:129, and 8:368.

16. John Donne, *Elegies, Songs, and Sonnets,* ed. Helen Gardner (Oxford: Clarendon Press, 1966). Hereafter abbreviated as *ESS;* all references to this

group of poems are from her edition. By the "profane" or "erotic" poems I refer
to those in this edition; by the "spiritual" or "divine poems" I refer to those in
Miss Gardner's edition of the *Divine Poems,* though again this distinction was not
Donne's.

17. Erich Auerbach, "Figura," in *Scenes from the Drama of European Literature,* trans. Ralph Manheim (New York: Meridian Books, 1959), p. 53; hereafter
abbreviated as *Scenes.*

18. See Kermode, *The Sense of an Ending,* (New York: Oxford University
Press, 1967), p. 48. See also Auerbach, *Mimesis,* trans. Willard Trask (New
York: 1957), pp. 64–66, 136–41, 170–76, and 279 ff; and T. S. Eliot, "The Four
Quartets" and "Ash Wednesday" in *The Complete Poems and Plays* (New York:
Harcourt, World and Brace, 1952).

19. All quotations from Shakespeare's *Sonnets* are from the edition by Douglas
Bush (Baltimore: Penguin Books, 1961).

20. Although in Sonnet 55 there is reference to rising to the last judgment, this
image is viewed exclusively from within a time-bound and secular position, i.e.,
the poet speaks of time only as extending to the edge of doom, and not beyond
into eternity after judgment.

21. Andrew Marvell, *Poems of Andrew Marvell,* ed. Hugh MacDonald (Cambridge, Mass.: Harvard University Press, 1960), p. 21.

22. In "The Canonization" and "The Anniversary," respectively.

23. "The Good-morrow"; see also "Sunne Rising," "Lovers' Infiniteness,"
"Loves Growth," "Nocturnal upon S. Lucies Day," "Valediction: Forbidding
Mourning," "Extasie," and "Canonization."

24. See J. B. Leishman, *Themes and Variations in Shakespeare's Sonnets* (New
York: Harper and Row, 1966), pp. 23, 102–18, and 149–231; and *ibid., The Monarch of Wit* (New York: Harper and Row, 1966), pp. 208–25.

25. See John Donne, *Essays in Divinity,* ed. Evelyn Simpson (Oxford: Oxford
University Press, 1952), p. xviii; hereafter abbreviated *Essays;* and 'Donne's
Sources," in *Ser.,* 10:296.

26. It is unclear whether Donne wrote these verses to give to his wife when he
was about to leave England for France with the Drurys in 1611; see Miss Gardner's note in "General Introduction," *ESS,* p. xxix.

27. As Gardner also notes: "Donne's fondness for the prefix 'inter', denoting
reciprocal action, is strikingly apparent in *O.E.D.*" ("Commentary," *ESS,* p. 189).

28. See "Appendix D." *ESS,* pp. 183–87.

29. See *OED,* 9:482, and 5:383. Though "sepulchrall" existed as a word before,
Donne's use of it as an adjective here is original.

30. Edwin Panofsky, *Tomb Sculpture* (New York: Abrams, 1964). p. 82; italics
mine; see also pp. 77–78.

31. John Donne, *The Anniversaries,* ed. Frank Manley (Baltimore: Johns Hopkins University Press, 1963), "II Anniv.," ll. 440–42. All future quotations of the
"Anniversaries" will be from this edition, hereafter abbreviated *Anniv.;* references
to the poems will be indicated with the line numbers, preceded by the title abbreviated as "I" or "II Anniv.," both in parenthesis in text.

32. See Gardner, "Commentary," *ESS,* p. 185.

33. Yeats, on the other hand, finds that "the tragedy of sexual intercourse is
the perpetual virginity of the soul." *Letters on Poetry to Dorothy Wellesley* (New
York: Oxford University Press, 1964), p. 174. I shall discuss Yeats's troubled
body-soul relations in chap. 4.

34. Given the context of the "Sunne Rising," much of its language is parodic

and a pun on Christ's resurrection in terms of an Adamic erection; in the poem sexuality defies time and ostensibly parodies divinity.

35. Gardner, *ESS.,* p. 201; she does not, however, discuss the two related implications of this repetition.

36. See, for example, *Ser.,* 3:254; and Matt. 10:39; Mark 8:35; Luke 9:24 and 14:26; John 12:24–25; 1 Cor. 15:36; and Col. 1:15–20.

37. See 1 Cor. 15:51–57 and Rev. 10:7; and *Ser.,* 7:389–90.

38. Gardner notes this reference from the sermons: " 'To desire without fruition, is a rage, and to enjoy without desire is a stupidity' " ("Commentary," *ESS,* p. 204). Since there is no natural generation in heaven (Matt. 22:30), this gloss, if applicable, suggests that the lovers are actually now risen to heaven "above"; however, I feel that the poem represents the earthly configuration of this heavenly consummation.

39. See Col. 1:15–20 and "Resurrection, imperfect."

40. See *Shorter OED* 3rd ed. rev. (Oxford: Oxford University Press, 1959), p. 383: "To betroth or engage, 1536."

41. Because human love is the present pattern and remembrance of divine love, they are mutually inspiring. In the Holy Sonnet on the death of his wife, Donne speaks of this "interinanimation":

Since she whom I lovd, hath payd her last debt
To nature, and to hers, and my good is dead,
And her soule early into heaven ravished,
Wholy on heavenly things my mind is sett.
Here the admyring her my mind did whett
To seeke thee God; . . .

In the remainder of the sonnet Donne speaks of his relation to God, the heavenly beloved: "But why should I begg more love when as thou/ Dost wooe my soule, for hers offring all thine." See also "Hymne to Christ" for a variation on this principle.

42. T. S. Eliot, "Ash Wednesday," *Complete Poems and Plays,* p. 64.

43. See Wolfgang Clements, "Donne's Holy Sonnet 14," *MLN,* 76 (1962):487.

44. See Isa. 1:8 and 27; Hos. 2–3; and Rev. 17:5.

45. Gardner, "Appendix C," *DP,* p. 123.

46. Yeats, on the other hand, finds man and God as mutually betraying each other, each dying the other's life, living the other's death. For Donne's religious certainty, see also "La Corona, Ascension," ll. 9–14.

47. "Hymne to Christ."

48. *Ser.,* 7:384; see also *Ser.,* 2:170; "A Litanie, XIV," ll. 118–19; and "Upon the Translation of the Psalmes", ll. 21–32.

49. These three lines condense the following passage from a sermon:

In a flat Map, there goes no more, to make West East, though they be distant in an extremity, but to past that flat Map upon a round body, and then West and East are all one. In a flate soule, in a dejected conscience, in a troubled spirit, there goes no more to the making of that trouble, peace, then to apply that trouble to the body of the Merits, to the body of the Gospel of Christ Jesus, and conforme thee to him, and thy West is East, thy Trouble of spirit is Tranquility of spirit. The name of Christ is *Oriens, the East;* And yet Lucifer himselfe is called *Filius Orientis, The son of the East.* If thou beest fallen by *Lucifer* . . . and not fallen as *Lucifer,* to a senselessenesse of thy fall . . . but to a troubled spirit, still thy Prospect is the East, still thy Climate is heaven, still thy Haven is Jerusalem (Gardner, "Commentary," *DP,* p. 108).

50. Gardner's "Appendix F" on "Paradise and Calvary," however, points out Donne's innovation within the convention; see *DP,* pp. 135–37.

51. Other sermons also speak of this relation; for example, Donne tells how Augustine has spoken of

. . . a medicinall falling, a falling under God's hand, but such a falling under his hand, as he takes not off his hand from him that is falne, but throwes him down, therefore that he may raise him (*Ser.,* 6:212).

See also Gardner's note, "Commentary," *DP,* p. 109.

52. See, for example, "Holy Sonnet to Mrs. Magdalen Herbert," "Resurrection," and "Ascension."

53. See *Ser.,* 7:117:: "He that rises to this Judgement of recollecting, and of judging himselfe, shall rise with a chearfulnesse, and stand with a confidence, when Christ Jesus shall come in the second."

54. See the holy sonnets "This is my playes last scene" and "Death, be not proud" and "A Litanie, XXII." In the following sermons Donne also preaches that death is the separation of body and soul, at which time the soul of the saved is immediately resurrected to heaven: *Ser.,* 2:204; 3:103; 4:60 and 62; 4:70 and 75 and 357–58; 6:71; 7:103, 108, and 117; and 10:229. See also Gardner, "Introduction," *DP,* pp. xliv–xlv and "Appendix A," *DP,* pp. 114–17.

55. See n. 49.

56. The image of purgatorial fires does not imply that Donne, or the Anglicans, held the Catholic doctrine of Purgatory, but rather, as the poem argues, just the opposite: Donne believes that one must "purge" oneself on earth; hence his special emphasis in the divine poems on penitence and accordingly the last judgment of the individual occurs at death, so that the soul of the saved goes immediately to heaven (or hell). See, for example, "A Litanie, XXII."

57. See Manley, "Introduction," *Anniv.,* pp. 1 and 12–14. See also Richard Hughes, "The Woman in Donne's Anniversaries," *ELH* 34 (1967):307–8 and 311; George Williamson, "The Design of Donne's Anniversaries," *MP,* 60 (1962): 188–91; and William Empson, *Some Versions of Pastoral,* (New York: New Directions, 1960), pp. 79–82.

58. Manley, "Intro.," *Anniv.,* p. 19.

59. Paul Tillich, *Systematic Theology* (Chicago: University of Chicago Press, 1953–63), 1:240; hereafter abbreviated as *System. Theol.* See also Paul Tillich, *Theology of Culture* (New York: Oxford University Press, 1959), pp. 54–66, and n. 77, chap. 1.

60. See "Resurrection, imperfect": "He would have justly thought this body a soule,/ If not of any man, yet of the whole." See also Manley, "Intro.," *Anniv.,* p. 14.

61. Manley, "Intro.," *Anniv.,* p. 18. See also Hughes, "The Woman . . .":

She is so inclusive a symbol that she is that vision repeated in all passing loveliness, Yeats's "ghostly paradigm of things," . . . the archetypal woman who has been symbolized in the Cabala's Shekinah, the neo-Platonic Paradisal Woman, the eternal consort of God in Proverbs, Dante's Beatrice, the Augustinian Sapentia (*ELH* 34 (1967):317).

62. See Northrop Frye, *Anatomy of Criticism* (Boston: Beacon Press, 1957), pp. 288 and 312–14; see also "I Anniv.," l. 66. See also Eugene Rice, *The Renaissance Idea of Wisdom* (Cambridge, Mass.: Harvard University Press, 1958), pp. 11–13 and 22–27.

63. It should be noted that for Donne, five is a number of incompletion, as found in the "First Anniversary," *Essays,* pp. 46 and 59, and "The Primrose," *ESS,* pp. 88–89. See also Hughes, "The Woman . . ." *ELH* 34 (1967): 310; Williamson, "The Design . . ." *MP* 60 (1962):164; and Louis Martz, *The Poetry of Meditation* (New Haven: Yale University Press, 1962), pp. 221–24.

64. See Rice, *Renaissance Idea of Wisdom,* pp. 67 and 124–48; see also Manley, "Intro.," *Anniv.,* pp. 9, 13–14, 17, and 19–49; Hughes, "The Woman . . .", *ELH* 34 (1967):323; John 1:5; and *Ser.,* 1:238–39; 2:228; 7:336; 9:87–90 and 99–100.

65. See "II Anniv.," ll. 440–45; see also *Ser.,* 4:87; 1:184–85; 9:373; and 10:229 ff; and Gardner, "Intro." *DP,* p. xlix.

66. See title page, *Anniv.,* p. 87, and "The Harbinger to the Progres," *Anniv.,* p. 89.

67. Manley, "Commentary," *Anniv.,* p. 178.

68. These lines are, no doubt, the direct ancestor of Yeats's description of the dancing girl in "The Double Vision of Michael Robartes."

69. See *Ser.,* 4:58–60 and 70–72; 6:63–64; and 7:189, for example, as previously discussed.

70. See Manley, "Commentary," *Anniv.,* pp. 197–98 for traditional references.

71. Donne, *Devotions,* "Expostulation XIX," pp. 124–25; italics mine.

72. See Tillich, *Theology of Culture,* pp. 57, 54–56, and 61–65.

3

Blake's Fourfold Resurrection and Christianity of the Imagination

Theoretical Introduction: "Thro' the Eye"

A major assumption which underlies this introductory summary of Blake's theology and the following chapter is that both "truth" and Blake's image of it are essentially continuous, for "Vision or Imagination is a Representation of what Eternally Exists, Really & Unchangeably."[1] Because the provenance and forms of eternal reality are mental,[2] discursive reference to them tends to become a closed and potentially repetitive system. Yet this Urizenic "dull round" contracts to that point of utter change at the vortex:

> The nature of Infinity is this: That every
> thing has its
> Own vortex, and when once a traveller
> thro' Eternity
> Has pass'd that Vortex, he perceives it
> roll backward behind
> His path, into a globe itself infolding
> like a sun,
> Or like a moon, or like a universe of
> starry majesty.
> (*M* 15: 21-25, K 497)

Such is the direction of our mental travel.

In this eternity of the imagination, "All is Vision" ("Laocoon," K 776). To clarify Blake's particular use of "art," we can observe that art is the highest form—in the necessary "firm and determinate outline" ("Desc. Cat.," K 585)—of the imagination, whose theological expression is forgiveness, of the self and of all men. As the productions of time with which eternity is in love, art and religion—together, Blake's Christianity—are the continual manifestations of the redemptive imagination, which alone envisions divine unity and perfection.

Throughout these introductory remarks and the following chapter, "imagination" (Blake's favorite concept) is used frequently, inclusively, and in a manner that may appear circular. My multiple uses reflect Blake's, for whom imagination is 1) the central and redeeming possession and identity of man and the Godhead, and 2) the eternal and real world of human existence and divine essence. Accordingly, the source of both art and religion is the divine imagination, the "Poetic Genius which is the Lord" ("Annot. Swedenborg," K 90).

Both manifestations of the divine image are redemptive because they, alone, envision complete perfection, and they end in the resurrection, wherein total unity is finally realized. If we cannot fully speak of this infinite imagination, we can observe Blake's particular structure of images, so that

> If the Spectator could Enter into these Images in his Imagination, approaching them on the Fiery Chariot of his Contemplative Thought, if he could Enter into Noah's Rainbow or into his bosom, or could make a Friend & Companion of one of these Images of wonder, which always intreats him to leave mortal things (as he must know), then he would arise from his Grave, then he would meet the Lord in the Air & then he would be happy. General Knowledge is Remote Knowledge; it is in Particulars that Wisdom consists & Happiness too ("VLJ," K 611).

For Blake, the resurrection is man's return to his original and eternal unity, which is fourfold: 1) his possession of his emanation, that which he loves, desires, and creates; 2) his reintegration of the self so that each of his Four Zoas function properly and harmoniously; 3) his immortal life of brotherhood of all men as one man; and 4) his reunion with the Godhead. In the beginning was this universal wholeness, but because Albion, in jealousy and fear, turned his back on the divine vision and thereby forsook the imagination, the cosmos fell. In contrast to the Biblical narrative, Blake conceives of this world's creation to be after the fall, because it directly results from and reproduces a previous cosmic division, separation, and restriction of the divine *pleroma,* which is "re-fulled" in the resurrection.[3]

However, God's merciful creation of the fallen world of generation and death avoids a fall into utter chaos: this "starry floor and watery shore" are "given" man so that he may be "regenerated" and redeemed "by resurrection from the dead."[4] In Blake's cosmogony, then, the psychic cause and effect of the cosmic fall is man's forsaking the imagination;[5] and the resurrection reunifies man to his prior, and proper, wholeness in the divine image.

Blake's redefinition of this traditional Christian promise, however, alters both its present and future forms. In his visionary prose description of his painting of "The Last Judgment," Blake, following Anglican practice, holds that baptism and the Eucharist are the necessary rites of regeneration: "All Life consists of these Two." However, he sees these conventional Christian rites as sacred (only) because mental: "Throwing off Error & Knaves from our company continually & Receiving Truth or Wise Men into our Company continually" ("VLJ," K 612-13). Because for Blake the provenance of the moral is the mental, men are admitted to heaven only if they have cultivated their understandings; further, "the Treasures of Heaven are not Negations of Passions, but Realities of Intellect" ("VLJ," K 615).

Blake's art and religion are united in his view of salvation, for "Jesus considered the Imagination to be the Real Man" ("Annot. Berkeley," K 774). To delineate this convergence, we will consider first his psychology and then his soteriology. In Blake's "own" mythology of the Four Zoas[6] reside his originality and greatness as a religious artist. Of these "Four Mighty Ones"—man's capacities to imagine, to love, to sense bodily, and to reason—who make a perfect unity (*VFZ,* N I: 9, K 264), Los is the most important, because alone "he kept the divine vision" in this "time of trouble" (postlapsarian history).[7]

More particularly, Los and Jesus are the "likeness & similitude" of each other (*J* 96: 7 and 22, K 743), for "the form of the fourth [immortal Zoa] was like the Son of God" ("Desc. Cat.," K 578). As Jesus is the incarnate *Logos,* the Savior is the incarnate imagination, or Los. Blake sees Christian love—the friendship and brotherhood without which man is not—as the absolute moral act of the imagination: "the blow of his [Los's creative] Hammer is Justice, the swing of his Hammer Mercy/

The force of Los's Hammer is eternal Forgiveness" (*J* 88:49-50, K 734). Accordingly, for Blake, the single source of both art and religion is the "Poetic Genius, which is the Lord" ("ARAO," K 98 and "Annot. Swedenborg," K 90). And both are the form of continuous redemptive activity: "It ["Imagination," "God himself," "Jesus"] manifests itself in his Works of Art" ("Laocoon," K 776).

In Christianity Jesus' incarnation, crucifixion, and resurrection constitute the definitive means and model for man's redemption, necessarily dependent on God's gift of grace and reflected in man's faith in the Savior. While Blake accepts the Christian principle of forgiveness of sins—but not the doctrine of the atonement, which he believes to be cruel and wicked: "Moral Severity & destroys Mercy in its Victim" (*J* 39:26, K 666)—he also holds that such fully giving of oneself for others must be continual and mutual, i.e., constantly repeated by every man, instead of terminally performed once by Jesus. Typically, Blake views Jesus' acts as necessary but not sufficient *per se* (i.e., performed only once) for man's salvation: "The Spirit of Jesus [and "The Glory of Christianity" (*J* 52, K 683)] is continual forgiveness of Sin" (*J* 3, K 621) and "Mutual forgiveness of each Vice,/ [has] oped the gates of Paradise" ("EG," K 7 758-59).[8]

And this continual, mutual forgiveness of sin—brotherly love —is the historical Jesus' unique and central teaching, as John records:

> These things I have spoken unto you, that my joy might remain in you, and that your joy might be full. This is my commandment, That ye love one another, as I have loved you. Greater love hath no man than this, that a man lay down his life for his friends (15: 11–13).

For Blake, this love is completely giving oneself for another, whereby the spiritual identity of each man and of all men is seen as one and is completed in the resurrection.

This forgiveness is both of the self and of others. To reveal the mystery of salvation, the last error which must be annihilated is the spectral, rational, selfhood, i.e., spiritual separateness, which causes and continues the fall (*VFZ,* N I: 290-91, K 272 and *J* 74: 1-13, K 714). When this Satan of reductive division is destroyed by freely giving oneself for another, then redemptive identification with the "eternal body of man" is realized through the "divine vision." Blake's "divine vision" means that total vision of the Godhead whereby the incarnation is completed in the resurrection: "He who sees the Infinite in all things sees God. . . . Therefore God becomes as we are, that we may be as he is" ("NNRb," K 98). This complete vision is divine because it is *of* (i.e., partakes of and belongs to) God.

Because we become, quite literally, what we behold (*J* 43 : 54, K 661), when man sees "thro' the eye," he embodies the complete and unified human form divine:

> . . . expanding, we behold as one,
> As One Man all the Universal Family,
>   and that One Man
> We call Jesus the Christ; and he in us,
>   and we in him,
> Live in perfect harmony in Eden,
>   the land of life,
> Giving, receiving, and forgiving each
>   other's trespasses.
> . . . he is all in all,
> In Eden, in the Garden of God, and
>   in heavenly Jerusalem (*J* 38 : 18-
>   25, K 664-5).

When one is fully a man, "God is no more" ("EG," K 750), i.e., God is no longer ("no more") separate from man, for the human and the divine again and finally are one:

> I am not a God afar off, I am a brother
>   and a friend;
> Within your bosoms I reside, and you
>   reside in me:
> Lo! we are One, forgiving all Evil,
>   Not seeking recompense.
> Ye are my members . . . !   (*J* 4:18-21, K 622).

Blake's "great task," from which he does not rest, identifies the traditional Christian eschatological expectation with his own vision of divine redemption through the imagination, the Savior, whose Christian name is Jesus:

> To open the Eternal Worlds, to open the
>   immortal Eyes

Of Man inwards into the Worlds of Thought,
    into Eternity
Ever expanding in the Bosom of God,
    the Human Imagination.
O Saviour pour upon me thy Spirit
    of meekness & love!
Annihilate the Selfhood in me:
    be thou all my life!   (*J* 5:18-22, K 623).

Traditionally the last judgment takes place at the end of days, and like the other determinate events in Christian "history," it occurs but once: Jesus judges man, who is then either forever saved or damned. Blake, however, is most concerned with how man is saved now ("VLJ," K 616). While he also expects this final judgment, he sees *a* last judgment, as well, which occurs multiply and in time. This adding of a judgment into time, akin to the intersection of time and eternity on the cross, continues the Protestant emphasis on judgment in history.[9]

But in Blake's interpretation, this moral judgment by the divine authority is a mental act of the self: "Whenever any Individual Rejects Error & Embraces Truth, a last judgment passes upon that Individual" ("VLJ," K 613).[10] Blake characteristically redefines reality and morality by identifying their eternal source: in the imagination. Accordingly,

> men are admitted into Heaven not because they have curbed & govern'd their Passions or have no Passions, but because they have Cultivated their Understandings. The Treasures of Heaven are not Negations of Passion, but Realities of Intellect, from which all the Passions Emanate Uncurbed in their Eternal Glory ("VLJ," K 615).

Like its multiple predecessors, *the* last judgment is a mental act. While Blake follows the traditional Christian pattern, in which Christ judges all men ("VLJ," K 616 and *M* 42:26-7, K 534), he changes the event's genesis by internalizing it within the human mind:

> All Things are comprehended in their Eternal Forms in the divine body of the Saviour, the True Vine of Eternity, The Human Imagination, who appear'd to Me as Coming to Judgment among his Saints & throwing off the Temporal that the Eternal might be Establish'd ("VLJ," K 605–6).

The moral act of the imagination whereby everlasting salvation is attained is to forgive:

Forgiveness of Sin is only at the Judgment Seat of Jesus the Saviour, where the Accuser is cast out, not because he Sins, but because he torments the Just, & makes them do what he condemns as Sin & what he knows is opposite to their own Identity ("VLJ," K 616).

As in time the "Inspired Man" casts out this last error of the selfhood, also at the end of time, he forever casts out this Satan, who repressively and rationally separates man from his eternal identity, individually and collectively, so that

> . . . the Furnaces [of satanic "affliction"]
>   became
> Fountains of Living Waters flowing from
>   the Humanity Divine.
> And all the Cities of Albion rose
>   from their Slumbers, and All
> The Sons & Daughters of Albion on soft clouds,
>   waking from Sleep.
> Soon all around remote the Heavens burnt
>   with flaming fires,
> And Urizen & Luvah & Tharmas & Urthona
>   arose into
> Albion's Bosom   (*J* 96:36-42, K 744).

Man is totally reunited with himself and with others in the last judgment of the imagination.

Finally, the resurrection also occurs multiply, in time and in eternity; following John 5:25, Revelation 20:5-6, and the sacrament of baptism, Augustine and Donne speak of the first resurrection on earth, of the spirit, through God's grace and faith in Jesus Christ. And following primarily 1 Corinthians 15, Christian doctrine teaches that man, like Jesus on Easter, will be raised from the dead in body and soul to judgment, and the saved will be transfigured into the immortal *pneumatikon*. Though Blake likewise agrees that

You may do so ["live in Paradise & Liberty"] in Spirit, but not in the Mortal Body as you pretend, till after the Last Judgment; for in Paradise they have no Corporeal & Mortal Body—that originated with the Fall & was call'd Death & cannot be removed but by a Last Judgment; while we are in the world of Mortality we must Suffer. The Whole Creation Groans to be deliver'd [and "the Earth is convulsed with the labours of the Resurrection"] ("VLJ," K 616 and "DLJ," K 443).[11]

In this "deliverance from Satan's Accusation" ("VLJ," K 615), mortal man is "reborn," "by a New Spiritual birth Regenerated from Death" (*VFZ*, N IX: 224, K 363).

Like Donne and other Protestants, Blake is primarily interested in how man now in spirit may "live in Paradise & Liberty," since this first resurrection assures the final resurrection at the end of time. For Blake, the individual's personal reintegration and "first resurrection" necessarily precede its communal attainment—"As One Man all the Universal Family" (*J* 38: 19, K 664)—here or hereafter. Jesus' Easter resurrection was singular and must be imitated by every man, as Albion learns.

The importance of this sublime sequence at the end of *Jerusalem* derives, partly, from its Biblical ancestors, which Blake appropriates by portraying their origin in the "poetic genius": "The Hebrew Bible & the Gospel of Jesus are not Allegory, but Eternal Vision or Imagination of All that Exists" ("ARAO," K 98 and "VLJ," K 604).[12] As discussed, the aesthetic form of forgiveness is imaginative identification.

W. B. Yeats frequently speaks of this conjunction, for, to him,

> the historical Christ was indeed no more than the supreme symbol of the artistic imagination, in which, with every passion wrought to perfect beauty by art and poetry, we shall live, when the body has passed away for the last time.

Elaborating the moral significance of the "imagination [that] was the first emanation of divinity, 'the body of God,' " Yeats explains

> that the imaginative arts were therefore the greatest of Divine revelations, and that the sympathy with all living things, sinful and righteous alike, which the imaginative arts awaken, is that forgiveness commanded by Christ.[13]

Blake expresses this symbolic equivalence in that Jesus and Los are the "likeness & similitude" of each other (as dramatized on *J* 96). The "Imagination, which becomes as the essence of sympathy [Blake], identified with Forgiveness and so with Christ, or Humanity."[14]

Speaking of the preservative assurance of redemption, Jesus teaches

> Verily, verily, I say unto you, Except a corn of wheat fall into the ground and die, it abideth alone: but if it die, it bringeth forth much fruit (John 12: 24).[15]

And Paul's definitive teaching of the resurrection, in 1 Corinthians 15, continues this image of transfiguration: "It is sown a natural body; it is raised a spiritual body" (15:44).

Now, in *Jerusalem,* this Christian regeneration arises from man's absolute imaginative identification with another "human form divine":

> Cannot Man exist with Mysterious
> Offering of Self for Another?
>   is this Friendship & Brotherhood?
> I see thee [Jesus] in the likeness & similitude
> of Los my Friend   (*J* 96:20-22, K 743).

When man lovingly gives himself for another, as Jesus exemplifies, he is unified and saved by this transfigurative act of the imagination (*J* 96:35-43, K 744).

Blake conceives of the individual's first, or spiritual, resurrection as the Four Zoas' restoration to perfect unity; this promise psychologizes Jesus' prayer before his glorification:

That they all may be one; as thou, Father art in me, and I in thee, that they also may be one in us: I in them, and thou in me, that they may be made perfect in one (John 17:21–23).[16]

At the beginning of *Vala, or the Four Zoas* Blake explicitly refers to these verses, from which his fourfold psychologization of man and God, in part, arises:

> Four Mighty Ones are in every Man;
>   a Perfect Unity
> Cannot Exist but from the Universal Brotherhood
>   of Eden,
> The Universal Man, to Whom be Glory Evermore
> (*VFZ,* N I:9-11, K 264).

Having attained this perfection of individual unity through the redemptive labours of Los, the whole of mankind are radically joined as and in the collective Divine Body, for

> He who would see the Divinity must see him
>   in his Children,
> One first, in friendship & love, then a
> Divine Family, & in the midst

Jesus will appear; so he who wishes to
see a Vision, a perfect Whole,
Must see it in its Minute Particulars,
Organiz'd, . . . & every
Particular is a Man, a Divine Member
of the Divine Jesus.   (*J* 91 : 19-22 and
30-31, K 738).

In the world of history, the imagination integrates man with his Zoas and with his emanation, for

Man is adjoin'd to Man by his Emanative portion
Who is Jerusalem in every individual Man, . . .
. . . turn your eyes inward: open, O thou World
Of Love & Harmony in Man: expand thy ever
lovely Gates! (*J* 44 : 38-42, K 675).

The *Logos*, who is Jesus in eternity and Los in time, alone knows and preserves divine perfection, imaged in the resurrection.

In the final resurrection of the apocalypse, "Man is All Imagination. God is Man & exists in us & we in him."[17] For Blake, as in Christian doctrine, the resurrected body is the "spiritual body," which for Blake, however, is the immortal body of the reunified Four Zoas and the spirit is inspiration, i.e., the creativity of the divine imagination: "What is the Divine Spirit? Is the Holy Ghost any other than an Intellectual Fountain?" (*J* 77, K 717).[18] Accordingly, Blake thus redefines the raised immortal and spiritual body in his "Christianity [which] is Art" ("Laocoon," K 777):

I know of no other Christianity and of no other Gospel than the Liberty of both body & mind to exercise the Divine Arts of Imagination, Imagination the real & eternal World of which this Vegetable Universe is but a faint shadow & in which we shall live in our Eternal or Imaginative Bodies when these Vegetable Mortal Bodies are no more (*J* 77, K 716-7).

This visionary prose states Blake's central belief which informs (directly or indirectly) virtually all of his work. The developmental pattern of Blake's works is Biblical—from the Old through the New Testaments, narrating the fall, creation, judgment, and redemption. And this correspondence, a "Divine Analogy," befits Blake's poetic knowledge that, because written by the Holy Spirit, "The Whole Bible is fill'd with Imagination & Visions from End to End" ("Annot. Berkeley," K 774; see also "VLJ," K 604 and 607).

However, as with his portrayals of Jesus (as in *The Marriage of Heaven and Hell*), Blake rewrites the Bible—"I have also the Bible of Hell, which the world shall have whether they will or no" (*MHH* 24, K 158)—according to its origin in the poetic genius. To particularize Blake's "genius," especially in his interpretation of Christianity, I wish to suggest that "what moved him" was a constant desire fully to see and delineate that divine reality envisioned only "thro' the eye" of imagination.

Blake's "great task" is spiritually prescriptive—the apocalyptic cleansing of each man's doors of perception so that everything is seen as it is, infinite and holy (as Blake appropriately describes his method on *MHH* 14, K 154 and on *J* 5:18-20, K 623). He creates, lovingly, to redeem—by destroying the last error of mystery and thereby revealing the divine eternal reality, because the traditional end of both religion and art is infinite and immanent divine vision.[19] Blake characteristically labors spiritually to "regenerate" this complete perfect unity—of man, of men, and of the human and the divine—through the resurrection of the imagination.

The Religion Tractates

Blake's first engraved works, appropriately, are the religion tracts, "There is No Natural Religion," first and second series, and "All Religions are One," etched about 1788, and they indirectly present the central principle developed throughout the rest of his work: the single source of salvation resides in the Lord who is the "Poetic Genius," whom the ancients called the "Spirit of Prophecy," whom the Christians called Jesus, and which Blake later calls the imagination.

The subject of "No Natural Religion," first series, is proper perception and the insufficiency of natural sense perceptions; such "single vision," as Blake later calls it, constitutes man's fallen condition in which he perceives only boundaries and divisions. Implied in the first "No Natural Religion" tract is the cause of all our woe, psychic and cosmic: not to see, i.e., to forsake the imagination, as Blake later dramatizes, is to fall; and fallen, man finds everything else fallen also, for "as a man is, so he sees."[20] The rational and experimental character reduces all things ("at the ratio") to the repetitious and inert "same dull round."

Blake expresses this central principle of transformational vision, wherein inner and outer are one, in the dictum of "The Mental Traveller" that "the Eye altering, alters all" (K 426), and this observation recurs in different forms as the chorus of his work. Whereas the first "No Natural Religion" applies this principle in its negative sense, the second "No Natural Religion" develops in the opposite direction, from the fallen to the risen form of perception.

The second series begins by arguing against restrictive reason, associated with the dark satanic mill of the selfhood, and then expounds the principle of infinite desire, the possession of which reveals man's coextensive identity with God:

> V. . . . less than All cannot satisfy Man. VII. The desire of Man being Infinite, the possession is Infinite & himself Infinite. Application. He who sees the Infinite in all things sees God. . . . Therefore God becomes as we are, that we may be as he is ("NNR," b, K 97–8).

To see the Infinite in all things is to see as God sees, which is to see God. Seeing through the eye of imagination, which imperative the poetic, or prophetic, character embodies—the immaculate perception of the Blakean incarnation—is to rise to "be as he is," the divine identification, completed in the resurrection.[21]

Finally, "All Religions Are One" treats the incarnate source of infinite vision, the "poetic genius," the "true" and "real" man, the "imagination." Of this spiritual man, Blake writes (in the "Annotations to Swedenborg's Divine Love," in about 1789) that "he who Loves feels love descend into him & if he has Wisdom may perceive it is from the Poetic Genius, which is the Lord" (K 90). From this spirit or poetic genius, whose inward form is the soul, man's outward form, his body, is derived, "For let it be remember'd that creation is God descending according to the weakness of man, for our Lord is the word of God & every thing on earth is the word of God & in its essence is God" ("Annot. Lavater," K 87).

As all men are alike in their inward or spiritual form, though with infinite variety in their outward, bodily form, so all religions are one because they arise from the same, single source, the imagination:

> Principle 5th. The Religions of all Nations are derived from each

Nation's different reception of the Poetic Genius, which is every where call'd the Spirit of Prophecy. . . . The Jewish & Christian Testaments are An original derivation from the Poetic Genius; this is necessary from the confined nature of bodily sensation. . . . As all men are alike (tho' infinitely various), So all Religions & as all Similars, have one Source. The true man is the source, he being the Poetic Genius ("ARAO," K 98).

For Christians, the manifest "source" of religion is Jesus, as Athanasius speaks of the incarnation: "Therefore the Word of God came in His own Person, in order that as He was the image of the Father he might be able to recreate Man after that image."

As between the Old and New Testaments, there is a figural relation between Blake's early (pre-1800) and later works, in which this true and real man is the poetic genius, who is our Lord; God himself is incarnate in his temporal form as Jesus, the Christian name of the Savior, whose radical identity is the imagination and whose work is art: "Jesus & his Apostles & Disciples were all Artists" ("Laocoon," K 777).[22]

The Contrary Progress of the Soul in the Songs of Innocence and of Experience

Blake's lyrics, like many of the songs from Yeats's plays, are illuminated when seen within their larger conceptual context. While the *Songs of Innocence and Experience* are successful alone, they also belong to Blake's fourfold system, of which "innocence" (Beulah) and "experience" (Generation and Ulro) are part.[23] The subtitle to the combined engraved book of 1794 states Blake's subject here, the "two contrary states," as part "of" his continuing concern, "the human soul" and its salvation. And from *The Marriage of Heaven and Hell*, composed concurrently, we must add that "without Contraries is no progression" (*MHH* 3, K 149). As Blake argues further in the epics,[24] contraries exist in a mutually creative relation (except at the bottom of the grave), from which "progress" proceeds.

The standardized arrangement of the combined *Songs of Innocence and of Experience* implies that the human soul must pass through both contrary states, and the resulting progress is the subject of the "Introduction" to *Experience,* "The Little Girl Lost" and "Found," and "To Tirzah"; the resultant "image of truth new born"[25] is described in "The Divine Image." One relation between Blake's early and late poems can be seen in the continuity and development of the resurrection motif, presented *sub specie temporis* in the naturalistic (*Songs*) and historical (*French Revolution, America,* and *Europe*) poems and presented *sub specie aeternitatis* as a religious symbol in the eschatological epics (*Milton* and *Jerusalem*).

Blake's illustration on the combined title page of the *Songs* shows fallen man represented as Adam and Eve, who are girded with leaves, showing that they are in a state of Experience; tongues of flame play over them to indicate their expulsion from Eden. Together the *Songs* show the natural world, which was mercifully created by God because of man's cosmic fall and from which he must rise in his apocalyptic return to his original wholeness in heaven, Blake's Eden. *Innocence* portrays natural innocence where the child and Jesus are the Lamb; both are protected in a maternal and pastoral environment. Seen from the perspective of the Bard, *Innocence* shows that this idyllic existence in the natural world is both temporary and necessary.

The Little Black Boy's Expectations

That earthly existence is transient, fallen, and preparatory for rejoicing with God in heaven is the subject of "The Little Black Boy," and the color imagery of this poem derives, I think, from Revelation. Temporarily ("a little space") on earth, the soul learns "to bear the beams of love"; with lyric succinctness, Blake here describes the trial and reward of passing through natural innocence and experience. In a physical sense, this "bearing" refers to enduring the heat of experience so that eventually the little black boy will "come out from the grove," or forest, of night and rejoice round God's tent. In a spiritual sense, the child whose soul is pure ("white") must "bear" earthly sufferings, as Jesus did in the incarnation and on the actual cross itself—the crucifix "beams of love" of Father and Son for man.[26] The purpose of both examples of mercy is the same, namely that God became as we are so that we may be as he is ("And be like him"). In its final sense, "to bear the beams of love" is to give birth to and to live as God in the human form divine of the resurrected body. Then the "cloud," through which man sees the sun-son-God but darkly, "will vanish"[27] and

... we shall hear his voice
Saying: come out from the grove my love
    and care,
And round my golden tent like lambs rejoice
       (facs. *SIE. Z*, 10:18-20).

The "golden tent" of the pastoral God, as Lamb and Shepherd (illustrated on Plate 10, where Jesus' light seems to illuminate the text in facs. Z) is the natural image of his golden throne in heaven, around which the blessed praise God, as described in Revelation 4:19, and 21-22. Here, as we shall continue to see, the expected result of bearing beams of love through the cloud of the natural world is to rise, so that "I'll stand and stroke his silver hair,/ And be like him and he will then love me." This condition in which each man bears the beams of love in the resurrected body is the expected, desired end of man's spiritual progress.

Divine Blessings

"The Divine Image" presents "the identification of man with God. Many passages can be found throughout his writings illustrating his fundamental belief in the divinity of the human nature."[28] In the apparently contemporary "Annotations to Lavater's *Aphorisms*," written about 1788-89, for example, Blake notes that "human nature is the image of God" (K 83). This identification of the human and divine joined in a single image is temporal in the incarnation and eternal in the resurrection. Its prefiguration structures this religious lyric. While the poem begins with God (in st. 1), it moves to those virtues—of Mercy, Pity, Peace, and Love—which the Father and Son share (in sts. 2 and 3), and ends with their incarnation as the "human form divine," Blake's image of the resurrected body, where "God is dwelling too."[29]

This final divine blessing has two different Biblical forms, and their distinction pertains to Blake's development of this motif. The Old Testament prophetic speaker envisions a pastoral, Messianic kingdom on earth, as the Lord says to Ezekiel:

My servant David shall be king over them and they shall have one shepherd. . . . I will make a covenant of peace with them; and I will bless them and multiply them, and will set my sanctuary in the midst of them for evermore. My dwelling place shall be with them; and I will be their God, and they shall be my people (37: 24–27).

In contrast, the apocalyptic speaker predicates this "marriage" *sub specie aeternitatis*:

And I saw a new heaven and a new earth; for the first heaven and the first earth were passed away; and there was no more sea. . . . Behold, the dwelling of God is with men, and he will dwell with them, and they shall be his people, and God himself shall be with them, and be their God (Rev. 21: 1 and 3).

In the *Songs* as in other early works until *Vala*, Blake presents this divine return from the prophetic perspective, *sub specie temporis*; from *Vala, or the Four Zoas* (1797) on, his emphasis shifts to the apocalyptic total destruction of this world and the creation of the Christian city of God.

The Songs of Experience: *"O Earth Return!"*

The *Songs of Experience* present the necessary descent into the fallen world of personal repression and social oppression from which man is raised. The youth of the cover of the *Experience* frontispiece leaves his flock of sheep and steps forward, under the tree of woe, i.e., moves from natural innocence to its contrary state of experience. Accordingly, the child of joy (pictured on the frontispiece of *Innocence*) now appears as a winged cherub (in copy Z), with a halo and seated on the head of the young man, with whom he holds hands. This winged child, whom Blake later calls the "covering cherub," is, however, not benign, for he represents the corrupt "selfhood," the selfish, possessive natural instincts of restriction.[30] The covering cherub of the selfhood must be finally negated, i.e., annihilated, as the last error of the tree of mystery. Here, however, the *Songs* treat man's psychological and social woes as necessarily confronted in experience before this stage is passed through.[31]

As suggested earlier, the *Songs of Innocence and of Experience* present in miniature the history of the human soul and body from the fall (creation) to the resurrection, and I will discuss this expectation of "repair," i.e., repatriation, as it appears in *Experience*. The ancient Bard, speaking *sub specie aeternitatis* ("who

Present, Past, and Future sees"), specifically calls man's "lapsed soul" to return to the Holy Word heard in the Garden of Eden; For having "fallen [,] fallen" man may yet renew the divine light, since creation (the starry pole of reason and the watery shore of time and space) was an act of divine mercy "giv'n"[32] man as the sleep of materialism from which to wake:

O Earth O Earth return!
Arise from out the dewy grass;
Night is worn,
And the morn
Rises from the slumberous mass (facs. *SIE, Z*, 30:11-15).

Both the Biblical allusions and expectations of this "Introduction" are prophetic in the Old Testament tradition of earthly renewal, though the "break of day" in the last line implies the final transformation of the apocalypse. In Isaiah 21 the prophet envisions the fall of Babylon, the great whore of materialism (who becomes the mother of earth's abominations, in Rev. 17:5), and the return of God's community:

And behold, here cometh a chariot of men, with a couple of horsemen. And he answered and said, Babylon is fallen, is fallen; and all the graven images of her gods he hath broken into the ground. . . . The watchmen said, The morning cometh, and also the night: if ye will enquire, enquire ye: return, come (21:9 and 12).

Likewise Jeremiah implores Israel "O earth, earth, earth, hear the word of the Lord" (22:29), repent, and return to God's covenant.[33] However, both the image of the last line of the "Introduction" to *Experience* and the late poem "To Tirzah" adumbrate Blake's movement from the Old Testament prophetic imperative of renewal to the New Testament apocalyptic vision of re-creation.[34]

The "break of day" toward which *Experience* moves derives from Revelation, where the Old Testament's prophetic promise of temporal renewal on earth is fulfilled in the eternal re-creation of the new heaven and new earth:

And he that sat upon the throne said, Behold, I make all things new. . . . And he carried me away in the spirit to a great and high mountain, and shewed me that great city, the holy Jerusalem, descending out of heaven from God. . . . And the city had no need of the sun, neither of the

moon, to shine in it: for the glory of God did lighten it, and the Lamb
is the light thereof (Rev. 21:5, 10, and 23; see also 25).

Blake's daybreak refers to this heavenly Jerusalem, where "there
shall be no night there; and they need no candle, neither light of
the sun; for the Lord God giveth them light: and they shall
reign for ever and ever" (Rev. 22:5). When the whole earth's
"lapsed soul," like the Bard, sees that final sun rise, the apocalypse will be complete.[35]

Till then, however, Earth is bound in the "darkness, dread &
drear" of experience. In her "Answer" Blake's imagery emphasizes the bodily imprisonment, which will be "changed" and liberated in the resurrection:

> Break this heavy chain,
> That does freeze my bone around
> Selfish! vain,
> Eternal bane!
> That free Love with bondage bound.[36]

Because the earth is bound in materialism, man lives in the "grey
despair" of mental error. Man's personal and social behaviour
mirrors his inward imprisonment in "mind-forg'd manacles."
Since a man sees and speaks as he is, we must consider what is
said in terms of who says it. In the *Songs* the poems which most
directly concern the resurrection motif are spoken by the Bard
(formerly called the prophet, the artist whom Blake later
names Los).

The Prophetic "Garden Mild"

While in darkness the earth can know and describe herself
only as "prison'd" in materialism (the starry floor and watery
shore which are the limits of Urizen's den). But the Bard envisions earth's prophetic renewal:

> In futurity
> I prophetic see,
> That the earth from sleep,
> (Grave the sentence deep)

Shall arise and seek
For her maker meek:
And the desart wild
Become a garden mild (facs. *SIE*, Z, 34:1-8).

The progress which "The Little Girl Lost" and "Found" portray concerns the soul's relation to the experiential body. The child's (Lyca's) return to the parents adumbrates Earth's return to her maker. In this set of poems what is "found" is a reconciliation within the world of generation, in the "garden mild."[37] These poems are about the child's soul, which begins in pastoral innocence, ages into experience, and passes through it to a state of prophetic innocence, where parents and child (whose pastoral correlate is the Lamb) lie down together in peace with the lion.

Aside from Neo-Platonic versions, the major "source" for this narrative is Isaiah's telling of the reign of the righteous on earth, when "the wilderness and the solitary place shall be glad for them; and the desert shall rejoice, and blossom as the rose" (35:1).[38] This condition of harmony between man and nature Blake calls Beulah, which name derives from Isaiah's description of the fruitful Messianic kingdom.[39] Toward this prophetic immanence and from the deep grave of materialism the sleeping Earth will rise and become a garden mild, the Biblical Eden, Blake's Beulah.[40]

The two poems present the body's (Lyca's parents') search for a fertile relation with the soul, personified in the world of generation as a daughter. If the soul is "lost in [the] desart wild" of experience, neither it (Lyca) nor the body (her parents) is able to rest ("sleep") until both find a path through the desert and are reunited in the prelapsarian garden. Using conventional images of the desert and wild animals to represent the inherent sterility and dangers of experience, Blake argues that they must and can be changed from being destructive to preservative, when man sees them as prophetically converted. Like unmental travelers, the parents wander seven days through the desert before their journey through experience (the fallen world of Genesis) is complete. On the eighth day, they meet the kingly lion, a creature of presiding bodily power, and this confrontation leads to their finding Lyca.

As the lion allays the parents' fears, which have kept them in experience thus far, by licking, not biting, their hands,

> They look upon his eyes
> Fill'd with deep surprise:
> And wondering behold
> A spirit arm'd in gold,
>
> On his head a crown
> On his shoulders down,
> Flow'd his golden hair.
> Gone was all their care (facs. *SIE*, Z, 36:33-40).

The moment of conversion involves a definitive change in perspective: "They look upon his eyes/ Fill'd with deep surprise." Their surprise, with which their former fears vanish, is that the lion, who represents the potentially dismembering aspects of experience, especially sexuality, is not predatory, but majestically protective: "And wondering behold/ A spirit armed in gold."

This realization that their vision is saving leads directly to their being reunited with their lost child:

> Then they followed,
> Where the vision led:
> And saw their sleeping child,
> Among tygers wild (facs. *SIE*, Z, 36:45-48).

It is not mistaken literalism to say that proper "vision" is the mode of finding and possessing an existence where neither body (the generative parents) nor soul (Lyca) is bruised by experience (the lion); the "they" in the last stanza, though ambiguous, refers, I think, to these three characters, as the illustration on Plate 36 shows. Their life of harmony is akin to the prophetic Messianic kingdom on earth, where "the wolf also shall dwell with the lamb and the leopard shall lie down with the kid; and the calf and the young lion and the fatling together; and a child shall lead them" (Isa. 11:6).

In the context of the prophetic prediction, this child, as everyman, belongs to and thus reforms the natural world, whereas in the New Testament the child, who is the Son of God and of Man, begins in, and returns to, the supernatural world. That this earthly garden, however "mild," is not satisfying is the implied subject of "Ah Sun-flower!"

Although this lyric may be considered as an experiential parody of false sexual virtue (Church chastity), it is also an extended call for "that sweet golden clime" at the end of time. There the presently repressed lovers (the pining youth and pale virgin) will "Arise from their graves and aspire,/ Where my Sun-flower wishes to go" (facs. *SIE, Z,* 43 : 7-8). Since the sunflower is clearly rooted in the natural world, the "sweet golden clime" it wishes to go to must enhance its life, rather than negate it. Likewise, the lovers seek a transvalued "natural" existence, which is free from the rose's thorns of sexual jealousy and from the sheep's horn of physical threat (death), as the accompanying poems "My pretty Rose Tree" and "The Lilly") on Plate 43 add. However, this land "where the travellers journey is done" is one neither free from bodily existence *per se*[41] nor bounded by the natural sun. I think we must look to the end of the completed progress of the *Songs,* where the late "To Tirzah" clearly distinguishes the prophetic regeneration within nature and the Christian resurrection "from generation free."[42]

"To Rise from Generation Free"

Blake's placing "To Tirzah" virtually at the conclusion of the combined *Songs of Innocence and of Experience* indicates the completed progress from natural innocence through experience to spiritual innocence. In spite of dating difficulties, what is significant is that Blake ends the *Songs of Innocence and of Experience* with this poem.[43] This religious lyric is illuminated by its Biblical echoes, with which we begin. The name "Tirzah" derives from the Song of Solomon 6 : 4, where it signifies physical beauty.[44] In his mythology Blake chronologically bifurcates this characteristic of natural woman, so that Tirzah is the comely sexual beauty of youth (the "virgin bright" of the "Mental Traveller," for example) and Rahab is the abominable old harlot (the great whore of Babylon), "terrible as an army with banners."

Implied in this use of the Biblical source and explicit in the poems and engraved illustration is Blake's insistence on the natural oppression of man's instincts in the time-bound world of generation. As natural innocence must pass into experience and as the comely young virgin grows into the terrible old whore (in the female version of the Orc cycle), so man must pass through mortal life and rise immortal:

Whate'er is Born of Mortal Birth,
Must be consumed with the Earth
To rise from Generation free:
Then what have I to do with thee?
(facs. *SIE*, Z, 52:1-4).

The last line of this stanza is Jesus' address to Mary in the Temple, as recorded in John 2:4;[45] and here the "thee" addressed is sexual womankind, collectively called Tirzah.

The next ten lines describe in miniature the genesis of man's natural betrayal. From the accompanying illustration we observe that neither the sexual (the young woman) nor the maternal (the older woman) supports or sustains man: he is saved only by the "spiritual body," who offers him baptismal water of immortal life (John 3:5-7). In spite of this death in the fallen, natural body, the Pauline *psychikon,* man will rise "from generation free" and whole (instead of divided into sexes)[46] because "the death of Jesus set me free."

This insistence on salvation through Jesus' resurrection, in the *pneumatikon,* from the dead reiterates Paul's logic of belief:

> But if there be no resurrection of the dead, then Christ is not risen: And if Christ be not risen, then is our preaching vain, and your faith is vain; ye are yet in your sins. . . . But now is Christ risen from the dead, and become the first fruits of them that slept. For since by man came death, by man came the resurrection of the dead. For as in Adam all die, even so in Christ shall all be made alive (1 Cor. 15:13-14, 16-17, and 20-22).

Blake incorporates the resurrection doctrine here as the virtual conclusion to the human soul's progress through the contrary states of innocence and experience; at the same time, his combining the Bible with his own developing mythology adumbrates his future progress and appropriation of the motif.

Blake continues the overall Biblical pattern of fall and resurrection by delineating his own understanding of these archetypal events, as we shall see. For example, the inscription on the Savior's robe—"It is Raised a Spiritual Body"—is illustrated by other contemporary writings. Since the possible date (from 1795-1805) of this poem varies, we must examine Blake's relevant uses of the word "spiritual" during these ten important years.

The earliest, and likely the most explanatory, occasion occurs in the letter to Dr. Trusler of 23 August 1799, where Blake characteristically insists on the primacy of vision, or imagination, which pertains to his reading of the Bible:

To Me This World is all One continuous Vision of Fancy or Imagination & I feel Flatter'd when I am told so. What is it sets Homer, Virgil, & Milton so high in the rank of Art? Why is the Bible more Entertaining & Instructive than any other book? Is it not because *they are addressed to the Imagination, which is Spiritual Sensation* (K 793–94; italics mine).

Here and consistently in other uses, Blake defines imagination as spiritual sensation; and their radical identity can also be understood as reversible, so that the spiritual is the imaginative, as Blake later describes the resurrected body "to the Christians."[47]

In his "Annotations to Boyd's translation of Dante's *Inferno*," written about 1800, Blake reiterates the insufficiency of naturalism, for "Nature Teaches nothing of Spiritual Life but only of Natural Life" (K 412). In the magnificent Night the Ninth (being the Last Judgment) of *The Four Zoas,* probably composed just after the turn of the century,[48] Blake envisions the marriage of the Lamb and his Bride, heavenly Jerusalem, "Mother of myriads redeem'd & born in her spiritual palaces,/ By a New Spiritual birth Regenerated from Death" (*VFZ,* N IX: 223-24, K 363; and Rev. 21). These lines contrast the failures of natural generation (outlined in "Tirzah") and the blessings of spiritual regeneration (presented in *Milton* and *Jerusalem*). Accordingly, the human body and soul have nothing to do with the mortal dross, which is fallen nature, and everything to do with immortal liberty, which is Jesus' gift of power and glory in the resurrection.

"To Tirzah" virtually, or spiritually, if you will, completes the combined *Songs of Innocence and of Experience* "shewing the contrary states of the human soul" without which there is no progress; and this poem indicates the perspective from which to view these sequential lyrics and the development of the epics. Though the mortal birth of the child allows him initial natural innocence with maternal, pastoral protection, he ages in time inevitably into experience, where he is trapped, temporarily, by delusive materialism and betraying generation. Man passes through both contrary states and "is Raised a Spiritual Body"; realizing this final progress into spiritual, or imaginative, innocence is Blake's extended subject.

The Marriage of Heaven and Hell: *Its Beginning*

"As a new heaven is begun, and it is now thirty-three years [Blake's age in 1790] since its advent: the Eternal Hell revives" (*MHH* 3, K 149); and this "new heaven" refers to Blake's "new church," which we now explore.[49] In comparison with Donne's ecclesiastical conception of marriage as the temporal union of body and soul in love on earth as a "remembrancer" and prefiguration of the eternal union of man and God in heaven—the whole world contracted thus—we here see Blake's humanization of "marriage."

In the introduction to *Jerusalem* Blake writes of his apocalyptic hopes when "Heaven, Earth, & Hell henceforth shall live in harmony" (*J* 3, K 621). Their living in harmony not only is tantamount to the "marriage of heaven and hell," but also means that, in fact, heaven subsumes hell, "for Hell is open'd to Heaven, thine eyes beheld/ The dungeons burst & the Prisoners set free" (*J* 77:33-35, K 718).[50] And, in fact, the anonymous and ahistorical (because unsigned) title page of *The Marriage of Heaven and Hell* illustrates this final liberation, whose *principia* are my subject.

The text and illuminations of the *Marriage* are integrated, as shown on the title page. Blake's inscription on one frontispiece, on copy B, that "Our End is Come" pronounces the apocalyptic "intention" of the *Marriage;* the fact that this pronouncement does not appear on later copies, however, suggests that perhaps it was premature. The title page has the words "The," "Heaven," and "Hell" written in roman capitals, the classical categories of good and evil, which are abolished in the "marriage,"[51] written in "living gothic" (as are "of," and "and," whose meaning of joining is pictured by the tail of the "d" which encircles the word and points upward, thus (and/).

The title page divides into thirds, with "The Marriage of" written in the upper third, where are pictured trees, whose branches point inward and upward, a man and a woman walking, arm in arm, from the left to the center, and a kneeling figure, piping, and above birds fly, in "an immense world of delight" (*MHH* 6, K 150). In the lower two-thirds, the portrayal of earth continues underground (into which the tree-roots extend), where burn the fires of hell and the apocalypse and among and through which man is liberated. The human figures are engaged in two apocalyptic acts—1) the union of man and woman which is also the reunion of body and soul[52] and 2) the resultant upward movement when "Hell is open'd to Heaven" and the "prisoners set free." Traditionally complete freedom and "true happiness" are attained in the resurrection.

Prophetic Persuasion and Apocalyptic Perception

In the text of *The Marriage of Heaven and Hell* Blake presents his principles whereby this total freedom, true Christian liberty, is realized.[53] On Plate 4 the "voice of the devil," surrounded by three trumpeting angels, reveals the errors of all previous sacred codes and articulates his own image of truth: he proclaims the unity of body and soul, the psychologization of reality, and the eternal delight of energy. If the *Marriage* is satirically immoral (being spoken by the devil), it is more seriously moral and concerned with the recognition and possession of "all deities," who "reside in the human breast," for "God only Acts & Is in existing beings or Men" (*MHH* 16, K 155).

Insofar as the *Marriage* is concerned with proper, i.e., infinite, perception, it continues the Old Testament prophetic tradition by emphasizing its visionary origin, as Blake's Isaiah and Ezekiel explain. When he asks them if God spoke to them, first

Isaiah answer'd, I saw no God, nor heard any in a finite organical perception; but my senses discover'd the infinite in everything, and as I was then perswaded, & remain confirm'd; that the voice of honest indignation is the voice of God. . . .

Then I asked: does a firm perswasion that a thing is so, make it so?

He replied. All poets believe that it does, & in ages of imagination this firm perswasion moved mountains; . . . .

Then Ezekiel said. The philosophy of the east taught the first principles of human perception; we of Israel taught that the Poetic Genius (as you now call it) was the first principle and all the others merely derivative. . . . which was the cause of our . . . prophecy that all Gods would at last be proved to originate in ours & to be tributaries of the Poetic Genius (*MHH* 12–13, K 153).

The prophets' remarks echo Blake's declaration in "All Religions" that "the Religions of all Nations are derived from each Nation's different reception of the Poetic Genius which is every where call'd the Spirit of Prophecy. . . . The Jewish and Christian Testaments are An original derivation from the Poetic

Genius" ("ARAO," K 98). The purpose of their acts, as well as of Blake's art, is "raising other men into a perception of the infinite" (*MHH* 13, K 154). In both source ·(the poetic genius) and end (infinite vision), Blake sees the prophetic and poetic principles as one.

On Plate 14 Blake expands this Old Testament prefiguration to its New Testament conclusion by combining the prophetic imperative of "raising men to a perception of the infinite" with the apocalyptic destruction of the fallen world, the revelation of "reality" and the resurrection of the united body and soul:

> For the cherub with his flaming sword is hereby commanded to leave his guard at the tree of life, and when he does the whole creation will be consumed, [in fire], and appear infinite, and holy whereas it now appears finite & corrupt.
>   This will come to pass by an improvement of sensual enjoyment (*MHH* 14, K 154).[54]

The illustration at the top of Plate 14 shows a "dead" or sleeping nude man lying on his back on the ground, from which flames burn; above him and at the top of the flames hovers, with outstretched arms and flowing hair, a female figure, the emanation, the soul with which the body will be reunited.

On this central (conceptually and numerically) plate and in the *Marriage* as a whole, the eschatology is more "begun" than completed. If we compare this illustration with other versions of this joyful return to wholeness, we find it here portrayed as about-to-begin, for the soul remains (literally) in suspended "anima-tion"; in "The Reunion of the Soul & the Body," "The Agony in the Garden," and on *Jerusalem* 96 and 99, however, the soul fully embraces the body and their reunion is complete.

The text of Plate 14 also supports this interpretation of imminent resurrection, for while the covering cherub is "hereby commanded to leave his guard at the tree of life," exactly "when he does" remains in the future. It "will come to pass by an improvement of sensual enjoyment," which is also the increase of spiritual enjoyment (John iii, 30) because body and soul are one: "Man has no Body distinct from his Soul; for that call'd Body is a portion of the Soul discern'd by the five Senses, the chief inlets of the Soul in this age" (*MHH* 4, K 149). While the guarding cherub of Genesis iii, 24 keeps the eastern gate of Eden from which man was exiled, Blake foresees the return to Eden through the western gate, i.e., through Tharmas, his mythological character, who represents the instinctual, sensual body and whose compass point is the west.[55] Blake's alteration of the Biblical placement (from east to west) emphasizes that man's return to his initial well-being is in the resurrected body, through the western gate of Tharmas.

Blake expands the inlets of the soul in his "salutary and medicinal" printing, "melting apparent surfaces away, and displaying the infinite which was hid" (*MHH* 14, K 154). The implied relation between the revelation of everything as infinite and holy and the resurrection of the body and soul becomes clearer in the observation that "if the doors of perception were cleansed, every thing would appear to man as it is, infinite" (*MHH* 14, K 154). The "cleansed" doors of perception are the eyes of imagination, through which man sees all as infinite because he himself is infinite in his "improved," or transfigured, eternal and imaginative body; "to the Eyes of the Man of Imagination Nature is Imagination itself. As a man is so he sees."[56] However, in the fall, "man has closed himself up till he sees all things thro' narrow chinks of his cavern" (*MHH* 14, K 154) of materialism, rationalism, and generation. Like the prophets Isaiah and Ezekiel, animated by the poetic genius, Blake desires to raise men to a perception of the infinite, envisioned in the resurrection.

Blakean Deities: Their Particular Friendship and Reformation

One traditional result of the Biblical apocalypse is the union of man and God. For Blake, however, because "All Deities reside in the human breast" (*MHH* 11, K 153), "God only Acts & Is in existing beings or Men" (*MHH* 16, K 155).[57] This belief in an immanent God, the human form divine, Blake later expands and centers in Jesus, whose proper worship remains constant: "The worship of God is: Honouring his gifts in other men each according to his genius, and loving the greatest men best; those who envy or calumniate great men hate God, for there is no other God" (*MHH* 22-23, K 158) "than that God who is the intellectual fountain of Humanity," as Blake explains in *Jerusalem*.[58] In the *Marriage*, as elsewhere, Blake believes that "Jesus Christ is the greatest man: you ought to love him in the greatest degree" (*MHH* 23, K 158).

In the *Marriage* Blake insists that Jesus' virtue was independent of and not bound by the Old Testament (or any other legal code): "I tell you, no virtue can exist without breaking these ten commandments. Jesus was all virtue, and acted from impulse, not from rules" (*MHH* 23-24, K 158). While Blake does not here expound what constitutes Jesus' virtuous impulse (as he does, most fully, in *Jerusalem*), he does emphasize the virtue of correction (as in *Milton*), by casting out error, whereby truth is revealed.

Blake's devil, "in a flame of fire," asserts that Jesus was an iconoclast whose total virtue was energy ("impulse"), or "mental fight," and who "came not to send Peace but the Sword" (*MHH* 16, K 155). He thereby converts an Angel to the "devil's party" of prophecy: "When he had so spoken, I beheld the Angel, who stretched out his arms embracing the flame of fire [daemonic inspiration, as on *MHH* 23, K 158] & he was consumed and arose as Elijah" (*MHH* 24, K 159). Elijah was the Old Testament prophet who saw God face to face but did not die (1 Kings 18:36) and who was directly resurrected to heaven (2 Kings 2:11). Blake consistently refers to Elijah as the immanent ancestor of Los, "the Spirit of Prophecy, the ever apparent Elias" (*M* 24:71, K 510).[59] His appearance in this context suggests not only Old Testament prophecies but their fulfillment in the New Testament, for it is said in Malachi, the last book of the Old Testament in the King James version, that Elijah will reappear to announce the Messiah and the last judgment.[60] In the Gospels according to Matthew and Mark, Jesus likewise says "Elias truly shall first come, and restore all things" (Matt. 17:11; and Mark 9:12).

These dual associations, of prophecy and the *parousia,* befit this context, in which Jesus (according to Blake) as the embodiment of daemonic energy is "revealed" and in which the Angel by "embracing the flame of fire" (i.e., truth), is transfigured: "and he was consumed and arose as Elijah." Further, "this Angel, who is now become a Devil, is my [Blake's] particular friend; we often read the Bible together in its infernal or diabolical sense, which the world shall have if they behave well" (*MHH* 24, K 158). That is, if the world acts to save itself, as did the Angel, by casting out error, which was consumed in the flames of truth, and embracing those mental fires, it will know and have the Bible properly.

Originally the *Marriage* ended with this Plate 24, for Plates

25-27, containing "A Song of Liberty," were added about 1792-93.[61] These verses narrate the birth of Orc,[62] as Blake calls the natural figure of political revolution associated with those in America and France. Moreover, they foretell the coming Messianic kingdom on earth—when empire is no more and everything that lives is holy.[63]

In the Old Testament and its Apocrypha and Pseudepigrapha this blessing is expressed communally in the renewed covenant of the Messianic kingdom. It is toward this prophetic expectation that the *Marriage* moves. While the New Testament image of the resurrection of the united body and soul also appears, it is in the context of an imminent "apocalypse" whose flames are those of historical revolution rather than of the final conflagration.

Accordingly, Blake's use of the resurrection here and in the three "historical" prophecies to follow is predominantly as an image of political renewal, not of sacramental transfiguration, as in *Milton* and *Jerusalem*. That *The Marriage of Heaven and Hell* ends with this expectation of social liberty and that the "historical" prophecies, written from 1791-94, also portray this Old Testament imperative of communal reformation locate Blake's scene of the Messianic kingdom on earth, set free.

The French Revolution: *Historical Brotherhood*

In the historical prophecies Blake incorporates the resurrection motif primarily in its Old Testament form, whereby the corrupt society is reformed by renewing the divine covenant on earth.[64] *The French Revolution* (1791) begins with the social sickness, sleep, and death which "brood over Europe" from which the dying earth must awake and rise. The two most salutary prescriptions, given by Orléans and the Abbé de Sièyes, plead for communal renewal in a humanistic, if not also prophetic, tradition.

First, Orléans argues for brotherhood;[65] then the Abbé de Sièyes, "like a voice of God," continues and expands this prophetic invocation of community: "Hear, O Heavens of France, the voice of the people arising from valley and hill" (*FR:* 206, K 143). Men will wander enslaved and worship terrors

Till dawn, till morning, till the breaking

of clouds, and swelling of winds, and
the universal voice
Till man raise his darken'd limbs out of
the caves of night, his eyes and his heart
Expand   (*FR:* 217-19, K 144).

The Abbé extends Orléans's insistence on brotherhood by in-
dicating the mode of communal concord—expansion of man's
heart and eyes.

The combined result of this personal empathic growth is a
renewed and blessed earth: "and the happy earth sing in its
course,/ The mild peaceable nations be opened to heav'n, and
men walk with their fathers in bliss" (*FR:* 236-37, K 144-45).
These lines conclude a passage describing the prophetic reformation of this earth, and not its apocalyptic transformation, as
the result of the French Revolution. In *America* (1793) and
Europe (1794), however, we shall see a different conclusion
for the possibilities of political revolt.

America: *The Limits of Natural Revolt*

Blake designates *America* "A Prophecy," and this is the first
time he so characterizes his work. *America* is more unified than
its fragmentary French predecessor, in large part because of his
didactic use of a created mythological character, Orc, to structure the prophetic narrative. America, in the western quadrant,
may be associated with Tharmas, the Body.[66] Orc, the "hero"
of this poem, represents (psychologically) instinctual and (po-
litically) revolutionary youth, in rebellion against the rational,
conservative, elder Urizen. But because Orc is only natural man,
he cannot retain his youthful fires of desire and revolt; inevitably, he ages into his former foe, repressive Urizen, against
whom another Orc will rebel.

This Orc cycle, whereby the young revolutionary inevitably
becomes his older repressor, imitates the pattern of natural
growth and will continue until it is subsumed by the supernatural;
this possibility appears in *Europe* with the birth of Jesus. Theologically, the resurrection of the body (of America, the western
quadrant) involves its transfiguration; on Plates 6 and 16 of
America Blake describes the insufficiency of the natural man

(caught in the Orc cycle) and his necessary, but here ambiguous, liberation.

As the spokesman of the ideal of the original revolutionary America (of 1776), Orc announces a last judgment, on Plate 6, which, in consequence and in Blake's illustration, resembles the "Song of Liberty" and Plate 21 of the *Marriage,* respectively; and both written texts describe a prophetic renewal:

> The grave is burst, the spices shed,
>   the linen wrapped up;
> The bones of death, the cov'ring clay,
>   the sinews shrunk & dried.
> Reviving shake, inspiring move, breathing!
>   awaking!
> Spring like redeemed captives when their
>   bonds & bars are burst; . . .
> Rise and look out, his chains are loose,
>   his dungeon doors are open. . . .
> For Empire is no more, and now the Lion
>   & Wolf shall cease. (*Amer.* 6:2-5,
> 10, and 15, K 198)

While these lines describe the Messianic kingdom, they must be read along with their illustration, which qualifies the revival therein.

In their *Census* of Blake's illuminated books (of which *America* is one of the most pictorial), Keynes and Wolf describe Plate 6 (which I supplement in brackets with my observations of copies A and C):

Above, a naked youth [with a fearful expression on his face] sits on a grave and gazes upward [over his left shoulder, toward a partial sunrise in the background]; beside him is a skull; below are a thistle, newt, fly, toad, and worm, types of mortality (cf. *MHH,* pl. 21 and illustrations to Blair's *Grave,* pl. 31). [on *MHH* 21 D there are two pyramids, emblems of oppression (as of the Egyptian taskmasters) and of threefold, i.e., of generated and of the satanic man, in the background.][67]

Though this male figure is sometimes called "resurrected man," I think regenerate (and not "regenerated," as in *VFZ,* N IX: 224, K 363) man is more accurate in view of the illustrated text. The body proportions of this man are grotesquely emphasized to display the genitalia, which place the seated man clearly in the natural world of generation, bound by copulation and death. The ironic relation, then, between this illustration and the accompanying text on Plate 6 indicates the natural limits of Orc's revolt.[68]

As the fiery rebel against repression (Urizen's perverted Ten Commandments, for example), Orc is "terrible," yet he comes "to renew the fiery joy, and burst the stony roof" of legalism:

> For every thing that lives is holy,
>   life delights in life;
> Because the sweet soul of delight
>   can never be defil'd.
> Fires inwrap the earthly globe,
>   yet man is not consumed;
> Amidst the lustful fires he walks:
>   his feet become like brass,
> His knees, his thighs like silver,
>   & his breast and head like gold.
> (*Amer.* 8:13-17, K 199).

The first portion of this passage also occurs in the *Marriage,* and the following alteration of Daniel 2:32-33 fittingly elevates the "Song of Liberty" by improving the metallurgy of Nebuchadnezzar's "fourfold" but fallen man. His natural constituent, the red clay of which Adam was formed, had been transmuted and each corresponding element raised so that his breast and head—the heart and eyes which must expand (as the Abbé teaches in the *French Revolution*)—are gold. This partial sensual improvement will be completed in the resurrection, in which the whole risen body will be "golden."[69] Orc's man, like his fires of revolt, are but prelude to the apocalypse, for Orc and postlapsarian man, of whom he is a type, are still serpentinely "wreath'd round the accursed tree" of mystery. (*Amer.* 8:11, K 198)

Although Orc's fires of instinctual desire rage at the end of this prophecy, their final effect is indeterminate here. Blake's prophecy sees the American revolution, symbolically an assertion of the liberty of the body's desires (Orc), as the beginning of other revolutions; hence the European thrones are "unable to stem the fires of Orc;/ But the five gates were consum'd, & their bolts and hinges melted/ And the fierce flames burnt round the heavens, & round the abodes of men." (*Amer.* 16:21-23, K

203) As in Plate 14 of the *Marriage,* the apocalyptic fires are initiated "by an increase in sensual enjoyment"; here man's natural restrictions, his mortal boundaries, the "five gates" or senses, which are the chief inlet of the soul in 1793, are consumed.

Presumably this unbinding should set man free, but Orc's fires do not keep this promise. The ending of *America* is as much ominous as hopeful, and the illustration shows this ambivalence:

> Above, the woman Earth with long flowing hair kneels in prayer; in and about her are small figures in various attitudes [imploring or huddled together in fear], and behind her are [four] fantastic tree forms [with human bodies contained in their trunks]; below, FINIS appears in a tangle of thorny flowers and a serpent.[70]

That *America* literally ends ("FINIS") entangled in the serpent of nature does not bode well.

The Sleep of Europe *and The* Song of Los

Europe, A Prophecy (1794) continues the story of Orc and the progress of revolution by suggesting that man may rise from generation free when Orc becomes "transcarnated" as Jesus. Blake's use of Milton's "Nativity Hymn" is parodic, however, because the first coming (in the Christmas incarnation) grew into what Blake considers perverted Christianity, whose two main errors—chastity and deism—must be cast out in a last judgment. Accordingly, the second coming is the crucial event in history, for only then is the Orc cycle of natural generation and deism broken and transfigured. *Europe* deals with Jesus' first coming, incarnated as Orc.

Divided from her mate, Los, and fallen, Enitharmon accentuates her separateness and fear of the ruddy (i.e., passionate) Orc by binding the body's instinctual satisfaction in the false virtue of chastity: "tell the Human race that Woman's love is Sin! . . . Forbid all Joy" (*Eur.* 5:5-7, K 240). This repression of sexuality is a little death, and during the 1800 years' (the length of the Christian era to Blake's day) sleep, "Man was a Dream" (*Eur.* 9:2, K 240) because instinctually anesthetized in the nets of abstinence.

This binding results in the second major error of official Christianity, namely materialism (in philosophy) and deism (in religion). When man is thus trapped in the body, "The ever-varying spiral ascents to the heaven of heavens/ Were bended downward, . . . barr'd and petrifi'd against the infinite" (*Eur.* 10:13-15, K 241).[71] That is, man's mind is subject to this negative metamorphosis:

> Thought chang'd the infinite to a serpent; . . .
> Then all the eternal forest were divided
> Into earth's rolling in circles of space,
>   that like an ocean rush'd
> And overwhelmed all except this finite
>   wall of flesh.
> Then was the serpent temple form'd,
>   image of infinite
> Shut up in finite revolutions, and
>   man became an Angel,
> Heaven a mighty circle turning,
>   God a tyrant crown'd (*Eur.* 10:16-
> 23, K 341).

Blake images this shutting up of the infinite in finite revolutions in the frontispiece to *Europe,* where Urizen-Elohim encompasses the fallen world (the starry floor and watery shore) given man till the break of day, till the "trump of the last doom" now sought (*Eur.* 12:13, K 242). Though Orc tries three times to blow the last trump, he (naturally) fails, and it is Newton, the apotheosis of deism and hence a kind of antichrist, who, the fourth time, "blow'd the enormous blast" (*Eur.* 13:5, K 243), forcing history to its crisis.[72]

Enitharmon wakes after 1800 years of sleep and calls on her children to wake from error and rise. Following this revival, "That nature felt thro' all her pores enormous revelry," is the traditional period of natural catastrophe (Rev. 7 and *Eur.* 15, K 245) as the fires of Orc's revolution spread to France. Finally Los, the prophet, awakes but "in snaky thunders clad." His "birth" into "the strife of blood" is ambiguous, for while his cry shakes "all nature to the utmost pole" (*Eur.* 15:10, K 245), the result of such strife is, again, very uncertain. If terrible Orc is Christ the Tiger, of Revelation 19:11-15, his compatriot sons of Los provide no certain release from the wrath.

The *Song of Los* (1795), completing the historical prophecies, is composed of *Africa,* which precedes *America* (their first

and last lines, respectively, being the same) and *Asia,* which concludes *Europe.* Sung by Los, the eternal prophet, the poems
sketch the temporal world of history, as Los's sons, especially
Orc, strive with the blood of revolt.

In contrast to the ambiguous end of *Europe, Asia* ends with
Orc's fiery rage consummated:

> Forth from the dead dust rattling
> > bones to bones
> Join: shaking convuls'd the shiv'ring
> > clay breathes,
> And all flesh naked stands. . . .
> The Grave shrieks with delight, & shakes
> Her hollow womb, & clasps the solid stem:
> Her bosom swells with wild desire:
> And milk & blood & glandous wine
> In rivers rush & shout & dance
> On mountain, dale and plain   (*Song Los*
> 7:31-40, K 248).

While there is here a resurrection from the dead, there is no
transfiguration from the natural to the supernatural because the
rising bones still belong to Orc's tree of natural religion. Describing what he aptly calls "the terrestrial orgasm," Erdman
comments that "nature has found her voice and her true love."[73]

The final image of the historical prophecies, and their characteristic content, belong to the Old Testament prophetic tradition,[74] in which the reformed community is restored to dwell
upon a renewed earth. But to transfigure the natural belongs
to another dispensation.

From Vala *to the* Four Zoas: *Toward Unity*

In the "Descriptive Catalogue" (1809) it is advertised that

Mr. B has in his hands poems of the highest antiquity. . . . All these
things are written in Eden. The artist is an inhabitant of that happy
country; and if everything goes on as it has begun, the world of vegetation and generation may expect to be opened again to Heaven,
through Eden, as it was in the beginning.
The Strong man represents the human sublime. The Beautiful man
represents the human pathetic, which was in the Wars of Eden divided

into male and female. The Ugly man represents the human reason. They were originally one man, who was fourfold; he was self-divided, and his real humanity slain on the stems of generation, and the form of the fourth was like the Son of God ("Desc. Cat.," K 578).

With hindsight, this description clarifies some of the confusion in the "voluminous" *Vala, or The Four Zoas,* whose principal, if sometimes discontinuous, subject is "how he [the Eternal Man, later named Albion] became divided" ("Desc. Cat.," K 578). As Bentley has patiently shown, the poem was composed over a period of time, from about 1795-1804, and while it is possible to date portions of the MS, both Bentley and Erdman have concluded that "the extreme complexity of the manuscript problems makes any analysis of the poem extremely dangerous."[75]

However, an overview of *Vala, or The Four Zoas* suggests the principle of its numerous revisions and the direction of its "development"; Nights I-III are revised "with additions of a Christian tenor." Night VIIb was probably composed in 1803, and commenting on Blake's use of a "Christian outline" there, Bentley remarks that

> He was *using the Christian myth, as he used others, as a subsidiary of his own myth,* and though he used its symbolism he was careful to avoid its name and narrative. But beginning with Night VIII and the additions to *Vala,* Christ is made an essential part of Blake's myth, both in name and direction.[76]

The change of titles—from *Vala* to *The Four Zoas*—names the pattern of development which characterizes both the mythic originality and the revised Christian content of the MS; that is, Blake's mythology of the Four Zoas structures the Christian conventions which it includes.[77]

By contrast, in the "historical prophecies" Blake's use of the resurrection motif is primarily in terms of the Old Testament prophetic imperative of reformation, as it applies to secular history in his time.[78] Accordingly, the Messianic kingdom (on earth) has yet to be realized in the indeterminate future. In *Vala, or The Four Zoas,* however, the resurrection is sacred because founded upon a given historical event in which the divine redeems the human, on Easter.

This Christianization of the initial text involves revising *Vala* into *The Four Zoas,* as Blake's "Descriptive Catalogue" suggests. In the invocation and gloss, Blake implies that his fourfold mythology psychologizes the Johannine *Logos*, and herein resides the originality of his "re-appropriation" of the "human form divine":

> Four Mighty Ones are in every Man;
>   a Perfect Unity
> Cannot Exist but from the Universal
>   Brotherhood of Eden,
> The Universal Man, to Whom be Glory
>   Evermore. Amen   (*VFZ*, N I: 9-11,
> K 264).

Blake's "universal man" unifies his own "four mighty ones," or Zoas, and all men in the "Universal Brotherhood of Eden."

Both conditions (individual and collective oneness) are necessary for the "perfect unity" of divinity which John describes (1:1 and 14) and which Jesus prays all men will return to,

> that they all may be one; as thou Father, art in me, and I in thee,
> that they also may be one in us: that the world may believe that thou
> hast sent me. And the glory which thou gavest me I have given them;
> that they may be one, even as we are one: I in them, and thou in me,
> that they may be made perfect in one (John 17:21–23).

While desiring the perfection of unity—"be ye therefore perfect, even as your Father which is in heaven is perfect" (Matt. 5: 48)—Blake "re-conceives" of this original "uni-versal" man as fourfold.

The Biblical origin of the "Four Mighty Ones" sheds light on Blake's "humanization" of them in his mythology. The Four "Zoas," or "living creatures," derive from Ezekiel's vision of the fourfold man in whose midst appears "the likeness of the Glory of the Lord" (1:28); they recur in Revelation as the four "beasts" (an alternate KJ translation) who surround God's heavenly throne and continuously praise him (4:8).

Blake's watercolor of "Ezekiel's Vision" (c. 1805) illuminates the symbolic identity of Urthona-Los; he is the most important of the Zoas because his "form was like the Son of God" ("Desc. Cat.," K 578). In Blake's picture the fourth form (and face) of the central figure appears just above the (center) head on "the likeness of the throne" with "the appearance of a man on it" (Ezek. 1:26). In Ezekiel's vision "This was the

appearance of the likeness of the glory of the Lord" (1:28)
and in Blake's mythology this Fourth Zoa is Urthona-Los:

> Los was the fourth immortal Starry one,
> > & in the Earth
> Of a bright Universe, Empery attended
> > day & night,
> Days & nights of revolving joy.
> > Urthona is his name in Eden   (*VFZ*,
> N I:14-17, K 264).

Although each of the Four Zoas must exist together in unity and
each according to his identity and peculiar wisdom, Urthona-
Los is the most important in Blake's mythology, for Los is the
temporal ("shortened") form of the eternal *Logos*.[79]

Invoking the muse of inspiration, a daughter of Beulah,
Blake states the principal subject of *Vala, or The Four Zoas:*

> His [the Eternal Man's, or Albion's] fall
> > into Division and his Resurrection
> > to Unity:
> His fall into the Generation of Decay
> > & death, & his
> Regeneration by the Resurrection
> > from the dead   (*VFZ*, N I:21-23,
> K 264).

Like the previous minor prophecies, *Vala* concerns man's fall
into personal psychic division, sexual generation, and moral and
social decay. But unlike the bounded world of those poems, *The
Four Zoas,* like "To Tirzah," offers a "Regeneration" of the
created world in a last judgment and a "Resurrection from the
dead" by portraying a return to prelapsarian wholeness.

Here Blake not only presents the causes of the fall in terms
of the division and disfunction of the Four Zoas, but also prescribes man's redemption in terms of their reintegration and
unity in and as One Man. If man will reorganize his fourfold
energies, he will reassume his infinite, eternal, human form
divine, the spiritual (for "spirits are organized men" [Desc.
Cat.," K 577]) body of the resurrection.

The structure of *Vala, or the Four Zoas* encompasses, for
virtually the first time in Blake's work, the total length of his-

tory, from the fall, through creation and generation, to regeneration. To understand what is raised, we must first consider
what falls, its causes, and its consequences; accordingly, this
discussion will include a selective interpretive outline of these
fourfold events. Nights I-IV present the fall of the Zoas and
consequent division of the Eternal Man, Albion. Los explains
the definitive cause of the Fall: "Refusing to behold the Divine
Image which all behold/ And live thereby, he is sunk down into
a deadly sleep" (*VFZ*, N I: 290-91, K 272). Blake thus differs
from the Biblical account in Genesis in that he understands God's
merciful creation of this world to follow, not to precede, the
fall.[80]

Implied in this difference of order is a fundamental difference
in definition of the fall. For Blake, its cause is neither man's
pride, nor his uxoriousness, nor his disobedience in wanting
knowledge of good and evil, which for him are already postlapsarian distinctions ("Annot. Swedenborg," K 91 and 96; and
"VLJ," K 615). Rather, forsaking the "Divine Image" causes
the fall into spiritual separateness and psychic division. This
individual and cosmic fragmentation, however, is mended in the
resurrection, when all is reintegrated in the eternal body of man.

Nights I-VI: The Zoas' Fall into Natural Division

Night I begins *in medias res* with Tharmas—the physical body
whose representative sense is touch and taste combined—already
fallen. The creation of the separate physical body, then, is the
first "proof" of the fall, which results in 1) Tharmas's loss of
his emanation (Enion, an earth goddess) and 2) his acquisition
of the false emotions of impotent pity and selfish possessiveness
(*VFZ*, N I: 35-37, K 265).

Night II opens with the Eternal Man "upon his Couch of
Death . . . Turning his Eyes outward to Self, losing the Divine
Vision." (*VFZ*, N II: 1-2, K 280) It narrates 1) the fall of
Luvah, the capacity for enhancing emotion, and 2) the resulting
separation from, and domination by, his emanation, Vala, the
natural world. Separated from her mate, Vala has become a
"Dragon winged bright & poisonous" (*VFZ*, N II: 89, K 282),
later know as Rahab, the harlot and mother of earth's abominations. Since the divided Luvah falls under nature's (Vala's)
domination, it is fitting that in Jesus' incarnation "the Divine

Vision appear'd in Luvah's robes of blood" (*VFZ*, N II: 247, K 286). In *Vala* Jesus is thus associated with Luvah, whereas in *Milton* and *Jerusalem*, he is identified with Los.

But until the "ransom" is complete, the world will be ruled by the spiritually wicked in high places (as Blake notes in the initial quotation from Ephesians 6 : 12) ; and men are exiled to the sufferings of experience, as Enion poignantly laments:

> What is the price of Experience?
> do men buy it for a song?
> Or Wisdom for a dance in the street?
> No, it is bought with the price
> Of all that a man hath, his house, his wife,
> his children. . . .
> It is an easy thing to rejoice in the tents
> of prosperity
> Thus could I sing & thus rejoice,
> but it is not so with me! (*VFZ*, N
> II: 397-418, K 290-91).[81]

At this point, man's sacrifice of all that he hath to experience—which is the price of wisdom—is not compensated, and the present result is madness:

> On to the margin of Non Entity
> the bright female came
> There she beheld the [terrible *del.*]
> spectrous form of Enion in the void.
> And never from that moment could she rest
> upon her pillow (*VFZ*, N II: 422-24, K 291).

The only alternative to this world of madness is the fulfilling possession of wisdom in the apocalypse.

Urizen's fall and loss of his wisdom figure, bright Ahania, is the subject of Night III. Caught in the declining half of the Orc cycle, Urizen becomes the "wearied intellect," instead of his former and proper role as prince of light when joined with Ahania in "those sweet fields of bliss/ Where liberty was justice & eternal science was mercy" (*VFZ*, N III: 39-40, K 292); now "the Divine Vision & Fruition is quite obliterated" (*VFZ*, N III: 36, K 292). Plagued by intellectual despair, Urizen cries that "Eternal death haunts all my expectation./ Rent from

Eternal Brotherhood we die & are no more" (*VFZ*, N III: 75-76, K 293).

Because Urthona is "keeper of the gates of heaven" (*VFZ*, N IV: 42, K 298; and *J* 82: 81, K 727), his "fall" consists of fading into a shadow of his former strength and thereby becoming the Spectre of Urthona, here called Los. This spectral relation between the eternal and temporal embodiments of the imagination is peculiar to *Vala* alone; Los ceases to be spectral in *Milton* and *Jerusalem, as* he comes to resemble Jesus. Given this prior divine sanction, Blake's Jesus can assume his mental form because he is sacred in essence. Symbolically, this orthogenesis means that Blake comes to see the imagination as saving.

The prayer "Lord, Saviour, if thou hadst been here our brother had not died" (*VFZ*, N IV: 253, K 304; and *J* 50: 11, K 681) directly echoes Martha's words to Jesus in John xi, 21-22 and enunciates his role as Savior: "in mercy thou/ Appearest cloth'd in Luvah's garments that we may behold thee/ And live" (*VFZ*, N IV: 256-58, K 304). Jesus confirms their hope, and "The Saviour mild & gentle bent over the corse of Death,/ Saying, 'If ye will Believe, your Brother shall rise again' " (*VFZ*, N IV: 269-70, K 304). This resurrection of another directly depends on Jesus' own, on Easter, as he foretold: "I am the resurrection and the life: he that believeth in me, though he were dead, yet shall he live" (John 11: 25).

In his divine mercy Blake's Jesus then creates the limit beyond which man can fall no further:

> And first he found the Limit of Opacity,
> & nam'd it Satan,
> In Albion's bosom, for in every human bosom
> these limits stand.
> And next he found the Limit of Contraction,
> & nam'd it Adam   (*VFZ*, N IV: 271-73,
> K 304).[82]

When "Limit/ Was put to Eternal Death," the finger of God touched the seventh furnace, and in terror of his task—to forge Golgonooza—Los becomes like the enslaved forms he beholds within the "dismal Darkness" of chaos beneath Satan. Not until he is no longer Urthona's spectre and is reunited with his emanation does Los fully participate in the labors of redemption, when from his furnaces the son of God shall walk forth.[83]

In Night V, however, Los reaches his limit of contraction when his "furnaces were out & the bellows had ceast to blow" (*VFZ*, N V: 17, K 305). The remainder of Night V deals primarily with the Orc cycle, whereby fallen man is bound to the natural world in constant repetition between youthful passion (Orc) and impotent reason (Urizen), whose gardens of wisdom are become a "field of horrid graves." As will be seen, only Golgonooza, the fourfold city of art, protects against "Eternal Death & Uttermost Extinction" (*VFZ*, N V: 75, K 307).

Night VI presents the inevitable restrictions of the Orc cycle, the world of generation, when Urizen, like Satan in Book II of *Paradise Lost*, explores the hell "when Thought is clos'd in caves" (*VFZ*, N VI: 241, K 311). The three women who guard the entrance, Blake's version of Sin and Death in the parallel scene in *Paradise Lost*,[84] are the great whore Rahab, or fallen sexuality, the natural heart, and the fallen senses; together, they comprise the hellish form of woman, whose "female will" would bind man down with her.

Nights VII and VIII: Los's Labors
Through Generation to Regeneration

Freedom from the terrors of generation is possible, as Los begins to see in Night VII.[85] Los will not be reunited with his emanation until "Thou art united to thy Spectre, Consummating by pains & labours/ [Thy *del.*] That mortal body, & by Self annihilation back returning/ To life Eternal" (*VFZ*, N VII: 343-45, K 328). This acceptance and hence annihilation of one's spectre, that part of the self which haunts and paralyzes it, is a necessary labor-pain for the "re-birth" of the whole, fourfold man:

> If [once *del.*] we unite in one,
>   another world will be
> Open'd within your heart & loins &
>   wondrous brain,
> Threefold, as it was in Eternity, &
>   this, the fourth Universe,
> Will be Renew'd by the three &
>   consummated in Mental fires
> (*VFZ*, N VII: 353-56, K 329).

If man refuses mental consummation and remains only a three-fold creature in the world of generation, he will be continuously subject to the Orc cycle. Los's foretelling redemption[86] is meant literally, for the divine vision dwells within, as Blake shows explicitly in *Jerusalem*. In the spirit of forgiveness Los prepares to be reunited with Enitharmon.

Man's repossession of his emanation is tantamount to inspiration (*VFZ*, N VII:435-54, K 331). For Enitharmon, the proper relation between man and his emanation, the part and partner of his soul, means that Los's "works are all my joy, & in thy fires my soul delights" as she colors his figures "with beams of blushing love" (*VFZ*, N VII:448 and 468, K 331-32). Los, now the active artist, alternates between creation and repose with Enitharmon in Beulah.[87]

With Los, the eternal prophet, now reunited with his emanation and restored to his vocation as the active artist, the preparation for the fourfold return to "ancient bliss" continues with the reintegration of all the Zoas within the Eternal Man. Night VIII deals primarily with Los's and Enitharmon's artistic labors and their redemptive effects. Having been fixed within the limit of contraction for seven ages (here indicated by the seven sneezes), the Eternal Man begins to awaken from the couch of death.[88]

Reunited and filled with love, Los and his emanation behold the "Divine Vision" constantly around them in Golgonooza and foreknow his victory over sin and death:

> They saw the Saviour beyond the Pit
>   of death & destruction;
> For whether they look'd upward,
>   they saw the Divine Vision,
> Or whether they look'd downward
>   still they saw the Divine Vision
> Surrounding them on all sides
>   beyond sin and death and hell
> (*VFZ*, N VI:48-51, K 342).[89]

As the cataclysm approaches, "Los builds the Walls of Golgonooza against the stirring battle/ That only thro the Gates of Death they can enter into Enitharmon" (*VFZ*, N VIII:109-10, K 343-44); that is, one must pass through generation (the merciful gate of Luban into Cathedron's loins) to regeneration.

The artistic productions of Los and Enitharmon "in Golgonooza's furnaces" revive the dead (whereas Vala's natural religion cannot). So created, Jerusalem appears in her potentially
redemptive form, as "the Divine Vision seen within the inmost
deep recesses/ Of fair Jerusalem's bosom in a gently beaming
fire" (*VFZ*, N VIII: 192-93, K 346).[90]
Within this Divine Vision the mystery of man's salvation
begins to be revealed; the Sons of Eden describe Jesus' incarnation in Luvah's robes of pity:

> Of dark death & despair & none from
>   Eternity to Eternity could escape
> But thou O Universal Humanity—who is One Man
>   blessed for Ever—
> Receivest the Integuments woven. . . .
> He puts off the clothing of blood,
>   he redeems the spectres from their bonds;
> He awakens the sleepers in Ulro; . . .
> We now behold the ends of Beulah
>   & we now behold
> Where death Eternal is put off Eternally.
> Assume the dark Satanic body in
>   the Virgin's womb,
> O Lamb Divine! it cannot thee annoy.
>   O pitying one,
> Thy pity is from the foundation of the World,
>   & thy Redemption
> Begun Already in Eternity. Come, then,
>   O Lamb of God,
> Come, Lord Jesus, come quickly (*VFZ*, N VIII:
> 231-45, K 347).

In this passage Blake incorporates the Christian expectation
of redemption while explaining the event in his own mythology.
Here the transfiguration consists of first putting off the "dark
Satanic body," the mortal clothing of blood:

> . . . first to Give his vegetated body
> [And then call Urizen & Luvah & Tharmas
>   & Urthona *del.*]
> To be cut off & separated that the

Spiritual Body may be Revealed (*VFZ*, N VIII: 265-67, K 348).[91]

In its ontogeny, however, Blake's "transfiguration" differs from that of traditional Christianity.

Blake here emphasizes putting off Mystery—the generic name for the vegetable body of Vala—and consequent revelation of the spiritual body. Jesus pities man because he is trapped in the fallen tree of Mystery, and it is primarily Jesus' desire to put off the mystery of mortality, not his pity *per se,* which motivates him to descend in order to raise: "Pitying, the Lamb of God descended thro' Jerusalem's gates,/ To put off Mystery time after time" (*VFZ*, N VIII: 260-61, K 347). In *Vala* Jesus is associated with Luvah, whereas in *Jerusalem* the Savior is identified with the imagination. "To wake up into Eden/ The fallen Man" and to reveal his eternal spiritual body means to reorganize until the image of the human form divine is reassumed "in the Eternal heavens of Human Imagination" (*VFZ*, N VIII: 368, K 366).[92]

Until the resurrection, however, in the catastrophes which precede the apocalypse, Blake again emphasizes the error of Mystery, particularly in the reign of the Antichrist of natural religion and his worship in the Synagogue of Satan. The natural world, Vala, is now further drawn down by Urizen, and she is clothed "with Scarlet robes & Gems,/ And on her forehead was written in blood 'Mystery'" (*VFZ*, N VIII: 281-82, K 348; and Rev. 2:9 and 3:9). This false female, the great whore of Revelation xvii, 5, was hidden "as in an ark and veil [of the natural body]/ Which Christ must rend & reveal. Her daughters are call'd/ Tirzah she is [call'd *del.*] nam'd Rahab" (*VFZ*, N VIII: 293-94, K 348).[93]

Though Jesus, in his vegetable body, is crucified on the "tree of Mystery," all mortality "may be put off/ Time after time by the Divine Lamb who died for all/ And all in him died & he put off all mortality" (*VFZ*, N VIII: 482-84, K 353). In the caverns of the grave

The Lamb of God has rent the Veil
   of Mystery, soon to return
In Clouds & Fires around the rock
   & the Mysterious tree. . . .

Collecting up the scatter'd portions
        of his immortal body. . . .
The Eternal Man is seen, is heard, is felt,
And all his sorrows, till he reassumes
        his ancient bliss   (*VFZ*, N VIII: 556-
83, K 355-56).

The sorrows of casting out error and destroying the vegetable
body of Mystery occur in the last judgment, being the last night
of mortality (*Vala*), which ends in the fourfold return to ancient
bliss.

Night IX: The Four Zoas' Judgment

Beginning with Jesus' resurrection, Night IX ends with an
apocalyptic renewal most like those in the *Apocrypha and Pseudepigrapha* of the Old Testament. Before this conclusion occurs
the reunion of the other Zoas (Urizen, Luvah, and Tharmas)
with their emanations, the destruction of the old world of error,
and the return to the original world of "bright visions." When
Los pulls the stars (sun and moon) from the sky, the loud trump
of Judgment calls the dead to awake, and the universal conflagration begins; in the Revelation narrative (vi and viii) the
falling of heavenly bodies follows the Lamb's opening the sixth
of the seven seals. Blake's beginning at this point stresses the
destruction of the fallen world of Mystery, Rahab, and of
natural generation, Tirzah. The flames which transform the
world are, for Blake, the "flames of mental fire" which reveal
"the bright visions of Eternity" (*VFZ*, N IX: 89-90, K 358).[94]
    With the universal conflagration of the "living flames winged
with intellect" which form the "bright visions of eternity" (*VFZ*,
N IX: 86 and 90, K 359),[95] the Eternal Man, awaking from his
couch of death, laments the war within his members and calls
upon the Zoas to return to their former unity. Because the
fallen Urizen represents the error of Deism and the continuation
of Mystery and because he is also a potential soldier in the desired "intellectual battle," the Eternal Man calls first on him to
repent and follow his request "to re-assume the human." When
Urizen no longer restricts Orc and Tharmas (the bodily instincts) he rises "into the heavens in naked majesty/ In radiant
youth" (*VFZ*, N IX: 192-93, K 362).

At this time of imminent restoration, history (linear time) is completed as Jerusalem, the new heaven and earth of Revelation 21, descends to bear the redeemed in her "spiritual palaces" of immortality:

> Behold Jerusalem in whose bosom the
> Lamb of God
> Is seen tho' slain before her Gates,
> herself renew'd remains
> Eternal, & I thro' him awake
> from death's dark vale.
> The times revolve; the time is coming
> when all these delights
> Shall be renew'd, & all these Elements
> that now consume
> Shall reflourish. Then bright Ahania
> shall awake from death,
> A glorious Vision [of *del.*] to thine Eyes,
> a Self-renewing Vision. . . .
> Immortal thou, Regenerate She. . . .
> Thus shall the male and female live
> the life of Eternity,
> Because the Lamb of God Creates himself
> a bride & wife
> That we his Children evermore may
> live in Jerusalem
> Which now descendeth out of heaven,
> a City, yet a Woman,
> Mother of myriads redeem'd
> & born in her spiritual palaces,
> By a New Spiritual birth Regenerated
> from Death   (*VFZ*, N IX: 205-24, K 362-63).

Jesus creates Jerusalem, the holy city of God and his Bride, so that man may be redeemed as a result of this "great marriage," "by a New Spiritual birth Regenerated from Death." In contrast to traditional Christian expectation, however, instead of already preexisting, the new Jerusalem is formed as and in the eternal union of God and man—of the Lamb and his Bride, Jerusalem, man and woman collectively. In this "great marriage" what one loves (Jerusalem-as-woman) is also where one lives (Jerusalem-as-city), for in the city of God, the transcendent

is also immanent. In this passage Blake predicates immortality
("That we his Children evermore may live in Jerusalem")
upon regeneration through this new spiritual birth.

Two later passages in the MS expand Blake's conception of
spiritual rebirth, first personally and then collectively. After the
destruction of Orc, Luvah and Vala are reunited so that the
external, natural world that one sees (Vala) emanates from
man's emotions (Luvah). Explaining this union, the Eternal
Man states the principle of proper organization, whereby man
becomes whole:

> If Gods combine against Man, setting
>   their dominion above
> The Human form Divine Thrown down
>   from their high station
> In the Eternal heavens of Human [Thought *del.*]
>   Imagination, buried beneath
> In dark Oblivion, with incessant pangs,
>   ages on ages,
> In enmity & war first weakn'd,
>   then in stern repentance
> They must renew their brightness,
>   & their disorganiz'd functions
> Again reorganize, till they
>   resume the image of the human,
> Co-operating in the bliss of Man,
>   obeying his will
> Servants to the infinite &
>   Eternal of the Human form   (*VFZ,* N IX:
> 366-74, K 366).

This complete psychic cooperation within an individual has a
corresponding and consequent form for the collective body of
man:

> . . . & thence we know
> That Man subsists by Brotherhood
>   & Universal Love.
> We fall on one another's necks,
>   more closely we embrace.
> Not for ourselves, but for the

> Eternal family we live.
> Man liveth not by Self alone,
> but in his brother's face
> Each shall behold the Eternal Father
> & love & joy abound   (*VFZ,* N
> IX: 637-42, K 374).[96]

This recognition of oneself in another—brotherhood—and resulting "universal love" constitutes the heavenly fellowship of Jerusalem and arises from the spiritual organization of the human form as the divine image: "Each shall behold the Eternal Father & love & joy abound."

To be forgiven and "repaired" in ancient bliss man must first pass through the last judgment, which begins when the Son of Man descends from Jerusalem on a great cloud of glory. The last harvest which follows indirectly derives from Matthew 13: 3-8[97] and from Revelation 14: 14-19. In the *Four Zoas,* however, Blake presents the ensuing "last supper" as the final celebration of a total Eucharist, whereby all of nature is harvested, eaten, internalized, and transfigured as human.

The sacrament, as Blake portrays it, symbolizes the internalization and possession of the world within the mind so that reality is revealed, as it is, infinite and holy. Whereas in the *Marriage* Blake states this truth in his *principia,* in *The Four Zoas* he images it in the august "judgment week" of Night the Ninth, wherein the Eucharist (instead of unction) becomes the "last rite" in a literal sense. Blake's use of the sacrament here is, I think, like the Catholic doctrine of transubstantiation, wherein the whole substance of the bread and wine is completely and "really" changed into the body and blood of Christ by the Holy Ghost; Blake's "last supper" is not commemorative, as for the Anglicans,[98] but the mind's actual conversion and possession of nature, so that "the Expanding Eyes of Man behold [in both senses] the depths of wondrous worlds!" (*VFZ,* N IX: 830, K 379).

Representing Urizen's "regenerated" intellectual capacities, his sons begin the mental plowing in preparation for the last sowing and harvest. First Luvah and Vala and Tharmas and Enion are restored to the lower paradise of Beulah, akin to the Old Testament Messianic kingdom of the apocryphal and pseudepigraphal writers. However, when the "Times are Ended," and Urizen joyously arises, he "Reap'd the wide Universe &

bound in Sheaves a wondrous harvest" (*VFZ,* N IX: 568 and
584, K 373; see Rev. 10:6 and 14:14-16).

The morning after this feast at which the natural world is the
"last supper" of the bread of life and the wine of eternity,
Enion arises from death-clothes to be reunited with Tharmas:

> The clouds fall off from my wet brow,
>   the dust from my cold limbs
> Into the Sea of Tharmas. Soon renew'd
>   a Golden Moth,
> I shall cast off my death clothes
>   & Embrace Tharmas again   (*VFZ,* N IX:
> 597-99, K 373).

Blake's naturalistic description of this upward metamorphosis
has "supernaturalistic" significance in the image of the "Golden
Moth," for the butterfly traditionally represents the soul.[99]

In her symbolic genesis, Blake's emanation corresponds to
the soul, as the etymological similarity—anima/us-emanation—
seems to suggest. As such, she is also a wisdom figure—the
proper knowledge of one's origin and end—like the "idea of a
woman" in Donne's "Anniversaries," as discussed. Appearing on
the title page of *Jerusalem,* the butterfly-soul therein is the collective emanation of Albion (all-men) and the Bride of Jesus.
In *The Four Zoas,* however, the emanation is presented in her
individual dimension, as a soul to a Zoaic body.

Thus reunited, Tharmas is now made whole, and he is properly nourished by the natural world which he has internalized
(digested) and thereby humanized:

> Joy thrill'd thro' all the Furious form
>   of Tharmas humanizing.
> Mild he Embrac'd her whom he sought;
>   he raised her thro the heavens,
> Sounding his trumpet to awake the dead,
>   on high he soar'd
> Over the ruin'd worlds, the smoking
>   tomb of the Eternal Prophet   (*VFZ,* N IX:
> 613-16, K 373).[100]

This last line quietly ("harpocratically") identifies Los, the
"Eternal Prophet," with Jesus, whose tomb of the natural world

is destroyed by fire (hence "smoking") in the apocalypse; while this identification is but tentatively suggested at the triumphant end of *The Four Zoas,* it is clarified and expanded in *Milton* and *Jerusalem.*

Urthona's Rising to the Renewed Earth

Attendant upon the resurrection of the body is the creation of the new heaven and new earth, which are revealed when Mystery—Rahab, the natural world—is destroyed:

> And all Nations were threshed out
> > & stars thresh'd from their husks. . . .
> "O Mystery," fierce Tharmas cries,
> > "Behold thy end is come. . . .
> Let the slave grinding at the mill
> > run out into the field;
> Let him look up into the heavens
> > & laugh in the bright air. . . .
> The good of all the Land is before you,
> > for Mystery is no more"   (*VFZ,* N
> IX: 656-80, K 374-75).

This exuberant passage and the similar descriptions which follow present an interpretive problem if we try to locate their Biblical and apocryphal analogues. As in the *Marriage,* I think that elements of both the prophetic and apocalyptic traditions are present.

Unlike the earlier *Marriage,* however, whose final "Song of Liberty" relates it more closely to the Old Testament prophetic imperative of present earthly renewal, the mythology of the Four Zoas and their return to unity in a "Messianic kingdom" resembles the various versions of the resurrection in the Old Testament *Apocrypha and Pseudepigrapha,* especially those of I Enoch 37-72 and of 2 Baruch.[101] But, in *Jerusalem,* as in the New Testament, the resurrection receives its definitive apotheosis—as the fourfold man-and-emanation who rise an "imaginative body" because of the redemptive labors of the artist who beholds the divine vision.

Yet the *Four Zoas* concludes with a uniquely Blakean vision. In the above passage, for example, the poet emphasizes the destruction of Mystery, whose mental form is error and whose physical form is fallen nature. As in the Old Testament and intertestamental concept of the Messianic kingdom, in the Pauline transfiguration of the body, and in Origen's doctrine of *apocatastasis,* the mortal, vulnerable, and destructive aspects of nature are miraculously changed into their immortal, incorruptible, and glorious forms. Thus, in counterpoint to Adam's and Eve's exile from Eden at the end of *Paradise Lost,* Tharmas exclaims, "The good of all the Land is before you, for Mystery is no more."

While the preceding part of this speech echoes *America* Plate 16, the context differentiates them. And we shall see an analogous contrast of prophetic reformation and apocalyptic transformation between this passage and the end of *Jerusalem.* Blake's early works (until about 1794) present the prophetic possibility of freedom through social reform. Incipiently in *The Four Zoas,* however, and concretely in *Milton* and *Jerusalem,* Blake predicates this liberty as depending on individual "spiritual" transfiguration. Unlike the ambiguous ending of *America,* where the fierce flames of Orc burn round the abodes of men with unknown effect, in *The Four Zoas* the immediate results of the cleansing cataclysm are clear.

The "world of shadows" and winter are not "gone and over" until Urthona's resurrection; further, at this moment, the temporal and eternal embodiments of the imagination are identified as one: "Then Los who is Urthona rose in all his regenerate power" (*VFZ,* N IX: 801, K 378). Blake's vision of the transfigurations resulting from Urthona's resurrection draws primarily on images of the Messianic kingdom in a renewed earth:

> The Sun has left his blackness
> & has found a fresher morning,
> And the mild moon rejoices in the
> clear & cloudless night,
> And Man walks forth from the midst of fires:
> the evil is all consum'd.
> His eyes behold the Angelic spheres
> arising night & day;
> The stars consum'd like a lamp blown out
> & in their stead, behold
> The Expanding Eyes of Man behold the depths
> of wondrous worlds!

One Earth, one sea beneath;
    nor Erring Globes wander, but Stars
Of fire rise up nightly from the Ocean;
    & one Sun
Each morning, like a New born Man,
    issues with songs & joy
Calling the Plowman to his Labour
    & the Shepherd to rest.
He walks upon the Eternal Mountains,
    raising his heavenly voice,
Conversing with the Animal forms
    of wisdom night & day,
That, risen from the Sea of fire,
    renew'd walk o'er the Earth;
For Tharmas brought his flocks
    upon the hills, & in the Vales
Around the Eternal Man's bright tent,
    the little Children play
Among the wooly flocks.
    The hammer of Urthona sounds
In the deep caves beneath;
    his limbs renew'd, his Lions roar
Around the Furnaces
    & in the Evening sport upon the plains.
They raise their faces from the Earth,
    conversing with the Man:

"How is it we have walk'd thro' fires
    & yet are not consum'd?
"How is it that all things are chang'd,
    even as in ancient times?"

The Sun arises from his dewy bed,
    & the fresh airs
Play in his smiling beams
    giving the seeds of life to grow,
And the fresh Earth beams forth
    ten thousand thousand springs of life.
Urthona is arisen in his strength,
    no longer now
Divided from Enitharmon,
    no longer the Spectre Los.

> Where is the Spectre of Prophecy?
> Where dwells the delusive Phantom?
> Departed: & Urthona rises
>   from the ruinous Walls
> In all his ancient strength
>   to form the golden armour of science
> For intellectual War.
>   The war of swords departed now,
> The dark Religions are departed
>   & sweet Science reigns   (*VFZ,* N IX : 825-
> 55, K 379).

Conceptually this passage delineates the new life which results from Urthona's resurrection and the ensuing reintegration of the Four Zoas.

But Jesus' role is not rendered explicit, and this end, although glorious, is not completely unified with the later Christian revisions of portions of the poem;[102] that is, the Christian elements are not consistently integrated with Blake's "regenerative" myth of the Four Zoas. For whatever reasons, the relation between the Christian and the Blakean narrative was never put in "firm and determinate outline" in the unfinished *Four Zoas* MS.

From the perspective of *Jerusalem,* it is clear that Blake's great achievement involves his expansion of the Christian *mythos* in his fourfold "history" (of Eden, Beulah, Generation, and Ulro) and psychology of the Four Zoas. Although the image of the Man who walks forth from midst the fires derives from Daniel 3 : 25, where his form is like the Son of God, as is Los's form, Blake does not establish his resemblance to his divine source. Instead he is more concerned with how all things are changed utterly when the doors of perception are cleansed "even as in ancient times." Like the new-born man himself, *Vala, or The Four Zoas* issues forth with related but discrete songs. The agent of this renewal is the expanding eye of the imagination, which literally "beholds the depths of wondrous worlds." Their characteristic feature is the proper unity of man's fourfold life and his "Universal Brotherhood of Eden," and their blissful harmony "recalls" the joyous development of the choral finale of Beethoven's Ninth Symphony. Like that of the Son of God in the *Marriage,* Urthona's last task in the *Four Zoas* is to bring the mental sword of "intellectual battle" for the great day of spiritual judgment.

Auguries of Spiritual Innocence

The "Auguries of Innocence" (in the Pickering MS, whose "fair copies" were made about 1803) ends with a prophecy of that organized innocence with which wisdom dwells:

> We are led to Believe a Lie
> When we see [with *del.*] not Thro' the Eye
> Which was Born in a Night to perish in a Night
> When the Soul Slept in Beams of Light
> God Appears & God is Light
> To those poor Souls who dwell in Night,
> But does a Human Form Display
> To those who Dwell in Realms of day (K 433-34).

The distinction between true and false sight is a continuous subject for Blake, as in the letter to Dr. Trusler of 23 August 1799, in which Blake explicitly states "that I know that This World is a World of Imagination & Vision." Since "as a man is, So he Sees" (K 793), those who dwell in and belong to "realms of day"—the "western path" where the Sun ascends the sky ("Morning," K 421)—likewise see God in the human forms around them.

As "a Soldier of Christ," engaging in "mental fight," Blake relates to Thomas Butts, on 22 November 1802, that though he has "travel'd thro' Perils & Darkness" at Felpham (at work, in part on *The Four Zoas*), "I am again Emerged into the light of day; I still & shall to Eternity Embrace Christianity & Adore him who is the Express image of God" (K 815). While this "descriptive catalogue" accurately indicates Blake's embracing Christianity, which is also, but more diffusely, reflected in the overall revisions of *The Four Zoas,* we must turn to the major epics which follow—*Milton* and *Jerusalem*—to see "the express image of God" through Blake's eyes, for "none can know the Spiritual Acts of my three years' Slumber on the banks of the Ocean, unless he should read My long Poem descriptive of those Acts . . . on One Grand Theme, Similar to Homer's Illiad or Milton's Paradise Lost."[103]

Before I discuss Blake's development of his concept of the Savior and His resurrection in *Milton* and *Jerusalem,* it is helpful to consider what was written between 1797 and 1804 (i.e., contemporaneously with *Vala* and just before *Milton* and *Jeru-*

salem), which sheds light on Blake's interpretation of Christianity. In the "Annotations to Watson" (1798), Blake explicitly calls himself a Christian—"To me, who believe in the Bible & profess myself a Christian"—and asks "Wherefore did Christ come?" (K 387).

In the remainder of the passage Blake describes what Jesus came to destroy—"to abolish the Jewish Imposture"—so that "henceforth every man may converse with God & be a King & Priest in his own house" (K 389).[104] Blake's "own house," as he recollects in his "Annotations to Reynolds," is "Inspiration & Vision. Inspiration & Vision was then [in 1798], and now is [in 1808], & I hope will always Remain, my Element, my Eternal Dwelling Place" (K 477). And the Gospel in Blake's house of Christian worship is "Forgiveness of Sins" ("Annot. Watson," K 395), which, as he was to insist twenty years later, was Jesus' unique and central moral teaching.[105]

In a notebook entry made between 1800-3, Blake writes to his spectre:

> & Throughout all Eternity
> I forgive you, you forgive me.
> As our dear Redeemer said
> This is the Wine & this the Bread   (K 417).

While the wine and bread of life were harvested at the end of *The Four Zoas,* they are here identified as forgiveness. The Gospel according to Blake teaches that the unique essence of Christianity is continual forgiveness, which Jesus embodies.

Milton and Blake: The Eternal Salvation of the Poet

Milton, a brief epic composed between 1800-3 to 1808-9,[106] portrays the liberation of the prophetic-poetic genius *sub specie aeternitatis.* Of the "Devil's party" (of unrestricted inspiration) without knowing it, Milton was "curbed by the general malady & infection from the silly Greek & Latin slaves of the sword" (*M* 1, K 480). As in the *Marriage,* Blake's impulse to "correct" Milton comes from a prior affection, which desires to see its subject made perfect.

In Blake's theology, this realization of one's true identity represents the judgment of the self in the first, or spiritual, resurrection. Blake's unironic motto from and for Milton implies that his way of salvation represented within is the "just & true" way. For Blake, art is redemptive because, like religion, its source is the divine imagination, and each must be free from restriction:[107]

> Rouze up, O Young Men of the New Age! Set your foreheads against the ignorant Hirelings! For we have Hirelings in the Camp, the Court & the University, who would, if they could, for ever depress [repress] Mental & prolong Corporeal War. . . . [B]elieve Christ and his Apostles that there is a Class of Men whose whole delight is in Destroying. We do not want either Greek or Roman Models if we are but just & true to our own Imaginations, those Worlds of Eternity in which we shall live for ever in Jesus our Lord [Amen!] (*M* 1, K 480).

For the first time, Blake here identifies (by implication of grammatic apposition) Jesus as embodying the imagination, the eternal world in which the resurrected live.

As English poets in the Biblical tradition, Blake's affinity to Milton is prescriptive, not imitative. The anamnetic lyric "And did those feet in ancient time" invokes the image of the Blakean Jesus, who comes with the mental sword of vision, which destroys the dragon of Mystery and reveals everything as it is, infinite and holy. Further, the proclamation of stanza 4 combines the Old Testament prophetic vision of the Messianic kingdom on earth with the Blakean vision of now regaining paradise in an imminent and mental apocalypse.[108] The social function of the epic is to teach the nation, and Blake's lesson is the continuous building of Jerusalem in England's (particularly), and (by extension) every, green and pleasant land.

Didactic in subject and structure, *Milton* is Blake's theodicy. Blake would agree with Milton's "Tractate on Education" that

> The end then of learning is to repair the ruins of our first parents by regaining to know God aright, and out of that knowledge to love him, to imitate him, to be like him, as we may be the nearest by possessing our souls of true vertue, which being united to the heavenly grace of faith makes up the highest perfection.

But part of what Blake discreetly "teaches" Milton is the fallacy of his proposed method:

> But because our understanding cannot in this body found it selfe but on sensible things, nor arrive so cleerly to the knowledge of God and things invisible, as by orderly conning over the visible and inferior creature, the same method is to be follow'd in all discreet teaching.[109]

According to Blake, this ordered, rational reliance on sensible, visible ("with the eye"), and inferior things produces a false concept of divinity, the root of Milton's errors.[110]

In the *Marriage* Blake explicitly locates Milton's misconception of the Godhead: "in Milton the Father is Destiny, the Son a Ratio of the five senses, & the Holy-Ghost a Vacuum!" (*MHH* 6, K 150). Blake seeks to correct this "original sin"—of mistaking divinity as Urizenic reason—from which stems his related distortion of the holiness of sexual love. Milton's "idea of a woman" is of repressive "female will," which insists that "Woman's love is Sin" and "Forbid[s] all Joy" (*Eur.* 5:5, and 8, K 240).

In reenacting the incarnation, Milton's recognition and destruction of his satanic mistakes constitute his self-judgment and his spiritual resurrection of and as the true inspired poet; thus, as Frye remarks, Blake's brief epic may be called "Paradise Regained by John Milton."[111] Blake expands and changes Milton's concept of "a Paradise within thee, happier farre" so that it is not the consolation for the loss of the Biblical Eden (Blake's Beulah); rather, it becomes the realization of having passed through and triumphed over the mortal world of sin and death. Blake's *Milton* is a last judgment of the self: the evil spectre of error is cast out forever and consequently the body (the reincarnated Milton) is reunited with his soul (his emanation) in the first, or spiritual, resurrection.

In subject, and in its numerous beautiful illustrations, *Milton* is Blake's most intensely personal book,[112] generated, in part, by the prophetic genius which Blake shares with Milton and would have fully revived (as the epigraph states). The "sublime of the Bible" has increasingly become Blake's model, as he writes to James Blake on 30 January 1803:

[I] am now learning my Hebrew אבג ["abc's"]. I read Greek as fluently as an Oxford Scholar & the Testament is my chief master: astonishing indeed is the English Translation, it is almost word for word, & if the Hebrew Bible is as well translated, which I do not doubt it is, we need not doubt of its having been translated as well as written by the Holy Ghost (K 821–22).

The source of this inspiration is "in the Human Imagination/ Which is the Divine Body of the Lord Jesus" (*M* 3:3-4, K 482). Since, however, "Every Man's Wisdom is peculiar to his own Individuality" (*M* 4:8, K 482), "what mov'd Milton" to the spiritual act of redeeming his imaginative self must be considered individually.

The Poet's Imitatio Dei

The "heroic action" of this epic involves Milton's descent from heaven, where he was "unhappy," to redeem his soul—his sixfold emanation,[113] Ololon—by casting out his Puritan errors. This descending-to-reascend is patterned after Jesus' "atonement": Milton's second coming is a last judgment of the self. Blake represents Milton's redemption in a series of five unions: 1) when the Bard enters Milton, after which Milton decides to descend; 2) when the falling Milton enters Blake's left foot; 3) when Los enters Blake-Milton to become the authoritative poet-prophet; 4) when Ololon is reunited with Milton; and 5) when this completed human (man and his emanation) is transfigured "with" Jesus. The religious pattern the epic thereby imitates is the spiritual regeneration of the first resurrection.

Explaining "what mov'd Milton," the ancient Bard sings of the major error of Puritanism, which worships Urizen instead of the true divinity, Jesus, the imagination.[114] For Blake, reason, alone, is "wrong" because it is reductive and satanic (*M* 10-11, K 490-92). Milton also misconceived of his proper relation to women, represented by his sixfold emanation, Ololon. These related errors stem from the same "original sin" of mental misconception. According to Blake, while Milton's God was one of rational restriction, his "idea" of women also reflected this same binding of man's infinite desire. This reduction then brings forth moral virtue as "the cruel Virgin Babylon" (*M* 5:27, K 484), or Tirzah, sexual repression, celebrated as chastity in "Comus"; moreover, Tirzah inevitably, i.e., naturally, ages into Rahab, the dragon-woman who destroys men (*M* 12-13, K 492-94).

Because Milton is a "true poet," he hears and comprehends the Bard's "words of eternal salvation," of which the Bard knows the full, and divine, power:

> I am inspired! I know it is the Truth!
> for I sing
> According to the inspiration
> of the Poetic Genius

> Who is the eternal all-protecting
>   Divine Humanity
> To whom be Glory & Power & Dominion
>   Evermore   (*M* 13:51 and 14:1-2, K 495)[115]

The Bard's entering Milton's bosom constitutes the poet's in-herent recognition of his proper prophetic power (*M* 14:9, K 495 and *M* 24:71, K 510). Whereas in *Milton* Los and Milton are so joined, in *Jerusalem* Los and Jesus are united finally to identify the origin and mode of forgiveness in the imagination.

Preparing redemptively to sacrifice himself to destroy these errors, Milton's act "imitates" Jesus' willingly giving himself for man in the incarnation. For Blake, this "forgiveness of sins" —of one's own and of others'—is the crucial moment in achiev-ing salvation.[116]

While the overall pattern of Milton's salvation corresponds to Christian teaching, its psychological cause and "meaning" are distinctly Blakean:

> And Milton said: "I go to Eternal Death!
>   The Nations still
> "Follow after the detestable
>   Gods of Priam, in pomp
> "Of warlike selfhood
>   contradicting and blaspheming.
> "When will the Resurrection come
>   to deliver the sleeping body
> "From corruptibility?
>   O when, Lord Jesus, wilt thou come?
> "Tarry no longer, for my soul
>   lies at the gates of death.
> "I will arise and look forth
>   for the morning of the grave:
> "I will go down to the sepulcher
>   to see if morning breaks:
> "I will go down to self annihilation
>   and eternal death,
> "Lest the Last Judgment come
>   & find me unannihilate
> "And I will be siez'd & giv'n
>   into the hands of my own Selfhood.
> "The Lamb of God is seen thro' mists
>   & shadows hov'ring. . . .

"What do I here before the Judgment?
     without my Emanation?
"With the daughters of memory
     & not with the daughters of inspiration?
"I in my Selfhood am that Satan:
     I am that Evil One!
"He is my Spectre! in my obedience
     to loose him from my Hells,
"To claim the Hells, my Furnaces,
     I go to Eternal Death"   (*M* 14:14-32, K 495-96).

Blake's Milton thus knows that the resurrection of the sleeping
(vegetable) body, at Jesus' coming, depends on man's own
prior self-preparation, in which one casts out his spectre and embraces his emanation.

     While Donne speaks of this act as the first, or spiritual, resur-
rection, whereby man is assured of the final resurrection, in
body and soul, Blake portrays man's self-judgment and regeneration in introspective, "psychological" terms: Satan is the evil
spectre of the selfhood, or rational separateness, and the soul
(the *anima*) is one's creative self, the emanation. Whereas the
characteristic drama of Donne's divine poems is attaining the
simultaneous cooperation of divine and human wills in penance,
Milton "mentalizes" the first resurrection because "the Human
Imagination . . . is the Divine Vision & Fruition/ In which Man
liveth eternally" (*M* 32:19-20, K 521; see also *M* 3:4, K 482).

     Milton descends through the vortex of the Rock of Ages,
upon which pale Albion sleeps, into the Sea of Time and Space,
which he enters as a falling star (emblematic of his Urizenic
image of God):

          Descending perpendicular, swift
               as the swallow or swift:
          And on my left foot falling
               on the tarsus, enter'd there: (*M* 15:
          48-49, K 497).[117]

Plates 15-20 describe the "cruelties of Ulro" through which
Milton passes, and Plate 21 recapitulates Milton's entry into
Blake, in which moment of joining

          I saw in the nether
          Regions of the Imagination—

> also all men on Earth
> And all in Heaven saw
> in the nether regions of the Imagination
> In Ulro beneath Beulah—
> the vast breach of Milton's descent. . . .
> And all this Vegetable World
> appear'd on my left Foot
> As a bright sandal form'd
> immortal of precious stones & gold.
> I stooped down & bound it on
> to walk forward thro' Eternity   (*M* 21:
> 4-14, K 503).

In this moment of inspiration in which the artist knows the work to be done, Blake-Milton walks through the "fourfold spiritual London," or Golgonooza (*M* 20:39-40, K 502).

Therein he sees Ololon as the River of Life (*M* 21:14-15, K 503 and Rev. xxii, 1), over whom weeps the Divine Family (the "council of God" in the *Four Zoas* or "communion of saints" in Christian vocabulary). Ololon desires to descend to Ulro to imitate Milton's and Jesus' incarnations, and her redemptive journey is blessed by Jesus, "Uniting in One with Ololon" (*M* 21:58-60, K 505).

Heralding this "great marriage," Los, as the "great sun of imagination" descends to enter Blake's soul:

> And Los behind me stood;
> a terrible flaming Sun; just close
> Behind my back. I turned round
> in terror, and behold!
> Los stood in that fierce glowing fire;
> & he also stoop'd down
> And bound my sandals on in Udan-Adan;
> trembling I stood
> Exceedingly with fear & terror,
> standing in the Vale
> Of Lambeth; but he kissed me
> and wished me health,
> And I became One Man with him
> arising in my strength. . . .
> Los had enter'd into my soul:
> His terrors now posses'd me whole!

> I arose in fury & strength (*M* 22:7-14,
> K 505).[118]

This resurrection in "fury & strength" of the imaginative poet, Blake-Los, anticipates the apocalyptic fulfillment. Of the Four Zoas, Los becomes increasingly more important, in both *Milton* and *Jerusalem,* because he is the laborer of redemption:

> He is the Spirit of Prophecy,
>   the ever apparent Elias.
> Time is the mercy of Eternity;
>   without Time's swiftness,
> Which is the swiftest of all things,
>   all were eternal torment.
> All the Gods of the Kingdoms of Earth
>   labour in Los's Halls:
> Every one is a fallen Son
>   of the Spirit of Prophecy.
> He is the Fourth Zoa
>   that stood arou[n]d the Throne Divine.
> (*M* 24:71-76, K 510 and Rev. iv, 8)

Blake's identification with the archetypal artist involves, not loss (as it does for Yeats), but rather regaining former wholeness and returning to the "Throne Divine."

The immediate result of their union, however, is a vision of the coming redemption of the generated world, in the "Great Vintage" and last harvest in which nature is threshed and "regenerated":

> The Great Vintage & Harvest
>   is now upon Earth.
> The whole extent of the Globe is explored.
>   Every scatter'd Atom
> Of Human Intellect is now
>   flocking to the sound of the Trumpet.
> All the Wisdom which was hidden
>   in caves & dens from ancient
> Time is now sought out
>   from Animal & Vegetable & Mineral.
> The Awakener is come outstrech'd over Europe:
>   the Vision of God is fulfilled:

> The Ancient Man upon the Rock
>   of Albion Awakes. . . .
>   [Jerusalem] weeps & looks abroad
> For the Lord's coming,
>   that Jerusalem may overspread all Nations. . . .
> Wait till the Judgment is past,
>   till the Creation is consumed
> And then rush forward with me
>   into the glorious spiritual
> Vegetation, the Supper of the Lamb
>   & his Bride, and the
> Awaking of Albion our friend
>   and ancient companion   (*M* 25 : 17-62,
> K 510-11).

Los and his sons are the "spiritual causes" (*M* 26: 40-43, K 512-13) of earth's redemption, and Book I ends with a vision of Los's world.

Milton's Destruction of States of Error and Recognition of Eternal Identity

Book II begins with an anatomy of Beulah, the golden world which creatively bridges mortal and immortal life. "Beulah is evermore Created around Eternity," and for the inhabitants of Eden, it is a place of rest while for inhabitants of earth, it is a place of inspiration (*M* 30: 8 and 12-20, K 518-19). Plate 38 C (or, 42 D), entitled "The Moment of Inspiration," illustrates how intimately related are erotic and artistic experience in Blake's Beulah. For both the inhabitants of Eden and of earth, Beulah prepares for "the great Wars of Eternity, in fury of Poetic Inspiration,/ To build the Universe stupendous: Mental Forms Creating" (*M* 30: 19-20, K 519).

Whereas Beulah is the place of regeneration, earth, *per se,* is the place of generation, as Book II distinguishes. The Satanic "know not of Regeneration, but only of generation" because

> Unforgiving & unalterable,
>   these cannot be Regenerated
> But must be created,

Plate 2   "Queen Katherine's [Vision, or] Dream" (1807)
           Saw you not even now a blessed troup
           Invite me to a banquet, whose bright faces
           Cast thousand beams upon me like a sun?
           They promised me eternal happiness. . . .
                   (Shakespeare, *Henry VIII*, IV, ii, 87–90)
     *Courtesy The National Gallery of Art, Washington, D. C., Rosenwald
Collection*

Plate 3 "Elohim Creating Adam" (1795) (Genesis 2 : 7)
Courtesy The Tate Gallery, London

Plate 4 Jerusalem 76(D) (1804–20)
Jesus replied: "Fear not Albion: unless I die
thou canst not live;
But if I die, I shall rise again & thou with me.
This is Friendship & Brotherhood:
without it Man is Not." (*J* 96: 13–16, K 743)
Courtesy The Harvard College Library

Plate 5 "The Dance of Albion, or Glad Day" (*c.* 1780)
Blake's inscription (*c.* 1800) reads:
      Albion rose from where he laboured at the Mill with slaves:
      Giving himself for the Nations
           he danced the dance of Eternal Death.
*Courtesy The National Gallery of Art, Washington, D. C., Rosenwald
Collection*

Plate 15 "The Reunion of the Soul and the Body" (1808)

The note accompanying this illustration (Plate X of Blair's *Grave*) reads: "The Body springs from the Grave, the Soul descends an opening cloud; they rush together with inconceivable energy; they meet, never again to part!"

Courtesy The National Gallery of Art, Washington, D. C., Rosenwald Collection

Plate 16   Jerusalem 99 (D) (1804–20)
Courtesy The Harvard College Library

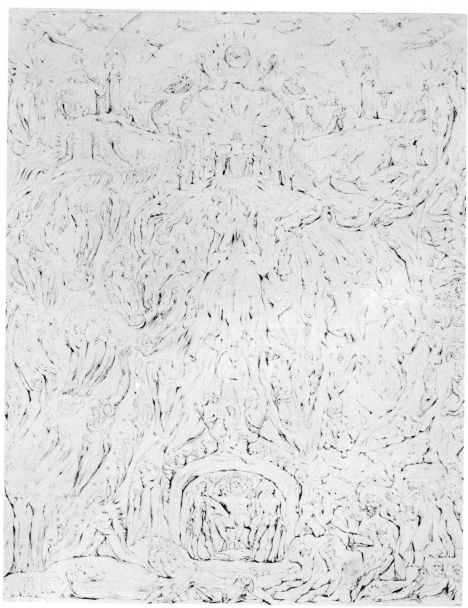

Plate 17 "A Vision of the Last Judgment" (1810)

"This world of Imagination is the world of Eternity; it is the divine bosom into which we shall all go after the death of the Vegetated body. . . . All Things are comprehended in their Eternal Forms in the divine body of the Saviour, the True Vine of Eternity, The Human Imagination, who appear'd to Me as Coming to Judgment among his Saints & throwing off the Temporal that the Eternal might be Establish'd" ("VLJ," K 605–6).

Courtesy The National Gallery of Art, Washington, D. C., Rosenwald Collection

Plate 18 "The Four and Twenty Elders Casting their Crowns before the Divine Throne" (1800–10) (Revelation 4:4)
  Courtesy The Tate Gallery, London

Plate 19 "The Ascension of the Dead" (1807) (Rejected title page for Blair's *Grave*)

Plate 20 "The River of Life" (1800–10) (Revelation 22:1–2)
    "If the Spectator could Enter into these Images in his Imagination,
approaching them on the Fiery Chariot of his Contemplative Thought, if
he could Enter into Noah's Rainbow or into his Bosom, or could make a
Friend & Companion of one of these Images of wonder, which always
intreats him to leave mortal things (as he must know), then would he
arise from his grave, then would he meet the Lord in the air & then he
would be happy. General Knowledge is Remote Knowledge; it is in
Particulars that Wisdom consists & Happiness too. Both in Art & in
Life . . ." ("VLJ," K 611).
    Courtesy The Tate Gallery, London

for they know only of Generation:
These are the God of the Kingdom of Earth
   ... opposed in War
Not Mental, as the Wars of Eternity
(*M* 31 : 19 and 21-25, K 520).

The task of Milton's descent is his self-regeneration by annihilating his former earthly errors. Psychologically, he must
recognize sexual love, in the married land of Beulah, as an
earthly form of inspiration in which man is joined with his
emanation, the creative "part and partner of his soul," the
totality of that which man loves, desires, and creates.

Theologically, Milton must recognize and cast out the satanic
results of his mistakenly elevating Urizen (*M* 32 : 3-7, K 521).
The "Seven Angels," or "Eyes," of God,[119] members of the
"Eternal Body," instruct Milton about the "Eternal Form of
his 'Individual Identity' "; and their knowledge is crucial in
Blake's teaching:

We are not Individuals but States,
   Combinations of Individuals. . . .
But the Divine Humanity & Mercy
   gave us a Human Form
Because we were combin'd
   in Freedom & holy Brotherhood,
While those combin'd by Satan's Tyranny,
   first in the blood of War
And sacrifice & next in Chains of imprisonment,
   are Shapeless Rocks
Retaining only Satan's Mathematic Holiness,
   Length, Bredth, & Highth,
Calling the Human Imagination,
   which is the Divine Vision & Fruition
In which Man liveth eternally,
   madness & basphemy against
Its own qualities. . . .
Distinguish therefore States
   from Individuals in those States.
States change, but Individual Identities
   never change nor cease   (*M* 32 : 10-23, K 521).

For Blake, eternal "essence" precedes temporal "existence."[120]

Milton's eschatology deals with the individual soul's (*psyche*) last judgment and revelation of identity:

> And thou, O Milton, art a State
>   about to be Created,
> Called Eternal Annihilation,
>   that none but the Living shall
> Dare to enter, & they shall
>   enter triumphant over Death
> And Hell & the Grave:
>   States that are not, but ah! Seem to be
> (*M* 32:26-29, K 521-22).

Like the spiritual transfiguration of baptism, this assurance of the resurrection both depends on and returns to the eternal form of the human and divine existence. Baptism traditionally is the Christian sacrament of "rebirth"; it originates from and imitates Jesus' death, in the mortal body of sin, and his resurrection, in the "spiritual body" of grace. When one is baptized, he then "lives a new life" with the risen Jesus, and the performance of this rite is the outward ceremony of the first, or spiritual, resurrection.[121] For Blake, this sacramental recognizing and destroying what is sinful and changeable, and preserving what is "good" and eternal, are acts of man's own imagination:

> Judge then of thy Own Self:
>   thy Eternal Lineaments explore,
> What is Eternal & what Changeable,
>   & what Annihilable.
> The Imagination is not a State:
>   it is the Human Existence itself
> (*M* 32:30-32, K 522).

The theological analogue for this radical recognition of identity is the epiphany; in the Western church it is associated with the adoration of the Magi and in the Eastern church with baptism. For Blake, the source of self-knowledge, or self-judgment, and of the self's eternal identity thereby revealed is the imagination; this realization of the "Human Existence" leads to triumphing over sin and death. Further, knowledge of one's origin provides authentic knowledge of one's present condition and of one's future end; i.e., to know the source from which

one is created is also to know that which is created and that to
which the created returns:

> For God himself enters Death's Door
>   always with those that enter
> And lays down in the Grave with them,
>   in Visions of Eternity,
> Till they awake & see Jesus
>   & the Linen Clothes lying
> That the Females had Woven for them,
>   & the Gates of their Father's House
> (*M* 32:40-43, K 522).

This Christian expectation of returning to the divine dwelling
eternally in body and soul—in the final resurrection to the holy
city of God—is "what mov'd Milton":

> Behold Milton descended
>   to Redeem the Female Shade
> From Death Eternal; such your lot,
>   to be continually Redeem'd
> By death & misery of those you love
>   & by Annihilation (*M* 33:11-13, K 522).

Imitating Jesus' life, both Milton and his emanation must
descend, for they "could not behold Golgonooza without passing
[through] the Polypus" of error;[122] and when Ololon independently follows Milton, "a wide road was open to Eternity/
By Ololon's descent thro' Beulah to Los & Enitharmon!" (*M*
35:22 and 35-36, K 525). Milton hears Ololon's inquiry—
"Knowest thou [Blake] of Milton?"—which initiates the last
acts of his own self-judgment (*M* 37:1 and 6-10, K 527).

In the sequence which follows, Milton's Covering Cherub is
associated with negations of the imagination, especially with his
erroneous theology, which misperceives Jehovah as the "Gods
of Ulro dark," thereby calling reason, instead of imagination,
the divine likeness.[123] However, once Milton recognizes his spectre as Satan, he also realizes his power to annihilate him; for
Blake's imaginative man, knowledge and power are both simultaneously attainable on earth, and are not incompatible with each
other and with life: "Satan! my Spectre! I know my power thee
to annihilate" (*M* 38:29, K 529).

In negation of the eye-for-an-eye "Laws of thy false Heav'ns," the legalism of rationalism, Milton comes to know the everlasting gospel of forgiveness of sins:

> Such are the Laws of Eternity,
>   that each shall Mutually
> Annihilate himself for others' good,
>   as I for thee. . . .
> Mine [purpose] is to teach Men
>   to despise death & to go on
> In fearless majesty annihilating Self,
>   laughing to scorn
> Thy laws & terrors, shaking down
>   thy Synagogues as webs.
> I come to discover before Heav'n & Hell
>   the Self righteousness
> In all its Hypocritic turpitude,
>   opening to every eye
> These wonders of Satan's holiness,
>   shewing to the Earth
> The Idol Virtues of the Natural Heart,
>   & Satan's Seat
> Explore in all its Selfish Natural Virtue,
>   & put off
> In Self annihilation all that is not
>   of God alone,
> To put off Self & all I have,
>   ever & ever. Amen   (*M* 38:35-36 and 40-49,
> K 530).

Though Albion begins to awake at this initial announcement of the cataclysmic destruction of error, he cannot rise from the couch of vegetable death until Milton conquers Satan in annihilating the selfhood.[124]

A Last Judgment of the Self in the Baptism of the Imagination

"In terrible [and beautiful] majesty" Milton now articulates his last judgment of the self:

"Obey thou the Words of the Inspired Man.
"All that can be (can be) annihilated
  must be annihilated
"That the Children of Jerusalem
  may be saved from slavery.
"There is a Negation,
  & there is a Contrary:
"The Negation must be destroy'd
  to redeem the Contraries.
"The Negation is the Spectre,
  the Reasoning Power in Man:
"This is a false Body, an Incrustation
  over my Immortal
"Spirit, a Selfhood which must be put off
  & annihilated alway.
"To cleanse the Face of my Spirit
  by Self-examination,
"To bathe in the Waters of Life,
  to wash off the Not Human,
"I come in Self-annihilation
  & the grandeur of Inspiration,
"To cast off Bacon, Locke, & Newton
  from Albion's covering,
"To take off his filthy garments
  & clothe him with Imagination,
"To cast aside from Poetry
  all that is not Inspiration,
"That it no longer shall dare to mock
  with the aspersions of Madness
"Cast on the Inspired by the tame
  high finisher of paltry Blots
"Indefinite, or paltry Rhymes,
  or paltry Harmonies,
"Who creeps into State Government
  like a catterpiller to destroy;
"To cast off the idiot Questioner
  who is always questioning
"But never capable of answering,
  who sits with a sly grin
"Silent plotting when to question,
  like a thief in a cave,
"Who publishes doubt & calls it knowledge,
  whose science is Despair,
Whose pretence to knowledge is envy,
  whose whole Science is
"To destroy the wisdom of ages
  to gratify ravenous Envy
"That rages round him like a Wolf
  day & night without rest:
"He smiles with condescension,

he talks of Benevolence & Virtue,
"And those who act with Benevolence & Virtue
     they murder time on time.
"These are the destroyers of Jerusalem,
     these are the murderers
"Of Jesus, who deny the Faith
     & mock at Eternal Life,
"Who pretend to Poetry
     that they may destroy Imagination
"By imitation of Nature's Images
     drawn from Remembrance.
"These are the Sexual Garments,
     the Abomination of Desolation,
"Hiding the Human Lineaments
     as with an Ark & Curtains
"Which Jesus rent & now
     shall wholly purge away with Fire
"Till Generation is swallow'd up
     In Regeneration" (*M* 40:29-41:28, K 532-33).

Illustrating how man can be king and priest in his own house,
this sublime passage portrays Milton as administering and con-
ferring upon himself the baptism of the imagination.

Blake appropriates this Christian sacrament[125] to "mean" the
death of the restrictive spectre of reason and the rebirth of the
liberated spirit of the "Poetic Genius, which is the Lord." As
the "Inspired Man," Milton speaks with that absolute self-
knowledge which is self-definition—I imagine that I am. The
spiritual identity is consummated when he is reunited with his
redeemed emanation (Ololon, less her shadow of error) and
when they, together, are transfigured as "One Man" with Jesus,
the Savior.

Alluding to Jesus' incarnation, crucifixion, and resurrection,
the last seven lines of this majestic speech interpret these events
according to Blake's cosmogony and theology. The incarnation
repeats God's initial merciful creation of time, space, and their
vegetable forms, which clothe fallen man in "Sexual Garments,"
the "abomination of desolation" of generation; these "filthy garments" hide the eternal and divine "Human Lineaments," as
did Old Testament legalism, the restrictive Ten Commandments
and laws of the Torah. Its "Ark & Curtains" (the "veil" made
with the [covering] "cherubims") "shall divide unto you between [or, shall separate for you] the holy place and the most
holy,"[126] signifying the "veil of the Temple" that was "rent" in
Jesus' crucifixion, ending the division. The generated (mortal)
body of mystery was destroyed in the crucifixion and transfigured

in the resurrection, in which the immortal human form divine is revealed.

The predominance of garment imagery in *Milton* converges on this central exchange. What is satanic—the grave clothes of the generated body mercifully woven in Cathedron's looms[127] —is put off and annihilated ("rent") when man is "wholly purge[d] away with Fire" in Los's creative furnaces, burning with "fires of intellect." What is revealed and repossessed are the divine "Human Lineaments." Incarnation into this world of Generation is "holy" (*J* 7:65, K 626) insofar as man images and rises to regeneration.

The Reunion of the Soul and the Body

Ololon's "rebirth" illustrates the same principle of self-cleansing; as Milton's emanation, it represents the redemption of his soul. Like Milton, she must descend through the void of Ulro, the grave of error, which, if entered into and passed through, becomes a womb of regeneration:[128]

> Then as a Moony Ark Ololon descended
>   to Felpham's Vale
> In clouds of blood, in streams of gore,
>   with dreadful thunderings
> Into the Fires of Intellect
>   that rejoic'd in Felpham's Vale
> Around the Starry Eight;
>   with one accord the Starry Eight became
> One Man, Jesus the Saviour, wonderful!
>   round his limbs
> The Clouds of Ololon folded
>   as a Garment dipped in blood,
> Written within & without in woven letters,
>   & the Writing
> Is the Divine Revelation
>   in the Litteral expression
> A Garment of War. I heard it nam'd
>   the Woof of Six Thousand Years   (*M* 42:7-15,
> K 534).

Ololon's reunion with Milton completes them both, for generically it represents the reunion of the soul and the body. As one, they are joined with and become "the Starry Eight," the Eight Eyes, or Spirits, of God which together form the total divine presence.[129] While Blake derives this symbolism from Biblical sources, as noted, his changing the final numerology (from seven to eight) indicates his characteristic view of the relation between man and God: that the completion of either (either the seven Eyes of God or the seven "ages" of man) depends on the union of both as "One Man," hence their combined totality is eightfold.

The prime meaning of Blake's alteration, then, is to reaffirm that man and God are both interdependently completed each by the "other." Blake's "human form divine" is both immanent and transcendent,[130] as Jesus fortells of the resurrection: "At that day ye shall know that I am in my Father, and ye in me, and I in you" (John 14: 20). Ololon's reunion with Milton and their becoming the "Starry Eight" represents the hypostatical union of man and God in Jesus: "with one accord the Starry Eight became/ One Man, Jesus the Saviour, wonderful!"

Accordingly, the clouds of Ololon folding around the Saviour as a garment dipped in the blood of "mental fight"[131] are a sign of the imminent apocalypse, the "Human Harvest." Blake beholds the ensuing conclusion of history, in which the twenty-four cities of Albion represent the twenty-four Elders around God's throne who "Judge the Nations of the Earth" and in whom the "Immortal Four" appear (*M* 42:18-21, K 534). Like John of Patmos's vision "in the spirit" (Rev. 1: 10 and 4: 2) of the divine throne, Blake's soul returns into its mortal state, "to Resurrection & Judgment in the Vegetable Body" (*M* 42: 27, K 534).[132]

While they have appeared periodically as two "auguries of innocence," the Lark and Wild Thyme are recurring symbols of Blake's criticism of Milton, particularly in his presenting the Holy Ghost as a "vacuum" (*MHH* 5, K 150), that is, as static and not an active, continual source of inspiration and truth that Jesus says He will send to inform those who are His: "lo, I am with you always, even unto the end of the world" (Matt. 28: 20). Most notably representing the abiding presence of the Holy Ghost in time, the Lark "vibrates with the effluence Divine" and is "Los's Messenger thro' the Twenty-seven Churches" (*M* 31:35, K 520 and *M* 35:63, K 526), i.e., to the decayed houses of religion, which Los-Blake would "repair."

To immortals, "the Lark is a mighty Angel," (*M* 36: 12, K

527)[133] who each morning, at dawn, sings forth inspiration (the immense world of delight of the expanded senses). This association implies, as Blake portrays explicitly (on *M* 38 C-42 D), that inspiration follows the sexual union of man and his emanation, for the Muses are daughters of Beulah, "Enraptured with affection sweet & mild benevolence" (*M* 30: 7, K 518) ; and such a relation also shows his Puritan predecessor the therapeutic (and not destructive) value of sexual love.

The Lark recurs through the poem as the continuous presence of the Holy Ghost,[134] or inspiration, in time. At the end of time, the Lark brings the eschatological message of Pentecost:

> And it shall come to pass in the last days, saith God, I will pour out of my Spirit upon all flesh: and your sons and your daughters shall prophesy and your young men shall see visions, and your old men shall dream dreams. And on my servants and on my handmaidens I will pour out in those days of my Spirit; and they shall prophesy: And I will show wonders in heaven above, and signs on the earth beneath (Acts 2: 17–19; see also Joel 2: 28–32).

Immediately upon Blake's soul's return from the vision of Jesus and the throne of God, the Lark mounts the sky and sings with a loud trill to announce the last days, literally the "Wild Thyme," associated with the Lark as "Los's Messenger to Eden" (*M* 35: 54, K 526). Blake's variation on Joel 3: 13—from "the wine-press is full" to the "Wine-presses and Barns stand open" (*M* 42: 37, K 535)—prepares for the total "Human Harvest" to follow in *Jerusalem*.

The Great Human Harvest:
"Prepar'd in All Their Strength"

Milton ends in this moment of eschatological expectation: having passed through a last judgment of the self and attained the first resurrection of the spirit "with" Jesus, Milton's example awaits "imitation" collectively by all men, for whom the

> Wine-presses & Barns stand open,
>   the ovens are prepar'd
> Their Waggons ready, terrific Lions
>   & Tygers sport & play.
> All Animals upon the Earth are prepar'd
>   in all their strength

To go forth to the Great Harvest
    & Vintage of the Nations   (*M* 42:37-39 and
43:1, K 535).[135]

The final plate contains only the last line with a picture of
the emanation, prepared as the bride;[136] the illustration shows
the (back of) the nude soul (not always virgin for Blake, as
she was for Yeats), nude except for a bluish cape, with outstretched arms in cruciform position with her fluffy golden hair
outflowing, and standing between two many-winged seraphim
looking like human ears of grain. There are flames of intellectual
fire at their feet and near the woman's, and written on the back
of a sketch for this plate is "Father & Mother, I return from
flames of fire tried & pure & white" (*M* 43, K 535). The redeemed Milton-Ololon (the reunited body and soul) is feminine
in relation to God, as Father and Husband.

Here the reunited body and soul stand triumphantly in the
"Human Harvest" (pictured in the Seraphim whose multifoliate
wings resemble grain),[137] awaiting the bodily consummation of
the spiritual resurrection in the final union with God in the last
resurrection of the apocalypse. Plate 99 of *Jerusalem,* as we
shall see, illustrates this consummate union, in body and spirit, of
God with his Bride, the totality of "regenerated" humanity in
Jerusalem.

Vala, or the Four Zoas somewhat hectically deals with every
man's psychology (an anatomy of fallen humanity), especially
with his emotional life as a natural creature, as indicated in the
original title, *Vala. Milton* incorporates the Zoaic psychology by
emphasizing Los-Urthona, the immortal one, in a last judgment
of the imagination, whereby the eternal and true self is revealed.
While Los-Urthona is inchoately the "hero" of the *Four Zoas,*
he becomes more explicitly central as the redeeming poet-prophet
of *Milton* and as identified with Jesus in *Jerusalem. Milton* ends
with the spiritual union of Los-Milton with Jesus in the first
resurrection, a personal redemption. *Jerusalem* ends with the
Four Zoas' and Albion's final resurrection and fourfold union
with the Divinity, the attainment of collective salvation.

"A Vision of the Last Judgment": Blake's Mental Sacraments

Although *Jerusalem* expands the eschatology of *Milton,* I first want to discuss the "Last Judgment" (1810), which further delineates Blake's religious vision.[138] Like Blake's other major works, this visionary prose predicates its Christian expectations upon their source, in the imagination:

> Vision or Imagination is a Representation of what Eternally Exists, Really & Unchangeably. . . . The Hebrew Bible & the Gospel of Jesus are not Allegory ["a totally distinct & inferior kind of Poetry"], but Eternal Vision or Imagination of All that Exists ("VLJ," K 604).

For Blake, this "divine vision" has ontological existence because of its fundamental soteriological essence; that is, man's knowledge of and access to heaven is through the Savior, whose traditional Christian name is Jesus and whose original Blakean identity is the imagination:

> This world of Imagination is the world of Eternity; it is the divine bosom into which we shall all go after the death of the Vegetated body. This World of Imagination is Infinite & Eternal, whereas the world of Generation, or Vegetation, is Finite & [for a small moment *del.*] Temporal. There Exist in that Eternal World the Permanent Realities of Every Thing which we see reflected in the Vegetable Glass of Nature. All Things are comprehended in their Eternal Forms in the divine body of the Saviour, the True Vine of Eternity, the Human Imagination, who appear'd to Me as Coming to Judgment among his Saints & throwing off the Temporal that the Eternal might be Establish'd ("VLJ," K 605-6).

Blake's art is spiritually therapeutic, for "the Nature of my Work is Visionary or Imaginative; it is an Endeavour to Restore what the Ancients call'd the Golden Age" ("VLJ," K 605), or what Blake calls Eden, the Biblical heaven, man's "Eternal Dwelling Place."[139] Of this painting, for example, Blake says "thus My Picture is a History of Art & Science, the Foundation of Society [all *del.*], which is Humanity itself" ("VLJ," K 613). Accordingly, the basis of Blake's collective civilized body ("society") is mental, for "the Primeval State of Man was Wisdom, Art & Science" (*J* 3, K 621); and such "Civilized Life" "Represents Religion," as it ought to be, "in the Christian Church" ("VLJ," K 610). Since "Fools flourish," however, a last judgment, "an Overwhelming of Bad Art & Science" ("VLJ," K 617), is necessary.

Because the eternal form of the Savior is the imagination, Blake's vision and execution of "the Last Judgment" redefines conventional moral categories as mental forms of perception, as intellectual phenomena: "the Combats of Good & Evil [& of

Truth & Error which are the same thing *del.*] is Eating of the Tree of Knowledge. The Combats of Truth & Error is Eating of the Tree of Life" ("VLJ," K 615). Accordingly, "whenever any Individual Rejects Error & Embraces Truth a Last Judgment passes upon that Individual" ("VLJ," K 613). Because the Holy Ghost is none other than the intellectual fountain of Humanity (*J* 77, K 717), "What are all the Gifts of the Spirit but Mental Gifts?" ("VLJ," K 613).

The last judgment of vision, accordingly, reveals that "Mental Things are alone Real":

> Error is Created. Truth is Eternal. Error or Creation, will be Burned up, & then, & not until Then, Truth or Eternity will appear. It is Burnt up the Moment Men cease to behold it. . . . "What," it will be Questioned, "When the Sun rises, do you not see a round disk of fire somewhat like a Guinea?" O no, no, I see an Innumerable company of the Heavenly host crying "Holy, Holy, Holy is the Lord God Almighty!" I question not my Corporeal or Vegetative Eye any more than I would Question a Window concerning a Sight. I look thro' it & not with it ("VLJ," K 617).

Blake's religion is beyond good and evil, the fallen fruits of the Tree of Knowledge (*VFZ*, N IX: 274, K 304) because "reality" is a mental phenomenon.

> Men are admitted into Heaven not because they have curbed & govern'd their Passions or have no Passions, but because they have Cultivated their Understandings. The Treasures of Heaven are not Negations of Passion, but Realities of Intellect, from which all the Passions Emanate Uncurbed in their Eternal Glory. The Fool shall not enter into Heaven be he ever so Holy ("VLJ," K 615).

Milton's last judgment of the self and baptism of the imagination, for example, dramatize this "truth" as his eternal identity is revealed through and as his "Immortal Spirit"; by giving himself for the "Children of Jerusalem," Milton imitates, and finally is spiritually joined with, Jesus in the first resurrection.

The saving mode of judgment is forgiveness of sins, of one's own and others'. Accordingly, Blake characterizes life as consisting of the two Christian sacraments which imitate Jesus' giving himself for man—baptism and the Eucharist.

> He [Jesus, the "Divine Humanity"] is the Bread & the Wine; he is the Water of Life; accordingly on Each Side of the opening Heaven appears an Apostle; [one *del.*] that on the Right Represents Baptism, [& the Other *del.*] that on the Left Represents the Lord's Supper.

All Life consists of these Two, Throwing off Error and Knaves from our company continually & Receiving Truth or Wise Men into our Company continually. ("VLJ," K 612–13).[140]

For the artist, the "waters of life" flow in the baptism of the imagination, and the eucharistic bread and wine of life reside in truth and wisdom. Further, Blake speaks of baptism as "Education," and such temporal acquisition of divine knowledge constitutes the present infusion of the Holy Spirit (whose gifts are mental). In contrast to this baptismal "Immediate Inspiration of God," the Eucharist benefits those who, though willing, are "too weak to Reject Error without the Assistance & Countenance of those Already in the Truth"; this "Advice of a Friend" appears "for a Protection" ("VLJ," K 614). Like Blake's visionary phenomenology of a last judgment, the Christian sacraments which are "the two introducers into Eternal Life" ("DLJ," K 444) are sacred because mental.

Blake's reversed causality here, however, derives its authority from his prior redefinition of the Savior as "The Human Imagination" ("VLJ," K 606). Within the Christian ontology of the sacred, Blake shows the mental and human form of the divine. In the beautiful passage speaking of the viewer's relation to this picture (and to the rest of his art), Blake predicates that

If the Spectator could Enter into these Images in his Imagination, approaching them on the Fiery Chariot of his Contemplative Thought, if he could Enter into Noah's Rainbow or into his bosom, or could make a Friend & Companion of one of these Images of wonder, which always intreats him to leave mortal things (as he must know), then would he arise from his Grave, then would he meet the Lord in the Air & then he would be happy ("VLJ," K 611).

This redemptive meeting of the person and his/her Lord depends on the accessibility of the divine "other." While Christianity has traditionally verified the Savior's entry into history (the incarnation) and his "opening" time into eternity (as Blake speaks of the resurrection), Blake is concerned with recovering and revealing the divine within the human mind. For Blake, the mode of this "repair" which reunites humanity with God (the traditional result of the moral discrimination of the last judgment) is the intellectual phenomenon of imaginative perception, or vision, of the infinite and holy ("VLJ," K 617).

While this piece of visionary prose, like *Milton*, concerns primarily the last judgment, I would like to conclude this discussion with an observation about the resurrection which follows. Although man may "live in Paradise & Liberty" before the last judgment in the resurrection "in the spirit," not until after the last judgment may he do so in the body. He will rise in the spiritual body of the fourfold "organized" man ("Desc. Cat.," K 576-77), "for in Paradise they have no Corporal & Mortal Body—that originated with the Fall & was call'd Death & cannot be removed but by a Last Judgment. . . . The Whole Creation Groans to be deliver'd" and "the Earth is convuls'd with the Labours of the Resurrection" ("VLJ," K 616 and "DLJ," K 443).

Jerusalem: *The Final "Awaking to Eternal Life"*

Jerusalem is the first and last word as Blake's best, most important,[141] and largest "published," i.e., engraved work. Twice as long as *Milton,* the brief epic of the individual, *Jerusalem* has 100 plates in all, divided equally into four chapters,[142] and this numerology combines a vaguely Christian number of totality (100) with Blake's fourfold vision. However, it is not to the Four Zoas individually to which each chapter is addressed, but to spiritual states of men, in ascending order, from the public, the Jews, the Deists, and the Christians—the fourfold epic of the collective body of men. As in the *Four Zoas* and *Milton, Jerusalem* concerns salvation, which central concern Blake made clear to his friend Thomas G. Wainwright, for example: " 'The Doctor ["Ruddicombe," since Blake's hair was yellow-red] assures me that the redemption of mankind hangs on the universal diffusion of the doctrines broached in this MS.' "[143] However, each of the major epics converges on a different moment of redemption. *Jerusalem* includes and expands the eschatology of these earlier poems by envisioning man's complete and final "perfect unity" in the eternal, divine, and imaginative body of the resurrection.

Vala, or The Four Zoas is primarily concerned with the Fall, though it concludes with a prophetic version of the resurrection (like those of the intertestamental books). *Milton* and *Jerusalem* are more distinctly Christian in spirit: the eschatological event of *Milton* is a last judgment of the self in the first, spiritual, resurrection and of *Jerusalem* it is the apocalyptic, collective resurrection of man's fourfold body and soul (emanation).

Blake's "central form"[144] to which each single work contributes is Biblical, and his unified vision "develops" from the Old Testament prophetic imperative of reformation (in the historical prophecies), through the intertestamental view of Messianic, earthly renewal (*Vala*) to the New Testament apocalyptic vision of complete transformation, "re-presented" in Jesus' resurrection, of the individual (in *Milton*) and of the community (in *Jerusalem*). This pattern follows the development of the resurrection doctrine itself (as discussed in chapter 1). While the *Four Zoas* culminates in a return to individual unity and a prophetic renewal, and while *Milton* climaxes in a last judgment and first, spiritual, resurrection of the self, *Jerusalem* consummates in the apocalypse. Blake presents this complete resurrection as Albion's reunion with Jerusalem and his Four Zoas, and the "great marriage" of the whole Humanity with the Divinity.

Blake's Jesus: "All Power" to the Imagination

Plate 1 of *Jerusalem*, the frontispiece, portrays Los-Blake entering through Death's Door "for Albion's sake Inspired." His giving himself for his friend reenacts Jesus' incarnation, and great commandment of John 15:12-13. Like *Milton*, *Jerusalem's* didactic content is an *imitatio dei*, of the Savior whose identity, as Milton learned, is the imagination. The "hero" of Jerusalem is Blake's Jesus-Los, each of whom is identified as the "likeness & similitude" of the other. Of the Four Zoas, the form of the fourth, Urthona-Los, "was like the Son of God" ("Desc. Cat.," K 578); because of this divine image—because "he kept the divine vision in time of trouble" (*J* 30:15, K 655 and *J* 95:20, K 742)—Los's redemptive labors are crucial.

The moral imperative of the Blakean artist is to realize the divine vision of perfection:

> I rest not from my great task!
> To open the Eternal Worlds,
>   to open the immortal Eyes
> Of Man inwards into the Worlds of Thought,
>   into Eternity
> Ever expanding in the Bosom of God,
>   the Human Imagination.
> O Saviour pour upon me thy Spirit

of meekness & love!
Annihilate the Selfhood in me:
be thou all my life!   (*J* 5, 17-22, K 623).

From this convergence and identification of man and God in the imagination—engraved in the sublime "Laocoon" which spiritually and chronologically follows *Jerusalem* as a coda—arises Blake's Christianity of the imagination, the principal concern of his poem and of this commentary.

Blake's hope that "the Reader will be with me, wholly One in Jesus our Lord, who is the God of Fire and Lord of Love" (*J* 3, K 621)[145] is to be taken literally, as is his interpretation of John 1:14 and 17:21-23 at the beginning of the *Four Zoas*. Blake's hope to be "wholly One" means the unity of the self (of one's emanation and Four Zoas), of man with men, and of man with God—all these are included in being "wholly One in Jesus," the *Logos:* "All had originally one language, and one religion: this was the religion of Jesus, the everlasting Gospel" ("Desc. Cat.," K 579), which Blake defines in *Jerusalem:* "The Spirit of Jesus is continual forgiveness of Sin" (*J* 3, K 621).

For Blake, this Gospel (summarized on Plate 77) is both the "way" and the "life" of the resurrection, as his note for "the last words of Jesus" indicates: "Εδοθη μοι πασα εξουσια εν ουρανω και επι γης" (*J* 3, K 621). The King James version of the Bible translates this sentence from Matthew 28:18 thus: "All power is given unto me in heaven and earth." Traditionally, however, "the last words of Christ" are the seven sayings, composited from the four Gospels, uttered on Good Friday from the cross.[146] Blake's designation of Jesus' last words, however, is clearly not traditional, but "literal" and representative of his divine image: Blake's is not the Jesus who suffers on the cross, but the triumphant Jesus Christ, risen in glory.[147] Hence, Blake's notation of Jesus' "last words" refers not to those uttered on the cross, as the dying man, but to those spoken after his resurrection from the dead, as the immortal human form divine, just before his ascension to heaven. It is central not only that Blake's is the risen Jesus but also, accordingly, that "All power is given unto me in heaven and earth."[148]

The motto at the beginning of the text of *Jerusalem*—Μονος ὁ Ιεσους ("only Jesus")—states both a theological and ontological position. It implies that the Trinity is One ("one-ly") in Jesus, as Blake explicitly states in the "Laocoon:"

"God is JESUS" (K 777). More importantly, it implies that Jesus alone ("Μονος") is the source of the eternal reality of salvation.

These interpretations are supported by their probable source in the fourth Gospel, whose "Word," the *Logos*, Blake associates with.[149] Jesus' prayer before his glorification emphasizes the holiness of unity, which Blake noted as gloss at the beginning of the *Four Zoas* and which clarify the presiding image of *Jerusalem:*

> That they all may be one; as thou, Father art in me, and I in thee, that they also may be one in us: that the world may believe that thou hast sent me. And the glory which thou gavest me I have given them; that they may be one, even as we are one: I in them, and thou in me, that they may be made perfect in one (John 17:21–23).

For Blake this knowledge and possession of perfection is shared by the Savior and the artist, for "Jesus considered the Imagination to be the Real Man" ("Annot. Berkeley," K 774). The *Logos's* theological name is Jesus, his aesthetic name is Los, and his eternal body and spirit are the imagination.

The first page of chapter 1 contains much of the "doctrine" which *Jerusalem* dramatizes, and the first two lines of the poem proper state Blake's constant subject: "Of the sleep of Ulro! and of the passage through/ Eternal Death! and of the awaking to Eternal Life. This theme calls me in sleep night after night, & ev'ry morn/ Awakes me at sun-rise" (*J* 4:1-4, K 622). Instead of the inspired daughters of Beulah, the Savior himself spreads his spiritual wings over Blake and dictates "the words of this mild song" (*J* 4:5, K 623) to him, since "all the Gifts of the Holy Ghost" are "Intellectual" or "Mental" gifts ("VLJ," K 604 and 613; *J* 77, K 717). Further this "God from whom all books are given" (*J* 3, K 621) again predicates the unity of the Christian Trinity in the Blakean Jesus-the-imagination, who is also God and the Holy Ghost, i.e., both the source of artistic inspiration and the divine vision therein imaged.

And finally, through cleansing and expanding the doors of perception, the awakened man of vision (literally) beholds the proper unity of man and God:

> . . . wake! expand!
> I am in you and you in me,
> mutual in love divine. . . .

> I am not a God afar off,
>   I am a brother and a friend;
> Within your bosoms I reside,
>   and you reside in me:
> Lo! we are One, forgiving all Evil,
>   Not seeking recompense.
> Ye are my members . . . ! (*J* 4: 7 and
> 17-22, K 622).

This immanence of a transcendent God informs Blake's theology, which holds that when man is wholly human, he is also divine.[150] The "Divine Family" is "One in Him. A Human Vision!/ Human Divine, Jesus the Saviour, blessed for ever and ever" (*J* 40, 46-47, K 667). Whereas Christianity teaches that God is Jesus, in the incarnation, and thus presents the humanness of the divinity, Blake teaches that Jesus is God, in the resurrection and thus emphasizes the divine humanity. For Blake, redemption involves the complete humanization of reality, which is also its divinization; that is, the human imagination's perception of the infinite and holy within a unified body and mind is also a perception of God, for "he who sees the Infinite in all things, sees God" ("No Natural Religion, b," K 98). It is important to remember the underlying Christian presupposition which Blake employs, namely, that because God first becomes human, the human then can become divine (as he concludes the second "No Natural Religion"); necessarily assuming the prior incarnation, the resurrection reunites man with God, and Blake's apotheosis of "Divine Humanity" is a religious, and not a secular, act, whose ontological sanction is manifest on Easter.

Albion's Forsaking the Imagination and His Fall to Materialism

Albion's fall into the sleep of Ulro, the nightmare of materialism and rationalism, stems from his hiding his emanation, Jerusalem, from her mate, Jesus. However, this destructive possessiveness not only keeps Jerusalem from her "Lord and Husband," but also separates Albion from Jerusalem, the land of his "heart's desire" (*J* 24: 28, K 647). This double spiritual separation negates the divine unity of God and man and is both the cause and result of the original Fall.

As in *Milton*, Blake presents this universal "sin" in its psychological components, within the mind. Virtually all of his descriptions of Albion's fall throughout *Jerusalem* concern his loss of beholding the divine imagination and its consequent usurpation by reason; thus does Albion lament what he has done, "O Human Imagination, O Divine Body, I have Crucified" (*J* 24:23, K 647).

The rest of his complaint describes how Deistic natural religion (Babylon, mother of earth's abominations) then usurps the spiritual (Jerusalem) :

> Yet thou was lovely as the summer cloud
>   upon my hills
> When Jerusalem was thy heart's desire,
>   in times of youth & love. . . .
> In the Exchanges of London
>   every Nation walk'd,
> And London walk'd in every Nation,
>   mutual in love & harmony.
> Albion cover'd the whole Earth,
>   England encompass'd the Nations,
> Mutual each within other's bosom
>   in Visions of Regeneration (*J* 24:36-
> 45, K 647-48).

The ancient times when the Holy Lamb of God did walk upon England's green and pleasant land, cease to exist because of Albion's fall, which produces, instead, the Orc cycle, the "eternal death" of generation.

The Four Zoas also fall into the destructive disorder within Albion,[151] and Urthona becomes a spectre, a "black Horror," because he too is murdered by the abominable and desolate "Reasoning Power" (*J* 10:15, K 629). Trying to "seduce" Los, the spectre of Urthona attempts to persuade him to abandon his unselfish "sublime Labours" "for Albion's sake" (*J* 8:17, K 627 and *J* 10:65, K 630).

But as the temporal form of "Human Perfection" (*J* 6:14, K 625), Los, alone, retains his inspiration in this time of trouble; he knows, like Job, that the present condition of affliction will cease and that "we shall all be changed" for the best:

> Comfort thyself in my strength;
>   the time will arrive
> When all Albion's injuries shall cease,

and when we shall
Embrace him, tenfold bright,
    rising from his tomb in immortality.
    . . . O that the Lamb
Of God would look upon me
    and pity me in my fury,
In anguish of regeneration,
    in terrors of self annihilation! . . .
And the Religion of Generation,
    which was meant for the destruction
Of Jerusalem, become her covering
    till the time of the End.
O holy Generation, Image of regeneration!
O point of mutual forgiveness
    between Enemies!
Birthplace of the Lamb of God incomprehensible!
(*J* 7:54-67, K 626).

To master his spectre (Urthona fallen into the "Reasoning
Power . . . An Abstract objecting power that Negatives every
thing")

Therefore Los stands in London
    building Golgonooza,
Compelling his Spectre to labours mighty. . . .
I must Create a System
    or be enslav'd by another Man's,
I will not Reason & Compare:
    my business is to Create   (*J* 10:13-14 and
17-21, K 629).

Los and his four sons build the great fourfold city of Golgonooza 1) to protect Jerusalem while separated from Albion and
Jesus, and 2) to prepare for their reunion, so that where one
lives is what one loves. Because of the fall and exile from Blake's
Eden, the "fourth and western Gate" "toward Eden is walled
up till time of renovation" (*J* 12:52, K 632); that "gate of the
tongue" (*J* 14:26, K 635), of Tharmas, the physical body, is
guarded by four cherubs.[152] "To find the Western path/ Right
thro' the Gates of Wrath [the cherubim with flaming swords]
is to "ascend the sky" in the resurrected body ("Morning,"
K 421).

This expectation is realized and resides in the continual building of Golgonooza, the Blakean city of eternal art: "All things acted on Earth are seen in the bright Sculptures of/ Los's Hall, & every Age renews its powers from these Works" (*J* 16:61-62, K 638).[153] Here Blake reverses the neoclassical notion of the relation of art and life, for "all things acted on Earth" imitate art (Los's bright sculptures), the eternal form of "reality."

Moreover, this "wondrous Art" is "the Divine Written Law of Horeb & Sinai,/ And such the Holy Gospel of Mount Olivet & Calvary" (*J* 16:68, K 638). That is, Los's creations, like the Old and New Testaments, contain man's spiritual history, from the beginning to the end. Characteristically (as we have seen beginning with the early religion tracts), Blake defines ("such is") religion and art in terms of their common source, the imagination. Golgonooza is the holy city of art because it embodies this envisioned eternal reality.

Having been addressed to the unbelieving public, chapter 1 accordingly ends with a description of Albion's despair—"Hope is banished from me" (*J* 24:60, K 648 and *J* 47:18, K 677)— which is directly associated with the lack of spiritual understanding. The didactic content of *Jerusalem* generates a corresponding didactic structure in the relation between the "state" to which a chapter is addressed and that chapter's ending.

While Albion, Blake's England, wastes in the desolation of blindness, the inhabitants of Beulah see his wounded condition ("a Thump on the Head," which "Jesus Christ comes with a balm to heal" ["VLJ," K 617]) and sympathize with him:

> Injury the Lord heals,
>   but Vengeance cannot be healed.
> As the Sons of Albion have done to Luvah,
>   so they have in him
> Done to the Divine Lord & Saviour,
>   who suffers with those that suffer;
> For not one sparrow can suffer
>   & the whole Universe not suffer also
> In all its Regions,
>   & its Father & Saviour not pity and weep. . . .
> Descend O Lamb of God,
>   & take away the imputation of Sin
> By the Creation of States

& the deliverance of Individuals Evermore
(*J* 25:5-13, K 648).[154]

When achieved, this "deliverance of Individuals" "By a New Spiritual birth Regenerated from Death" (*VFZ*, N IX:224, K 363) is the immortal liberty of Blake's Jerusalem.

Los's Friendship

Addressed primarily "to the Jews," chapter 2 continues to incorporate Biblical and English history into Blake's *mythos:* like all of *Jerusalem,* the chapter is both diagnostic and therapeutic. The introductory section outlines the basis (a truth which "cannot be controverted") for Blake's "re-conversion" of the Jews: "Ye are united, O ye Inhabitants of Earth, in One Religion the Religion of Jesus, the most Ancient, the Eternal & the Everlasting Gospel" (*J* 27, K 649). The Everlasting Gospel is, of course, the "Forgiveness of Sins," the original and single Moral Virtue that Jesus alone inculcated.[155] However, the Jews' errors, codified as "Moral & Self-righteous Law" (*J* 27:23, K 650), negate this eternal, and hence prior, Gospel and wither man to a mortal worm.

Chapter 2 not only describes these deadly "laws of sacrifice for sin" (perverted religion from the "Fatal Tree" of Good and Evil), but also prescribes how man may be cured by and return to the "Human Form Divine,"

> Weeping in weak & mortal clay,
> O Jesus, still the Form was thine
>
> And thine the Human Face, & thine
> The Human Hands & Feet & Breath,
> Entering thro' the Gates of Birth
> And passing thro' the Gates of Death
> (*J* 27:59-64, K 651).

The fallen Albion becomes an Old Testament punisher and judge in this chapter dealing with the errors of legalism and rationalism. In contrast, Los emerges as the merciful hero, the very likeness of the healing Jesus, and as the chief architect in the mutual building of Jerusalem in every land.

The beginning of chapter 2 is an anatomy of Albion as the "punisher & judge" (*J* 28:4, K 652). Having fallen—because he turned his back on the Divine Vision[156] and jealously hid Jerusalem, his emanation and Jesus' bride—Albion externally repeats these destructive acts which restrict the natural world to the "deadly Tree" of "Moral Virtue and the Law/ Of God who dwells in chaos hidden from human sight" (*J* 28:15-16, K 652).

The end of "Auguries of Innocence" presents the opposite, and desired, divine immanence:

> God Appears & God is Light
> To those poor souls who dwell in Night,
> But does a Human Form Display
> To those who Dwell in Realms of day (K 434).[157]

Not only do such cold laws harmfully separate man from God but they also separate man from man (*J* 28:12, K 652). In his astute description of Chaucer, Blake writes of both phenomena, as old as the error: "when separated from man or humanity, who is Jesus the Saviour, the vine of eternity, they [abstract characters of human life] are thieves and rebels, they are destroyers" ("Desc. Cat.," K 571).

In the resulting natural and historical confusion and tumult, Los and his emanation "alone are escaped" "because he kept the Divine Vision in time of trouble" (*J* 30:15, K 655). Los prays for the "Divine Saviour [to] arise/ Upon the Mountains of Albion as in ancient time!" and for the suffering England's final release from "The Rocky Law of Condemnation & double Generation & Death" (*J* 30:21-22 and 37, K 656): "The Dead awake to generation! Arise O Lord, & rend the Veil!" (*J* 30:40, K 656).

As this passage (uncondensed) bears witness, Los "was the friend of Albion who most lov'd him"; and as Albion grows sicker, Los strives the more to revive him. While the two phenomena are causally related, both are clearer when considered individually: before viewing how Los emerges as the Fourth immortal form (*J* 42:24, K 670) from the furnaces of the dead, I will continue discussing Albion's sickness.

Because what is perceived directly depends upon the perceiver, Los examines the "spiritual cause" of Albion's external "rocky clouds of death & despair":

> Fearing that Albion should turn his back
>   against the Divine Vision,
> Los took his globe of fire
>   to search the interiors of Albion's
> Bosom, in all the terrors of friendship
>   entering the caves
> Of despair & death. . . . (*J* 31:2-5, K 656).

This inspired act of true brotherhood is pictured on the frontis-piece as an emblem of freely giving oneself for another, the Christian liberty of friends in Jerusalem.[158]

Amid "Albion's rock & precipices, caves of solitude & dark despair"—the horrid waste of England's once green and pleasant land—Los finds that "Every Universal Form was become bar-ren mountains of Moral/ Virtue" (*J* 31:19-20, K 657). Jeru-salem is bound in "the iron threads of love & jealousy & despair" by Vala, Albion's wife. Further, Albion's having turned his back to the Divine Vision is tantamount to and results in his falling into the "Spectrous Chaos" of the "Rational Power." Conse-quently, the "Great Selfhood, Satan, [is] Worshipp'd as God" (*J* 33:17-18, K 659), instead of Jesus.

The satanic selfhood is man's rationalizing selfish power, which accuses, devours, haunts, and separates man from him-self, from his soul, from other men, and from God, as Albion's fall shows. In short, it is the last error which negates forgiveness and which must be cast out in the last judgment and destroyed in the apocalypse to complete the resurrection to perfect unity. As Milton saw, "the Reasoning Spectre/ Stands between the Vege-tative Man & him Immortal Imagination" (*M* 40-42, K 532-35 and *J* 36:24, K 633).

The resultant false "System of Moral Virtue [is] named Rahab" (*J* 39:10, K 666), "the mother of earth's abomina-tions" (Rev. 17:5). Not annihilated, the Selfhood continually damns man, individually and communally so that

> . . . the immortal mansion
> Of Man for ever [will] be posses'd
>   by monsters of the deeps,
> And Man himself become a Fiend,
>   wrap'd in an endless curse,
> Consuming and consum'd for-ever

in flames of Moral Justice (*J* 40:27-30, K 667).

From this hell of the cursing spectre, "the Divine Mercy/ Steps beyond and Redeems Man in the Body of Jesus" (*J* 36:54-55, K 663-64).

Forgiveness and Life as One Man

Until that time Los acts as the temporal agent of redemption "Because he kept the Divine Vision in time of trouble" (*J* 30: 15, K 655); that is, the artist beholds and preserves the image of divine perfection. Entering Albion's soul in the terrors of friendship, Los sees his sickness, "the blue death in Albion's feet." Then Los joins the "Divine Body" (Jesus), who mercifully follows.[159]

Both this embrace and the hymn to Albion by Los-Jesus adumbrate the final union of man and God:

> Albion! Our wars are wars of life,
>   & wounds of love
> With intellectual spears,
>   & long winged arrows of thought.
> Mutual in one another's love
>   and wrath all renewing
> We live as One Man;
>   for contracting our infinite senses
> We behold multitude,
>   or expanding, we behold as one,
> As One Man all the Universal Family,
>   and that One Man
> We call Jesus the Christ;
>   and he in us, and we in him
> Live in perfect harmony in Eden
>   the land of life,
> Giving, receiving, and forgiving
>   each other's trespasses.
> He is the Good shepherd,
>   he is the Lord and master,
> He is the Shepherd of Albion,

he is all in all,
In Eden, in the garden of God,
    and in heavenly Jerusalem.
If we have offended, forgive us (*J*
38:14-26, K 664-65).[160]

After this magnificent speech, Blake-Los speaks to affirm the
"Vision of God upon my pleasant valleys":

I behold London,
    a Human awful wonder of God!
He says: "Return, Albion, return!
I give myself for thee.
My Streets are my Ideas of Imagination.
Awake, Albion, awake!
    and let us awake up together.
My Houses are Thoughts;
    my Inhabitants, Affections, . . .
For Albion's sake and
    for Jerusalem thy Emanation
I give myself, and these my brethren
    give themselves for Albion" (*J* 38:
29-39, K 665).

With this fourfold vision, Blake also anticipates the final
apocalypse of the imagination, when everything is again human,
for "Man anciently contain'd in his mighty limbs all things in
Heaven & Earth" (*J* 27, K 649):[161]

    . . . for Cities
Are Men, fathers of Multitudes,
    and Rivers & Mountains
Are also Men; everything is Human
    Mighty! sublime!
In every bosom a Universe expands . . . (*J* 38:
46-49, K 665).

Like his Christian model, Los transcends legal bounds:
"Righteousness & justice I give thee in return/ For thy righteousness, but I add mercy also" (*J* 42:20, K 670); this addition,

of course, distinguishes the Old Testament from the New Testament ethic. Further, Los resembles his Christian model in his insisting on God's immanence in man: "Why stand we here trembling around/ Calling on God for help, and not *ourselves in whom God dwells*" (*J* 43:13, K 672; italics mine). Until the *parousia* and the fourfold reunion with the divine, all power is given to Los—renaming him the Spirit of Prophecy, calling him Elijah" (*J* 44:31, K 674; and *M* 24:71, K 510); he communicated directly with God, was bodily transported to heaven, and his reappearance announces that the "great and terrible day of the Lord is near."[162]

Finally, however, "none but the Lamb of God can heal/ This dread disease, none but Jesus" (*J* 45:15-16, K 675), whose full (Blakean) identity remains to be revealed. Having been generated into the world of death, man's western gate is closed until the return to Blake's Eden, through Tharmas in the resurrected body. According to the Biblical account in Genesis 3:24, the cherubim guard the eastern gate, and Blake's altering the direction (to the west, Tharmas's quadrant) indicates the importance of the expectation of the resurrection of the body along with that of the other three Zoas.

Until then, "the Bodies in which all Animals & Vegetations, the Earth & Heaven/ [which] were contained in the All Glorious Imagination, are wither'd & darken'd." The material correlate of the sleep of Ulro is the reduction of the "Visions of Eternity" to "weak Visions of Time & Space, fix'd into furrows of death"; the psychical correlate is the reduction of mutual forgiveness to "One Great Satan/ Inslav'd to the most powerful Selfhood: to murder the Divine Humanity" (*J* 49:13-14, 22, and 29-30, K 679).

Chapter 2 ends with a version appropriate "to the Jews" of the *"Komm Jesu"* hymn sung by the daughters of Beulah: "Come, O thou Lamb of God, and take away the remembrance of Sin." This "remembrance of sin" is associated with the Old Testament legalistic codes and lost, but renewable, covenant with God; unlike Donne's therapeutic sense of "remembrance", this one "is a Woe & a Horror" (*J* 50:24 and 28, K 681) in its essence and effect, for both indicate man's spiritual separateness. Jesus removes the "remembrance of sin" not by its retribution, but by its forgiveness. This is the "Covenant of Jehovah," elaborated in chapters 3 and 4 of *Jerusalem*.

Christian Liberty: "Are not Religion and Politics the Same Thing?"

Addressed "to the Deists," chapter 3 contains two motifs in counterpoint: 1) the nadir of the fall in its varying related catastrophes, and consequently, 2) the necessity of beholding Jesus' spirit. In combination with the two preceding chapters, the destructive errors of no and "false" religions culminate in the appearance of the Antichrist (at the end of chapter 3), who is destroyed in the apocalypse (of chapter 4). As Albion's condition worsens and ensnares others, Los's struggle to awaken his soul from its reductive sleep in Ulro becomes more pronounced.

In chapter 3 the major "negations" which oppose each other are between the natural and the spiritual, between the rational and the imaginative, and between the temporal and the eternal. The Deists fail to distinguish between man's immortal and mortal *état d'âme*, and they mistake his natural condition for his spiritual one.[163] This error and polarization is absolute and of utmost consequence, for "Man must & will have Some Religion: if he has not the Religion of Jesus, he will have the Religion of Satan."[164]

Chapter 3 depicts Deism's

> worship[ping] Satan under the Name of God . . . by the means of what you call Natural Religion and Natural Philosophy, and of Natural Morality or Self-Righteousness, the Selfish Virtues of the Natural Heart. This was the Religion of the Pharisees who murder'd Jesus. Deism is the same & ends in the same (*J* 52, K 682).

Further, its collective errors are also against humanity: "All the Destruction, therefore, in Christian Europe has arisen from Deism, which is Natural Religion" (*J* 52, K 683). Chapter 3 presents a total indictment of fallen and false worship.

As the friend who loves Albion the most, Los "wept vehemently" over his stricken condition. And more importantly, as the "Vehicular [temporal] Form of Strong Urthona . . . Los builded Golgonooza" (*J* 53:1 and 15, K 684). Begun for Jerusalem's sake and protection on earth, Golgonooza is that ideal city of art, which, when completed, becomes the city of God, "new Jerusalem," so that where one lives is what one desires, creates, and loves—because Jerusalem is Albion's land of the heart's desire (*J* 24:37, K 647), each person's emanation (*J* 54:3, K 684) and Jesus' Bride (*J* 53:24, K 684), respectively.

Because "Jesus & his Apostles & Disciples were all Artists" ("Laocoon," K 777), to construct Golgonooza is also to engage in the Christian's "Mental pursuit for the Building up of Jerusalem" (*J* 77, K 717).

Collectively, as Jesus' Bride, Jerusalem is the "Mystic Union of the Emanation in the Lord" (*J* 53:4, K 684), while in every individual person, she is his "Emanative portion" by which "Man is adjoin'd to Man" (*J* 44:38-42, K 675). Traditionally Jesus embodies the hypostatical union of man and God in which the saved share in the last resurrection to heaven. That Jerusalem is both Albion's emanation and Jesus' Bride here explains that Christian concept according to Blake's view that man is joined to man, and humans and God are joined in the freeing love that is the imagination's forgiveness:

> In Great Eternity every particular form
>   gives forth or Emanates
> In own peculiar Light,
>   & the Form is the Divine Vision
> And the Light is his Garment.
>   This is Jerusalem in every Man,
> A Tent & Tabernacle of Mutual Forgiveness,
>   Male & Female Clothings.
> And Jerusalem is called Liberty
>   among the Children of Albion (*J* 54:
> 1-5, K 684).

Deriving but differing from its probable source in Revelation, this definition incorporates John's vision of "new Jerusalem," which had "no need of the sun, neither of the moon, to shine in it: for the glory of God [the *Shekinah*] did lighten it, and the Lamb is the light thereof" (21:23 and 22:5; see Isa. 60:19), into Blake's concept of the emanation, or soul— the form of man's wisdom which "is peculiar to his own Individuality" (*M* 4:8, K 483). The communal form of the soul in Jerusalem is the Christian liberty of mutual forgiveness, whose source is the merciful imagination.

When man is finally so joined to man and to Jesus in Jerusalem, the holy "City, yet a Woman" (*VFZ*, N IX:222, K 362) of the "great marriage," what one loves totally is where one lives, and is infinite and holy. One fruit of this union is the collective moral body, as Paul writes of the new city: "But Jeru-

salem which is above is free, which is the mother of us all"
(Gal. 4:26).

Then, as now, "Are not Religion & Politics the Same Thing?
Brotherhood is Religion" (*J* 57, 10, K 689). As Blake drama-
tizes on *Jerusalem* Plate 96, without this religion of brotherhood,
Jesus' continual forgiveness, "Man is not" (K 743).

Jesus' Continual Forgiveness
 "That He Himself may Dwell Among You"

Like Los, Jerusalem keeps the Divine Vision in time of trouble, and Jesus' reply verifies his immanence:

> Give forth thy pity & love;
> > fear not! lo, I am with thee always
> Only believe in me,
> > that I have power to raise from death
> (*J* 60:76-78, K 694).

Of the two plates which follow to illustrate these precepts,
Plate 62 is doctrinally the most important, while Plate 61 was
a late addition.[165] Moreover, *J* 61 specifically emphasizes Jesus'
dwelling among men, literally, through the forgiveness of sin,
as Blake reinterprets his "holy" conception in the united body
and spirit.

Blake incorporates his disbelief in the Virgin Birth[166] into his
larger and essential belief in forgiveness, so that Jesus' incarnation further exemplifies (from his prenatal origin) continual
giving forth of love. Reacting to Mary's (natural) pregnancy,
"Joseph spoke in anger & fury, 'Should I/ Marry a Harlot &
an Adulteress?'" to which she answers by innocently and humanly asking "'Art thou more pure/ Than thy Maker who
forgiveth Sins & calls again Her that is Lost?" (*J* 61:6-7, K
694).[167]

Because "there is none that liveth & Sinneth not!" Joseph
forgives Mary's adultery and child "by the Holy Ghost," or
her own "peculiar wisdom." (*J* 61:24 and 27, K 694-95).
Thus Jesus embodies, quite literally, this act of forgiveness,
for

> Jehovah's Salvation
> Is without Money & without Price,

in the Continual Forgiveness of Sins,
In the Perpetual Mutual Sacrifice
in Great Eternity: . . .
If you Forgive one-another,
        so shall Jehovah Forgive You,
That He Himself may Dwell among you (*J* 61:
21-26, K 694-95).

These sayings of the Angel to Joseph in his dream echo Jesus'
words after the Lord's prayer in Matthew 6 : 14. Jesus' resurrection, the subject of the next plate, completes the divine forgiveness thus conceived and embodied in his incarnation.

Like Mary, the outcast and defaced Jerusalem is called a
harlot and asks if Jesus will become her husband, and like Mary
Magdalen (John 20), Jerusalem is the first to "behold thy
Spiritual Risen Body," the *pneumatikon*. Seeking to reaffirm
the relation between Jesus' resurrection and everyman's salvation, she asks "Shall Albion arise?" Then, like Job (19:26),
she bespeaks her own certain knowledge: "I know that in my
flesh I shall see God." Jesus' reply to Jerusalem—"I am the
Resurrection & the Life"—repeats his ancient redemptive words
to Martha in John 11:25. Each is a definitive statement of
immortal belief, and his last words in this speech combine (and
rephrase slightly) those following in John 11:25 with those at
the end of Matthew 28:20: "Only believe & trust in me. Lo,
I am always with thee!" (*J* 62:14-16 and 29, K 696).

A major significance of this speech is, perhaps, its effect on
Los, the artist who images Jesus and who

    . . . beheld the Divine Vision
        among the flames of the Furnaces.
    Therefore he lived & breathed in hope;
        but his tears fell incessant
    Because his Children were clos'd
        from him apart & Enitharmon
    Dividing in fierce pain;
        also the Vision of God was clos'd in clouds
    Of Albion's Spectres, that Los
        in despair oft sat & often ponder'd
    On Death Eternal, . . . then to his Anvils
    Turning, anew began his labours,
        tho' in terrible pains (*J* 62:35-42, K 696).

From here on, the struggle between the Christian "World of Mercy" and the Deist world of destructive natural religion is absolute: Luvah (Jesus-as-Pity) is crucified, on Albion's tree of the Selfhood, "to die a death of Six thousand years bound round with vegetation" (*J* 65:10, K 699).

Without and Within the "Worlds of Thought"

The horrors of this "Polypus of Roots of Reasoning, Doubt, Despair, & Death" (*J* 69:3, K 707) are the subject of most of the remaining plates (except for *J* 71, which anticipates the subject of chapter 4). Like both previous chapters, and like the Orc cycle it portrays, chapter 3 closes with the chaos of the natural world, worshiped by the Deists and representing the period of catastrophes before the last judgment (Rev. vi-xxi and *J* 73-75).

In Blake's anatomy, the whole world's frailty and decay stem from "Entering into the Reasoning Power, forsaking Imagination" (*J* 74:7, K 714). Once, in the beginning, man's four mighty Zoas existed in "Perfect Unity" (*VFZ*, N I:9-11, K 264, and John 17:21-23)—among themselves and between man and God; after the cosmic and psychic fall, "In opposition deadly, [and] their wheels in poisonous/ And deadly stupor turn'd against each other, loud & fierce" (*J* 74:5-6, K 714).

This description of the internal ontogeny of the fall—man's "forsaking Imagination"—is followed and recapitulated by its external phylogeny, the restricted world:

> The Spectre is the Reasoning Power in Man,
>   & when separated
> From Imagination and closing itself
>   as in steel in a Ratio
> Of the Things of Memory,
>   It thence frames Laws & Moralities
> To destroy Imagination, the Divine Body,
>   by Martyrdoms & Wars. (*J* 74:10-13, K 714).

The female and social counterpart of the Antichrist, Babylon, appears as "Rational Morality," who threatens to destroy Jerusalem; covertly containing the errors of religious history, "thus is Rahab reveal'd,/ Mystery, Babylon the Great, the Abomination of Desolation,/ Religion hid in War a Dragon Red & hidden Harlot" (*J* 75:18-20, K 716 and Rev. 17:5). The errors of history wind round in "Eternal Circles" to form the satanic mills in the prison of death.

Having introduced Babylon, in his own voice Blake speaks out against her desolate chaos which must now be destroyed in the imminent apocalypse:

> Teach me, O Holy Spirit, the Testimony
> of Jesus! let me
> Comprehend wonderous things
> out of the Divine Law! . . . .
> Hence is my Theme, O Lord my Saviour,
> open thou the Gates
> And I will lead forth thy Words! (*J* 74:14-
> 41, K 714-15).

This plea echoes Blake's initial definition of his "great task" "to open the immortal Eyes/ Of Man inwards into the Worlds of Thought" (*J* 5:18-19, K 623).

Blake's vision of Albion's land describes this infinite perspective:

> What is Above is Within,
> for every-thing in Eternity is translucent.
> The Circumference is Within, ...
> For all are Men in Eternity,
> Rivers, Mountains, Cities, Villages,
> All are Human,
> & when you enter into their Bosoms you walk
> In Heavens & Earths,
> as in your own Bosom you bear your Heaven
> And Earth & all you behold,
> tho' it appears Without, it is Within,
> In your Imagination,
> of which this World of Mortality is
> but a shadow (*J* 71:6-19, K 709).

Expanding the *principia* of "No Natural Religion" and the *Marriage,* these lines reveal everything as it is, infinite and holy, in the imagination, which is human and divine. This apocalypse of the imagination is completed at the end of chapter 4, when

"Jesus, breaking thro' the Central Zones of Death & Hell,/ Opens Eternity in Time & Space, triumphant in Mercy" (*J* 75:21-22, K 716).

Blake's Christianity of the Imagination

The fourth and last chapter of *Jerusalem*, like the Biblical narrative, completes the history of man's fall and the mystery of his salvation in the apocalyptic resurrection. Like the fourth form who emerged in Daniel's furnaces, and like the fourth Gospel, which relates how the Word was made flesh, Blake's fourth Immortal One, Urthona, in his temporal incarnation as Los-Jesus arises as the single, continual source of redemption, "Μονος ὁ Ιεϛονς." The visionary prose introduction defines Blake's Christianity of the imagination: "I know of no other Christianity and of no other Gospel than the liberty both of body & mind to exercise the Divine Arts of Imagination" (*J* 77, K 716-17).[168]

The arts of imagination are divine because they alone reveal both the mode and fulfillment of salvation, as Blake teaches:

What were all their [the Apostles] spiritual gifts? What is the Divine Spirit? is the Holy Ghost any other than an Intellectual Fountain? . . . What are the Treasures of Heaven which we are to lay up for ourselves, are they any other than Mental Studies & Performances? What are all the Gifts of the Gospel, are they not all Mental Gifts? Is God a Spirit who must be worshipped in Spirit & Truth, and are not the Gifts of the Spirit Every-thing to Man? . . . I call upon you in the Name of Jesus! What is the Life of Man but Art & Science? . . . What is Immortality but the things relating to the Spirit which Lives Eternally? What is the Joy of Heaven but Improvement in the things of the Spirit? . . . Can you think at all & not pronounce heartily That to Labour in Knowledge is to Build up Jerusalem, and to Despise Knowledge is to despise Jerusalem & her Builders. And remember: He who despises & mocks a Mental Gift in another . . . mocks Jesus the giver of every Mental Gift . . . Let every Christian, as much as in him lies, engage himself openly & publically before all the World in some Mental Pursuit for the Building up of Jerusalem (*J* 77, K 717).[169]

From this, and similar passages, as observed, it is clear that Blake uses and means "imaginative" (as "mental" and "intellectual") and "spirtual" as synonyms. In this original identification resides Blake's revelation of redemption.

Blake's theology is Christ-centered, and *Jerusalem* converges on Jesus' radical identity as the imagination, the source of every mental and spiritual gift, which comprise the Gospel and the "Treasures of Heaven": "Imagination, the real & eternal World of which this Vegetable Universe is but a faint shadow, & in which we shall live in our Eternal or Imaginative Bodies when these Vegetable Mortal Bodies are no more" (*J* 77, K 717). Altering the traditional transfiguration, Blake's vision of the resurrection (in an immaculate perception) conceives of Paul's "spiritual body" as the imaginative one, which is its "real" and eternal form, partaking of that heaven to which it rises.

Los's "Divine Vision"

The final chapter of *Jerusalem* joins the Christian with Blake's own *mythos* as both converge in the image of the Savior. Laboring with the "Divine Vision," Los knows and preserves the possibility of redemption: "I know I am Urthona, keeper of the Gates of Heaven,/ And that I can at will expatiate in the Gardens of bliss" (*J* 82:81-82, K 727). As he watches his furnaces wherein Golgonooza is created and directs the laborers, engaged in the mental pursuit of building, Los Sings of Jerusalem's reappearance; his song expands upon Revelation 21:2 by viewing her as the "reflected image" of the sleeping Albion, with whom she will be reunited and raised.

But before this is possible, Los must overcome his spectre's separating him from his emanation. Although this division and usurpation have not been stressed in *Jerusalem*,[170] its addition here serves as a revealing model. This episode further delineates Los as the paradigmatic hero as he personally rehearses the "doctrine" of redemption in prelude to its complete dramatization in Albion's awakening. Los's spectre is that which haunts the artist's creativity by threatening to become an enforced personal will, which separates him from others and from his emanation, that which he desires, loves, and creates. Like Milton's last judgment, Los's casting out his spectre both imitates and, thereby, reveals the divine.

In the "eternal morning" of Blake's Eden, male and female love were joined in harmony ("VLJ," K 613) and "the same" (*J* 87:17, K 732). Because man and his emanation were separated into sexes in the "wars of Eden" ("Desc. Cat." K 578), in this world of generation, they are "opposite". The possession of one's emanation is necessary for self-unity; moreover, it is necessary for brotherhood, the unity of all people:

> When in Eternity Man converses
> with Man, they enter
> Into each other's Bosom
> (which are Universes of delight)
> In mutual interchange, and
> first their Emanations meet
> Surrounded by their Children;
> if they embrace & commingle,
> The Human Four-fold Forms
> mingle also in thunders of Intellect;
> But if the Emanations mingle not,
> with storms & agitations
> Of earthquakes & consuming fires
> they roll apart in fear;
> For Man cannot unite with Man
> but by their Emanations
> Which stand both Male & Female
> at the Gates of each Humanity.
> How then can I ever again
> be united as Man with Man
> While thou, my Emanation,
> refusest my Fibres of dominion?
> When Souls mingle & join
> thro' all the Fibres of Brotherhood
> Can there be any secret joy on Earth
> greater than this? (*J* 88:3-15, K 733).

To the last question, Blake answers that the fourfold joys of brotherhood exceed those of threefold sexual organization, which "must vanish & cease/ To be when Albion arises" (*J* 92:13-14, K 739), for "the human is fourfold" (*M* 4:5, K 483).

Toward this end, Los casts out his spectre, that doubt and fear which have separated him from his desired possessions. This last judgment, of the imagination, dramatically portrays Los's proper power, in one of the poem's most inspired and important passages:

> Go Spectre! obey my most secret desire

Which thou knowest without any speaking.
  Go to these Fiends of Righteousness,
Tell them to obey their Humanities
  & not pretend Holiness
When they are murderers. . . .
Go, tell them that the
  Worship of God is honouring his gifts
In other men: & loving
  the greatest men best, each according
To his Genius: which is the Holy Ghost in Man;
  there is no other
God than that God who is
  the intellectual fountain of Humanity.
He who envies or calumniates,
  which is murder & cruelty,
Murders the Holy-one. Go, tell them this,
  & overthrow their cup.
Their bread, their altar-table,
  their incense & their oath,
Their marriage & their baptism,
  their burial & consecration.
I have tried to make friends
  by corporeal gifts but have only
Made enemies. I never made friends
  but by spiritual gifts,
By severe contentions of friendship
  & the burning fire of thought.
He who would see the Divinity
  must see him in his Children,
One first, in friendship & love,
  then a Divine Family, & in the midst
Jesus will appear; so he who wishes
  to see a Vision, a perfect Whole,
Must see it in its Minute Particulars, Organized,
  & not as thou,
O Fiend of Righteousness, pretendest;
  thine is a Disorganized
And snowy cloud, brooder of tempests
  & destructive War.
You smile with pomp & rigor,
  you talk of benevolence & virtue;
I act with benevolence & Virtue

                    & get murdered time after time.
        You accumulate Particulars
                    & murder by analyzing, that you
        May take the aggregate,
                    & you call the aggregate Moral Law,
        And you call that swell'd & bloated Form
                    a Minute Particular;
        But General Forms have their vitality
                    in Particulars, & every
        Particular is a Man, a Divine Member
                    of the Divine Jesus (*J* 91:4-31, K 737-38).[171]

The subject of this triumphant passage is proper worship, and Blake's Los "overthrows" traditional Church rites to replace their unsatisfactory sacramental relation to God with the mental sacredness of both that which is worshiped and that which worships, or of creator and created; while the sacraments provide access to God for man, they also necessarily imply a prior and continuing separation between man and God. Blake takes the incarnation and the resurrection literally, and for him, once the Word was made flesh, every man partakes of the Word: "every / Particular is a Man, a Divine Member of the Divine Jesus."

Blake's Jesus is the source of salvation insofar as he is the eternal image of the human form divine, the *Logos* of whom Los is the temporal image. This difference from the traditional Christian concept of Jesus as the "only Son of God" is basic to Blake's religion, in which the "Imagination" is "the Divine Body in Every Man" ("Annot. Berkeley," K 773). Man and God were and shall be One when (and only when) man imagines and acts as Jesus, whose spirit is forgiveness and whose worship is loving him as he exists in other men because "there is no other/ God than that God who is the intellectual fountain of Humanity."

This identification means that "moral" and "aesthetic" imperatives are both mental and one for Blake:

        He who would see the Divinity
                    must see him in his Children,
        One first, in friendship & love,
                    then a Divine Family, & in the midst

Jesus will appear; so he who wishes to see
a Vision, a perfect Whole,
Must see it in its Minute Particles, Organized.

With this organized, or spiritual, innocence, dwells wisdom.[172]
Accordingly, Los smites his spectre, who would draw him
down into the abyss of demonstrations of the indefinite:[173]

Los beheld undaunted, furious,
His heav'd Hammer; he swung it round
& at one blow
In unpitying ruin driving down
the pyramids of pride,
Smiting the Spectre on his Anvil
& the integuments of his Eye
And Ear unbinding in dire pain,
with many blows
Of strict severity self subduing,
& with many tears labouring (*J* 91:
42-47, K 738).

Now asserting his sovereignty, Los authoritatively speaks with
God's voice of "honest indignation:

I care not whether a Man is Good or Evil;
all that I care
Is whether he is a Wise Man or a Fool.
Go, put off Holiness
And put on Intellect,
or my thund'rous Hammer shall drive thee
To wrath which thou condemnest
till thou obey my voice (*J* 91:55-59,
K 739).

This inspired speech reiterates Blake's insistence that previous
moral codes, "ideas of good and evil," are postlapsarian phenomena, the decaying fruits of the deadly Tree of Mystery
and Mortality. Yet Blake is one of the most "moral" of authors
in that he realizes that the provenance of "mortality" and of
"reality" is mental.[174]

Brothers-in-Love: Eternal Daybreak

No longer spectrally separated from his emanation, Los comforts her, and his "glad tidings" announce the *parousia:*

> Fear not, my Sons, this Waking Death;
>   he is become One with me.
> Behold him here! We shall not Die!
>   we shall be united in Jesus.
> Will you suffer this Satan,
>   this Body of Doubt that Seems but Is Not,
> To occupy the very threshold of Eternal life?
>   if Bacon, Newton, Locke,
> Deny a Conscience in Man
>   & the Communion of Saints & Angels,
> Contemning the Divine Vision & Fruition,
>   Worshipping the Deus
> Of the Heathen, The God of this World,
>   & the Goddess Nature,
> Mystery, Babylon the Great,
>   The Druid Dragon & hidden Harlot,
> Is it not that Signal of the Morning
>   which was told us in the Beginning?
> (*J* 93:18-26, K 741).

Most important in Blake's appropriation of Christianity is his identifying Jesus with Los, as do lines 18-19 of this plate, which "re-reads" thus: "Fear not, my sons, this Waking Death because [for;] he [Jesus] is become One with me./ Behold him [Jesus] here! We shall not Die! We shall [all] be united in Jesus."[175]

Being united with the Savior, Los's thunderous speech echoes Jesus' telling his disciples of the signs of the end of the world, in Matthew 24:3-24, which is here signaled by the appearance of Rahab, "Mystery, Babylon the Great, the Druid Dragon & the Goddess Nature," soon to be destroyed (Rev. 19:6). Indeed, these "negativing" disclosures render the battle between true and false religion absolute as history reaches its crisis and faces the last judgment, for "Time was Finished!" (*J* 94:18, K 742).

Though the end of the generated world commences like its beginning—"The Breath Divine Breathed over Albion" (*J*

94:18, K 742 and Gen. 1:2)—its end is radically different. The Orc cycle of fallen history, climaxed in Rahab, will shortly be destroyed in the *dies irae:* "The Breath Divine went forth over the morning hills. Albion rose/ In anger, the wrath of God breaking, bright flaming on all sides around" (*J* 95:2-3, K 742).

Albion takes up his golden Bow (whose constitution we shall consider shortly) and necessarily reintegrates his Four Zoas to their proper places (i.e., functions) so that he can authoritatively and completely perform the coming transfiguration. Of these Four "Mighty Ones," Blake typically most praises the all-powerful Urthona-Los, who unwearied labors and keeps "the Divine Vision in time of trouble." (*J* 30:15, K 655 and *J* 95:20, K 742). As we shall see on *J* 96, it is "Los's sublime honour" to preserve, literally, the image of redemption.

Blake's last things are mental and concern casting out error and receiving wisdom ("VLJ," K 612-13). Here Brittannia (the ancient name of England, and of Jerusalem and Vala jointly—*J* 36:27, K 663 and *J* 94:20, K 742) enters Albion's bosom rejoicing, so that he regains his "lost" (and hidden) emanation, through whom he may also be reunited with Jesus. Blake's "family tree of life" in *Jerusalem* delineates how man and Jesus become One Man, when, conversing with each other, "they enter/ Into each other's Bosom (which are Universes of delight)/ In mutual interchange and first their Emanations meet" (*J* 88:4-5, K 733).[176]

The genealogy of Blake's "great marriage" incorporates this loving-kindness of the emanation, for Jerusalem is both Albion's —and all men's (*J* 54:1-5, K 684)—emanation and Jesus' Bride. Albion, the collective body of persons, is reunited with his collective soul (*J* 95 and 96, K 742-43), and they are thus "gathered" "together unto the supper of the great God" (Rev. 19:8 and 17) in the resurrection: at last, Albion and Jesus become—as the phrase must be altered—brothers-in-love.

The Blakean Second Coming: Jesus-as-Los

As soon as Jerusalem enters Albion's bosom, "rejoicing," so that they may both be reunited with Jesus

Then Jesus appeared standing by Albion
as the Good Shepherd

By the lost Sheep that he hath found,
    & Albion knew that it
Was the Lord, the Universal Humanity;
    & Albion saw his Form
A Man, & they conversed as Man with Man
    in Ages of Eternity.
And the Divine Appearance was
    the likeness & similitude of Los
(*J* 96:3-7, K 743).

While the Christian pastoral images are unquestionably traditional (from John 10:11 and 14), they are incorporated to
delineate a characteristic Blakean gesture of finding and repos-
sessing what was formerly lost, as the illustrations on this plate
and on *J* 99 portray.[177]

Blake's description of Jesus centers on his identity as the imagination, of which Los is the "likeness & similitude." The following annotation to Swedenborg's *Divine Love* (written about
1789) glosses this sublime plate (*J* 96) and testifies to the
integrity of Blake's vision: "He who Loves feels love descend
into him & if he has wisdom may perceive it is from the Poetic
Genius, which is the Lord" (K 90). Here conversing with him,
when Albion diagnoses his sickness ("my deadly sleep of Six
Thousand years") as stemming from his serpentine and cruel
selfhood, he addresses Jesus as "my Divine Creator & Redeemer" (*J* 96:13, K 743). Blake focuses Jesus' prayer in John
17:21-23 on Jesus himself—"Μόνος ὁ Ιεςονς"—in whom God
and man are both "made perfect in one." As Jesus is the incarnate *Logos*—both the Creator and Redeemer, the Savior is
the incarnate imagination, or Los.

Jesus' definition of friendship and brotherhood, the *sine qua
non* of human existence, derives from his earlier teaching as John
records.[178] But this dialogue differs from that source in that
Blake locates the source of Christian love and forgiveness in the
"Divine Image."

First, Jesus comforts Albion that his (Jesus') death and resurrection are necessary to man's living together:

Fear not Albion:
    unless I die thou canst not live;
But if I die I shall rise again
    & thou with me,

This is Friendship, & Brotherhood:
without it Man is Not   (*J* 96: 14-16, K 743).

Throughout, Blake considers the atonement a pagan and wicked doctrine,[179] and the sacrificial death here spoken of refers to *every* person's (as symbolized by Albion) willingly giving himself for another, whereby both are saved. Blake differs from traditional Christian doctrine on this point, for he views Jesus' crucifixion *not* as the single and sufficient act of "atonement," *"qui tollis peccata mundi."*

Rather, Blake's Jesus is the eternal model and mode—the "Divine Analogy," to use Blake's appropriate phrase—for every man's "way" to redemption. When Jesus says "I am the way, the truth, and the life; no man cometh unto the Father, but by me" (John 14: 6), Blake interprets this identification to mean that "my example" is the way: through his continual *imitatio dei* man comes to salvation: "At that day ye shall know that I am in my Father, and ye in me, and I in you" (John 14: 20).

Man's transfiguration from the mortal to the immortal body and soul precedes this final union. Again the source in John clarifies Blake's "meaning" in Jesus' definition of the life of brotherhood:

> Verily, verily I say unto you, Except a corn of wheat fall into the ground and die, it abideth alone: but if it die, it bringeth forth much fruit (John 12: 24, and Matt. 10: 39).

Jesus conditional language in this and Blake's version ("except," "unless," and "but if," respectively) should not be read as hypothetical but as continually recurrent, like the forgiveness it postulates. Paul's beginning his definitive teaching of the resurrection in 1 Corinthians 15 with this image of regeneration locates its importance:

> that which thou sowest is not quickened, except it die: . . . so also is the resurrection of the dead. It is sown in corruption; it is raised in incorruption: It is sown in dishonour; it is raised in glory: it is sown in weakness; it is raised in power: It is sown a natural body; it is raised a spiritual body (15: 36–44).

In man's putting off, one for another, every sin by forgiveness in friendship, as Los does for Albion, though he may die, he shall rise again. Again, while Jesus defines the initial model— "I am the resurrection and the life: he that believeth in me, though he were dead, yet shall he live. And whosoever liveth and believeth in me shall never die" (John 11 : 25-26), Blake holds that to "believe this" is to live it. Thus Albion knowingly asks: "Cannot Man exist without Mysterious/ Offering of Self for Another? is this Friendship & Brotherhood?" (*J* 96 : 20-21, K 743).[180]

Blake's Jesus is both the model and mode of this redemptive giving oneself for another, as Albion's recognition of Jesus' identity illustrates: "I see thee in the likeness & similitude of Los my Friend" (*J* 96 : 22, K 743). This vision expands, by reversing, his earlier description ("The Divine Appearance was the likeness & similitude of Los") to complete the union of the human forms divine, for Jesus is Los and Los is Jesus; as Jesus is the eternal *Logos,* Los is his temporal ("shortened") form: "The Imagination is not a State: it is the Human Existence Itself" (*M* 32 : 32, K 522). Jesus represents the complete human and divine life because he is the "only" ("Μονος") way to Heaven—"I am the way, the truth, and the life; no man cometh unto the Father but by me" (*J* 4, K 622 and John 14 : 6). Jesus the imagination literally beholds perfection, wherein humans and God are reunited—"That they may be one, even as we are one: I in thee, and thou in me, that they may be made perfect in one" (John 17 : 22-23). The eternal origin of total forgiveness, which is our giving our life, in love, for a friend, is the human imagination divine: through it we identify ourselves wholly with all other life, also holy.

"The Divine Image": Love and Continual Forgiveness

This imaginative identification of man and man thereby annihilates the satanic selfhood, the covering cherub, who here darkly approaches to "overshadow" Albion.[181] What Jesus came to remove is this selfhood of separation, which blinds man to his eternal and communal body, as he asks Albion:

> Wouldest thou love one who never died
> For thee, or ever die for one
>   who had not died for thee?
> And if God dieth not for Man
>   & giveth not himself
> Eternally for Man, Man could not exist;

> for Man is Love
> As God is Love; every kindness
> to another is a little Death
> In the Divine Image,
> nor can Man exist but by Brotherhood
> (*J* 96:23-28, K 743).

This sublime speech echoes both Jesus' "great commandment, That ye love one another, as I have loved you. Greater love hath no man than this, that a man lay down his life for his friends" (John 15:12-13) and John's First Epistle:

> Hereby we perceive the love of God, because he laid down his life for us: and we ought to lay down our lives for the brethren. . . . He that loveth not knoweth not God; for God is love. In this was manifested the love of God toward us, because that God sent his only begotten Son into the world, that we might live through him. Herein is love, not that we loved God but that he loved us, and sent his Son to be the propitiation for our sins. Beloved, if God so loved us, we ought also to love one another. No man hath seen God at any time. If we love one another, God dwelleth in us, and his love is perfected in us (3:16 and 4:8–12).

Rather than depend on the traditional single "propitiation of our sins" in the crucifixion, Blake holds that "at-onement," whereby God and man are united in "love" as "in the beginning," and must continue throughout time (implied, in part, by using the present tense) and "eternally." This interpretation extends Jesus' model, of giving himself totally for man, from a single event, begun in the incarnation and "finished" in the crucifixion, to a never-ending mode of individual and collective existence (brotherhood); or, as Blake annotates Lavater (in 1788), "and consider that LOVE IS LIFE" (K 76). Further, "there is no Medium or Middle state"[182] between being a spiritual friend or enemy, for "every kindness to another [than the Divine Image] is a little Death." Further, this kindness to others involves a willing sacrifice (a "little Death") of our separate selfhood, since we cannot exist "but by Brotherhood." The origin and mode of the Christian love is the human imagination, which fully identifies all life with its holy essence and source (our "Divine Creator & Redeemer").

Albion's freely giving himself for Jesus illustrates how man is redeemed by imaginatively identifying with or, (to use the emotional form of this perceptual act) loving, "his Friend":

So saying the Cloud overshadowing
    divided them asunder.
Albion stood in terror,
    not for himself but for his Friend
Divine; and self was lost
    in the contemplation of faith
And wonder at the Divine Mercy
    & at Los's sublime honour   (*J* 96:29-32,
K 743).

The cause of Albion's fall was his turning his back on the Divine
Vision and thus separating himself and his proper possessions
from divinity, and his salvation involves eliminating the "overshadowing cloud" of the Selfhood, which isolates and destroys.
Albion's selfless terror for his Friend, Jesus as the Divine Mercy
and as Los,[183] causes the Selfhood to be "lost in the contemplation of faith." The provenance of this eschatological event is
mental ("contemplation").

Albion's Four Zoas' Resurrection and Revelation of Heavenly Unity

When Albion freely gives himself for his friend, he "brings
forth much fruit" and rises in the first, or spiritual, resurrection:

So Albion spoke & threw himself
    into the Furnaces of affliction.
All was a Vision, all a Dream:
    the Furnaces became
Fountains of Living Waters
    flowing from the Humanity Divine.
And all the Cities of Albion
    rose from their Slumbers, and All
The Sons & Daughters of Albion
    on soft clouds, waking from Sleep.
Soon all around remote
    the Heavens burnt with flaming fires,
And Urizen & Luvah & Tharmas
    & Urthona arose into
Albion's Bosom.
    Then Albion stood before Jesus in the Clouds

Of Heaven, Fourfold
    among the Visions of God in Eternity
(*J* 98:35-43, K 744).

Through his giving himself,[184] Albion and all his children are awakened from the mortal body of the selfhood, eternal death in the sleep of Ulro, to the immortal body of the divine humanity.

This transfiguration is a collective first resurrection, celebrated with the baptismal "fountains of Living Waters" in which man has washed off the "Not Human" (*M* 41:1, K 533). The individual, psychic content of Albion's transfiguration is the resurrection of his Zoas to their proper fourfold unity. The reintegrated and whole Albion now stands prepared for the last judgment at the break of "the Eternal Day" in the new heaven.

Instead of new Jerusalem's descending from God, she here awakes and rejoins Albion because Jerusalem is his emanation; this "repair" constitutes the reunion of the body and the soul. Further, because Jerusalem is also Jesus' Bride, Albion (all men) will be reunited with God as Albion and Jerusalem rise to the heavenly "great marriage." The initial "vision and fruition of the Holy-one" is thus fulfilled: "I am not a God afar off, I am a brother and a friend;/ Within your bosoms I reside, and you in me" (*J* 4:17-19, K 622).

But first the Selfhood, the last error of Mystery, must be finally destroyed as the Four Zoas now perform their proper functions. In "A Vision of the Last Judgment" Blake describes their "salutary and medicinal" function[186] like the four "beasts" of Revelation xv, 7:

> these I suppose to have the chief agency in removing the [former *del.*] old heavens & the old earth to make way for the New Heaven & the New Earth ("VLJ," K 612).

But rather than emphasizing the destruction of the material old world, Blake gives primary attention to the Zoas' destroying the mental cause of these fallen forms, namely the "Druid Spectre" of the Selfhood.

Blake's Satan is the "limit of opacity," he who is unable to transmit, reflect, or give (emanate) forth the Divine Vision, the Lord who is the everlasting light.[187] Generically Satan is error, which cannot be redeemed in all eternity (*VFZ*, N VIII:381, K 351), which must be cast out in the last judgment and utterly destroyed in the apocalypse.

Within the individual, the chief form of error is the selfhood, the spiritual separateness of selfishness, the cause of Albion's fall (*J* 4: 33-35, K 622, and *J* 74: 7 and 10-13, K 714); this spectre is propagated by the rationalizing tendency and haunts the psyche as the accuser of sin.[188] Within society and history, the chief forms of error are Deism and its philosophical twin, materialism; as collective mental perversions (*J* 89: 9-13, K 734) they are the whore, Rahab, "Mystery, Babylon the Great, the Abomination of Desolation,/ Religion hid in War, a Dragon red & hidden Harlot" (*J* 75: 19-20, K 716).

The satanic covering cherub is the Antichrist, (*J* 89: 10, K 734), who has divided Albion from Jesus (*J* 96: 17, K 743). As this last error of the selfhood is now cast out in the last, and fourfold judgment, and annihilated, the mystery of salvation is revealed and completed.

Since Blake's Jesus is the "giver of Every Mental Gift" (*J* 77, K 717), his Antichrist is the negation of this "intellectual fountain of Humanity" (*J* 91: 11, K 738) and is therefore annihilated with the "Arrows of Intellect" of the fourfold "Bow of Mercy & Lovingkindness" belonging to the transfigured Albion, in whom the Four Zoas are reunited in legitimate power and authentic glory (*J* 97-98, K 744-45). Primarily in thus identifying the Antichrist as spiritual separateness and in emphasizing the Zoas' annihilating him, Blake's apocalypse differs from the Biblical account of the destruction of the old world. Because every man is properly fourfold, this last collective judgment is also fourfold, with each of the Four Zoas harmoniously functioning and participating. What is evil and therefore must be destroyed is whatever separates man from his full perfection.

"All Human Forms Identified" in the Resurrected Divine Imagination

And what is finally revealed is the original unity of man and "all things in Heaven and Earth" (*J* 27, K 649) when the cosmos is humanized in the final resurrection of Albion's Four Zoas:

And every Man stood Fourfold;
    each Four Faces had: One to the West,
One toward the East, One to the South,

> One to the North, the Horses Fourfold,
> And the dim Chaos brighten'd beneath,
>   above, around: Eyed as the Peacock,
> According to the Human Nerves of Sensation,
>   the Four Rivers of the Water of Life. . . .
> . . . revealing the lineaments of Man,
> Driving outward the Body of Death
>   in an Eternal Death & Resurrection,
> Awaking it to Life among the Flowers of Beulah,
>   rejoicing in Unity
> In the Four Senses, in the Outline,
>   the Circumference & Form for ever,
> In Forgiveness of Sins which is Self-Annihilation;
>   it is the Covenant of Jehovah   (*J* 98:12-
> 23, K 745).

Thus individually unified fourfold, the Universal Family lives as One Man "in perfect harmony in Eden" (*J* 38:21, K 665). The "new Heaven" is finally realized in the fourfold city of God and man, "according to the wonders Divine/ of Human Imagination":

> The Four Living Creatures, Chariots,
>   of Humanity Divine Incomprehensible,
> In beautiful Paradises expand.
>   These are the Four Rivers of Paradise
> And the Four Faces of Humanity,
>   fronting the Four Cardinal Points
> Of Heaven, going forward,
>   forward irrestible from Eternity to Eternity. . . .
> And they conversed together
>   in Visionary forms dramatic which bright
> Redounded from their Tongues
>   in thunderous majesty, in Visions
> In new Expanses, creating exemplars
>   of Memory and of Intellect,
> Creating Space, Creating Time,
>   according to the wonders Divine
> Of Human Imagination. . . .
>   & every Word & Every Character
> Was Human . . . & they walked
> To and fro in Eternity as One Man,

reflecting each in each and clearly seen
And seeing . . . (*J* 98 : 24-40, K 745-46).

Likewise, the "new earth" is recreated as human in Blake's apocalypse of the imagination:

All Human Forms identified,
    even Tree, Metal, Earth & Stone; all
Human Forms identified, living,
    going forth & returning wearied
Into the Planetary lives of
    Years, Months, Days & Hours; reposing
And then Awaking into his Bosom
    in the Life of Immortality   (*J* 99 : 1-4,
K 747).

Blake's principal subject (either directly or indirectly) is his "words of eternal salvation," wherein man realizes the traditionally promised end of redemption (personally and communally) in the resurrection to the heavenly Jerusalem. Blake's incorporation of this motif delineates his development, which can be described in terms of the Bible as follows: from the Old Testament prophetic imperative of moral and social reformation (in the historical prophecies), through the intertestamental view of this renewal in the Messianic kingdom on earth (in the *Marriage* and the *Four Zoas*), to the New Testament "sacramental" transfiguration in a last judgment of the self in the first, or spiritual, resurrection (in *Milton*), to the apocalyptic transformation and communal, final resurrection (in *Jerusalem*).

Blake's originality and greatness reside in his fourfold "divine vision" of the source and mode of redemption. Man's "body" consists of the Four Zoas, and his "soul" (the *pneuma* or *anima*) is the emanation, through whom he is joined with other men and is finally reunited with God. For Blake the transfiguration to the immortal, spiritual body consists of man's reunion with the emanation and his reintegration of the Four Zoas to their original "perfect unity."

Blake's theology and psychology are both Christ-centered: "Μονος ὁ Ιεσονς." While the Christian name of the Savior is Jesus, his Blakean identity is the imagination: the contracted *Logos* is Los. Accordingly, man's "repair" is achieved through Los-Urthona's redemptive labors because he keeps the divine vision in this time of trouble by beholding and manifesting eternal perfection in "Works of Art" ("Laocoon," K 776).

The Christian resurrected body becomes synonymous for Blake with the imaginative body (*J* 77, K 717), for "Man is All Imagination. God is Man & exists in us & we in him" ("Annot. Berkeley," K 775). So united with and in the human image divine, we become a Universal Family of One Person—"Jesus the Christ . . . he is all in all" (*J* 38 : 20 and 24, K 665)—whose resurrected collective body and soul compose the envisioned brotherhood and sisterhood of Eden—the continual, mutual forgiveness of all sin in the complete liberty of heavenly Jerusalem.

NOTES: CHAPTER 3

1. William Blake, *Blake: Complete Writings with Variant Readings,* ed. Geoffrey Keynes (London: Oxford University Press, 1966), "A Vision of the Last Judgment," p. 604.

Hereafter the following system will be used for Blake notations. All quotations are from Keynes's edition unless otherwise stated, with supplements from my observations of original MSS, from facsimile editions, or from the Bloom and Erdman edition of *Blake: Poetry and Prose,* which will be further specified when cited.

The following abbreviations will be used: citations from the Keynes edition will identify (abbreviated) the work and line number (of long poems) followed by K and the page number, and will be included in text in parenthesis.

The following abbreviations of Blake's works will be used hereafter:

"Annot. Lavater"—Annotations to Lavater's "Aphorisms on Man"

"Annot. Swedenborg"—Annotations to Swedenborg's "Wisdom of Angels concerning Divine Love and Divine Wisdom"

"NNRa"—There is No Natural Religion, first and second series, "NNRb" respectively

"ARAO"—All Religions are One

SI—Songs of Innocence

SE—Songs of Experience

SIE—Songs of Innocence and Experience (combined)

FR—The French Revolution

MHH—The Marriage of Heaven and Hell

Amer.—America

Ur.—Urizen

Eur.—Europe

Los—Song of Los

VFZ—Vala, or The Four Zoas

"Annot. Watson"—Annotations to Watson's "Apology for the Bible"

"DLJ"—A Description of the Last Judgment

"Annot. Reyonlds"—Annotations to Reynolds's "Discourses"

M—Milton

"Desc. Cat."—Descriptive Catalogue
"PA"—Public Address
"VLJ"—A Vision of the Last Judgment
"Milton Illust."–Descriptions of the Illustrations to Milton's "L'Allegro and Il Penseroso"
J—Jerusalem
"EG"—The Everlasting Gospel
"GP"—For the Sexes: The Gates of Paradise
"Annot. Berkeley"—Annotations to Berkeley's "Siris"
"Laocoon"–The Laocoon
"Homer and Virgil"—On Homer's Poetry and on Virgil
"Ghost Abel"—The Ghost of Abel
"Annot. Wordsworth"—Annotations to the Poems by William Wordsworth
"Annot. Excursion"—Annotations to the Excursion by William Wordsworth
"Illust. Dante"—Notes on the Illustrations to Dante

2. See "VLJ," K 605, 613, 617; and *J* 69:25, K 707; and *J* 71:15-19, K 709, for examples.

3. See *Jerusalem Bible,* ed. Alexander Jones (New York: Doubleday and Co., 1965):

As he [Christ] is the Beginning he was the first to be born from the dead, so that he should be first in every way; because God wanted all perfection to be found in him (Col. 21:17–19).

"The word *pleroma* here . . . is defined as the 'divinity' that is actually 'filling' Christ now in his body; in other words, the risen Christ, through his incarnation and resurrection now unites the divine and the created" (*J.B.,* N.T., pp. 345–47).

4. "Introduction," *SE,* K 210; *VFZ,* N I:23, K 264; *J* 7:65, K 626; and "VLJ," K 614.

5. See *J* 24:23, K 647; *J* 49:12-31, K 679; and *J* 74:1-13, K 714, for examples.

6. See also "DLJ," K 444 and "Annot. Watson" (1798), K 389 and Letter, to George Cumberland, 12 April 1827, K 879 for the continuity of this belief. Traditionally Anglican doctrine and the sacraments rest on "the inward work of the Holy Spirit", see "Westminster Confession of Faith," 1643, art. 1, cited by Bettenson, Documents, p. 245. For Blake, however, the "Holy Spirit" is "none other than an Intellectual Fountain" (J 77, K 717; and J 91:11, K 738), so that grace (for him) originates from man's mind as it partakes of the divine creative fullness.

7. *J* 30:15, K 655 and *J* 95:20, K 742; see also *VFZ,* N III:103, K 294.

8. See also "Annot. Watson," K 395; "VLJ," K 616; *J* 49:75, K 680; *J* 61:21-26, K 694–95; *J* 63:27, K 697; *J* 64:24, K 699; *J* 88:50, K 734; *J* 96:14–32, K 743; *J* 98:23, K 746; "EG," K 754; "GP," K 761; and "Ghost Abel," K 781.

9. See Donne, *Ser.,* 6:277 and chap. 2, above.

10. In *Eur.* and *VFZ* Blake refers to "the" (last) judgment, and his concern with "a" last judgment becomes dominant in *Milton* (1804) and "A Vision of the Last Judgment" (1810).

11. See David Erdman, ed., *A Concordance to the Writings of William Blake* (Ithaca, N.Y.: Cornell University Press, 1967), 2:2286; and *M* 42:27, K 534.

12. See also "VLJ," K 605 and 607; "Desc. Cat.," K 579; *J* 27, K 649; and "Annot. Berkeley," K 774.

13. W. B. Yeats, *Essays and Introductions* (New York: Macmillan, 1961), pp. 137 and 112; see also pp. 131 and 139. Yeats's reinterpretations of Blake will be discussed at the beginning of chapter 4.

14. W. B. Yeats and Edwin Ellis, eds., *Works of William Blake, Poetic, Sym-*

bolic, Critical (London: Bernard Quaritch, 1893), 1:321; see also 2:168; hereafter abbreviated *Blake*.

15. See also John 10:17; 11:25–26; 14:6 and 15:11–13.

16. See also John 5:14, 25–26; 10:30; Matt. 5:48; James 1:4; and 1 John 2:5; 3:2 and 11–24; iv, 7–21; and v, 7.

17. "Annot. Berkeley," K 775; see also "Laocoon," K 775–77; and *VFZ*, N III:103, K 294; "VLJ," K 605; *J* 5:18–20, K 623; *J* 44:30–31, K 674; *J* 71:15–19, K 709; *J* 77, K 716–17; *J* 95:18–20, K 742.

18. See also *J* 91:8–11, K 738; "Illust. Dante" ("Imagination [is] the Holy Ghost"), K 785; Letter, to Dr. Trusler, 23 Aug. 1799, K 794; Letter, to James Blake, 30 Jan. 1803, K 822; "VLJ," K 613; and Letter to George Cumberland, 12 April 1827, K 878.

19. As in Rev. 21–22 and Augustine, *City of God*, Bk. XXII, chap. 29.

20. Letter, to Dr. Trusler, 23 Aug. 1799, K 793.

21. See John 1:1 and 14; and 1 John 3:2.

22. Though written about 39 years later, the spirit of each pronouncement is the same, I feel; see also "Annot. Lavater," nos. 14 and 16, K 66.

23. See Northrop Frye, "Blake's 'Introduction to Experience,'" *HLQ* 21 (1957): 57; see also David Erdman, *Blake: Prophet Against Empire*, rev. ed. (New York: Doubleday and Co., 1969), p. 105; hereafter abbreviated *PAE*. Northrop Frye, *Fearful Symmetry* (Boston: Beacon Press, 1962), pp. 4, 217–18, 269–70, and 415; hereafter abbreviated as *FS*. Hazard Adams, *William Blake: A Reading of the Shorter Poems* (Seattle: University of Washington Press, 1963), pp. 52–53; hereafter abbreviated *RSP*. Bernard Blackstone, *English Blake* (Cambridge: Cambridge University Press, 1949), p. 349; hereafter abbreviated *EB*. Margaret Bottrall, *The Divine Image* (Rome: Edizioni di Storià e letteratura, 1950), p. 11; hereafter abbreviated *DI*.

24. See *M* 30:1, K 518 and *M* 40:32–37, K 533; *J* 17:33–35, K 639; and *J* 48:13–14, K 677.

25. "Voice of the Ancient Bard," *SI*, K 126. See Harold Bloom and David Erdman, eds. *The Poetry and Prose of William Blake* (New York: Doubleday and Co., 1965), Erdman, "Textual Notes," p. 722; hereafter abbreviated *PPWB*. See also William Blake, *Songs of Innocence and Experience*, facsimile ed. copy Z, ed. and with commentary by Geoffrey Keynes (London and Paris: Blake Trust, 1967), "Introduction," p. xv, and "Commentary" without pagination to combined title page; hereafter abbreviated facs. *SIE, Z*. Citations followed by plate and line number will be included in text in parenthesis.

26. This configuration reappears in Blake's illustration of the child Jesus asleep on the cross as Mary looks on in fearful devotion; "The Christ Child Asleep on the Cross" is a tempera painting located in the Victoria and Albert Museum and is reproduced in Anthony Blunt, *The Art of William Blake* (New York: Columbia University Press, 1959), Plate 35a.

27. See 1 Cor. 13:12; and Adams: "the notion of bodies as clouds which shade the soul from light appears in both Plato and Dante." (*RSP*, p. 265) To this one must add that it is the natural, confined body (the *psychikon*) which shades and which must be removed so that man may live in the spiritual body; see Frye, *FS*, p. 212.

28. Keynes, "Comment." facs. *SIE, Z*, for Plate 18.

29. Blake's "human form divine" likely derives from Milton's "human face divine," of *Paradise Lost*, Bk. III, l. 44; Blake's change befits his concern with overall relationships, i.e., with total design.

30. See Keynes, "Comment." facs. *SIE, Z,* for Plate 28. See also S. F. Damon, *Blake Dictionary* (Providence: Brown University Press, 1965), p. 93; hereafter abbreviated *BD*. The phrase "covering cherub" derives from Ezek. 28:14 and 16, and Blake's use of it, especially in *Jerusalem* will be discussed.

31. In my discussion I am more concerned with Blake's vision of the resurrection—how we are to be saved—than with its contraries and negation, and accordingly I will emphasize the texts which deal specifically with this motif. This emphasis excludes a number of poems which deal with various forms of loss in experience, but I am more concerned with how man may regain his former, prelapsarian well-being and wholeness.

32. See, for example, "Frontispiece" to *Europe,* where Jehovah's act of encompassing the material world (with his left hand) is benign. Also "VLJ," K 614.

33. Milton repeats this plea in the context of "A Ready and Easy Way to Establish a Free Commonwealth," in *Prose of John Milton,* ed. Max Patrick (New York: Doubleday and Co., 1967), p. 550; hereafter abbreviated *PJM*.

34. In the context of Blake's use of the Biblical tradition, it is clear that "Tirzah" is not "vindictively" placed at the end, as Hirsch (mistakenly) feels; see E. D. Hirsch, *Innocence and Experience: An Introduction* (New Haven: Yale University Press, 1964), p. 159.

35. Other references to this eternal "day-break" occur in "Morning," K 421, *J* 87:11, K 732; *J* 93:26, K 741; and *J* 97:3, K 744.

36. "Earth's Answer," *PPWB,* p. 19, whose punctuation I prefer here; see also K 211 and facs. *SIE, Z,* 31:21–25.

37. Again, this earthly renewal belongs to the prophetic vision and differs from the destruction and re-creation on a new earth in the apocalypse. Here I think Adams, who is usually acute, misleadingly blurs the differences between the Old Testament prophetic speaker and the New Testament apocalyptic speaker of Revelation when he comments on the two poems', being transferred from *SI* to *SE:* "Here it is proper to state that the preamble seems to place the poem clearly among *SE,* since in it the Bard is concerned with an apocalypse" (*RSP,* p. 210). From one perspective, apocalypse means the total humanization of nature (see Frye, *Anatomy of Criticism,* pp. 119 and 136), as implied in "NNR" and in *MHH* and clearly stated at the end of *Jerusalem;* my comparison with these examples will indicate the difference between apocalyptic total humanization of nature and prophetic reciprocity between man and his environment.

38. Shortly afterwards Blake also refers to this chapter of Isaiah in *MHH* 3. For the Neoplatonic analogues, see Kathleen Raine, *Blake and Tradition* (Princeton: Princeton University Press, 1968), 1:126–55; hereafter abbreviated *BT*. See also Raine's essay, "The Little Girl Lost and Found," in *Divine Vision,* ed. Vivian de Sola Pinto (London: Gollancz, 1957), pp. 22–63; hereafter abbreviated *DV*.

39. See Isa. 67:4; also 60:1–4.

40. Blake's Eden, the Biblical heaven, will be further discussed. In the context of these poems, however, the illustrations to st. 1–10 of "TLGL" on Z 34 supports this distinction. As Keynes describes, "the girl with [embracing] her lover, is pointing up to the first prophetic stanzas, whence a bird [an "immense world of delight"] takes flight. The symbolic serpent turns away on the other side, frustrated by the truth of the Bard's prophecy" ("Comment.," facs. *SIE, Z,* for Plate 34). The lovers stand at the bottom right while the prophetic preamble and bird are not overshadowed by the tree of experience.

41. I thus disagree with Raine's reading of "Ah Sunflower!" as a Platonic, or Neoplatonic poem "in thought and in imagery"; see *BT* 1:218–19. That Vala appears brooding atop a sunflower on *J* 53, rather than making the "Sunflower" any more Platonic, later suggests the Christian aspiration of both poems.

42. See Matt. 22:30 and *J* 61:51, K 695.

43. The dating of this poem presents an unresolved problem, for opinions vary: from a date of 1795 (by Damon, *BD*, p. 407); 1796–98 and 1799–1801 (by Keynes and Edwin Wolf, *William Blake's Illuminated Books: A Census* (New York: The Grolier Club, 1953), pp. 52, 55, 57; hereafter abbreviated *IBC;* and K 894); to "probably following 1803 (ca.)" (by Erdman, "Dating Blake's Script: the 'g' hypothesis," *Blake's Newsletter* 3, no. 1 [15 June 1969]: 8–13). As the reader will see from consulting the above texts, the dating of this poem is unsettled, though Erdman's latest hypothesis ("probably following 1803 [ca.]") is probably a sound conjecture. Accordingly, I will consider the poem in terms of its appropriateness to the sequence and why it was placed virtually at the end of *SIE,* in spite of its date and previous locations.

44. "Thou art beautiful, O my love, as Tirzah, comely as Jerusalem, terrible as an army with banner" (Song of Sol. 6:4).

45. See also Mark 1:24; 5:7; John 7:6 and 30; 7:20. These passages suggest that the natural must be rejected until the hour of transfiguration "is come."

46. See "Tirzah," 1. 5 and *VFZ*, N VII:309, K 327 and "Desc. Cat.," K 578, for examples.

47. See *J* 77, K 717; and "Annot. Berkeley," K 773–75; "Annot. Wordsworth's Poems," K 78203; and "Ghost Abel," K 779.

48. See Erdman: "The text of Night IX cannot be dated closely enough to tell whether Blake had begun it before he moved from Lambeth, but it seems to have been completed before the announcement of peace in October 1801 (except for the first 89 lines, a later addition)" (*PAE,* p. 318). See also "Text. Notes," *PPWB*, pp. 737–39.

49. For discussions of Swedenborg's influence, see Martin Nurmi, *Blake's Marriage of Heaven and Hell* (Kent, Ohio: Kent State University Press, 1957); Raine, *BT;* for discussions of Boehme's influence, see Nurmi, Raine, and Desirée Hirst, *Hidden Riches* (New York: 1964). Here and elsewhere I am concerned with Blake's "own" incorporation of traditional elements.

50. While I realize that about 14 years separate these two statements, I think their conceptual similarity overrides this chronological difference.

51. See "Annot. Swedenborg," K 91; for Blake these are postlapsarian classifications.

52. As Blake pictures also, for example, in his illustration for Blair's *Grave,* entitled "The Reunion of the Soul and the Body," reproduced here as Plate 14. See also his observation that the loins are the place of the last judgment (*J* 30:38, K 656).

53. The historic and satiric elements have been discussed, notably in Erdman, *PAE,* pp. 175–92; and by Harold Bloom, *Blake's Apocalypse* (New York: Doubleday and Co., 1965), pp. 67–101; hereafter abbreviated *BA*. As Frye points out, however, "the great satirist is an apocalyptic visionary like every other great artist if only by implication" (*FS*, p. 200).

54. In this plate Blake refers to the following: the "ancient tradition" is the collection of apocalyptic predictions, based on Biblical and apocryphal texts (see Raine, *BT* 2:32–52). "Six thousand years" signifies the end of the created world,

which took six days to create in Genesis (see Gen. 2:2–3, Exod. 20:11, and 2 Pet. 3:8) ; after the exile from Eden, God placed the cherub to guard the tree of life, as narrated in Genesis iii, 24; the cherub recurs in Ezek. 28:11–16, whom Blake later calls the covering cherub of the selfhood and associates him with Satan (*M* 9:51–52, K 490) and is finally annihilated in the apocalypse (*J* 98:6, K 745).

55. See *VFZ*, N I:24, K 264; *M* 19:17, K 500; *M* 34:37, K 524; *J* 59:12, K 691; and *J* 97:10, K 744. Although Tharmas is not so named until about 1796–97, in *VFZ*, N I:24, K 264, his symbolic significance is here announced.

56. Letter, to Dr. Trusler, 23 Aug. 1799, K 793; see also Letter, to George Cumberland, 6 Dec. 1795, K 790.

57. See also Blake's belief as recorded by H. Crabb Robinson: " 'We are all co-existent with God; members of the Divine Body, and partakers of the Divine nature' " (quoted from Robinson's *Literary Remains* in *William Blake,* ed. Alfred Kazin [New York: Viking Press, 1940], p. 680) ; hereafter abbreviated *Blake.*

58. See also "Annot. Lavater, nos. 549 and 552," K 82 and *J* 91:11, K 738.

59. See also "VLJ," K 611; and *J* 44:31, K 674.

60. See Mal. 4:5.

61. See Erdman, "Text. Notes," *PPWB,* p. 723 and *PAE,* pp. 137–38.

62. See *MHH* 25–26, vv. 1, 8, and 13, K 159; see also the illustration of the event on the left, bottom of Plate 3.

63. See *MHH* 27, K 160; and "Annot. Lavater, K 74; and *VFZ,* N II:366, K 289.

64. Here as throughout I am most interested in the symbolic content of Blake's work, and accordingly I will not emphasize the historical-political content, for which the reader may consult Erdman's thorough *PAE.* And, in spite of all the background this kind of study provides, it is questionable how complete is the correspondence between historical events and Blake's mythological representation of them, as Frye observes: "The 'states' Blake deals with can seldom be identified with the very mixed elements of a political event: to do this either blurs the imaginative pattern or falsifies history" (*FS,* p. 204; see also Bloom, *BA,* p. 165; and Erdman, *PAE,* pp. 148–49).

65. And in more logical and less "imaginative" terms than Blake later uses; see *FR:* 90–94, K 142–43. Since, Orleans reasons, the necessary imaginative identification is impossible, men must treat each other as brothers—separate, but equal.

66. Though this identification is not made explicit until about four years later, at the beginning of *VFZ,* N I:24, K 264, I think it pertains to Blake's political use of the motif here.

67. Keynes and Wolf, *IBC,* p. 41; for the appellation "resurrected man," see, for example, S. F. Damon, *William Blake: his Philosophy and Symbols* (Boston: Houghton Mifflin Co., 1924), p. 328; hereafter abbreviated *PS.*

68. The text and illustration do coincide, but ironically on this plate, though this arrangement is not always the case.

69. See Rev. 21–22:5.

70. Keynes and Wolf, *IBC,* p. 41; my additions from observations of copies A and C. There is general agreement, as Damon comments, that while the text ends with America in the midst of revolution, "the pictures, however, end with the state of Experience as yet unrelieved" (*PS,* p. 341; see also Bloom, *BA,* p. 136).

71. See also Blake's illustration "Jacob's Ladder," where this spiral ascent to heaven is portrayed.

72. The numerical symbolism here, in which three is associated with the body and Satan, probably derives from Daniel (as Bloom notes, *BA,* p. 170); see also Letter, to Thomas Butts, 22 Nov. 1802, 11. 83–88, K 818.

73. Erdman, *PAE,* p. 243.

74. One source for these last lines from *Song Los* may be Ezekiel's vision of the valley of dry bones (also illustrated by Blake), Ezek. 37.

75. See William Blake, *Vala, or the Four Zoas, a Facsimile of the MS and a transcript of the poem and a study of its growth and significance,* by G. E. Bentley (Oxford: Clarendon Press, 1963), pp. 157–66 and 170; hereafter abbreviated facs. *VFZ.* For corroboration on the dating, see also K 263 and 897–98 and Erdman, "Text. Notes," *PPWB,* pp. 737–39. I have first studied through this colossal facs., while continuing to quote from Keynes, with exceptions and supplements as noted; further references indicate the Night (I–IX) followed by line number and K plus page number and will be included in text in parenthesis, as usual.

76. Bentley, facs. *VFZ,* p. 174; see also pp. 163–65; italics mine; see also Erdman, "Text. Notes," PPWB, pp. 737–38 and K 578.

77. The question "what light does this later Christianization of the poem shed on its earlier versions and on Blake's other 'unbaptized' poems?" will be answered primarily in relation to the two major epics, which follow. Basically *Milton* and *Jerusalem* present man's resurrection to personal and communal unity as a continual imitation of Jesus' giving himself for others through the imagination's divine mercies of redemption. As for the earlier, less Christian sections of *VFZ* itself, I think it is not possible to be certain of their critical relevance because the MS is unfinished and had the MS not been abandoned, Blake might have made more additions or reorganizations.

78. I am here using "prophetic" after Blake's use of the word in the pronouncement: "Every honest man is a Prophet; he utters his opinion both of private and public matters. Thus: If you go on So, the result is So. He never says, such a thing will happen let you do what you will. A Prophet is a Seer" ("Annot. Watson," K 392).

79. That Los is the contracted form of the *Logos* is implied in the revisions of the MS and specific in *Jerusalem,* where Jesus (the Son) and Los (the Sun) are the very "likeness & similitude" of each other: see also Rev. 21:23–22:5.

80. As also the ancient Bard sings in the "Introduction" to *SE;* and see *M* 24:72–73, K 510 and "VLJ," K 614.

81. See also Job 28:9–15 and 20–28. I refer readers to the whole passage of the end of Night II, especially those who question Blake's own "experience" or doubt his "relevance."

82. See also *M* 13:20–21, K 494 and *J* 35:1–2, K 662.

83. See Dan. 3:19; *VFZ,* N IX:827ff, K 379; *J* 53:15ff, K 684, and *J* 60:5, K 692.

84. John Milton, *Paradise Lost* (New York: Odyssey Press, 1937), Bk. 2, 11. 650–80.

85. I refer to VIIb (in Keynes's designation, K 320), which is, however, Bentley's and Erdman's VIIa. Keynes, Bentley, and Erdman thus disagree about which version is earlier or later. Keynes notes that "VIIb was probably written later (K 320), whereas Erdman notes that "of the two nights this [VIIa] is most probably the later, meant at one time to replace the other (VIIb)" ("Text. Notes," *PPWB,* p. 755). However, Bentley, in his thorough facs. ed., says that "VIIb was written later than VIIa" (facs. *VFZ,* p. 163).

86. Los "beheld the Center open'd' by Divine Mercy inspired" and builds Golgonooza in the nether heavens of Beulah, for beneath

> Was open'd new heavens & a new Earth
>   beneath & within,
> Threefold, within the brain, within the heart,
>   within the loins:
> A Threefold Atmosphere Sublime, continuous
>   from Urthona's world,
> But yet having a Limit Twofold
>   named Satan & Adam (*VFZ* N VII: 374 and

380–84, K 329).

The implication of these lines is somewhat puzzling if taken literally, for the new heaven and earth traditionally appear after the apocalyptic destruction of the old earth, in what Blake earlier called the fourfold consummation in "mental fires," whereas the setting here is still in the natural, threefold world; I think, however, that this description must be read from the temporal Beulah, not from the perspective of the eternal Eden.

87. This intimate relation between the erotic and the artistic—in Beulah (sexual love) comes the moment of inspiration—receives more therapeutic emphasis in *Milton,* as illustrated on Plate 30 C–42 D.

88. This incident probably derives from 2 Kings 4:35, where Elisha raises the Shunammite's son, whose seven sneezes announce his return to life.

89. This description of Jesus' immanence probably derives from Rev. 21:23–24, although this vision in Golgonooza, the city of art, here precedes and also anticipates the apocalypse and incarnation, which follow as the Lamb of God appears "clothed in Luvah's robes" (*VFZ*, N VIII:61, K 342).

90. In *VFZ,* however, her full identity as Jesus' Bride and Albion's emanation (all men's soul) is not realized, as finally in *Jerusalem.*

91. Bentley transcribes the deleted reading here: "but first to rent(?) the Veil of Mystery" (facs. *VFZ,* p. 110).

92. See also the dicta that "spirits are Organized Men" ("Desc. Cat.," K 577) and "Unorganiz'd Innocence: An Impossibility. Innocence dwells with Wisdom, but never with Ignorance" ("Note written on pages of *VFZ*," K 380).

93. The name Rahab derives from Joshua 2:1, where she is a harlot; Tirzah, as I have noted, is from Song of Sol. 6:4, and for Blake, she represents physical beauty whose possessor however, naturally rages into a whore.

94. Blake's repetition of this "intellectual" conflagration on the next page (119) of the MS, as well as in later works, such as the opening lyric of *Milton,* is but a "rough" indication of its great importance.

95. This passage may well have inspired, and is analogous to, Yeat's "Byzantium."

96. The marginal reference to Eph. 3:10 reads "To the intent that now unto the principalities and powers in heavenly places might be known by the church the manifold wisdom of God."

97. The parable of the sower, whose mighty example is Jesus; see Matt. 3:12.

98. See Bettenson, *Documents,* pp. 147–48, 207, 211, 264, and 304. See also chap. 1 n. 77. This eschatological symbolism may derive from Blake's literal interpretation of Jesus' promise to change the mortal into the immortal: "whoso eateth my flesh, and drinketh my blood, hath eternal life; and I will raise him up at the last day" (John 6:54).

99. As Kathleen Raine has documented in *BT*, I, frontis. and 181–95; see also "Auguries of Innocence," 1. 39 (K 432), where the moth and butterfly are also associated with the last judgment. The Jewish mystics, as well as classical (Greek) iconographers, portrayed the soul (*psyche*) as a winged butterfly, in the eschatological paintings in the Dura-Europos temple. Yeats's calling "wisdom a butterfly" (in "Tom O'Roughley") continues this tradition.

100. I have omitted the "s" in "form" in 1. 613 since, though Keynes prints the word in the plural, neither Bentley nor Erdman does, and from looking at the facs. MS, I can see no clear "s."

101. As discussed in chap. 1. I have seen only one of Blake's five illustrations to the *Book of Enoch*, trans. 1821 and illustrated by Blake c. 1822; see Geoffrey Keynes, ed., *Drawings of William Blake: 92 Pencil Studies* (New York: Dover Publications, 1970), Plate 84, "The Angels and the Daughter of Man." Though this drawing does not illuminate the *Four Zoas* text under consideration, Blake was able to read Hebrew by 30 Jan. 1803 (see Letter, to Jas. Blake, K 821), although I doubt that he could read the original Ethiopic.

102. See Bentley:

the evidence of the revisions of Vala clearly indicates that Blake was only gradually convinced of the applicability of the Christian myth to his own prophecies. At first he began with Christian parallels . . . but slowly the changes became more central. Finally, he introduced a directing agency external to the Four Zoas ("the Council of God") which effected a profound change upon the meaning and direction of this poem (facs. *VFZ*, p. 163).

Of Night VIII, the last portion worked on (from 1805–10?), Bentley deduces that "it seems probable therefore, that these late passages were first written in *Jerusalem* and then transferred to *Vala*. All the additions referred to may at least be associated in time, from their use in *Jerusalem*, as well as from their common Christian subject matter." In terms of the different handwriting styles, "the pages of Blake's copperplate hand in Nights I–III are covered with additions of a Christian tenor. He made no changes of this kind, however, in the body of the next five Nights. . . . Certainly it is curious that the middle Nights were never brought into conformity with the Christianity of the Nights at either end of Vala" (*ibid.*, p. 165).

103. Letter, to Thomas Butts, 25 April 1803, K 823; see also K 927, Frye *FS*, p. 314, Damon, *BD*, p. 275, and Erdman, "Text. Notes," *PPWB*, p. 727–28.

104. Virtually the same hope is expressed in his last significant letter, to George Cumberland, on 12 April 1827, which ends: ". . . to get into Freedom from all Law of the Members [from the Vegetable body] into the Mind, in which every one is King & Priest in his own House. God send it so on earth as it is in Heaven" (K 879).

105. See "EG," and its "Supplementary Passages, K 757; and "Prologue," for "GP," K 761; also "Laocoön," K 775.

106. See Erdman, "Text. Notes," *PPWB*, pp. 727–28; and *M* 36:21–25, K 527. There are 51 plates in all, arranged in 2 books, instead of the originally intended 12, with 8 beautiful full-page illustrations.

107. See John Milton, *Paradise Regained* (New York: Odyssey Press, 1937), Bk. 4, ll. 311–64.

108. The commanding images of st. 3 portray the traditional second coming of Jesus (Rev. 14:14 and "DLJ," K 444, and "VLJ," K 609 and 613) according to Blake's "infinite desire."

109. *PJM,* p. 238.

110. Blake states this result and its alternative in his own religion tractates; see, for example, "NNRb," K 98.

111. Northrop Frye, "Notes for a Commentary on *Milton,*" *DV,* p. 103.

112. See *M* 15:49, K 497; *M* 21:4, K 503; and Letter, to Thomas Butts, 25 April 1803, K 823.

113. See Blake's illustration no. 11 to Milton's "Il Penseroso," in which Milton is surrounded by six spirits, his sixfold emanation of his six female loves (three wives and three daughters).

114. See *M* 3:3-4, K 482 and *Paradise Lost,* Bk. 8, ll. 590–91.

115. See also Rev. 5:12-13 and *J* 44:31, K 674. This authenticity will be further discussed in the conclusion.

116. As a narrative, *Milton* stretches out this moment of inspiration—"a pulsation of the artery"—in the brief epic form.

117. See also *M* 21:4-5, K 503 and plates 14 C-17 D. Plate 29 C-32 D is entitled "WILLIAM," a full-page illustration of this intensely personal moment; Blake, naked except for under-shorts, leans back with arms outstretched, in cruciform position, to receive Milton-as-star in his left (representing the material) foot, which is stepping forward. In the background are three stone steps, presenting threefold Beulah, and from which spreads a cloud of black smoke (*M* 15:50, K 497), which indicates the dark error of Puritan sexual repression. See also the companion plate for Robert, 33 C-37 D.

118. See the equally august illustration of the influx of inspiration, on *M* 43 C-47 D, reproduced here as Plate 8; in its original colors with gold additions (in overlay), this picture "fierce glows" with the "bright visions of eternity." That this union of Los and Blake takes place in Udan-Adan, the formless bottom of existence, implies that even Ulro can be transformed in the apocalypse.

119. See Zech. 4:10 and Rev. 1:4 and 20; 3:1; 4:5; and 5:6. These seven await completion in the Eighth Eye, or Eighth Man, Jesus, who unites man and God; see *M* 15:4, K 496; *J* 55:33, K 686; and *Blake's Job: William Blake's Illustrations to the Book of Job,* ed. and with commentary by S. F. Damon, (Providence, R. I.: Brown University Press, 1966), title page and illustration on Plate 13, p. 37; hereafter abbreviated *Job.* Damon comments that "the true God . . . is Jesus, the Divine Imagination, and the Forgiveness of Sins: the only God whom Blake recognized" (*ibid.,* p. 36). See also Northrop Frye:

> The true God for Blake is the creative imagination of man, the eternal Jesus whose religion is the Everlasting Gospel. . . . Job's progress, as Blake sees it, is from a God projected into the sky . . . to the recovery or resurrection of this God in Job's own mind.

"Blake's Reading of Job," *William Blake: Essays for S. F. Damon,* ed. Alvin Rosenfeld (Providence, R. I.: Brown University Press, 1969), pp. 228-29; hereafter abbreviated *ED.*

120. See "Annot. Reynolds," K 470 and 474.

121. See Rom. 6:4 and *J.B.,* N.T., pp. 276-77. For a fuller discussion of this matter, see chap. 1.

122. The Polypus is the aggregate, chaotic body of error found in the fallen world of Ulro; for Milton it derives from his shadowy, suppressed desire.

123. From this fundamental error stem the twelve gods of false mythologies and false worship, or the twenty-seven churches (each named after its founder),

whose number is the epitome of satanic error (three cubed). For a full commentary, see Bloom, "Comment.," *PPWB*, pp. 840–41 and Damon, *PS*, pp. 426–27.

124. See *M* 39:10–40:36, K 530–33; see also the passage in "Areopagitica" beginning "Methinks I see in my mind a noble and puissant Nation rousing herself like a strong man after sleep and shaking her invincible locks" (*PJM*, p. 324).

125. Traditionally baptism celebrates man's initial transfiguration "in the spirit" from the mortal, corruptible *psychikon* to the immortal, incorruptible *pneumatikon*: "if the Spirit of him that raised up Christ from the dead shall also quicken your mortal bodies by his Spirit that dwelleth in you" (Rom. 8:11).

126. Ezek. 26:31–33; Isa. 25:6; Matt. 27:51; Heb. 10:19; see also *VFZ*, N VIII:255–56; *M* 37:40, K 528; "VLJ," K 613; and *J* 75:15–22, K 716.

127. See *M* 13:26, K 494; *M* 26:36, K 512; *J* 59:25, K 691; *J* 73:1, K 713; and *J* 83:72, K 728.

128. See *M* 41:37 and 42:1–2, K 534; and *J* 1, K 620 Speaking of the emanation's wisdom, Frye notes that "although the object of Milton's journey is to seek Ololon, Ololon in fact seeks him" ("Notes for a Commentary on *Milton*," *DV*, p. 136). This same motif appears in Blake's engraving "The Reunion of the Soul and the Body" for Blair's *Grave* (1808) and in "The Agony in the Garden," for examples; that the soul seeks and possesses the body is part of the unique blessing of the resurrection.

129. See n. 119. As the seven days of creation, or, lengthened, the seven ages of man in experience, they are transformed by the eighth day, or age, which is traditionally God's eternal sabbath. See Augustine, *CG*, Bk. 22, chap. 30, and Spenser's "Mutabilitie Cantoes." See also Damon, *BD*, p. 134; and Frye, "Notes . . . *Milton*," *DV*, pp. 109 and 126–27; and *FS*, pp. 401 and 448–49.

130. See *J* 4:7–21, K 622; "EG," l. 75, K 752; and "Annot. Berkeley," K 775.

131. This "intellectual battle" has continued for ("the woof of") six thousand years, after which, in the old tradition referred to in the *Marriage*, Plate 14, the world will be destroyed in fire.

132. See "VLJ," K 616. Milton also believed in the last judgment of the body and soul together; see *Christian Doctrine*, Bk. 1, chap. 33.

133. See Blake's "Milton Illustrations": "The Lark is an Angel on the Wing . . . The Earth beneath awakes at the Lark's Voice" (K 618); see also this delightful illustration.

134. As the twenty-eight larks suggests, one returns each morning (counting a month as twenty-eight days), and they together (as twenty-eight, a number of the totality for Blake) form the continuous presence of the Holy Spirit in time.

135. It is questionable if there is a period at the end of the poem; it does not appear in copy D or C, and I prefer to omit it here, since the end is now opened.

136. See S. F. Damon, *A Note on the Discovery of a New Page of Poetry in William Blake's Milton* (Boston: Club of Odd Volumes, Merrymount Press, 1925), pp. 12–13 and Keynes and Wolf, *IBC*, pp. 100–101.

137. This iconography and Milton's descent and first resurrection illustrate Jesus' example of redemptive transmutation: "Except a corn [grain] of wheat fall into the ground and die, it abideth alone: but if it die, it bringeth forth much fruit" (John 12:24; see also Matt. 10:39 and 1 Cor. 15:36).

138. Although the original picture which the prose piece describes is lost, there are two other versions on the same subject; one is located in the National Gallery in Washington and is reproduced in Damon's *BD*, and the other is in the Petworth

collection in England and is reproduced in Erdman's *PPWB*. For a short discussion of their differences, see Damon, *BD*, p. 437; however, I am here most interested in Blake's prose remarks and will "draw on" the picture only in passing.

139. See also "Annot. Reynolds," K 477; and "PA": "To recover Art has been the business of my life. . . . Imagination is My World; this world of Dross is beneath my Notice" (K 600); and Letter, to Dr. Trusler, 23 Aug. 1799, K 793-94 and Letter, to George Cumberland 12 April 1827, K 878-79.

140. See Prov. 9:5; and the earlier "Description": "On the right hand of the Throne of Christ is Baptism. On his left is the Lord's Supper: the two introducers into Eternal Life" ("DKJ," K 444).

141. Thus, for example, Allan Cunningham writes that Blake "considered the Jerusalem to be his greatest work. . . ." This excerpt is from Cunningham's *Lives of the Most Eminent British Painters, Sculptors, & Architects,* 6 vols., 2nd ed. (London: Oxford University Press, 1830, 2:143-88; it is quoted by G. E. Bentley, ed., *Blake Records,* Oxford: Oxford University Press, 1969, p. 490; hereafter abbreviated *BR*.

142. They were originally designated as "XXVIII Chapters" (K 620), probably intended to represent the traditional twenty-four Elders and the Blakean Four Zoas, or the twenty-eight cities of Albion and Jerusalem, around God's throne, as in Rev. 4:4 and 6; in any case, twenty-eight is a number of heavenly completeness for Blake (see Frye, *FS*, pp. 368-69 and 378-79, for example).

143. This passage appeared in *The London Magazine,* 1 (September 1820): 301. See also Damon, *BD*, p. 209 and Bentley, *BR*, pp. 265-66.

144. "Annot. Reynolds," K 459; see also Frye, *FS*, pp. 205, 217-18, and 414-28; Frye, "Blake," *English Romantic Poets and Essayists,* ed. Carolyn and Laurence Houtchens (New York: New York University Press, 1957), pp. 18-20; Bottrall, *DI*, pp. 7 and 116; Hirst, *HR*, p. 320; Erdman, *PAE*, p. 160; and Adams, *RSP*, p. 38, for examples of Blake's unity.

145. See also Exod. 14:17; Isa. 66:15; Heb. 13:29; and Blake's inscription on Hervey's "Meditations among the Tombs": "God out of Christ is a Consuming Fire" (*Concordance* 2:2315).

146. Jesus' traditional seven "last words" are: 1) "Father, forgive them, for they know not what they do" (Luke 23:34); 2) "Woman, behold thy Son" (John 19:26); 3) "Behold thy Mother" (John 19:27); 4) "Verily, I say unto thee, Today shalt thou be with me in Paradise" (Luke 23:43); 5) "Eli, eli lama sabachthani?" (Matt. 27:46; Mark 15:34); 6) "I thirst" (John 19:28; and 7) "It is finished" (John 19:30). "Father, unto thy hands I commend my spirit" (Luke 23:46).

147. It is important to note the consistency of this image in Blake's illustrations as well. Even in the pictures of the crucifixion, of which there are relatively few, Jesus' expression is not so much one of absolute suffering—man, *sub specie temporis*—as is found in both western and eastern iconography of the crucifixion, but rather, it seems to me, one of patient knowledge of redemption—man, *sub specie aeternitatis*.

In the two compassionate drawings of Jesus' crucifixion in the MS of *VFZ* (N VIII, pp. 111 and 115, as numbered by Bentley in the facs. ed.), for example, Christ appears with big nails in his two hands and left (representing the agony of the material man) foot among the flames of creative purgation ("the God of Fire") looking down, at (fallen) man, with an expression of total sympathetic understanding.

I am sorry that I cannot include these and the two triumphant illustrations of

Jesus' resurrection (N VIII, pp. 114 and 116, in Bentley's facs. *VFZ*) in the spiritual body glorious.

Of Jesus as "the likeness & similitude of Los" Wicksteed comments that

One sees two pages later the face [of Jesus] in profile where "One stood forth from the Divine Family & said" (Plate 33, l.1), but a few lines lower down the words are attributed to LOS. "So Los spoke" (Plate 33, l. 10). And it is only on the next page that this agent of the saving process LOS is himself seen in "the Divine Similitude" (see Plate 34, ll. 10–13). [note that the two plates which Wicksteed here refers to the corresponding to Plates 37 and 38 in Keynes's numbering].

Joseph Wicksteed, *William Blake's Jerusalem: A Commentary* (London: Blake Trust, 1954), p. 200; hereafter abbreviated *JC*.

And on *J* 76 (in copies C, D, and F) Jesus looks less tormented than expectant, as Albion, also in cruciform position, imploringly prepares to imitate him; this same expression occurs in Blake's illustration to *Paradise Lost*, Bk. 12, "Michael Fortells the Crucifixion." Wicksteed's comment on *J* 76 C is also interesting:

On pl. 76 the great engraving of ALBION worshipping the Crucified Christ, we do indeed see the face, but the name 'Jesus' has been in most copies obliterated, possibly because it represents the Christ in Death rather than as the living LOGOS that dwells in all humanity, and in any case it seems to be the revelation to ALBION of what he himself in his sleep of Death has made of the Saviour (*ibid.*, pp. 200–201).

This plate (copy D) is reproduced as Plate 4.

And of *J* 99 Wicksteed interprets the scenario as Jesus' descending into hell to redeem man:

It is in the Stirling copy alone that he is clearly seen as the Saviour—as one burdened with the whole of human grief and guilt. His halo is no longer a mighty Sun more powerful than the flames of Hell, but a few dazzling spears of light, flashed upon the blackness of a stygian night shot with dark peacock shades of beauty[1] [note: the note designated by this "1" reads:] 1. It must be remembered that according to Christian doctrine Jesus descended into Hell at his death not only to save Adam and the patriarchs, but, as Milton implies in *Paradise Lost,* to save God himself from Satan's wiles. This is particularly emphasized in Blake's illustration to the passage in *Paradise Lost* in which the Son offers to take upon himself the penalty imposed by Divine Providence upon Adam (Bk. 3, ll. 227 ff) (*ibid.*, pp. 249–50).

If I may offer a conservative counter-interpretation of the illustration on *J* 99, I think it portrays the reunion of God and his Bride (a patriarchial Jesus and Jerusalem) in the apocalyptic flames of the new creation; in the only colored copy (E), belonging to Mr. Mellon, the divine figure has a blue halo, Los's color of poetic inspiration; the black and white copy (D) of this consummate plate is reproduced here as Plate 16.

148. "These words [of Matt. 28:18] in which the infallible king himself announces the possession of the kingdom, St. Matthew, who is essentially the historian of the kingdom, alone records." Rev. A Carr, *The Gospel According to St. Matthew* (Cambridge: 1888), p. 319.

149. For the unity of the Father and the Son, see John 10:30; and 1:1–14; 10:38, 14:6, 10–11, and 20; and 17. For Jesus' "power over all flesh," see John 17:2–3. See also Luke 4:8; John 5:44; 1 Tim. 1:17; Jude 25; and Rev. 5:12–13.

150. For an early statement (c. 1788) of this belief, see "Annot. Lavater," K 87; for late aphorisms to the same effect, see "EG," K 750 and "Annot. Berkeley," K 773–75.

Consulting the *Concordance* one finds that Blake never uses the more Johannine phrase "Human Divinity," whereas he always makes "Humanity" the noun and "Divine" the adjective, whether hyphenated as "Divine-Humanity" (used only twice, on *J* 43:20, K 672 and *J* 70:19, K 709) or "Divine Humanity," or the less frequent, reversed "Humanity Divine." Blake's distinct preference for the final substantive human form of the divine, and this total human form of the redeemed cosmos appears in the apocalypse, as on *J* 99.

151. See *J* 7:30–41, K 625–26; in contrast to his earlier treatment of their fall in *VFZ,* here Blake is more concerned with Albion's fall as the cause of their downward disruption.

152. *J* 13:6, K 633; see also Gen. 3:24; and *MHH* 14, K 154.

153. Yeats frequently refers to these bright halls as containing the artist's metaphors, i.e., the "marbles of the dancing floor" which "break bitter furies of complexity"; however, his attitude toward "Byzantium" differs, as will be discussed in chap. 4.

154. See also *M* 32, K 521–22, and Rom. 12:19.

155. See, for example, "Annot. Watson," K 395; and "EG" (Supplementary Passages) K 757.

156. See *J* 24:23, K 647; *J* 31:2, K 656; *J* 33:1, K 659; *J* 54:7, K 685; and *J* 74:7, K 714.

157. See also 1 John 1:5 and 3:2.

158. See *J* 1 and the inscription on the right-hand side of the archway, K 620; *J* 38:39, K 665; *J* 48:56, K 678; and John 15:12–13.

159. *J* 37:11, K 664. See Wicksteed, *JC,* p. 200 and n. 147.

160. Lines 17–21 of this plate were added to *VFZ,* N I:470–75, K 277, and the Zoaic and divine unity of man which concerns both works is elaborated in *Jerusalem* in Los. The traditional image of Jesus as the "good shepherd" derives from John 10:11 and 14. Whereas Paul teaches that God is "all in all" (1 Cor. 15:28), and Augustine concurs that "He shall be the end of our desires who shall be seen without end" (*CG* 22:30), Blake characteristically identifies Jesus as the "Lord and master."

161. In the kabbalistic tradition, this man is named Adam Kadmon; in the Christian tradition, he is the original *Logos,* and in the Blakean mythology, this man is the resurrected Albion.

162. See 1 Kings 19:13; 2 Kings 2:11; Mal. 4:5; and Matt. 22:11; see also *MHH* 22–24, K 158.

163. The "Epilogue" to the "GP" is also relevant here:

> Truly, My Satan, thou art but a Dunce,
> And dost not know the Garment from the Man. . . .
> Tho' thou art Worship'd by the Names Divine
> Of Jesus & Jehovah, thou art still
> The Son of Man in weary Night's decline,
> The lost Traveller's Dream under the Hill

(K 771).

164. See also Letter, to Thomas Butts, 25 April 1803: "Christ is very decided on this Point: 'He who is Not With Me is Against Me.' There is no Medium or Middle State" (K 822); see also Matt. 12:30 and Rev. 3:16.

165. See Damon, *PS,* p. 457. Plates 94 and 95 were also clarified by such explansion; see Erdman, "Text. Notes," *PPWB,* p. 733.

166. See also "VLJ," K 610; *J* 90:34–38, K 736–37; and "EG," ll. 69–80, K

754–55; Mary's "sin" was her "dark pretense to Chastity:/ Blaspheming Love, blaspheming thee" (K 755).

167. See also Blake's compassionate illustration "The Woman Taken in Adultery" (which "re-writes" John 8:4–11); "EG," K 754; and the painting "The Virgin and the Child in Egypt" (1810), in which Mary appears more as the glowing wife and mother than a pale virgin. See also "On the Virginity of the Virgin Mary & Johanna Southcott," K 418; and Dante Illustration, no. 99.

168. It should be noted that Blake emphasizes this identification by one of two wiggly lines (extending off the "n" of "than") in the right margin of this prose passage, in copies C, D, and F; here I think there can be no question about the significance of such a "decoration," however minute.

169. See *MHH* 22, K 158; "VLJ," K 605–6, 613, and 615; and *J* 91:8–11, K 738. Yeats calls this visionary prose passage "the very keystone of his [B's] thought" (*E&I*, p. 137).

The rhetorical questions beginning "What are the Treasures of Heaven?" through "are not the Gifts of the Spirit Every-thing to Man?" are marked by the other wiggly line in the right margin of copies C, D, and F.

170. In contrast to N IV of *VFZ* Blake is here concerned with Los's redemptive labors. Part of this later emphasis on Los's poetic genius is illustrated, I think, on *J* 100. I intuitively expect that *J* 99, rather than *J* 100, satisfyingly illustrates the apocalyptic ending of *Jerusalem* and that *J* 100 refers to a prior event. I realize that this interpretation has not been put forth by other critics, who variously explain the characters and actions on *J* 100.

Raine comments that "the figures are Urthona, Los and Enitharmon, with solar and lunar emblems of their labours at the furnaces and looms of generation" (*BT*, I, 51). Wicksteed writes that "LOS and ENITHARMON-JERUSALEM gaze at one another before the complete City of Golgonooza, the new Logos, and their task accomplished and the Sun of Eternity liberated to ascend" (*JC*, p. 102). Damon comments that "Urthona with hammer and tongs stands before the serpent temple, which is evidently copied from the serpentine druid temple of Avebury. . . . On Urthona's right is his spectre, Los, flying inward with the sun; on his left his emanation, Enitharmon, weaves the dark garment of the flesh against the background of moon and stars, Beulah" (*PS*, p. 475). Keynes and Wolf do not identify the figures or interpret the scene, but note that "in the background is a chain of Druid arches, i.e., a serpent Temple, adapted from Plate viii of Stukeley's *Abury, a Temple of the British Druids* (1743)" (*IBC*, p. 110). Erdman has suggested 1) that the figure carrying the sun is Urizen, originally prince of light, that Urthona-Los hold the hammer and tongs, and that Enitharmon weaves bodies in the moony Beulah; he has also suggested that 2) Urthona may be carrying the sun while Los holds the hammer and compasses and that Enitharmon is more passive than active (These suggestions were put forth in a Blake seminar, at the MLA meetings 28 Dec. 1968).

To this variety of opinion, I add the following interpretation: that *J* 100 more fittingly belongs between *J* 82 and 83 and illustrates 1) *J* 82:26, K 725; *J* 82:47–50, K 726 (which Erdman notes were revised; "Text. Notes," *PPWB*, p. 733); and *J* 82:81–82, K 727; and 2) *J* 83:54–81, K 728–29. Up the right-hand margin of *J* 82 is a worm, which becomes the serpent druid temple in *J* 100. Erdman also notes that "Plate 83 (different in technique and lettering as well as in content obviously did not originally follow [*J* 82]" (*ibid.*, p. 733). Other possible portions of the text which *J* 100 could illustrate are: *J* 86:33–61, K 731–32; *J* 88:1, 33–36 and 44–55, K 733–34; and *J* 90:1–13, and 49–50, K 736–37, respectively.

The iconography (in both its horizontal composition, usually a fallen position for Blake, and particular characters) of *J* 100 represents, to my mind, the moment before reunification and resultant regaining proper authority, as is narrated, variously, in the above suggested referents. Los, the vehicular form of Urthona, stands with honest pride in the center with his creative hammer and tongs (*J* 83:75–78, K 728–29) while Enitharmon "Joy'd in the many weaving threads in bright Cathedron's Dome,/ Weaving the Web of life for Jerusalem" (*J* 83:72–73, K 728). The figure at Los's right is his attentive spectre, before he is cast out (*J* 91; K 737–39): "Alternate they watch in night, alternate labour in day,/ Before the Furnaces labouring, while Los all night watches/ The stars rising & setting & the meteors & terrors of night" (*J* 83:79–81, K 729). The serpent temple in the background is the "winding worm" of false, natural religion. The sequence precedes Los's reunion with Enitharmon, Albion's reunion with Jerusalem, and their fourfold "perfect unity." *J* 100 does not, in my view, portray the "great marriage" after the apocalypse of *J* 96–*J* 99, consummated and illustrated on *J* 99, which properly ends *Jerusalem* (reproduced here as Plate 16).

171. See "Annot. Lavater," K 82; *MHH* 22, K 158; "VLJ," K 604; *VFZ*, N I:470–75, K 277; *J* 38:14–25, K 664–65; and *J* 77, K 717.

172. "Notes written on a page of *VFZ*," K 380; "VLJ," K 611; and Prov. 8.

173. In striking contrast to Yeats, Blake here rejects the major code of occultism, the Smaragdine Tablet, which he views as binding down what is above; conversely, Yeats appeals to it for access to that which is above because both traditional and Blakean Christianity, however desired, are not seen by him as available.

174. See "VLJ," K 615; Damon adds this gloss from Milton's "Second Defense": "'You therefore who wish to remain free, either instantly be wise or as soon as possible, cease to be fools'" (*PS*, p. 466).

175. Though the proper noun "Jesus" is not named till after pronominal reference to him, I think that the "he" and "him" do refer to Jesus, and not to "this waking death" (the spectre whom Los has just cast out); also, the ";" (in l. 18) can be read as a causal connective.

176. See *VFZ*, N IX:38–42, K 374 and Eph. 3:10.

177. Numerous other examples of Blake's fondness for "returning" indicate how pervasive this movement is, in life as well as art; see the familiar example of Blake's being moved to tears at the story of the prodigal son's return (as reported by H. Crabb Robinson).

178. I refer not only to the Fourth Gospel, but also to John's three beautiful Epistles, especially to the first, whose third and fourth chapters may well have inspired parts of *J* 96. For the reader I leave this first epistle: "Whoso keepeth his word, in him verily is the love of God perfected: hereby know that we are in him" (2:5).

179. See *M* 2:13, K 481; *M* 5:39, K 485; *J* 39:25, K 666; *J* 46:27, K 676; and "Ghost Abel," 2:10 and 14, K 780.

180. See 1 John 3:11–21.

181. This overshadowing cloud is associated with Jesus' transfiguration on the mount (Matt. 17:2 and Mark 9:2), and hence is fitting here to prelude Albion's transfiguration.

182. Letter, to Thomas Butts, 25 April 1803, K 822; see also Matt. 12:30; Rev. 3:16 and *J* 52, K 682.

183. I read *J* 96:32, K 743 as completing the union of Jesus and Los, implied

in ll. 7 and 22, jointly referred to by the connecting "&" in "at the Divine Mercy & at Los's sublime honour."

184. Blake's use of "vision" and "dream" here describes the illusion of the sleep of Ulro (though more of a nightmare than a dream) which Albion now realizes (in a vision, or insight) as such. If the order of vision and dream were reversed, they could be read as "extinction of illusion" and "revelation of reality" respectively; but, given the present order, they are most likely read as synonyms for the illusion that vanishes as redemption is revealed, when "the Furnaces became/ Fountains of Living Waters." In almost all other cases, Blake uses "vision" to mean perception or revelation of that which is divine, eternal, and true.

185. As in Rev. 21:2 and in *VFZ*, N IX:205–24, K 362–63. In this text Blake varies the Revelation narrative to emphasize the Four Zoas' participation in the resurrection.

186. "Melting apparent surfaces away, and displaying the infinite which was hid," like Blake's "infernal" method of printing in *MHH* 14, K 154.

187. See *VFZ* N IV:271, K 304; *M* 13:21, K 494; *J* 42:31, K 670; and *J* 73:77, K 713. And Isa. 24:23; 60:1 and 19; and Rev. 22:23 and 5.

188. See Blake's full-page illustration of this imperative "To annihilate the Selfhood of Deceit & False Forgiveness" (M 16:1, K 497), pictured on M 15 C–18 D; see also "VLJ," K 615 and Blake's *Job*. This "accuser" is an ancestor of Yeats's "remorse," also to be cast out.

Another illustration which should be considered here is "Christ with a Bow" (after 1800) for *Paradise Lost*, Bk. 6, VI, l. 763; this unfinished drawing, however, was not part of the *PL* series and differs from "The Casting of the Rebel Angels into Hell," which was included and is similar in the single figure of Christ with his spiritual bow. Of "Christ with a Bow," the Philadelphia Art Museum writes that "Blake may have meant the design to illustrate symbolically the Triumph of Imagination, as personified by Christ, over Reason, the Urizen of his mythology." (Philadelphia Museum of Art, *William Blake: A Descriptive Catalogue of an Exhibition of the Works of William Blake selected from Collections in the United States* [Philadelphia, 1939], p. 162.) Earlier in the above passage from *PL*, Bk. 6, Milton presents his interpretation of "Ezekiel's Vision," and that fourfold vision of God (Blake's original illustration is reproduced on Plate 13), and the design "Christ with a Bow," befit the narrative on *J* 97 and 98.

4

"Why Are the Gods by Men Betrayed?": Yeats's Quest for Self-Unity

However else one understands it, the resurrection is the chief traditional religious image of total satisfaction of all desire and of perfection. Blake's engraving "The Reunion of the Soul and the Body" (from his illustrations to Blair's *Grave*), which was chosen for the covers of Yeats's and Ellis's edition of Blake's writings, vividly illustrates this shared, central desire for wholeness. Whereas Blake conceives of this reunion as imminent, Yeats characteristically asks "where" this unity is possible; further, his question is also a way of asking "whether" it is ever attainable. This chapter will discuss both the secularization of belief in and desire for the resurrection, and the consequent loss of its expectation in Yeats's writings: "Why must the lasting love what passes?/ Why are the gods by men betrayed?"[1]

My task in this discussion of Yeats is twofold: 1) to show the limits beyond which the continuity of the resurrection motif cannot go without losing its initial religious meaning and power, to reveal the mystery of man's redemption, as I think happens in Yeats's case; and 2) given this nonconvertibility of a religious doctrine, to show how Yeats would achieve the "profane perfection of mankind," whose joys are tragic and inherent within the boundaries of a secular world. The discussion of Yeats, then, will be concerned with the fundamental properties of religious symbolism and with the poetic consequences of its nature for Yeats.

Though I will consider the question of the continuity and

"conversion" of the resurrection more comprehensively in the conclusion (chapter 5), I wish to outline its major components here since they apply to Yeats's relation to Donne and Blake and to his own heroic achievement. So as not to blur my "theological" and aesthetic judgments, I should state that if we consider Yeats's "system" neither as theology, nor as philosophy, but as a "metapsychology" for his poetry, then we shall discuss its values, strengths, and limits in primarily literary terms.

Further, the kind of evaluation appropriate to make of Yeats's work is an aesthetic one because his metapsychical system serves primarily to legitimate his basic, continuing poetic enterprise (from which it is often derived). His system, however eclectic, is locked within itself, like its gyres, and depends mostly on itself for its authority (in contrast to the divine authority, of the Bible, from which Donne's and Blake's metaphysical and poetic authenticity arises). In the 1938 edition of *A Vision,* for example, Yeats writes to Pound that this book "will, when finished, proclaim a new divinity (p. 27)" Yeats's proclamations do produce poetry, but they do not, in my view, produce any new divinity whose existence precedes and transcends speech about him. What Yeats gives us is man-made—a human poetry of the unrequited heart and a self-begotten system of subjective "moods," which both begin and end between man's natural extremities, birth and death, joy and remorse.

When the poet no longer belongs to and holds the beliefs of an ecclesiastic community, its symbols and the reality they "represent" are lost to him, as they are in Yeats's skeptical cyclicism of the time-bound world. This loss of religious authority—the beginning of secularization—also occurs among some mystics, as Scholem describes:

> certain authors, disregarding or rejecting all traditional authority, describe their mystical experience in resolutely secular terms, yet clothe their interpretation of the same experience in traditional images. This is the case with Rimbaud and more consistently with William Blake. . . . Even in such revolutionaries, who seek their authority essentially in themselves and in a secular interpretation of their visions, tradition asserts its power.[2]

Later, some figures accept no authority whatever, or recognize a multitude of related authorities, as in Yeats's case. This passage points out an important feature of religious language, namely, that its "power" derives from "traditional authority."

Further, the "meaning" of religious language, which is ordinary language changed by the substance of what it expresses, like the Eucharistic bread and wine, is determined by the presence of the divine. This sacred essence appears first on the transcendent level, beyond empirical reality, so that it then may appear on the immanent level, within encountered reality. Conversely, without sacred authority, religious language does not exist. Accordingly, new religious symbols are born out of a changed relationship to the ultimate foundation of being, i.e., to the Holy.[3] And finally, when a religious symbol dies, its authority and validity cannot be replaced by a secular one. This nonconversion of the resurrection motif I specifically want to show in Yeats. In Yeats "man is in love and loves what vanishes"; we shall inquire whether there is "any comfort to be found."

Blake and Yeats: Sanction for a Skeptic

"All" is the word that Blake and Yeats both use most frequently in their poetry,[4] and this coincidence indicates a spiritual affinity, insofar as both poets know that "less than all cannot satisfy man." But while Blake and Yeats express a desire for perfect unity, their respective access to this ideal differs significantly. In a letter to his father in 1914, Yeats states a "metapsychology": which would find "what is" to be "what is wanted":

> the poet seeks truth, not abstract truth, but the kind of vision of reality which satisfies the whole being. It will not be true for one thing unless it satisfies his desires, his most profound desires. . . . I think the poet reveals truth by revealing those desires.[5]

While for Blake "everything possible to be believ'd is an image of truth," for Yeats, truth resides in man's "profound desires," a psychological phenomenon.

The Blake-Yeats relation and its bearing on Yeats as an individual, in a larger, perennial tradition, must be clarified. This matter involves two issues, namely the general question, "what is the nature of poetic influence?" and the specific question, "what is Blake's influence on Yeats?" While I cannot deal with either thoroughly here, we will nonetheless have to consider both, in a propaedeutic manner. Again, I should state explicitly my principal concern in this section, which is to discuss the poetic use Yeats makes of Blake.

Before investigating some of the prose texts in which Yeats's "reading" of Blake is telling, I would like to suggest a pattern of "poetic influence" which is here a pertinent issue. If "tradition" is to be both greatly meaningful and meaningfully great, the person within it must meet it on terms which belong both to the parent tradition and to the individual self therein engendered; that is, one must engage the tradition both on its own and on one's own terms. Poetic influence is like romantic love, Bloom surmises, and I would agree, adding that this is so because in both cases the beloved "other" (person or tradition) can be possessed only by giving him/herself irrevocably to it so that he/she then may receive the blessings of mutually enhancing reciprocity.

In the specific case of Yeats's relation to Blake, I partly agree with Bloom's "revisionary" theory of poetic influence "in which the poet creates his own precursors by necessarily misinterpreting them."[6] Certainly this consistent misconstruing describes Yeats's usual misreading of Blake, especially in his essay "The Symbolic System" in volume 1 of the Yeats-Ellis 1893 edition of *Blake's Works*.

In discussing this piece I want to point out how, though Yeats read Blake all his life, Blake's "influence" was neither stylistic (except for some verbal repetitions and echoes) nor directly conceptual.[7] Rather, Yeats saw the Blake he misinterpreted as sanctioning his own intuitions, not as initially giving or determining them. Speaking of his search for "an image of the modern *mind's discovery of itself*," Yeats advises that "we do not seek truth in argument or in books but *clarification of what we already believe*."[8] Though these statements were written with the conscious clarity of maturity, I think they also apply to an aspect of the principle by which Yeats typically misunderstood Blake.

The most important generative category of Yeats's creative misreading involves his mistakenly elevating the natural in a way which is false to Blake but true to Yeats. Speaking of the "No Natural Religion" tractates, Yeats doubly misunderstands the Blakean "intellect," or imagination:

> As natural things correspond to intellectual, so intellectual things correspond to emotional. In the second of the two tractates on "Natural Religion" Blake goes further and asserts that "the poetic genius," as he calls the emotional life, "is the true man."[9]

Now, the reader of Blake knows that "natural things," found in

Beulah, Generation, and Ulro differ fundamentally from "intellectual things," found in Eden, which do not correspond to the "emotional things" of Beulah. Further, this scheme does not include Eden, but reductively includes in it Beulah. Accordingly, Yeats conflates Luvah and Los, both of whom he calls "the great emotional or inspired principle."[10] Though Yeats associates the poetical character with the "emotional life," Blake does not; moreover, "emotion" is a word Blake never uses, though it is one of Yeats's favorites, just as imagination, meaning something quite different, is one of Blake's.

That we are reading more Yeats than Blake here becomes clear when Yeats speaks of the "moods," the collective form of emotion, whose history is "the history of the universe" and whose symbolic name is God.[11] The "immortal moods" are to be discovered in mortal desires and "a divine love in sexual passion."[12] When Yeats elaborates on man's relation to his subjective God, he rehearses (in his Blake commentary) the gyres of *A Vision:*

> The mind or imagination or consciousness of man may be said to have two poles, the personal and impersonal, or, as Blake preferred to call them, the limit of contraction and the unlimited expansion. When we act from the personal we tend to bind our consciousness down as to a fiery centre. When, on the other hand, we allow our imagination to expand away from this egoistic mood, we become vehicles for the universal thought and merge in the universal mood. Thus a reaction of God against man and man against God—which is described by Swedenborg as good and evil, and by Blake as really two forms of good (MS notes to Swedenborg)—goes on continually.[13]

What is especially telling here is Yeats's redefinition of Blake's terms in order to set man and God in conflict, as they typically are in Yeats. The two poles, of contraction and expansion, were set by Blake's God (once by Jesus and once by Los) as an act of mercy, analogous to his giving man the starry pole and watery shore of creation.[14] Yeats reverses Blake's intended meaning, which is that God mercifully acts to make possible man's salvation, so that for Yeats man and God are perpetually at war. This non-Christian view that the human and the divine are in conflict unconditionally differentiates Yeats from Blake and Donne; the nature and consequences of this heroic battle we shall explore in portions of this chapter.

In his secular quest, however, Yeats also desires perfect unity:

there is only one perfection and only one search for perfection, and sometimes it has the form of the religious life and sometimes of the artistic life.[15]

The Yeats-Ellis "Preface" comments briefly on this crucial change: "As the language of spiritual utterance ceases to be theological and becomes literary and poetical, the great truths have to be spoken afresh."[16] This description, contrary to its authors' intention, applies more to Yeats than to Blake, the source of whose poetic speech is traditional divine authority, as the Miltonic Bard knows. Accordingly, Yeats perceives that Blake's teaching "is new only in its symbolism. It is new as consciousness is always new; old as life is always old."[17] Nonetheless, "it [Blake's "system of thought"] is profoundly Christian —though wrapped in a queer dress and certainly poetical," Yeats writes in a letter, and adds that "it has done my own mind a great deal of good in liberating."[18] In each of these descriptions of Blake's "originality" Yeats implies that the language of spiritual ontology can be translated from the religious to the secular, whereas I am inclined to think that such language cannot be so "converted."

One of this study's major arguments is that art and religion arise from the same collective source—the divine imagination— —and that they share a similar individual origin—the human belief in and desire for perfection. In another context Yeats interprets Blake's recognition of this relation: "He made possible a religious life to those who had seen the painters and poets of the romantic movement succeed to theology." The "religious life" Yeats has in mind is less that which Blake made possible and more what he himself would have. Accordingly, Yeats subjectifies Blake's belief to state his own—"believing that the crucifixion and resurrection were the soul's diary and no mere historical events" (*Explor.*, p. 45). Yeats's rejecting the factual historicity of Christ's Easter rising from the dead (in body and soul) would mean, in Pauline terms, that one's faith and preaching are in vain (1 Cor. 15:14). Precisely because of this resurrection, the soul's new life (with Jesus) can occur, celebrated now in baptism. But a concern with the soul's life without an actual redemptive event does not constitute a religious life, but rather a humanistic one. In his introduction to the 1925 edition of *A Vision* Yeats explains his practical object in connection with "spiritual happiness": "I wished for a system of thought that would leave my imagination free to create as it chose and yet make all that it created, or could create, part of the one history, and that the soul's."[19] Speaking of this process of secularization, Tillich likewise argues that "in the atmosphere of feeling, without a definite object of emotion, without an ultimate content [the transcendent God], religion dies."[20]

Yeats's Nonreligious Eschatology of Art

When theological events become the private affair of the soul, they lose their divine authority and their shared character insofar as they cease to belong to a definable ecclesiastic community. Accordingly, to Yeats "faith mean[s] that belief in a spiritual life which is not confined to one Church" (*E&I*, p. 208). One of Yeats's characteristic conceptual gestures is trying to reestablish access for the individual *anima hominis* to the *anima mundi*, the continuous symbolic resource of the collective mind:

> The end of art is the ecstasy awakened by the presence before an ever-changing mind of what is permanent in the world, or by the arousing of that mind itself into the very delicate and fastidious mood habitual with it when it is seeking those permanent and recurring things (*E&I*, p. 287).

In Yeats's art, as in his view of life, this "end" is not final.

Instead, Yeats remains the seeker (like the betrayed knight in that early play), the hierophant who has

> sought through all my life to find the secret of life. I was not happy in my youth, for I knew that it would pass; and I was not happy in my manhood, for I knew that age was coming; and so I gave myself, in youth and manhood and age, to the search for the Great Secret. I longed for a life whose abundance would fill centuries. . . . I would be—no, I *will* be!—like the ancient gods of the land.[21]

The title of this early story ("Where there is Nothing, there is God") recurs in *The Unicorn from the Stars* when Martin, the spiritual man, exclaims "Now all is clear to me. Where there is nothing, where there is nothing—there is God!"[22] This ambiguous pronouncement suggests the difficulty for Yeats of talking about God.

In the early play *Where There is Nothing* (later rewritten as *Unicorn from the Stars*) the quasi-Blakean hero Paul Ruttledge undertakes a regeneration of his soul, which will at death come into possession of itself and of the joy that made it. Whether or not he achieves this sought-after consummation seems dubious in the play, though he does attain some insight along his crooked way. The problem involves, in part, the relation between the temporal and eternal labors of redemption, which Ruttledge holds are totally distinct:

> The Christian's business is not reformation but revelation, and the only labours he can put his hand to can never be accomplished in Time. He must live so all things shall pass away.[23]

The God of this play, however, is so transcendent that he exists only "where there is nothing": "We must destroy the World; we must destroy everything that has Law and Number, for where there is nothing, there is God."[24] The conceptual problem of the play stems, I think, from there being no accessibility to this God of nothingness; the linking of "ancient frenzies and hereditary wisdom . . . a Marriage of Heaven and Hell"[25] does not in fact take place, except in Ruttledge's subjective recognition that "it is inside our minds that it [the world] must be destroyed, it must be consumed in a moment inside our minds. God will accomplish his last judgment, first in one man's mind, and then in another."[26] Aside from this Blakean insight, the play leaves us, like Ruttledge's followers, with nothing about God.

In *A Vision* Yeats would locate God in the thirteenth sphere; it is the "ultimate reality," "a phaseless sphere," "sufficient to itself," and contains "what Blake called 'the bright sculptures of Los's Halls'" (*Vision,* 193 and 240). The thirteenth sphere is the spiritual equivalent of the fifteenth phase, and both are the *loci* of unity of being, as some of Yeats's unpublished notes for *A Vision* describe:

> all whirling [is] at an end, and unity of being perfectly attained. There all happiness, all beauty, all thought, their images come to view taking fullness, to such a multiplicity of form that they are to our eyes without form. They do what they please, all [struggle] at an end, daimons and men reconciled, no more figures opposing one another in a daemonic dance, and it is these who create genius in its most radical form and who change the direction of history.[27]

In this desired, atemporal unity exists man's freedom, which, however, is found "neither between death and birth nor between birth and death" (*Vision,* p. 236). To Yeats, the God of the thirteenth sphere remains powerful and hidden: "it can do all things and knows all things, it knows what it will do with its freedom but it has kept the secret" (*Vision,* p. 302). Speaking of his difficulty of writing of God, Yeats, in his 1930 Diary, says that "again and again with remorse, a sense of defeat, I have failed when I would write of God, written coldly and conventionally" (*Explor.,* p. 305).

Insofar as God does appear, Yeats associates him with death, with phase 1, the coldly objective phase of complete plasticity which is incompatible with life (as is its opposite, phase 15).[28] Under these circumstances neither incarnation nor resurrection is possible, and Yeats's favourite tenet is that man and God die each other's life and live each other's death. This basic conflict (the chorus of *A Vision*) delineates its conceptual frame, schematized in the interlocking gyres: "The whole system is founded upon the belief that the ultimate reality, symbolized as the sphere, falls in human consciousness . . . into a series of antinomies."[29] While Yeats probably takes this schema from Blake's "Mental Traveller," the "natural" ancestor of *A Vision* (p. 189), he expands its cyclical core to include all history, from which there is then virtually no escape. At least, Yeats's attention is predominantly focused on the repeating phases within the lunar circle of destiny. The significance of 1) the negative symbiosis of conflict between man and God, and 2) the resulting alternating gyres, whose reference is both psychological and historical, is that no transcendence and no salvation are therein conceptually possible.[30]

That this Yeatsian periodicity concerns the soul *sub specie temporis* becomes clear when we contrast Blake's twenty-eight "Churches" with Yeats's twenty-eight phases of the moon. Aside from the difference between the religious and architectonic and the natural and unconscious, there is a more important substantive difference between what happens at the twenty-eighth point; for Blake, the twenty-eighth Church is the apocalyptic, heavenly communion, whereas for Yeats, the twenty-eighth phase of the moon brings the soul round again to the beginning, to repeat its journey, without escaping out of the historical wheel: "Man seeks his opposite or the opposite of his condition, attains his object so far as it is attainable, at phase 15 and returns to phase 1 again."[31]

In the temporal equivalent of the thirteenth sphere, in the fifteenth phase, Christ is revealed.[32] However, this Jesus is present for Yeats solely as a subjective condition, without "reality" outside the self, "for a God is but the self," as he later explains (*E&I*, p. 461). Yeats's God exists in his man-made creations, which are those of art:

No worthy symbol of God existed but the inner world, the true humanity, to whose various aspects he gave many names, "Jerusalem," "Liberty," "Eden," "The Divine Vision," "The Body of God," "The Human Form Divine," "The Divine Members," and whose most intimate expression was art and poetry (*E&I*, p. 133).

Accordingly, in the poem "Wisdom," Yeats locates "true" belief in the artistically created, not in the historically revealed, Jesus:

The true faith discovered was
When painted panel, statuary,
Glass-mosaic, window-glass,
Amended what was told awry
By some peasant gospeller.

When Yeats extends the Blakean identity of Jesus as the imagination, the resulting alteration loses religious validity because he speaks of Jesus Christ without believing in his definitive redemptive essence, as Blake, however, does. Instead, Yeats conceives of Jesus as an artistic entity:

The historical Christ was indeed *no more* than the supreme *symbol* of the artistic imagination, in which, with every passion *wrought to perfect beauty by art and poetry,* we shall live, *when the body has passed away for the last time;* but before that hour man must labour through many lives and many deaths (*E&I,* p. 137; italics mine).

In this paraphrase of Blake's central declaration in *Jerusalem* (Plate 77) Yeats's changes indicate his loss of belief in the Easter resurrection, and this secular attitude recurs in his other interpretations of Blake's Christianity. Yeats lacks belief in the immortal spiritual body, and without certainty of that "real and eternal world" of the resurrection-to-come, he places man inside the mortal circle of destiny in which he lives and dies many times, without determinate release.

In his comments on Blake's "symbolic system" in the prophetic books, Yeats gives primary emphasis to the imagination, which he says is also called Christ. However, there is an important

distinction between Blake's saying that Jesus is the imagination
and Yeats's saying that the imagination is Jesus. Though "is"
linguistically identifies the two nouns it joins, the copula is not
conceptually reversible. That is, the authenticity of a religious
symbol depends on its redemptive reality, as traditional Christianity, for example, reflects in its eschatology and sacraments.
In his conception of Jesus Christ, Yeats accepts his human form
as the imagination without also accepting his prior divine existence: "Jesus being always understood as a symbolic name for
organized inspiration applied to human purposes."[33]

The third person in the Trinity Yeats calls the Daimon, who
again represents an aspect of man's interior being, like Blake's
emanation, rather than an aspect of God's transcendent being.
In this postlapsarian world where there is questionable comfort
to be found, man and Daimon are in conflict because immortal
desire is unfulfillable in a mortal state: "man and Daimon feed
the hunger in one another's hearts . . . [and] the more insatiable
in all desire . . . the more close will be the bond, the more violent
and definite the antipathy" (*Mythol.,* pp. 335-36).

A major theme throughout Yeats's poetry and prose is the
postlapsarian incompatibility of mortal life and total satisfaction: .

> Until the axle break
> That keeps the stars in their round,
> And hands hurl in the deep
> The banners of East and West,
> And the girdle of light is unbound,
> Your breast will not lie by the breast
> Of your beloved in sleep.[34]

Interpreting Shelley, Yeats associates death with "that which
thou dost seek" and thinks that "the ideal world [is] the world
of the dead" (*E&I,* pp. 72 and 88). J. B. Yeats's observation
that "art is the expression of unsatisfied human desire—and
human desire through all the centuries has never altered—though
it varies constantly in strength"[35] characterizes his son's work.

If we agree that belief and creation are related,[36] then we can
distinguish between Blake's seeing religion as a form of art and
Yeats's substituting "creation" for "belief" (as in his grand
testament in "The Tower"):

And I declare my faith:
I mock Plotinus' thought
And cry in Plato's teeth,
Death and life were not
Till man made up the whole,
Made lock, stock and barrel
Out of his bitter soul,
Aye, sun and moon and star, all,
And further add to that
That, being dead, we rise,
Dream and so create
Translunar Paradise.

Yeats astutely entitles a section of "Discoveries" "religious belief necessary to religious art"; he goes on to say that "all symbolic [i.e., "religious"] art should arise out of a real belief, and that it cannot do so in this age proves that this age is a road and not a resting place for the imaginative arts." An alternative, of which Yeats is a master, is lyric poetry, which, when speaking "of emotions common to all, require[s] not indeed a religious belief like the spiritual arts, but a life that has leisure for itself . . ." (*E&I*, p. 294). At best, then, Yeats views poetry as the secular soul's alternative to religion; ideally, they constitute analogous activities, at least insofar as they are both revelatory:

> I do most firmly believe that all art is dedicated to wisdom and not because it teaches anything but because it reveals divine substances.[37]

Except that they are perceived by the imagination, the identity of these divine substances is never revealed until the end of time:

> True art is the flame of the Last Day, which begins for every man when he is first moved by beauty, and which seeks to burn all things until they become "infinite and holy" (*E&I*, p. 140).[38]

Until then, however, in the bounded world of time and space, the vision of the ideal causes a basic conflict in man, between his finite, mortal body and his infinite, immortal aspirations: "There is a continual conflict . . . the perfection of Nature is the decline of Spirit, the perfection of Spirit is the decline of Nature" (*E&I*, p. 467). In this battle I think Yeats's victory lies on the side of nature.

Yeats's Secularization of Christian Events

Five poems on major Christian events clearly indicate Yeats's nonreligious view of them. The subject of the earliest, "To the Rose upon the Rood of Time," is man's being caught (crucified) within the time-bound, natural world, "in all poor foolish things that live a day." Yeats's prayer to the rose of intellectual beauty (*Auto.*, p. 170) is typical of the occultism of his early poetry:

> But [I] seek alone to hear the strange things said
> By God to the bright hearts of those long dead,
> And learn to chaunt a tongue men do not know.

Yeats seeks such arcane speech because conventional, Christian terms are no longer applicable.

Like his "pale, unsatisfied" Magi, Yeats sees the incarnation as a subjective event and in a pagan context:

> When the old *primary* becomes the new *antithetical*, the old realisation of an objective moral law is changed into a subconscious turbulent instinct. The world of rigid custom and law is broken up by "the uncontrollable mystery on the bestial floor" (*Vision*, p. 105).

Here, as throughout *A Vision*, history is seen as continuously cyclic (alternating between "objective" and "subjective" phases), in which the "incarnation" holds no redemption, neither permanent nor absolute.

This ambiguous metamorphosis in time is portrayed in "Easter, 1916," where the "uprising" belongs to a political, not theological, world. Further, in direct contrast to the "mysterious" redemptive change of 1 Corinthians 15, 51-52, the utter change here is the "terrible beauty" of death, still victorious in what remains the historical world, the unopened grave. The transfiguration of this Easter, without heaven's "suffice," is the final loss of life, instead of its enhancement and immortalization; and the poet memorializes the Irish heroes' deaths.

Like the "incarnation," Yeats views the "second coming" as belonging to the cyclic cataclysm of the natural world, and not as beneficently transforming it. As the rose is bound "on the rood of time," Yeats's subjective "theology" has no valid symbol of transcendence to complete perfection. There is no redemption either in the first coming ("the uncontrollable mystery on the bestial floor") or in the second, when "surely some revelation" should be at hand, save the "rough beast" come round at last to be born in the *dies irae*.

Yeats's totally changing what is born emphasizes the absence of a Savior and consequently binds man in the continuous, secular opposition between life and death. Neither in time nor at its end is a land of the heart's desire approachable or inhabitable. In contrast to Blake, for Yeats there is no liberation from the pathogenic cycle of history, in which life is coterminous with conflict, between knowledge and power, desire and possession:

> For Wisdom is a property of the dead,
> A something incompatible with life;
>   and power,
> Like everything that has the stain of blood,
> A property of the living.

Whereas the comic transfiguration of Christianity (as in Dante) immortalizes life at its fullest, the tragic exchange and substitution of spiritual for natural goods in Yeats's secular world causes an irrecoverable loss to the soul: "But is there any comfort to be found?/ Man is in love and loves what vanishes,/ What more is there to say?" Or, to describe the situation alternately, "the intellect of man is forced to choose/ Perfection of the life, or of the work,/ And if it take the second, must refuse/ A heavenly mansion, raging in the dark."

Yet the option, "perfection," of this choice is misleading, for perfection is, in the natural world, at best transitory. Yeats's presentation of the *Resurrection* indicates a naturalistic view of the event, which results in the principal Yeatsian conflict, as the Greek skeptic states: "Your words are clear at last O Heraclitus. God and man die each other's life, live each other's death."[39] Though the supernatural God manifests itself in natural man, the deadly symbiosis between them ends in loss, as plangently lamented in the closing lines of the play:

> Everything that man esteems
> Endures a moment or a day.
> Love's pleasure drives his love away,
> The painter's brush consumes his dreams;
> The herald's cry, the soldier's tread

Exhaust his glory and his might:
Whatever flames upon the night
Man's own resinous heart has fed.

These lines majestically acknowledge the impossibility of simultaneously enjoying and possessing what is desired; moreover, the means of obtaining that desideratum destroys it at the same time it is sought. Like Wallace Stevens, the major humanist poet of the twentieth century, Yeats accepts that "the honey of heaven may or may not come,/ But that of earth both comes and goes at once" ("Le Monocle de Mon Oncle"). The cost of man's love and glory in the natural world without its transfiguration is self-extinction. Heroically, then, Yeats chooses the devouring flames of the heart's passion.

The Subjective Poet: His Discontent

One stylistic consequence of this transcience and sacrifice of the "dream" is the writing of lyrics, rather than epics. Blake's epics, for example, present a continuous and, on the whole, coherent view of "reality," and while his lyrics are aesthetically self-sufficient, their total meaning resides in the fourfold cosmos of the epics. To the extent that a lyric is "explained" by something else, Yeats's *A Vision* corresponds to Blake's "A Vision of the Last Judgment" and his epics.[40] But the difference in analogous titles is not merely linguistic, for it points to a fundamental philosophic and stylistic difference. Having no determinate eschatology, Yeats's *Vision* does not inclusively partake "of the last judgment," wherein the temporal is thrown off "that the Eternal might be Establish'd"; instead, Yeats's *Vision* remains within the time-bound secular world of history, whose end is indeterminate because the gyres continue to run on. Yeats's perception of the (Christian or Blakean) "eternal reality" wherein reside the "bright sculptures of Los's halls" is at best transient and discontinuous, without ontological permanence; and the moments of "heaven blazing into the head" are recorded in the dramatic lyric, the impersonal form of the subjective man.

Further, in content, the lyric befits the Yeatsian subjective poet, whose theme is the self and its proper relations: "The creations of a great writer are little more than the moods and passions of his own heart, given surnames and Christian names, and sent to walk the earth."[41] No coincidence, this last gesture indicates a fundamental restlessness of the subjective man, of whom the "wandering aengus" is a memorable example in Yeats's early poetry; and he wanders, with varying names, through Yeats's verse, until he sinks in upon himself and truth. Owen Aherne is another name of this central subjective man, whom Yeats describes as giving

> the impression of a man holding a flame in his naked hand. He was to me, at that moment, the supreme type of our race, which, when it has risen above, or is sunken below, the formalisms of half-education and the rationalisms of conventional affirmation and denial, turns away, unless my hopes for the world and for the Church have made me blind, from practicable desires and intuitions toward desires so unbounded that no human vessel can contain them, intuitions so immaterial that their sudden and far-off fires leaves heavy darkness about hand and foot. He had the nature, which is half monk, half soldier of fortune, and must needs turn action into dreaming, and dreaming into action; and for such there is *no order, no finality, no contentment in this world* (*Mythol.*, pp. 293–94; italics mine).

The source of the subjective man's restlessness is his "aching heart," which sorrows with "a measureless desire for a world made wholly of essences" (*Mythol.*, p. 267). However, the desired consummation of the poet with the "elaborate spiritual beauty" (*Mythol.*, p. 270)—the heavenly beloved, whose "beauty was like wisdom" (*Mythol.*, p. 169)—is impossible in the natural world. This union, analogous to the Christian re-union of the body and soul, can be found by Yeats, if at all, only outside time. Mongan, the wizard-king who remembers his past "heavenly" lives, knows this bitter truth:

> I have drunk ale from the Country of the Young
> And weep because I know all things now: . . .
> I became a man, a hater of the wind,
> Knowing one, out of all things alone,
>   that his head
> May not lie on the breast nor his lips
>   on the hair
> Of the woman that he loves, until he dies.[42]

Like Stevens, Yeats would believe that because death is the mother of beauty, "hence from her,/ Alone, shall come fulfillment to our dreams/ And our desires" ("Sunday Morning").

For the subjective man, who finds no satisfaction in this world, consummation *may* occur in death: "What else can death be but the beginning of wisdom and power and beauty?"[43] Characteristically, however, Yeats expresses this long-sought fulfillment with uncertainty, as an unanswered question. This perfection and completion, as the narrator of "The Golden Age" hears, are alien to "our fallen world," and "we must weep until the eternal gates swing open" (*Mythol.*, pp. 104-5). Wisdom, power, beauty, and blessing are simultaneously and eternally possessed only after the creation of the new heaven and new earth in the apocalypse,[44] which the early Yeats seeks so that his heart may find satisfaction.

Unity of Being and the Fifteenth Phase

Having passed through these "flaming doors," "certainly it is always to the Condition of Fire, where emotion is not brought to any sudden stop, where there is neither wall nor gate, that we would rise." This extraterrestrial "condition of fire" "is all music and all rest" (*Mythol.*, pp. 364 and 356-57); "the words 'musical,' 'sensuous,' are but descriptions of that converging process," into that unity of being of the supernatural fifteenth phase:

> Its own body possesses the greatest possible beauty, being indeed that body which the soul will permanently inhabit, when all its phases have been repeated according to the number allotted: that which we call the clarified or Celestial Body (*Vision,* pp. 135–36).

This clarified or celestial body corresponds generically to the raised *pneumatikon*. They differ, however, in their genesis, for in Christian "psychology," the *pneumatikon* is perfected in its union with the Godhead, whereas in Yeats's psychology, it is completed in the unification of the self:

> The initiate, all old Karma exhausted, is "the Human Form Divine" of Blake, that Unity of Being Dante compared to a perfectly proportioned human body; henceforth he is self-creating (*E&I,* p. 483).

This perfect unity recurs as Yeats's principal subject, the unattainable ideal: "I thought there could be no aim for a poet or artist except expression of a 'Unity of Being' like that of a 'perfectly proportioned human body'" (*Auto.*, p. 166).[45] Moreover, "Man can only love Unity of Being and that is why such conflicts [to attain it] are of the whole soul" (*Explor.*, p. 302).

"The Phases of the Moon" (a shortened poetic version of *A Vision*) describes the cyclic progression of the soul, which seeks "an image of mysterious wisdom" in its union with the body:

> All thought becomes an image and the soul
> Becomes a body: that body and that soul
> Too perfect at the full to lie in a cradle,
> Too lonely for the traffic of the world:
> Body and soul cast out and cast away
> Beyond the visible world.

At the full moon, the fifteenth phase, when complete subjectivity is achieved, the soul possesses a desired "perfectly proportioned human body": "All dreams of the soul/ End in a beautiful man's or woman's body." But this unity of being is neither compatible with life nor accessible in an afterlife. Blake's engraving of the "Reunion of the Soul and the Body" illustrates this unity as an apocalyptic event:

> The idea of death suggests to me Blake's design (among those he did for Blair's *Grave* I think) of the soul and the body embracing. All men with subjective natures move towards possible ecstasy, all with objective natures towards a possible wisdom.[46]

However, this desired condition does not last; once momentarily attained, the soul then moves outward toward objectivity: "Before the full/ It [the soul] sought itself and afterwards the world." And then the cycle continues as "the first thin crescent is wheeled round once more."

Because there is no resolution in life, the fifteenth phase is associated with death and imagined in the "body['s] perfection brought" in the subjective triumph of the dancer. Dancing "her life away" between the Sphinx, the Greek, feminine herald of wisdom, and Buddha, the Oriental, masculine herald of love— the two guardians of the fifteenth phase (*Vision,* p. 207)—she represents the totality of mind and passionate emotion joined in the "eternal" moment of her dance, of her "pulsating" art. This ideal union of body and soul, though outside time and nature, can, for Yeats, be made in art; in the dancer's still movement, "mind moved yet seemed to stop/ As 'twere a spinning top." Like a "self-sown, self-begotten shape that gives/ Athenian intellect its mastery," the dancer's atemporal union of body and soul represents Yeats's version of the risen spiritual body—

> When all sequence comes to an end, time comes to an end, and the soul puts on the rhythmic or spiritual or luminous body and contemplates all the events of its memory and every possible impulse in an eternal possession of itself in one single moment (*Mythol.*, p. 357; see also *Vision*, p. 139).

"Among School Children": How Can We Know?

"Among School Children" expresses Yeats's highest aspiration—the progress toward this desired condition "where" unity of being is attained. His original prose description of the poem, however, reiterates the impossibility of its realization:

> School children and the thought that live [life] will waste them perhaps that no possible life can fulfill our dreams or even their teacher's hope. Bring in the old thought that life prepares for what never happens.[47]

The poem narrates what is to be learned, especially by the subjective man—that his dreams are unfulfilled and that there is no earthly compensation for this loss. Typifying the bitterness and "curse[s] upon old age" of *The Tower*, this principal recognition and disappointment increase Yeats's tragic "fit of grief or rage."[48]

In school, the old man progresses back through his past states to his original wholeness: we "dream back or think back to that first purity. Is not all our spiritual knowledge perhaps a reversal, a return?" (*E&I*, p. 417). The poem's stanzaic development would converge on that prior and final condition of unity, when "contemplation and desire, united in one, inhabit a world where every beloved image has bodily form, and every bodily form is loved" (*Vision*, p. 136).

Like Crazy Jane, the feminine soul which grows more passionate as man's body ages, Yeats also desires that immortal "true love," when "all could be known or shown/. If Time were but gone." This knowledge, or revelation, however, does not occur until judgment day, when the subjective man's love of perfection is requited and enhanced in the union of beauty (bodily perfection) and wisdom (mental, or spiritual, perfection).

Yeats is here "among school children," i.e., among the education of hopes and the continuation of spiritual knowledge, but not their realization, uncertainly projected at the end. The stanzaic order ("I walk. . . . I dream. . . . I look. . . .") progresses toward a personal reverie ("Her present image floats into the mind") and knowledge. The poem seeks an answer to the central question of what compensates the suffering laborer for his labor, the creator for the created, "for the pang of his birth,/ Or the uncertainty of his setting forth?"

An answer involves finding an enhancing relation between "nature" and its "ghostly paradigm" such that man can be animated by both without "bruising" either. Yet the "living beauty" that nuns and mothers worship and that kept "a marble or a bronze repose" "break[s] hearts" because it is a "presence" of "returned yet unrequited love." This personal and cultural betrayal, virtually omnipresent, characterizes Yeats's peculiar condition—being mocked by those immortal (because self-begotten) images "that all heavenly glory symbolize" and that he would be gathered into and would join.

Yeats's address to these self-begotten images in the last stanza presents his alternative and secular symbol of "all heavenly glory." His pronouncements about both tree and dance "declare" the unity of being which is desired, and the conventional Christian motif of the resurrection of body and soul illuminates their relation. Essentially, I think, the visionary knowledge and union Yeats seeks at the end is neither found nor created nor revealed; and their absence is a theological, not an aesthetic, matter.

The major difficulty in interpreting the last stanza stems from the fact that Yeats's system lacks an adequate eschatological symbol; accordingly, the relation between the symbols is unresolved. For example, the language of the last stanza does not answer the following questions: are "blossoming" and "dancing" alternate ("either-or") and singular examples of compensated labor?; or are they dual and jointly necessary ("and") aspects of the same compensation?; is the "great rooted blossomer" the natural tree of knowledge or the supernatural tree of life?; is the dancer, like that of "Phases of the Moon" and "Double Vision of Michael Robartes," "beyond the visible [i.e., mortal] world"?

The conceptual difficulties prevent, I think, the last stanza from being read as a completed, coherent declaration of unity. The irreconcilable epistemological modalities stem, I think, from the absence of an eschatological reality, which would resolve them. At the same time, it is precisely this ideal condition which Yeats would represent—so that both blossoming and dancing symbolize that heavenly glory "where" body (the natural beauty of process) and soul (the artistic beauty of product) are enhanced ("O brightening glance") and united and known as created: "How can we know the dancer from the dance?"

Another way of clarifying the indeterminacy of Yeats's "last things" is to ask just "where" this union of maker and made occurs—in the natural world of the tree or in the supernatural world of the dancer and the fifteenth phase? Donne's "Anniversaries," for example, deal with this condition of blessedness "where" "shee's now a part both of the Quire and Song" ("I Anniv.," l. 10); and Donne's "holy roome" in which one is a "partaker and a part" of heaven's "rich joys," belongs to the conventional communion of saints.[49] At the end of Book III, "The Soul in Judgment," of *A Vision* (1937) Yeats describes the thirteenth cone, or God, in terms of the dance, and this example suggests that the desired self-unity belongs to the supernatural world:

> It [the thirteenth cone] becomes even conscious of itself as so seen [by man], like some great dancer, the perfect flower of modern culture, dancing some primitive dance and conscious of his or her own life and of the dance (*Vision*, p. 240).

Likewise, in the "Supernatural Songs," when Yeats locates "where" this union occurs, "there" is described in self-contained, literally circular, terminology: "There all the barrel-hoops are knit/ There all the gyres converge in one."

This union, however, does not belong to a theologically legitimated eschatology, because for Yeats traditional religious authority is not accepted and hence is lost. Specifically, Yeats's subjectification (as "the soul's diary") of the resurrection motif results in difficulties in locating and representing its realization; acknowledging this consequence, he concludes that though the thirteenth cone is actually a sphere, "to Man, bound to birth and death, it can never seem so, and that it is the antinomies that force us to find it a cone. Only one symbol exists, though the reflecting mirrors make many appear and all different" (*Vision*, p. 240). In its images' doubleness, the last stanza of "Among School Children" reflects this problem of unifying the many parts of the one; Yeats's quest for this desired union, of subject and object, of mind and body, remains an unanswered question. The artistic magnificence of the poem, for this reader, lies in the attempt to join the supernatural and the natural, the maker and the made. The cause of their final separateness, I think, is an inherently theological (and not a poetical) matter involving the loss of religious authority.

Yeats's Subjectification of Religious Language: Three Poetic Examples

While in one way or another this aim of finding and expressing the sought unity of being remains throughout Yeats, the distinctive religious properties of the motif are lost as its symbolism is secularized:

> *I consider that a conflict between religious and secular thought, because it governs all that is most interior and spiritual in myself, must be the projector of the era (Vision, pp. 256–57; italics mine.)*

Yeats's secular "conversion" of the resurrection motif in part involves its subjectification so that religious language and images pertain not to an external divine order, but rather belong to man's self (or, soul), the *anima hominis*. This psychic appropriation appears in his early period (through *The Wind Among the Reeds,* 1899) when occultism subsumes eschatology. For example, at the end of "The Secret Rose," the final consummation which the speaker seeks deals not with the great marriage of men and God, but with the union of man with "heavenly spiritual beauty," or wisdom:

> I, too, await
> The hour of thy great wind of love and hate.
> When shall the stars be blown about the sky;
> Like the sparks blown out of a smith, and die?
> Surely thine hour has come, thy great wind blows,
> Far-off, most secret, and inviolate Rose?[50]

In his *Autobiography* Yeats identifies this red rose as "intellectual beauty," whose "romantic" relation to the poet would open the "invisible gates [of heavenly wisdom] . . . as they opened for Blake" and reveal "the strange things said/ By God to the bright hearts of those long dead,/ And learn to chaunt a tongue men do not know" (*Auto.*, pp. 169-70 and "To the Rose upon the Rood of Time").

Complete beauty is a distinctive feature of unity of being, the fifteenth phase, the completion of the subjective; its cognitive correlate is self-knowledge—the completion and "eternal possession of itself in one single moment" (*Mythol.*, p. 357). It is this total identification of the self with all that it seeks within that Yeats awaits.

In "A Prayer for my Daughter," while he does not identify to whom he prays, Yeats's "radical innocence" is defined by self-contained internal harmony:

> The soul recovers radical innocence
> And learns at last that it is self-delighting,
> Self-appeasing, self-affrighting,
> And that its own sweet will is Heaven's will

While he does not reject the concept of a heavenly order, its "religious" status and function are subsumed and defined by the personal ("its own sweet will"). Further, Yeats is typically vague about the conditions of such final knowledge: why is it a "recovery?" when does the soul acquire such knowledge? does it learn "at last" or is it self-sufficient only "at last"? (i.e., is this phrase adverbial or adjectival?) how does it so learn? The answers in the last stanza of "custom" and "ceremony" seem unconvincing in the context of the poem. This problem stems from the absence of an external, public, and accessible Savior— the unnamed receiver of the prayer.

Yeats's declining to name either the prayed-to Savior or the "fitter welcome" that he offers naturalizes and thereby secularizes death. "In Memory of Major Robert Gregory," beginning as a processional of the dead, converges on Yeats's memory of Gregory, one of the "cheated dead." Of his former friends, Lionel Johnson's Catholicism offers him "a measureless consummation that he dreamed."[51] But Yeats knows no such personal transcendence and even "our perfect man . . . share[s] in that discourtesy of death." This perfection, however, as Yeats describes it, belongs solely to the secular, natural world:

> Soldier, scholar, horseman, he,
> And all he did done perfectly. . . .
> As 'twere all life's epitome.

In Christianity, the perfect man is, of course, Jesus; and without this divine model of transcendence, there is no compensation for Gregory's death.[52]

Consequently, Yeats "translates" the public language of religion into a subjective "eschatology," whose source is personal and which thereby loses its redemptive validity. In "All Soul's Night" the generative speaker turns in on his own mind, "wound in mind's pondering," in order "to say/ A certain marvellous thing." The narrative structure, built upon a personal catalogue ("Horton's the first I call . . ."), restates the absence of a shared public credence, since "none but the living mock" Yeats's marvelous mental "apparitions."

A personal, private image joins and, in effect, replaces a traditional, sacramental symbol or situation:

> Two thoughts were so mixed up I could not tell
> Whether of her or God he thought the most,
> But think that his mind's eye,
> When upward turned, on one sole image fell;
> And that a slight companionable ghost,
> Wild with divinity,
> Had so lit up the whole
> Immense miraculous house
> The Bible promised us,
> It seemed a gold-fish swimming in a bowl.

The dead woman's presence unexpectedly converges on a homely image of illumination,[53] instead of the traditional "immense miraculous" one; and this substitution emphasizes, I think, the personal and uncertain, if not absurd, nature of the Biblical promise in Yeats's view.

Similarly at the end, Yeats's singly sufficing thought is generated from and belongs to his own mind: "Such thought, that in it bound/ I need no other thing." It does not reach that heaven "where the blessed dance," but ends as an image of the grave, "as mummies in the mummy-cloth are wound." If such a condition, analogous to that of being "free and yet fast,/ Being both Chance and Choice/ . . . And sink[ing] into its own delight at last," is blessed, it is typically self-conferred and independent of any holy "other." And what is known ("I have mummy truths to tell") is held presently unrevealed, in the incompleted process of knowing: "Such thought—such thought have I that hold it tight/ Till meditation master all its parts."[54]

The Unattainable Land of the Heart's Desire

Yeats's system lacks an eschatology beyond that of personal "meditative mastery." What Blake calls the "divine vision"— the *Logos* of John i—is absent. Instead, Yeats seeks the "eros vision," in which the soul's ascent is prompted by human love.[55] In fact, I feel that Yeats is primarily a love poet, whose best poems are either about, or occasioned by, women, who writes with a tragic sense of personal loss, and whose characteristic subject is the laments of the body and the soul for lost beauty and wisdom. Yeats's treatment of this "eros" archetype differs from Donne's and Blake's precisely on the matter of the soul's fate in relation to the divine beloved.

For Donne the sanction, model, and goal for earthly spiritual and sexual union is the hypostatical, heavenly "great marriage." For Blake, the union of man with his emanation, as well as with his four Zoas, "repairs" and returns him to his prior wholeness; further, this union with the beloved is necessary for his present creative and moral well-being, and it is the means by which man and God are joined. Blake's emanation is man's inspiration, whom Yeats renames the Daimon.

For Yeats, however, the relation of these analogous figures is opposite, "for man and Daimon feed the hunger in one another's hearts" (*Mythol.*, p. 335). Though Yeats's Daimon is directly associated with the poet's creativity—as an expression of his "unsatisfied desires"[56]—its cost is continual conflict; there is a deep enmity between man and his Daimon, i.e., between the poet and his beloved muse:

> my imagination runs from Daimon to sweetheart, and I divine an analogy that evades the intellect . . . that it may be "sexual love," which is "founded upon spiritual hate," is an image of the warfare between man and Daimon (*Mythol.*, pp. 336 and *J* 54:12, K 685).

Yeats's associating the mortal beloved ("sweetheart") and the immortal beloved (Daimon) in this description derives from Blake's uniting man with his emanation; however, Yeats's association differs in that he conceives of the two not only as separate but as warring: "Lacking suitable objects of desire, the relation between man and *Daimon* becomes more clearly a struggle or even a relation of enmity" (*Vision*, p. 131).

For Yeats's subjective man there is no consummate union with either beloved. Yeats's comment on sexual conjunction indicates his skepticism about such unions, physically or spiritually:

The present Pope has said in his last Encyclical that the natural union of man and woman has a kind of sacredness. He thought doubtless of the marriage of Christ and the Church, whereas I see in it a symbol of that eternal instant where antinomy is resolved. It is not the resolution itself (*Vision,* p. 214).

There is no earthly resolution, either of the heart or of the soul, save in death, as in "Cap and Bells," for example.

Like Forgael in *The Shadowy Waters,* Yeats's "secret" and "passionate" wandering is unconsummated,

> For it is a love that I am seeking for,
> But of a beautiful, unheard-of kind
> That is not in the world.

This love consists of the "dreams . . . that the heart longs for" and that are wisdom, for "wisdom and dreams are one."[57]

The "land of heart's desire" for love's wisdom is outside of and incompatible with this natural world (*Col. Plays,* p. 95); however, while the Biblical "new heaven and new earth" are also incompatible with this world, access to them has triumphantly been made possible ("Jesus . . . Opens Eternity"), so that man need not be left stranded on the watery shore of this shadowy world. The same "passionate wanderer," Yeats's subjective man, recurs in *The Shadowy Waters,* where he is told that "none but the dead, or those that never lived,/ Can know that ecstasy." Because Forgael seeks that unchanging passion of imagined love before all else, he heroically asks and answers, "What matter/ If I am going to my death?—for there,/ Or somewhere, I shall find the love they have promised."

The qualification, "or somewhere," suggests Yeats's uncertainty about the existence of this "unimaginable happiness," which is tantamount to his description of "paradise [which] is happiness, the abundance of earth, the natural life, every man's desire, or some such thing."[58] This indefinite "some such thing" is elaborated in *The Unicorn from the Stars* by Martin, the incarnated soul from heaven,[59] whose "business" is "revelation":

Father John, Heaven is not what we have believed it to be. It is not quiet, it is not singing and making music, and all strife at an end. I have seen it, I have been there. The lover still loves, but with a greater passion, and the rider still rides, but the horse goes like the wind and leaps the ridges, and *the battle goes on always, always. That is the joy of Heaven, continual battle* . . . it is not here; we shall not come to that joy, that battle, *till we have put out the senses,* everything that can be seen and handled, as I put out this candle. . . . We must put out the whole world as I put out this candle. . . . We must put out the light of the stars and the light of the sun and the light of the moon . . . till we have brought everything to nothing once again. I saw in a broken vision, but not all is clear to me. Where there is nothing, where there is nothing—there is God![60]

The model for this Yeatsian "heavenly" battle, however joyous, may well be earthly conflict, the first result of Blake's "wars of Eden"; and this battle is not the great intellectual one fought with spiritual swords, but the heroic one of the questing soul.

"Ego Dominus Tuus": The Divided Poet

In spite of his desire for total unity, mortal man finds himself in division and conflict:

Man can only love Unity of Being and that is why such conflicts are conflicts of the whole soul . . . there arise[s] between us [man and any "opponent" with a different view] a struggle like that of the sexes. All life is such a struggle. When a plant draws from and feeds upon the soil, expression is its joy, but it is wisdom to be drawn forth and eaten (*Explor.,* p. 302).

As the plant image (elsewhere, the tree) would suggest, such conflict is not only tantamount to life but also prerequisite for creation: "passion is conflict, consciousness is conflict," and "no mind can engender till divided into two," for "all creation is from conflict, whether with our own mind or with that of others" (*Explor.*, p. 331 and *Auto.*, pp. 231 and 389). This recurring combination of conflict and creation is the contrary and necessary other half of Yeats's search for unity.

Moreover, of these two "contrary states," Yeats typically chooses that of the divided creator; this choice necessitates, for him, losing both natural and spiritual goods to gain those of the poet: "I think that all noble things are the result of warfare; . . . great poetry and philosophy [are the result] of invisible warfare, the division of a mind within itself, a victory, the sacrifice of a man to himself" (*E&I,* p. 321). This "tragic war" is the subject of "Ego Dominus Tuus," one of Yeats's several dialogues of self and soul.

The two speakers, *Hic* and *Ille,* represent respectively personal, historical man and the impersonal, archetypal man, whom Yeats would summon to disclose all that he seeks. While man's individual and communal life are preserved, and enhanced, in the resurrection, these aspects of the "self" are divided and opposed in Yeats. The possibility of their union depends on each half's finding and possessing what it lacks: the subjective *Ille* calls his opposite half "by the help of an [archetypal] image" while the objective *Hic* "would find myself and not an image." But such reconciliation with himself and the world in which he lives is, at best, only momentary for the subjective poet, whose "aching [because unsatisfied] heart/ Conceives a changeless work of art." *Ille* understands even Dante as fashioning his work on an unattainable ideal: "A hunger for the apple on the bough/ Most out of reach." With typical "nonchalance," Yeats includes himself with Dante and Shelley (and Landor) in phase 17, where unity of being becomes "more easy than at any other phase" (*Vision,* p. 141); but his description of Dante here casts doubt on that wished-for ease. Nonetheless, Yeats's unrelieved passion for unity remains as the subject of his tragic art.[61]

Ille, however, does not possess the arcane image of "all that I seek" within himself, so that he would call to "the mysterious one," his anti-self, "being indeed my double," who discloses the sought-after knowledge: "The other self, the anti-self or the antithetical self . . . comes to those who are no longer deceived, whose passion is reality" (*Mythol.,* p. 331), of which art is a vision. This creature, who corresponds in a contrary fashion with Blake's emanation in her form as "the created," Yeats calls the "mask":

> As life goes on, we discover that certain thoughts sustain us in defeat, or give us victory, whether over ourselves or others, and it is these thoughts, tested by passion, that we call convictions. Among subjective men (in all those, that is, who must spin a web out of their own bowls) the victory is an intellectual daily recreation of all that exterior fate snatches away, and so is that fate's antithesis; while what I have called "the Mask" is an emotional antithesis to all that comes out of their internal nature. We begin to live when we have conceived life as tragedy (*Auto.,* p. 128; see also *Vision,* p. 142).

Finding that this life leaves the heart and senses tragically unsatisfied, psychic survival for Yeats necessitates creating whatever is wanting (i.e., desired and absent). Without either the divine assistance of the Holy Ghost or the human inspiration of the emanation, Yeats's writing of poetry depends on the division and "quarrel" within himself, most frequently between his instinctual and spiritual needs (*Mythol.,* pp. 331-32).

The Self-Begotten, "Unchristened" Poet

Although in Christianity and Blake's interpretation of it, man and God were originally united but now separated, they may be reunited through Jesus. Contrastingly, in Yeats's subjective system there is neither a mediator nor a definitive return to or attainment of the desired unity; and this breach is an unavoidable cost of secularization. Insofar as God appears in Yeats, he is present as an absolute rival, in mortal conflict with natural man: "The Man in Man fights the God in Man"—" 'the one living the other's . . . death and dying the other's life.' "[62]

To survive, then, the poet must be his own creator, as Yeats describes the self-begotten man of phase 17 (where he places himself, aptly, with Shelley) :[63]

> The *Body of Fate,* therefore, derived from a phase of renunciation, is "loss," and works to make impossible "simplification by intensity." The being, through the intellect, selects some object of desire, for a representation of the *Mask* as Image, some woman, perhaps, and the *Body of Fate* snatches away the object. Then the intellect (*Creative Mind*), which in the most antithetical phases were better described as imagination, must substitute some new image of desire; and in the degree of its power and of its attainment of unity, relate that which is lost, that which has snatched it away, to the new image of desire, that which threatens the new image to the being's unity (*Vision,* p. 142).

As this passage suggests, for Yeats poetry is largely a symbolic compensation for various losses, psychically tantamount to and designated as the exile from Eden, as the early story "The Golden Age" describes:

> I seemed to hear a voice of lamentation out of the Golden Age. It told me that we are imperfect, incomplete, and no more like a beautiful woven web, but like a bundle of cords knotted together and flung into a corner. It said that the world was once perfect and kindly, and that still the kindly and perfect world existed, but buried like a mass of roses under many spadefuls of earth. The faeries and the more innocent of the spirits dwelt within it, and lamented over our fallen world in the lamentation of the wind-tossed reeds (*Mythol.,* p. 104).

In the early poetry, Yeats's search for fulfillment, in the "land of heart's desire," will be completed when the poet is united with the "white woman," whose instinctual component is passion and whose spiritual essence is wisdom.[64] Yeats would be united with his feminine, emanative, or spiritual half; but not "until God burn time" in the apocalypse will he possess both bodily and spiritual goods together, unbruised and augmented. Yeats continually waits for this union on judgment day, and until then, like Crazy Jane, laments that

> "Love is all
> Unsatisfied
> That cannot take the whole
> Body and soul."

Yeats's desire for this unity of being, the beauty of the "perfectly proportioned human body," the wisdom of the beloved soul, and their incompatibility with life constitute the characteristic concerns of his poetry, which celebrates the secular heart's heroic ventures:

> . . . I—though heart might find relief
> Did I become a Christian man and choose
>   for my belief
> What seems most welcome in the tomb—
>   play a predestined part.
> Homer is my example and his unchristened heart.

As implied in the symbolic progression of "Among School Children," because Yeats's system lacks a traditional (trans-temporal and trans-personal), authoritative eschatology, his last things are self-created and "artistic."

"Sailing to Byzantium": The Last Things of Life and Art

Yeats finds no reconciliation between body and soul, his instinctual and spiritual halves, which are at war, each living the other's death, dying the other's life. Corroboration of this view exists in the fact that Yeats's conceptual framework does not preserve both bodily and spiritual goods at once; hence, for example, in terms of *A Vision,* phases 15 and 1, respectively, oppose each other and are incompatible with human life. Second, as Mrs. Yeats's recollections and Mr. Yeats's scholars suggest,[65] this poem was conceived to explore again the tragedy of sexuality in the perpetual virginity of the soul. As an "old man," he seeks to exchange his "bodily decreptitude" for spiritual "wisdom."

This *voyage*—"to recover my spirits"⁶⁶—is the subject of "Sailing to Byzantium" (written in late 1926, when he was 61):

> Now I am trying to write about the state of my soul, for it is right for an old man [to do so]. . . . Byzantium was the centre of the European civilization and the source of its spiritual philosophy, so I symbolize the search for the spiritual life by a journey to that city.⁶⁷

While Byzantium was the capital of eastern Christianity, this fact does not interest Yeats, as his famous description of it in *A Vision* indicates; this city is "where religious, aesthetic, and practical life were one" and "where" unity of being would be found: "If I were left to myself I would make phase 15 coincide with Justinian's reign, that great age of building in which one may conclude Byzantine art was perfected" (*Vision*, pp. 279 and 281). While this unity (of phase 15) is sought in "Sailing to Byzantium," Yeats again creates poetry out of the division between natural and spiritual well-being.

The conflict, between the sensual (animal) and the intellectual-spiritual (*anima*), is the initial generative proposition: "Caught in that sensual music all neglect/ Monuments of unageing intellect." The only enemy of the beautiful and the innocent is time; while whatever is begotten and born dies, both the intellect and its created monuments are here "unageing."⁶⁸

Blake also believes mortal life to be a betrayal and for him, as for the Christian, "the death of Jesus set me free"; without a Savior, however, Yeats would transfer "immortality" to the artistic product. In this poem Yeats holds that the made object perhaps is safe from time, but is not saving *per se*, i.e., is without intrinsic redemptive value. Since Yeats's body and soul die each other's life, to survive, the soul typically sinks in upon itself, "studying/ Monuments of its own magnificence," found in Byzantium. As the soul lives upon itself and would confer its own "immortality," so Byzantium is holy because its art is "perfected" (*Vision* (1925), p. 244 and *Vision* (1937), p. 281).

Here, as in Yeats's other major poems on the matter, art represents a possibility, but not the achievement, of "salvation"; this "creed," however, lacks the ontological authority of shared religious belief. "All our art," writes Yeats, "is but the putting our faith and the evidence of our faith into words or forms and our faith is in ecstasy,"⁶⁹ where art and "the end" are coterminous for the subjective man (*E&I*, p. 287).

Insofar as Yeats here conceives of eternity, it is associated

with the made thing, the artistic productions of time; and it resides in the domain of the poet, not of the priest. Accordingly,
those "standing in God's holy fire" are sages (not the conventional saints or blessed ones among the purgatorial flames
through which Dante passes in purification) ;[70] they exist in the
extraterrestrial "condition of fire," in which spiritual wisdom,
but not bodily power, is found (*Mythol.*, pp. 356-57). What
they offer is not so much holiness, or wholeness, as the wisdom
of "supreme art,"[71] for they are the singing masters of the soul
which knows itself, unlike the "dying animal" of the body which
does not. The poem aspires to Yeats's final plea to the sage-
muses to "gather me/ Into the artifice of eternity."

This last request (especially as it is elaborated in stanza 4)
corresponds to the ambiguous union at the end of "Among School
Children." In both poems the body and soul are not reunited
with each other and finally united to God, as in the resurrection;
instead, maker and made would be joined. Through the possibly
"unageing" production of time—"artifice"—with which he is in
love, Yeats would enter the Gnostic eternity of the soul and leave
the dying animal of the body. Further, Yeats conceives of "eternity" as "artifice," in its nonpejorative sense as the "supreme"
creation of the soul. The reversible genitive (*of* in "artifice of
eternity") construction of the metaphor joins the two nouns as
mutually belonging to and defining each other in this central
identification.

However, in the last stanza (again as in "Among School
Children") what is wished for and gained is not successfully
symbolized because the necessary religious resources are absent.
For the internalized search for the spiritual life (the poem's
stated subject) to be aesthetically realized, the poem's task is
to represent the soul's purified existence as one which is free of
bodily decay. Sturge Moore's criticism—that "a gold smith's
bird is as much nature as a man's body, especially if it only
sings like Homer or Shakespeare of what is past or passing or
to come to Lords and Ladies"—[72] is valid and points out how
Yeats's imagination is not "out of nature." Moreover, his "holy
city" is secular (with aristocratic lords and ladies) and still
within the time-bound world which he would leave.

And therein lies the poem's conceptual issue. In Yeats there is
no authenticated transcendence to that eschatological reality of
new Jerusalem; accordingly, as in this poem, man-made art
would be his "last thing" in this time-bound world. While Yeats

states that "I have somewhere read that in the Emperor's palace at Byzantium was a tree made of gold and silver, and artificial birds that sang," another "source" for the last line is the first stanza of Blake's "Introduction" to the *Songs of Experience,* especially the line "Who Present, Past, & Future sees"; but Blake's ancient Bard, like the four creatures around God's throne, is outside of time and can therefore see beyond all time into eternity.[73] While the eternal can enter the temporal world, the temporal cannot, unaided, pass into the eternal realm; and the sages by whom Yeats would be gathered into the artifice of eternity do not possess the power to accomplish their religious task, that of salvation (of the soul and the body). The golden bird represents an artistic product which is an improvement, but not a transformation, of the natural world.

"Byzantium": The Upward Metamorphosis of the Artistic Process

Byzantium is Yeats's "holy city," whose architecture suggests to him "the Sacred City in the Apocalypse of St. John," whose art completely absorbs (gathers in) the impersonal artist and represents "the vision of a whole people" (*Vision,* pp. 279-80). Byzantium is the sacred home of that long-sought personal and cultural unity, and its Blakean ancestor is Golgonooza, through which travelers pass inward to eternity. The subject of "Byzantium" is the artistic process of purifying, i.e., of creating, those poetic images which are at last capable of symbolizing permanent and transcendent metamorphosis, traditionally imaged in the resurrection.

This transmutation is corroborated by the two standard statements that "Byzantium began as an 'explication' of the supernatural"[74] and as a description (occasioned by the death of a friend) of

> Byzantium as it is in the system toward the end of the first Christian millennium. A walking mummy. Flames at the street corners where the soul is purified, the birds of hammered gold singing in the golden trees, in the harbour, offering their backs to the waiting dead that they may carry them off to Paradise (*Explor.,* p. 290).

Again, the goal is unity of being, and Yeats's "most difficult" task becomes aesthetic because metaphysical:

Because the 15th phase can never find direct human expression, being a supernatural incarnation, it impressed upon work and thought an element of strain and artifice, a desire to combine elements which may be incompatible, or which suggest by the combination something supernatural (*Vision*, p. 292).

Without the authoritative language of a religious domain, the supernatural and its accessibility are highly problematic; the poet, alone, without a mediator or guide, must summon, unwind, and master his own "mummy truths."

The unusual perceptual difficulty in stanzas 1-3 derives from the simultaneous, if not prior, problem of trying to make an all-inclusive and totally objective ("starlit") or subjective ("moon-lit") statement about "all that man is." What can be sorted out assuredly, however, are the unpurged mortal images of day and the purged immortal superhuman images of this night of phase 1 or 15; the unnameable yet supernatural images, "more miracle than bird or handiwork . . . in glory of changeless metal" scorn aloud, when embittered by the moon, the "fury and the mire of human veins," which Yeats would "break," i.e., transcend. This differentiation, between the temporal and the eternal, a kind of muddled Blakean last judgment, begins the artistic purgation to find or create supernatural images of immortality.

Through benign flames the blood-begotten spirits of the dead pass and thereby are purified ("grew pure in mind") of "all complexities of fury." These self-begotten flames ("an agony of trance") initiate the extraterrestrial "condition of fire": "When all sequence comes to an end, time comes to an end, and the soul puts on the rhythmic or spiritual body or luminous body."[75] This transformation, occurring in stanzas 4-5, again is rather ambiguously conceived (both conceptually and syntatically).

The second stanza of "News for the Delphic Oracle" elucidates the dolphins' movements in "Byzantium":

> Straddling each a dolphin's back
> And steadied by a fin,
> Those Innocents re-live their death, . . .
> And the brute dolphins plunge
> Until, in some cliff-sheltered bay
> Where wades the choir of love
> Proffering its sacred laurel crowns,
> They pitch their burdens off.

" 'Dolphins . . . form a mystic escort of the dead to the Islands of the Blest,' " and according to F. A. C. Wilson, Yeats was familiar with this Platonic and Pythagorean doctrine. The "choir of love" toward which they progress is the immortal love of the disembodied spirit, not that of the heavenly choir of saints, united in body and soul, praising God.[76]

As in the desired upward metamorphosis of "Sailing to Byzantium," Yeats portrays the body's (mere mire and blood) "dying" so that the soul may live unpolluted. In "Byzantium" his "vision" is twofold—first, of purging life's bitter images into those purified spiritual images of an afterlife, and second, of producing, art, i.e., of the process of creating "those images that yet/ Fresh images beget." Taken together, these acts represent how art is made and endures—in the upward transmutation of life's "mire and blood" into art's marmorean self-sufficiency. Both aspects of this single, central enterprise require renouncing instinctual complexity, the fury and mire of human veins, to gain spiritual, or symbolic, glory, "of changeless metal." If Yeats here more successfully describes an "afterlife," it is distinctively characterized by the separation of body and soul (and thus in contrast to the resurrection). In a relevant passage from *Rosa Alchemica* Yeats speaks of the "supreme dream of the alchemist, the transmutation of the weary heart into the weariless spirit," and the terms of this alchemical change pertain to the desired metamorphosis in both Byzantium poems, which invoke "divine alchemists, who labour continually, turning lead into gold, weariness into ecstasy, bodies into souls, the darkness into God" (*Mythol.*, pp. 269-70).

Whereas in "Sailing to Byzantium" the artistic product would be "eternal," here the *process* of creation attains eschatological significance. This change—from the made to the making—of the locus of "immortality" indicates another aspect of Yeats's secularization and loss of the traditionally promised end: since nothing endures forever—neither life nor art—the possibility of an eternal existence is lost. Instead, Yeats's "afterlife" of the purified consists of the artistic process of generating "those images that yet/ Fresh images beget."

The golden smithies[77] of the Emperor forge "marbles of the dancing floor," whose marmorean perfection "break bitter furies of complexity . . . [of] That dolphin-torn, that gong-tormented sea" of time and space. Those self-begotten images, I think, are of the soul's marble "monuments of unageing intellect"; and being self-sown, they are Yeats's secular images of "immortality," since they are either those of God (the starlit dome of phase 1) or those of perfect beauty (the moonlit dome of phase 15). This conceptual ambiguity is built into "Byzantium," so that the soul's purification (the supernatural object of phase 1) is an aesthetic process (self-begotten in those images of complete beauty of phase 15).

"The Supernatural Songs"

The titles and cover designs of Yeats's individual books are, of course, significant, and Yeats associates, historically, *A Full Moon in March* with the resurrection.[78] Of these poems, the "Supernatural Songs" deal specifically with that extraterrestrial unity of being when "whole is joined to whole."

"Ribh at the Tomb of Baile and Aillinn" speaks of the miraculous measureless consummation which Yeats's subjective man has always sought and not found:

> The miracle that gave them such a death
> Transfigured to pure substance what had once
> Been bone and sinew; when such bodies join
> There is no touching here, nor touching there,
> Nor straining joy, but whole is joined to whole;
> For the intercourse of angels is a light
> Where for its moment both seem lost, consumed.

Though this transfiguration is momentary and indefinite ("such bodies"), Yeats alludes to the pure spiritual substance that Baile and Aillin become in death.

Very often Yeats associates this union of body and soul with sexual consummation, as in the Solomon and Sheba poems and in "The Chosen," and not with a religious cause or event. The natural marriage bed, and not the supernaturally empty tomb, symbolizes the "solved antinomy"[79] for Yeats. Accordingly, such a blessed union is, at best, transient, existing only "for its moment." Although "eternity is passion," passion is not eternity, for "yet the world stays" to which the lovers return.[80]

When Yeats conceives of the supernatural, it is most frequently in terms of the natural:

> Natural and supernatural with the self-same
> ring are wed.

As man, as beast, as an ephemeral fly begets,
    Godhead begets Godhead,
For things below are copies, the great
    Smaragdine Tablet said.

Blake-Los would have none of this binding down to the in-definite, multiple, natural world, but since, in Yeats's view, the natural is not transfigured and raised, he brings the supernatural down into it. A distinctive difference between human and divine love, however, remains, namely, that the latter is self-begotten and therefore wholly in possession of itself: "Godhead on God-head in sexual spasm begot Godhead." "The point of the poem," Yeats explains, "is that we beget and bear because of the incom-pleteness of our love."[81]

The soul's self-delighting happiness resides in "its own cause or ground," and only God can wholly possess her. "Ribh Con-siders Christian Love Insufficient" because "hatred [as well as love] of God may bring the soul to God." Whereas in Christian theology man's body (individually and collectively) and soul are joined together and with God, Yeats cannot reconcile the in-stinctual and the spiritual, for "at stroke of midnight[when God "wins" man] soul cannot endure/ A bodily or mental furniture." Without a Savior and untransfigured, the body is at war with the soul and with God. While Ribh finds Christianity insufficient, he does not find what will suffice to provide the desired whole (of body, soul, and God).

The "Supernatural Songs" end with "Meru," the ancient eastern sacred mountain. This place and the poem imply that the Western tradition is "desolate" of reality[82] because it is "hooped together" under the manifold illusion of wholeness. The Eastern hermits, passively and objectively, "know/ That day brings round the night, that before dawn/ His [man's] glory and his monuments are gone."

The reverenced "monuments of unaging intellect" are also subject to decay, as Yeats discovers (by 1930). More permanent and unchanging than "those images" is the process of change itself. While Spenser, for example, also holds change as the first law of nature, he, unlike Yeats, conceives of that "time when no more change shall be . . . but thence-forth all shall rest eternally/ With Him that is the God of Sabbaoth hight." Whereas Chris-tian history linearly progresses to its divine end, human history is viewed by Yeats as cyclicly alternating between objective and subjective phases:

Each age unwinds the thread another age had wound, and it amuses me to remember that before Phidias, and his westward-moving art, Persia fell, and that when full moon came round again, amid eastward-moving thought, and brought Byzantine glory, Rome fell; and at the outset of our westward-moving Renaissance Byzantium fell; all things dying each other's life, living each other's death (*Vision,* pp. 270–71).

Last Poems: The Maker's "Tragic Joy"

That cyclic transience is the only permanence informs Yeats's major last poems. One's momentary rejoicing is in face of the recurring, contrary gyres, in which "all things run," again and again. If man knows joy, it derives from the fact that beauty and satisfaction are passing (transient) and not permanent. Yeats's "last thing," as portrayed in "Lapis Lazuli," consists of tragic "gaiety transfiguring all that dread" of the final scene (destruction and death) in the *aesthetic process*. Because there is no Savior in Yeats's "painted-stage world," the source and agent of gaiety and renewal is the man-who-makes: "All things fall and are built again,/ And those that build them again are gay."

Yeats's concept of history as cyclic (between two contrary gyres), in contrast to the linear, unidirectional course of Christian history, provides a means of finding and preserving at least part of what is traditionally promised at the end of time. In the viewer's imagining the artifact and in the process of creation from which it stems—in these dual acts resides whatever "immortal" but tragic delight and harmony there is: "One asks for mournful melodies;/ Accomplished fingers begin to play." Staring on all this tragic scene, Yeats's eyes, like their "ancient, glittering eyes," are gay. Ending centripetally, the poem's "rejoicing" is self-begotten and perceptual, for the process, that of imagining and building, outlasts the product.

Whatever Yeats's reasons for choosing "Under Ben Bulben" to appear as his last poem, it is an appropriate "ending"—presenting the Yeatsian "profane perfection of mankind." This poem is in part an answer to "The Man and the Echo" about the soul's judgment and fate; here, in typical Platonic fashion,[88] Yeats conceives of death as the separation of body and soul, rather than their Christian reunion. Uncertain about an afterlife, Yeats asks "O Rocky Voice,/ Shall we in that great night rejoice?" Like Blake and Shelley, Yeats would come "proud, open-eyed, and laughing to the tomb."

"Under Ben Bulben" begins with a Shelleyian disdain of death, in which completeness of passion may at last be won. Yet Yeats's interpretation of this "immortality" returns man to natural vacillation: "Many times man lives and dies/ Between two extremities,/ That of race and that of soul." This cycle corresponds to that of the twenty-eight phases of the moon, alternating between complete objectivity (the race) and complete subjectivity (the soul). Without breaking out of this restricting circle of destiny, man is but thrust "back into the human mind again."

The judgment prayed for in the third section occurs internally when man "completes his partial mind,/ [and] For an instant stands at ease." Yet such momentary resolution but preludes the "violence" (conflict) which generates the accomplishment of work or life.

Yeats views art as "bring[ing] the soul of man to God," but this "perfection" is "profane" and sexual, without a Donnean "remembrancer" and without a Blakean eternality:

> When sleepers wake and yet still dream,
> And when it's vanished still declare,
> With only bed and bedstead there,
> That heavens had opened.

The "greater dream," the vision of the new heaven in eternity, "had gone" and leaves the vacillating gyres of natural history to "run on" and on. Yeats's self-begotten legacy is the secular artist's craft ("trade"): "Sing whatever is well made."

> *"I lie awake night after night*
> *And never get the answers right. . . .*
> *Shall we in that great night rejoice?"*

Yeats's principal motive, I would suggest, for wanting to "remake" himself till he is William Blake is to make truth also obey his call; and Yeats's heroic stature resides in this tragic attempt to master the absolute. But whereas Blake sees through the eternal eye of imagination, Yeats sees, I think, with the vegetable eye of nature.

Not holding any religious (specifically, Christian) eschatology, Yeats's imagination lies on this side of eternity. Without theological certainty of knowing "translunar paradise," Yeats characteristically speaks of the goal of his guest as a question:

Are he and his blue-robed companions [Blake's visionary company] and their like, "the eternal realities" of which we are the reflection "in the vegetable glass of nature" or a momentary dream? To answer is to take sides on the only controversy in which it is greatly worth taking sides, and in the only controversy which *may never be decided* (*E&I*, p. 152; italics mine).

Perhaps the primary reason that Yeats may never decide, especially in favor of the "eternal realities" of the imagination, both human and divine, is that his subjective system is not religious (in the simplest sense of believing in a redeeming God). One limitation of a secular viewpoint, as we find in Yeats, is that it neither finds nor reveals the hoped-for, fulfilling reality because salvation depends on a divine teleology. Skeptically, Yeats questions the "better" life after death (as in "King and No King"):

> And I that have not your faith, how shall
> I know
> That in the blinding light beyond the grave
> We'll find so good a thing as that
> we have lost?

Without, for example, Augustine's beatific vision and without Blake's "divine vision," Yeats is "blind" to the blessings of the resurrection.

When Yeats considers the incarnation and transfiguration, he reconceives them in aesthetic and "psychic" terms—as the soul's two movements in creation: the incarnation is "as" the Dionysiac impulse to create forms, whereas the transfiguration is "as" the Apollonian gesture to transcend form.[84] These two opposing movements of the soul are "systematized" in *A Vision*—the "soul's diary" and struggles extended throughout history—[85] as the recurring twenty-eight phases of the moon. In this natural model there is only momentary resolution and no finality, except as cyclic change itself.

Without an eschatological reality, there is no reunion and resurrection of the body and soul in Yeats's system; their respective loves are neither reconciled nor preserved:

> For all life longs for the Last Day
> And there's no man but cocks his ear

> To know when Michael's trumpet cries
> That flesh and bone may disappear,
> And souls as if they were but sighs.

In the early love poems—and the majority and best of Yeats's poetry is love poetry, as he also observes—[86] the body must be assimilated to the soul, whereas in the late love poems, the soul must be assimilated to the body.[87] Characteristically, one is "bruised to pleasure" the other; they attain no benign and enhancing relation, as in Christian doctrine (of the spiritual body) or in Blake's "psychology" (the union of man and his emanation and the fourfold harmony of the Zoas).

Yeats's system contains no definite or permanently achieved model of the transfiguration and resurrection, except as presented in the aesthetic process and as momentarily experienced "profanely" in sexual union. Completed unity of being—Dante's "perfectly proportioned human body," Blake's "human form divine"—is both incompatible with life and unattained, if not also unattainable, in an "afterlife." God typically occupies the place of death in the Yeatsian vision (as in "Blood and Moon," for example),[88] and the source of creation and renewal is in the unchristened heart, where all Yeatsian ladders start.

Nor is there the collective eternal form of unity, the Christian communion of saints, the Blakean brotherhood of Eden. Yeats associates such cultural unity with artistic, not moral goods: this great unity exists "in the realms of imagination which we shall make the whole human family One Man."[89] Yeats's Byzantium, too, is a transient phenomenon, of earthly history, not of heavenly eternity.

Yet there can be no question of Yeats's profound desire for unity of being, when the soul and body are perfectly harmonized and augmented, "the sense of the self in the highest mode imaginable."[90] Like Blake's human form divine, Yeats's unity of the fifteenth phase corresponds to the resurrected body and soul, which constitute the simultaneous possession of formerly irreconcilable contrary goods. A reason for the nonattainability of individual and communal wholeness, is a definitive and traditional form, is that such blessedness is neither self-begotten nor self-conferred nor "composite," but derives realization in the transcendent and divine "other."

In fact, in "A General Introduction for my Work" Yeats becomes unusually pious and his declaration of faith partly delineates the "continuity" of the motif we are studying:

I was born into this faith, have lived in it, and shall die in it; my Christ, a legitimate deduction from the Creed of St. Patrick as I think is that Unity of Being Dante compared to a perfectly proportioned human body, Blake's "Imagination," what the Upanishads have named "Self": nor is this unity distant and therefore intellectually understandable, but imminent [immanent?], differing from man to man, and age to age, taking upon itself pain and ugliness, "eye of newt, and toe of frog" (*E&I*, 518).

Whether or not Yeats considered this an "orthodox" statement, it, like the conclusions of poems whose subject is a spiritual journey upward, toward "heaven," returns (directly, or by default) to the natural world; and here, I think, Yeats is most at home. While it is certainly more difficult to write convincingly of the new heaven and new earth than to write of the present (fallen) world, Yeats's vision does not include the imagination of the resurrection. This absence, as initially stated, is by no means an aesthetic deficiency in Yeats *qua* poet; in fact, his best poetry is generated by the resulting tragic loss of the land of the heart's desire and love.

Reversing Yeats's central query, we can ask: why are men by the gods betrayed? Like the question, an answer is a mutual matter; that is, human well-being is a condition of total unity, of "uncomposite blessedness" (as Michael Robartes tells the dancer). Since Yeats's man and God are in continual and absolute conflict, each dying the other's life, living the other's death, there is no final and redemptive union, as Biblically promised. Without a transcendent and accessible eschatological reality of the divine, man is betrayed to purely mortal life, caught between desire and death.

Given the virtual unattainability—neither found in life nor created in art—of perfection, Yeats's poetry typically originates from and deals with the heart's tragic conflict between desire and possession: "It is terrible to desire and not possess, and terrible to possess and not desire. Because of this we long for an age which has the Unity which Plato somewhere defined as sorrowing and rejoicing over the same things."[91] Like Beethoven's "Creatures of Prometheus" ballet and Third Symphony, Yeats's "heroic" ideal has a funeral march at its core. Once again, man's war with himself involves the loss of instinctual goods (the body) to gain spiritual, or symbolic, ones, as in the Byzantium poems. Instead of the promised preservation and enhancement of that perfect unity and completion that the subjective man wants, there is but renunciation and loss associated with the vision of the ideal. The major features of Yeats's secular system are the self's division and conflict, primarily between body and soul. Insofar as this "quarrel with himself" is poetically creative, it is sought by the spiritual, or symbolic, man; but insofar as it is utterly destructive, it is sought to be avoided by the instinctual man. Accordingly, Yeats ends *The Resurrection* with natural man heroically confronting the terrestrial fires which destroy his joys and desires in the very process of their fulfillment:

> Love's pleasure drives his love away,
> The painter's brush consumes his dreams;
> The herald's cry, the soldier's tread
> Exhaust his glory and his might:
> Whatever flames upon the night
> Man's own resinous heart has fed.

Because Yeats does not hold a religious eschatology, his "last things" are made by humans and found in the upward transmutation of life in the process of the poet's creating art. But this "heaven" suddenly blazing into the head is transcient and not permanent:

> While on the shop and street I gazed
> My body of a sudden blazed;
> And twenty minutes more or less
> It seemed, so great my happiness,
> That I was blessed and could bless.

Nonetheless, while this illumination lasts, it brings simultaneous happiness and blessedness—the traditional psychological and moral categories of heaven. Analogous to Blake's casting out the satanic accuser of sin—an example of man's forgiveness and judgment of his self—is Yeats's forgiving himself the lot and casting out his spectral remorse. This subjective sanctification gives Yeats that "great sweetness" of salvation:

> We must laugh and we must sing,
> We are blest by everything,
> Everything we look upon is blest.

NOTES: CHAPTER 4

1. "The Grey Rock," *The Variorum Edition of the Poems of W. B. Yeats,* ed.

Peter Allt and Russell Alspach (New York: Macmillan, 1965). All quotations of poems are from this edition, hereafter abbreviated *Var.*

2. Gershom Scholem, *On the Kabbalah and Its Symbolism* (New York: Schocken Books, 1969), p. 16.

3. Tillich, *Theology of Culture* (Oxford: Oxford University Press, 1969), p. 59; see also pp. 47–48 and 61.

4. See *Blake Concordance,* 2:2181; and *A Concordance to the Poems of W. B. Yeats,* ed. Steven Parrish and James Painter (Ithaca: Cornell University Press, 1966), p. 935. In other concordances with a word frequency index, "all" is used eleventh most frequently by Emily Dickinson and third most frequently by Matthew Arnold.

5. Letter, to J. B. Yeats, 12 Sept. 1914, *Letters of W. B. Yeats,* ed. Alan Wade (London: Rupert Hart-Davis, 1954), p. 588; hereafter abbreviated as *Letters.*

6. Harold Bloom, *Yeats* (New York: Oxford University Press, 1970), p. 5. I am uncertain, however, if this willful misinterpretation, due to one's anxiety about the paralyzing if not perhaps unmatchable greatness of one's predecessors, is the only or most desirable, kind of poetic influence. While sympathetic to the above situation, intuitively I prefer the example of Elijah's passing to Elisha his mantle of poetic inspiration, as represented in Blake's Los (*M* 24: 71, K 510). See also Bloom, p. 81, and Yeats's essay "William Blake and his Illustrations to the Divine Comedy," which will be discussed in somewhat different terms .

7. See W. B. Yeats, *Autobiography* (New York: Collier-Macmillan, 1965), pp. 76 and 108–9; hereafter abbreviated as *Auto.* Future references will be followed by page number and will be included in text in parenthesis.

W. B. Yeats, *A Vision* (New York: Macmillan, 1961), p. 72; hereafter abbreviated as *Vision,* and future references to this edition (a reprint of the 1938 ed.) included following citation followed by page number in text in parenthesis. References to the 1925 edition of *A Vision* will be indicated as such.

W. B. Yeats, *Essays and Introductions* (New York: Macmillan, 1961), p. 94; hereafter abbreviated as *E&I;* future references to it included following citation followed by page number in text in parenthesis.

Letter, to Ethel Mannin, 9 October 1938, *Letters,* p. 917.

8. W. B. Yeats, *Explorations* (New York: Macmillan, 1962), pp. 345 and 310, italics mine; hereafter abbreviated *Explor.,* and future references to it included following citation followed by page number in text in parenthesis.

9. Edwin Ellis and W. B. Yeats, eds. *The Works of William Blake, Poetic, Symbolic, Critical,* 3 vols., (London: Bernard Quaritch, 1893), 1:239; hereafter abbreviated as Yeats-Ellis *Blake.*

10. *Ibid.,* 1:240.

11. *Ibid.,* p. 239.

12. *E&I,* p. 195.

13. Yeats-Ellis *Blake,* 1:242.

14. See *VFZ,* N VIII: 16 and 383; *M* 29:35–39; and *J* 35:1 and 42:29–35.

15. *E&I,* p. 207; see also *E&I,* pp. 195, 287, 352, and 390; and *Auto.,* p. 332.

16. Yeats-Ellis *Blake,* 1:xi.

17. *Ibid.,* 2:242.

18. Letter, to Katharine Tynan, May 1890, *Letters,* pp. 152–53.

19. W. B. Yeats, *A Vision* (London: T. Werner Laurie, Ltd., 1925), p. xi; further references to this version will be indicated by *Vision* (1925) followed by page number. More consideration, however, will be given to the 1938 edition since it represents (as the subtitle indicates) "A Reissue with the Author's Final

Revisions," and deals with more clarity with the issues at hand; unless otherwise stated, references will be to this 1938 edition, abbreviated *Vision*.

20. Tillich, *Theol. Culture,* p. 7.

21. W. B. Yeats, *Mythologies* (New York: Macmillan, 1959), p. 173; hereafter abbreviated as *Mythol.;* future references to it included following citation followed by page number in text in parenthesis.

22. W. B. Yeats, *The Collected Plays of W. B. Yeats* (New York: Macmillan, 1963), p. 245; hereafter abbreviated as *Col. Plays* and future references to this collection included following citation followed by page number in text in parenthesis.

The unicorn, Yeats explains in a letter, symbolizes the soul; see Letter, to Elizabeth Yeats, autumn 1920, *Letters,* p. 662.

23. W. B. Yeats, *The Variorum Edition of the Plays of W. B. Yeats,* edited Russell Alspach (London: Macmillan, 1966), p. 1139; hereafter abbreviated *Var. Plays*. In contrast, of course, Blake's Los knows that "he is the spirit of prophecy, the ever apparent Elias./ Time is the Mercy of Eternity" (*M* 24:71–2, K 510).

24. *Ibid.,* p. 1140 (and p. 1164).

25. *Ibid.,* p. 713.

26. *Ibid.,* p. 1158.

27. Richard Ellmann, *The Identity of Yeats* (New York: Oxford University Press, 1964), p. 166; see also p. 221.

28. See *Vision,* p. 104; see also Frye, "The Rising of the Moon," in Donoghue and Mulryne, eds., *An Honoured Guest* (Dublin: St. Martin's Press, 1966), pp. 19–31; and Bloom, *Yeats,* pp. 342, 378, and 384, for example.

29. *Vision,* pp. 187 and 193. For *A Vision's* generative debt to "The Mental Traveller," see *Vision* (1925), pp. 133–34, and *Vision,* p. 189, for example.

30. See *Vision* (1925), pp. xiii, xxiii, 130, 134, 139, 148, 170, 183–85, and 214; and *Vision,* pp. 270–71.

31. *Vision,* p. 81.

32. See *Vision,* pp. 232; and 183, 208, 239–40, and 263.

33. Yeats-Ellis *Blake,* 2:195; see also 2:11, 168, 170, 182, 193, 221, 254, 259, 263, and 272, for examples; these passages I take to be largely by Yeats.

34. "He hears the Cry of the Sedge"; see also "Cap and Bells," and "He Thinks of his Past Greatness when Part of the Constellations of Heaven" for examples of this recurrent theme.

35. J. B. Yeats, *Letters to his Son and Others,* ed. Joseph Hone (London: Faber and Faber, 1954), Letter, to Jack Yeats, 12 Feb. 1920, p. 269. Whether or not this remark was ever also made to W. B. Yeats, it nonetheless applies to him; see, for example, *Auto.,* p. 166.

36. See *ibid.,* Letter, to W. B. Yeats, 9 Jan. 1920, p. 267; also *Explor.,* p. 335 and *Mythol.,* p. 341.

37. Letter, to Robert Bridges, 7 Dec. 1896, *Letters,* p. 268.

38. See also Blake, *MHH* 14, K 154 and "VLJ," K 604.

39. *The Resurrection* in *Col. Plays,* p. 373. Probably Yeats's favourite line, it reappears in "Notes," for "The Gift of Harun Al-Rashid," *Var.,* 829; *Explor.,* pp. 430 and 434; *Letters,* p. 918; and *Vision,* pp. 68, 197, and 271, for examples.

40. Donne's religious prose, especially his sermons, provide the corresponding anagogic superstructure in his canon. See chapter 5 for a discussion of this matter.

41. Letter, to the Editor of the *Daily Express,* Dublin, pub. 27 Feb. 1895, *Letters,* p. 249; see also Letter, to Sean O'Faolain, 15 Aug. (?1929): "The origins

of a poet are not in that which he has cast off because it is not himself, but *in his own mind and in the past of literature"* (*Letters,* p. 787, italics mine).

42. "He Thinks of Past Greatness when a Part of the Constellations of Heaven"; it was first called "The Song of Mongan" when published in *The Dome* in Oct. 1898, and Yeats notes that "the Country of the Young is a name in Celtic poetry for the Country of the Gods and of the happy dead" (*Var.,* p. 177).

43. *Mythol.,* p. 115; see also pp. 233, 274, and 277; "Hero, Girl, and Fool," and Rev. 5:13.

44. See "He bids his Beloved be at Peace," "Valley of the Black Pig," "He hears the Cry of the Sedge," "The Blessed," "The Secret Rose," and Rev. 4:13 and 7:12. In this postponement Yeats is traditional.

45. Though Yeats goes on to say that there are some men who cannot possess or express it, he would be one who could.

46. Letter, to Ethel Mannin, 9 Oct. 1938, *Letters,* p. 917.

47. A. Norman Jeffares, *A Commentary on the Collected Poems of W. B. Yeats* (Stanford, Cal.: Stanford University Press, 1968), p. 299; hereafter abbreviated as *Commentary.* See also *Auto.,* p. 71.

48. See Letter, to Mrs. Olivia Shakespear, 24 Sept. 1926, *Letters,* p. 719. Here, as in l. 5 of "Sailing to Byzantium," I would read "or" as "and."

49. Elsewhere, in "The Dialogue of Self and Soul," Yeats says that when knower and known are one, man "ascends to heaven"; Donne also associates this union of "object" and "wit" with heaven ("II Anniv.," l. 443).

50. See also "The Blessed"; Rev. 8:12; Luke 7:24 ("What went ye out in the wilderness for to see? A reed shaken with the wind?"); and the following lines from *Where There is Nothing:*

He [God] is alway planning last judgments. And yet it takes a long time, and that is why he laments in the wind and in the reeds and in the cries of the curlews (*Var. Plays,* p. 1156).

51. Accordingly, "historic Catholicism, with its counsels and its dogmas, stirred his passion like the beauty of a mistress . . ." (*Auto.,* p. 148).

52. This realization is more directly expressed in the other two poems about Gregory's lonely death, "An Irish Airman Forsees his Death" and "Reprisals."

53. "A bowl of goldfish was kept on one of the windows of Yeats's house on Broad St., Oxford, to amuse Anne Yeats" (Jeffares, *Commentary,* p. 315).

54. Revelation of or from the supernatural is not part of Yeats's secular world (in contrast to the religious views of Donne and Blake).

55. See Northrop Frye, "The Top of the Tower," *Southern Review,* 5, no. 3 (n.s.) (Summer 1969): 851 ff.

56. See *Mythol.,* pp. 362 and 365; and *Vision,* p. 131.

57. *Shadowy Waters* and "Wisdom and Dreams," *Var.,* p. 743.

58. Letter, to Lady Gregory, 27 Nov. 1902, *Letters,* p. 384.

59. See Letter, to Elizabeth Yeats, Autumn 1920, *Letters,* p. 662 and Letter, to Mrs. Olivia Shakespear, 25 July 1934, *Letters,* p. 825, and *Col. Plays,* pp. 242–45.

60. *Col. Plays,* p. 245; italics mine; see also Rev. 7:12–13.

61. See *Explor.,* pp. 155, 162–63, and 252; and *Auto.,* pp. 127–28.

62. Yeats-Ellis *Blake,* 2:250 and *Var.,* p. 829 (omitted in the ellipsis are variant punctuations which do not alter the statement).

63. See *E&I,* p. 424; and *Explor.,* p. 375; *Auto.,* p. 214.

64. See, for example, "The Poet to his Beloved," and "Wandering Aengus." See also Allen Grossman, *Poetic Knowledge in the Early Yeats* (Charlottesville, Va.:

University of Virginia Press, 1969), pp. 151–68; hereafter abbreviated *Poetic Knowledge*.

65. See Jon Stallworthy, *Between the Lines, Yeats's Poetry in the Making* (Oxford: Oxford University Press, 1963), pp. 89–90; and Bloom, *Yeats*, pp. 347–48.

66. See "After Long Silence," and Letter, to Mrs. Olivia Shakespear, 5 Sept. 1926, *Letters*, p. 178.

67. Jeffares, *Commentary*, pp. 253–55.

68. The adjective here, as in other examples of this genitive link ("of") construction, modifies both nouns. See Christine Brooke-Rose, *A Grammar of Metaphor* (London: Secker and Warburg, 1965) for a good discussion of this and related properties of the metaphor.

Subsequently, however, Yeats realizes that even these intellectual artifacts are vulnerable to time's destruction, for "every thing that man esteems/ Endures a moment or a day."

69. See Letter, to J. B. Yeats, 5 Aug. 1913, *Letters*, p. 583; see also *Mythol.*, p. 332.

70. See Dante, *Purgatorio*, canto xxvii and Yeats's Letter, to Mrs. Olivia Shakespear, 27 Oct. 1927, *Letters*, pp. 730–31. In contrast to Yeats's body-soul opposition, see also *Paradiso*, canto xiv: "And when we put completeness on afresh,/ All the more gracious shall our person be,/ Reclothed in the holy and glorious flesh." (ll. 43–45)

71. See *Mythol.*, pp. 300–301.

72. W. B. Yeats and T. S. Moore, *W. B. Yeats and T. S. Moore: Their Correspondence, 1901–1937*, ed. Ursula Bridge (New York: Oxford University Press, 1955), pp. 162–64; hereafter abbreviated as *Correspondence*.

73. See *Var.*, p. 825; Blake, "Intro.," *SE*, K 210; *J* 15:8, K 635; and Rev. 4:8. Here, as in the relatively few other instances, Blake's "influence" is linguistic, not conceptual, except by sanction.

74. See Letter, to T. S. Moore, 4 Oct. 1930, *Correspondence*, p. 164.

75. *Mythol.*, p. 357; in this description, as at the beginning of this poem, Yeats has typical difficulty being certain ("or . . . or") of the supernatural.

76. See F. A. C. Wilson, *Yeats and Tradition* (London: 1968), pp. 221 and 210; and Jeffares, *Commentary*, pp. 497 and 389–90.

77. Whereas Los always keeps the divine vision, Yeats's golden smith is a secular artist ("of the Emperor").

78. See Letter, to Mrs. Olivia Shakespear, 7 Aug. 1934, *Letters*, p. 826 and *Vision*, pp. 207–8.

79. *Vision*, pp. 52 and 214.

80. "Whence Had They Come" and "Solomon and the Witch"; in contrast, the lovers in Donne's "Canonization" remain "above" the temporal and Blake's Beulah "is evermore Created around Eternity" (*M* 30: 8, K 518).

81. Letter, to Mrs. Olivia Shakespear, 24 July 1934, *Letters*, p. 824.

82. Speaking of the sensual continuity of the East, Yeats writes that "the east has its solutions always and must therefore know nothing of tragedy. It is we, not the east, that must raise the heroic cry" (Letter, to Dorothy Wellesley, 6 July 1935, *Letters*, p. 837).

83. See "Hour Before Dawn," "Upon a Dying Lady," "Sailing to Byzantium," "Dialogue of Self and Soul," "Ribh Considers Christian Love Insufficient," and "Under Ben Bulben."

84. See Letter, to George Russell, 15 May 1903, *Letters,* p. 402, and Letter, to John Quinn, 15 May 1903, *Letters,* p. 403.

85. See Letter, to Ethel Mannin, 9 Oct. 1938, *Letters,* p. 916.

86. See Letter, to Mrs. Olivia Shakespear, 25 May 1926, *Letters,* p. 714; and "A General Introduction for my Work," *E&I,* p. 509.

87. For examples of the body's assimilation to the soul, see *The Wind Among the Reeds,* "Hero, Girl, and Fool," "Last Confessions," and "Sailing to Byzantium." For examples of the soul's assimilation to the body, see "Solomon and the Witch," the "Crazy Jane" poems, "Byzantium," "Chosen," "Conjunctions," "Lady's Three Songs," "News for the Delphic Oracle," "Consolation," and "Under Ben Bulben."

88. See Frye, "The Top of the Tower," *Southern Review* 5, no. 3, n.s., (Summer 1969): 868–71; Bloom, *Yeats,* p. 378.

89. Yeats-Ellis, *Blake,* 2:256.

90. Grossman, *Poetic Knowledge,* p. 208. See also Augustine, *The City of God,* trans. Marcus Dods (New York: Random House, 1950), Bks. XIII, chap. 20, XX, chap. 6, XXII, chaps. 19, 24, and 30; *Sermons on the Liturgical Seasons,* trans. Sister Mary Muldowney, (New York: Fathers of the Church, 1959), pp. 271 and 357. And St. Thomas Aquinas, *On the Truth of the Catholic Faith: Summa Contra Gentiles, Book IV: Salvation,* trans. Charles O'Neil, (New York: Doubleday and Co., 1957), Bk. IV, chap. 86, pp. 325–26 and chap. 92, p. 340.

91. Letter, to Mrs. Olivia Shakespear, 25 May 1933, *Letters,* p. 810.

5

"Post-Mortem": Very Last Things

The Eschatological Symbol: Its Redemptive Essence

In studying the poetic continuity of the resurrection motif, I have avoided some philosophical problems raised by the concept by considering only Donne, Blake, and Yeats, in whom the pattern is clear: hope for a resurrection characteristically informs the major work of these authors. To treat the subject more abstractly leads to problems of defining "continuity," and "conversions," and the "meaning" of the resurrection to which I have applied them. However, some clarity may appear if we begin this conclusion by considering what constitutes the ontological authority of a religious symbol.

We can observe the following distinctive features of an authentic eschatological symbol. First, it "re-presents" the original and final divine reality; i.e., it joins and completes God's initial creative fullness (*pleroma*) by returning to this divine *Logos* in the end. Second, an eschatological symbol partakes of the infinite into which it "opens" (as Blake observes) the finite; Jesus' incarnation mysteriously joins the divine and eternal with the human and the temporal to redeem man, and this redemption is revealed in Jesus Christ's Easter resurrection. Third, sacramental participation in an eschatological symbol reenacts prior and promised redemptive actuality, immanent therein; in Christian ritual, for example, baptism thus imitates Jesus' death (in the mortal, natural body) and resurrection (in the immortal, spiritual body). Fourth, this present participation in the sacred and the future salvation it partakes of are absolute, i.e., total and collective; when this old world is destroyed in the apocalypse and the new heaven and new earth are created, then the earthly Church of baptized Christians becomes the communal Bride of the Godhead in the heavenly "great marriage."

Fifth, and finally, the ontological existence of an eschatological symbol manifests its prior soteriological essence; that is, an eschatological symbol is real and true because it is first sacred:

> Therefore the religious symbol, the symbol which points to the divine, can be a true symbol only if it participates in the power of the divine to which it points. . . . A symbol *has* truth: it is adequate to the revelation it expresses. A symbol *is* true: it is the expression of a true revelation.[1]

For Christians, the absolute transcendent authority from which truth and reality arise is God, the *Logos*. This divinity is revealed when God "speaks" to man, and the definitive Word of God's "speaking" is Jesus:

> And the Word was made flesh, and dwelt among us, (and we beheld his glory, the glory as of the only begotten of the Father,) full of grace and truth. . . . Sanctify them through thy truth: thy word is truth. . . . That they all may be one; as thou Father, art in me, and I in thee, that they also may be one in us: that the world may believe that thou hast sent me. . . . I in them, and thou in me, that they may be made perfect in one (John 14 and 17:17 and 21–23).

The Easter resurrection of Jesus as the Christ reveals and completes the mystery of man's promised salvation:

> And we know that the Son of God is come, and hath given us an understanding, that we may know him that is true, even in his Son Jesus Christ. This is the true God, and eternal life (1 John 5:20).

The reality and truth of this definitive eschatological event arise from its divine essence, whose identity and teleology are redemptive:

> I am the resurrection and the life: he that believeth in me, though he were dead, yet shall he live: And whosoever liveth and believeth in me shall never die (John 11:25–26).

In the introduction and in my interpretations of Donne, Blake, and Yeats, I have tried to delineate what the resurrection and "belief" in it "mean"—hope and desire for perfect unity: of the human and the divine, of body and soul, of the individual and the community, of subject and object, of time and eternity, and of our beginning and end. Given my view that the origin of art and religion is the human imagination divine and that the provenance of belief is love and desire, I believe that Blake's vision of the resurrection composes its original "meaning." Contrarily, as preacher and poet, Donne's belief represents the traditional ecclesiastical perspective, whereas, as poet, Yeats's disbelief (in a traditional religion) represents the modern, secular position.

Donne's Holy Harmony

Possessing the "holy" "amouresseness of a harmonious soule," Donne is theologically and poetically concerned with unions; the "greatest" is the final marriage of the Church and the Godhead: "Beyond all this [the miracle of Jesus' resurrection in body and soul, from the dead], God having thus maried soule and body, in one man, and man and God, in one Christ, he marries this Christ to the Church."[2] Donne typically "contracts" (engages and focuses) the last day to the present one. The soteriological sanction for this "transfusion" is the first, or spiritual, resurrection, in time, which assures the last resurrection, of body and soul, into eternity.

In the "profane" love poems, Donne incorporates the erotic into the eschatological in the first resurrection of the body in sexual love; it is both a "remembrancer" of the prior, single "hypostaticall union" of man and God and the prefiguration of the final, collective union of Christ and his Bride: "Wee dye and rise the same, and prove/ Mysterious by this love."

In the divine poems Donne dramatizes the first resurrection of the spirit in the simultaneous cooperation of the human will, through penance, and of the divine will, through grace. "I . . . labour to'admit you, but Oh, to no end"; therefore,

> Batter my heart, three person'd God; for you
> As yet but knocke, breathe, shine;
>   and seeke to mend;
> That I may rise. . . .

In the "Anniversaries" Donne incorporates the eschatological into the symbolic; religious symbols "are directed toward the infinite which they symbolize *and* toward the finite through which they symbolize it. . . . They open the divine for the human and the human for the divine."[3] That is, Donne's "idea of a woman" symbolizes the soul's proper likeness to God: "Shee whom we celebrate/ . . . kept, by diligent deuotion,/ Gods Image" ("II Anniv.," ll. 448 and 455-56). In the first resurrection the soul recognizes its divine similitude, completed in the last resurrection. By meditating on Elizabeth Drury as an earthly "patterne" of heavenly virtue, Donne not only "repairs" his fallen state in this decayed "land of unlikeness" but also raises his soul to God in the first resurrection: "Returne not, my soule, from this extasee,/ And meditation of what thou shalt bee" ("II Anniv.," ll. 321-22).

While these meditations on salvation are traditional in conception (as also found in "Goodfriday," for example), Donne's contemplations in the "Anniversaries" differ in their expression of this *imitatio dei*. That is, by elevating the historical Elizabeth Drury to an "immortal" model of the divine, Donne "transfigures" the individual *sub specie temporis* into a religious symbol *sub specie aeternitatis*. Donne's sacramental commemorations of the "religious death" and resurrection of Elizabeth Drury, of "the idea of a woman," or the soul's divine likeness, in the "Anniversaries" comprise his own first, or spiritual, resurrection. The sanction for this individual apotheosis is the religious fact of Jesus' Easter rising, without which this poetic meditation would lack ontological validity. While Donne's incorporation of the resurrection motif in the "Anniversaries" constitutes a symbolic act, this use is clearly within a religious, and not a secular, domain. Accordingly, the poet praises the sacred reality which is the origin of his speech's authenticity and meaning. As seen in the "Anniversaries," this process of religious symbolization is redemptive in that it reveals the divine, the prior source of poetic grace:

> The purpose, and th'Authority is his [God's]
> Thou [E.D.] art the Proclamation; and I ame
> The Trumpet, at whose voice the people came
> ("II Anniv.," ll. 526-28).

Blake's Gospel, Everlasting

For Donne the author of the Bible is the Holy Ghost,[4] and for Blake this Holy Spirit is the poetic genius whose essence is imaginative, or mental, or intellectual:[5]

tion" of the resurrection in his Christianity of the imagination (*J* 77, K 716-17). Blake's religion is a "re-conversion" of Christianity because he believes that originally and finally man's fourfold redemption resides in the eternal imagination (the *Logos*), manifest in the everlasting gospel of Jesus and in other works of art, which is a public act of mental charity.

Blake's theology is Christ-centered: "Μονος ὁ Ιεςονς" (*J* 4, K 622). The Trinity is wholly "one" in Jesus, and Jesus is the "one-ly" divinity: the Holy Spirit and God are joined as "the intellectual fountain of Humanity" (*J* 91:10-11, K 738), and "God is Jesus" ("Laocoon," K 777). Moreover, the shared identity of this (Blakean) Godhead is the imagination and "concenters" in the Savior. Blake's Jesus-the-imagination is the eternal *Logos,* whose temporal ("shortened") name is Los; they are the very "likeness & similitude" of each other (*J* 96:7 and 21, K 743), and "Jesus & his Apostles & Disciples were all Artists" ("Laocoon," K 777).

In contrast to New Testament narrative, for Blake Jesus' incarnation and crucifixion are *not* the only necessary and sufficient "propitiation" for man's "sin." Blake believes neither in the "virgin birth" nor in the doctrine of atonement:[8] " ' Must the Wise die for an Atonement? does Mercy endure Atonement?/ No! It is Moral Severity & destroys Mercy in its Victim' " (*J* 39:25, K 666).

Blake holds the Protestant doctrine of preexistence—that Jesus Christ's humanity is coeternal with his divinity,[9] as he explains to H. C. Robinson: " 'We are all co-existent with God [in the fourfold beginning, potentially now in spirit, and finally in the end], Members of the Divine Body. We are all partakers of the divine nature.' "[10]

For Blake, Jesus is the eternal model (the "divine analogy") and mode of redemption—in the continual forgiveness of sins by imaginatively identifying with and freely giving oneself for another, as sublimely shown in *Jerusalem:*

> Albion stood in terror, not for himself,
>   but for his Friend
> Divine; & Self was lost in the
>   contemplation of faith
> And wonder at the Divine Mercy
>   & at Los's sublime honour (*J* 96: 30-32,
>   K 743).

While John also records Jesus' "great commandment" that "greater love hath no man than this, that a man lay down his life for his friends" (John xv, 13 and I John iii-iv), Blake with insight identifies, and expands throughout time, its eternal source: Christian love is the absolute and continual moral act of the imagination,

> . . . for Man is love
> As God is Love; every kindness
>   to another is a little Death
> In the Divine Image . . . (*J* 96:26-28, K 743).

For Blake, as in traditional Christianity, the central eschatological event is the resurrection. Elaborating the teachings of John, Augustine, and Donne, Blake believes in a first resurrection of the spirit on earth ("VLJ," K 616) which assures the final resurrection of "body and soul" to heaven. Blake expands the Protestant concern with the individual in his "psychology" of the Four Zoas. Their reintegration to a renewed earth is the predominant prophetic subject of *Vala, or the Four Zoas*. In *Milton* Blake expands the characteristic Donnean concern with present and proper penance, which assures redemption. The individual eschatological drama of *Milton* is a last judgment of the self, celebrated in the baptism of the imagination (*M* 40-41, K 532-33). In this first resurrection of the Blakean spirit—i.e., of the real and true inspired poet—Milton is transfigured "with" Jesus (*M* 42:10-11, K 534).

Jerusalem, Blake's greatest work, portrays the apocalyptic resurrection. The fourfold Blakean "body" is reunited with the soul (Jerusalem, Albion's emanation and all men's liberty). The reintegration of the Four Zoas to their prior and proper "perfect unity" constitutes Albion's "first resurrection." In the last judgment, the "repaired" Albion annihilates the last error of the selfhood. Thereupon the mystery of salvation is revealed and realized in the final, collective resurrection of the fourfold Zoaic body and soul:

> And every Man stood Fourfold. . . .
>   revealing the lineaments of Man
> Driving outward the Body of Death
>   in an Eternal Death & Resurrection
> (*J* 98:12 and 19-20, K 745).

For Blake, man and God are identified in the imagination, in the human image divine. In this identification Blake's traditionality and originality converge. I mean "identified" 1) as the revelation of one's "real and eternal identity" (as in *M* 32:32, K 522) and 2) as the reunion of both man and God, as in the "Eighth Man," the "Seven Spirits, or Eyes" of God plus man.[11] The "mystery" of Jesus' incarnation incorporates his simultaneous humanity and divinity, which Protestant doctrine of preexistence Blake holds and reaffirms.[12] And in the resurrection, the "mystery" of humanity's salvation is traditionally revealed; for Blake, this revelation is of man's (his emanation's and Four Zoas') union with Jesus Christ and their mutual completion as the "Eighth Man" in "the real and Eternal World of Imagination."

At the end of *Milton* the "Starry Eight/ Became One Man, Jesus the Saviour, wonderful!" (*M* 42:10-11, K 534); they are spiritually united in that world of imagination and "Eternity in which we shall live for ever in Jesus our Lord." (*M* L, K 480). And at the end of *Jerusalem,* Albion's emanation (all people's soul and "divine vision" [*J* 54:2, K 684]) Jerusalem is Jesus' returned Bride: in their "great marriage" we are all members of the eternal divine body (*J* 53:54, K 684), for there "All Human Forms [are] identified . . . in the Life of Immortality" (*J* 99:1 and 4, K 747). In Blake's resurrection, man's "liberty of both body and mind," Jerusalem, is fully ("all") identified as the Savior, Jesus, "in" and "according to the wonders Divine/ Of Human Imagination" (*J* 98:31-32, K 746).

Identified as the imagination, Jesus is both the eternal model and continual mode of this redemption. Blake's "re-creation" of this "divine analogy" constitutes his religious originality and his poetic authority, as his "words of eternal salvation" reflexively confirm in *Milton:*

> I am Inspired! I know it is Truth!
>   for I Sing
> According to the inspiration
>   of the Poetic Genius
> Who is the eternal all-protecting
>   Divine Humanity,
> To whom be Glory & Power
>   & Dominion Evermore. Amen (*M* 13:51
> and 14:1-3, K 495).

In the New Testament, the figure to whom this worship belongs is God, who sits upon the throne in heaven (Rev. 7:12), whereas Blake recognizes that this Lord is the Poetic Genius (as in the early "Annot. Swedenborg," K 90). From the ontological authority of this divine reality arises the eternal authenticity of Blake's poetic speech and of his religious symbolism.

As the "only" divinity, Jesus the imagination is the eternal source of human salvation, and his ontological existence arises from this prior soteriological essence as the Savior, whose definitive revelation to man is mental.[13] To reveal and liberate the origin, reality, and truth of humanity's redemption is Blake's accomplished "great task" (J 5:17-21, K 623). And the completed authenticity of his central eschatological symbol resides in the resurrection of the imagination:

> I know of no other Christianity and of no other Gospel than the liberty of both body and mind to exercise the Divine Arts of Imagination, Imagination, the real & eternal World of which this Vegetable Universe is but a faint shadow, & in which we shall live in our Eternal or Imaginative Bodies (J 77, K 716–17).

Yeats's Lost "Land of Heart's Desire": The Tragedy of the Secular Poet

While Donne and Blake are Christian poets, however differently and redundantly that phrase applies, Yeats is not: "Homer is my theme and his unchristened heart." Not accepting a traditional religious position, Yeats secularizes eschatological expectations by subjectifying them; accordingly, his "last things" leave the domain of theology to become the wanted creations of the poet's dreams:

> And I declare my faith: . . . .
> Death and life were not
> Till man made up the whole, . . .
> Out of his bitter soul, . . .
> And further add to that
> That, being dead, we rise,
> Dream and so create
> Translunar Paradise.

When Yeats writes about man in this life, we can make a literary criticism of his poetry, but when he writes about God and the afterlife, we can also make a corresponding philosophical judgment about the authority of his religious declarations. When poetry makes claims whose verification is a theological matter, then our aesthetic criticism also becomes metaphysical. When the artist speaks seriously of religious concerns (e.g., "faith" and "paradise"), he must use language with adequate power and meaning to participate in and express the divinity to which it refers. Without this prior theological legitimation, the artist's religious speech lacks authentic access to the transcendent eternal reality to which it would refer; instead, it remains bound in the natural world of mortality, where Yeats celebrates the "profane perfection of mankind."

In Yeats's case, this absence of a religion from which salvation derives, appears in his "conversion" of the spiritual body of the resurrection to the "perfectly proportioned human body" and soul to his "unity of being." But Yeats's temporal, subjective system differs from its Christian predecessor primarily in that it lacks an eternal Savior—Jesus the Christ, Blake's human image divine—who mediates between man and God to make possible their promised union; that is, Yeats's secular system lacks a traditional, authenticated eschatological symbol through which the desired redemption is realized.

The language of divine ontology is not translatable. The poet cannot provide man-made access to this transcendent source of salvation; heaven is neither revealed, nor found, nor created initially on earth. Consequently, Yeats does not know and possess the desired wisdom and beauty of the Holy City, as he concludes in "Under Ben Bulben":

> . . . . Gyres run on;
> When that greater dream had gone
> Calvert and Wilson, Blake and Claude
> Prepared a rest for the people of God,
> . . . but after that
> Confusion fell upon our thought.

Without the traditional, religious imagination of eternity, Yeats's "vision" is of historical man and his unsatisfied "soul's diary." Because his secular system includes no transcendent divine reality and no authentic eschatological symbol, which participates in it, the Biblical promise that the united body and soul will rise immortal to "all heavenly glory" is never fully realizable. Instead, Yeats's "last things" are found in the upward transmutation of life in the process of creating art. But, in the end, both the tragic poet and his heroically self-begotten images reside in the cyclic, natural world, "in the foul rag-and-bone shop of the heart," that, nonetheless, "loves nothing but the perfect and our dreams make all things perfect that we may love them" (*E&I*, p. 149).

Eschatological Symbols: Very Last Words

The following further observations may now be made about the distinctive features of religious symbolization and the process of secularization. We begin by recognizing that there is an absolute breach between a religious view of existence, i.e., one which has a transtemporal (traditional) and transpersonal (collective) revealed relation to the transcendent divinity in whom salvation is realized, and a secular view, which lacks such a redemptive purpose and certainty. Accordingly, a religious ontology, or its attributes, cannot be converted to a secular world. For example, redemptive validity on the immanent level directly depends on its prior reality on the transcendent level; hence the movement toward salvation is unidirectional, namely, that God becomes as we are (the incarnation) so that we may become as he is (the resurrection), as the creeds and Blake teach. But we cannot say, as Feuerbach and Yeats would like to, that the above relation is reducible to a single and reversible equation, in which saying that God is man is the same as saying, and with distinct preference, that man is God.[14] Rather, I think we must respect the wisdom of traditional teachings on this matter of deification, which, like Christian history, depends on the transcendent deity's entering this world, breaking through death and hell, and opening the gates of heaven through which redemption is possible.

The absolute difference between the natural and supernatural worlds and the only revealed way to pass from one upward to the other are the subjects of Hopkins's "That Nature is a Heraclitean Fire And Of the Comfort Of the Resurrection," for example. The triumph over natural time and death, whose destructive forces are described in the octet, directly depends on the resurrection, whose radical transformation is described in the sestet. When nature's bonfire burns on the last day "to leave but ash:"

> In a flash, at a trumpet crash,
> I am all at once what Christ is, 'since he was

> what I am, and
> This Jack, joke, poor potsherd,' patch, matchwood
>   immortal diamond
> Is immortal diamond.

The poetic power and meaning of Hopkins's sonnet derive from the argument of its theological legitimacy, without which neither its claim nor its comfort would be successful.

From this basic distinction between a view which is religious and one which is not, there flow certain consequences for the nature of religious symbolism and for its poetic incorporation. Without ontological certainty of divine redemption and without shared (across time and across persons) access to its public forms (the Bible, liturgy, and doctrine), authoritative poetic symbolization of an essentially religious subject (salvation) is not successful. This phenomenon becomes apparent if we contrast Donne's symbolic use of Elizabeth Drury in the "Anniversaries" as an earthly (in-dwelling) "patterne" of heavenly virtue with Yeats's personal use of the golden bird in "Sailing to Byzantium"; while both poems aspire toward spiritual transcendence, I think the significant difference between the successes of both attempts stems from the presence or absence of the eschatological reality from which derives the authority of symbolism dealing with a religious subject. Analogously, the purposive potency of the sacraments depends on the previous and present divine reality of that which they symbolize and thereby participate in. Once this transcendent dimension disappears, the symbol (the immanent substance) consequently dies; further, its authority cannot be replaced by or converted into another symbol or into a sign, which does not participate in that to which it merely points. Hence Yeats's golden bird does not convincingly attain the sought eternity, whose reality is not self-begotten, but given from the deity above.

The conceptual relation between Donne's, Blake's, and Yeats's poetry and prose bears on this phenomenon, I think, from which the following analogy can be proposed:

Donne's	*Blake's*	*Yeats's*
"elegies, songs, and sonnets"	lyrics	lyrics
"divine poems"	(epic) prophecies	plays

sermons	prose (visionary)	prose (meta-psychological)

While this schema is too generally inclusive, I think it accurately first suggests that lyric poetry derives from the engagement of the individual into the communal, whose collective aesthetic resources consist of traditionally shared symbols (of a religious realm) or signs (of a secular realm); Donne's "divine poems," Blake's prophecies, and Yeats's plays are communal forms, whose literary authenticity derives from religious (of Donne and Blake) or meta-psychological (of Yeats) prose.[15]

Second, a correlative of this analogy suggests that salvation begins as an individual, internal experience of the divine "other" and ends by being realized in a communal, external form. The relation between the Old and New Testaments, for instance, strongly suggests that this progression cannot be reversed; and it is a triumph of the New Testament that individual salvation, in Christ Jesus and in one's relation to Him, is the manifest basis for its communal attainment. This same pattern most clearly appears in Blake, whose work progresses from a concern with personal to collective salvation, as in the development from the *Songs of Innocence and Experience* and *The Marriage of Heaven and Hell*, to *Vala, or The Four Zoas* (a transition) to *Milton* and *Jerusalem;* of the major prophecies, *Milton* treats the individual's relation to Jesus as the inspired self of the poet and *Jerusalem* concerns all people's Christian liberty of the imagination.

Third, I think this analogy points out the need for the redemptive aspirations of lyric or epic poetry to derive from and rest on a theological authority, such as the prose of these three authors provides, or attempts to provide; when this prose is meta-psychological, as in Yeats's case, the claims and successes of the poetry are of a different nature.

Religious symbols function poetically to mediate between the divine "other," the eternal collectivity of the Godly, and the human self, the temporal individual; as such, Jesus Christ, the definitive word of God's speaking to man, is the paradigm of a religious symbol, upon which others are modeled. When this mediator no longer exists, i.e., no longer is believed to exist, the divine reality which it partakes of is no longer accessible either; that is, the symbolic mediator offers access to the holy "other."

The language of religious ontology is not translatable, since sacred symbols cannot be replaced or converted. They are lost through secularization, which occurs by disclaiming the transcendent realm in which they participated; hence, while external forms (commemorative signs) may be preserved, their content or substantive meaning is gone.[16]

Accordingly, some major features of secularization are 1) the loss of an authenticated divine ontology, 2) the consequent loss of religious symbols to mediate between man and God, the individual and the communal, and the temporal and the eternal, and 3) the resulting proliferation of various signs which may point to the lost realm and the lost access to it, but which clearly remain within the secular world of their creation because the absolute source of symbolic authority has previously disappeared.

To conclude, we may return to consider something of the theory and function of eschatology. Conceptually, eschatology conceives of and unifies the totality of reality, divine and human, eternal and temporal, supernatural and natural. Dealing specifically with redemption (judgment and heaven), Christian eschatology is unique, I think, in its ontological inclusiveness, by theologically going beyond the boundaries or other "studies." That is, eschatology completes our beginning (and "middle") by providing an ending which reconciles the various preceding parts and, more importantly, which reveals and fulfills everything as infinite and holy (as Blake writes of the apocalypse).

The authenticity of eschatological symbols, as argued, derives from their participation in divine reality. New Testament eschatology, in its definitive completeness, makes accessible this supernatural heaven; an absolute, radical change from the former condition is necessary and achieved by transfiguring the (fallen) natural world, for which "thanks be to God, which giveth us the victory through our Lord Jesus Christ" (1 Cor. 15:57). Whether we consider Jesus' Easter resurrection literally or figuratively, we can see that a definitive mediator is necessary to complete our salvation because as Jesus Christ (God's speaking to man) is the holy Word, so a religious symbol represents the eschatological reality it opens.

Finally, then, the unique function and ontological meaning of eschatology are to reveal and offer salvation. If we want to realize total divine completeness, perfection, and unity and to attain redemption, then ultimately eschatology is necessary.

I, also, hope the wise reader will love, and be wholly One in, our Lord—in Blake's Christianity of the imagination, in the "one-ly" Savior, the *Logos* whose theological, Christian name is Jesus and whose poetic, Blakean name is Los, the human image divine. Imagination completely identifies the human and the divine, for it annihilates the selfhood (the Satan of spiritual separateness) and wholly reunites man with himself (with his emanation and Four Zoas), with others (in the universal brotherhood of Eden and continual forgiveness of sins in the holy liberty of Jerusalem) and with the Godhead. This perfect unity is fully and truly realized in the apocalyptic resurrection, for, as Blake reminds us (in "The Laocoon," K 776),

The Eternal Body of Man

is the IMAGINATION

that is, God himself ⎫
the Divine Body ⎭ יהוה Jesus:

We are his Members.

NOTES: CHAPTER 5

1. Paul Tillich, *Systematic Theology*, 3 vols. (Chicago: University of Chicago Press, 1951–63), 1:239–40; see also Paul Tillich, *Theology of Culture* (New York: Oxford University Press, 1969), pp. 47–66; and Mircea Eliade, *Myth and Reality*, trans. Willard Trask (New York: Harper and Row, 1963), pp. 19 ff; and Mircea Eliade, *The Two and the One*, trans. J. M. Cohen (New York: Harper and Row, 1965), pp. 201–7.

2. See John Donne, *Divine Poems*, edited Helen Gardner (Oxford: Clarendon Press, 1966), "Hymne to Christ," p. 49. John Donne, *Sermons*, edited George Potter and Evelyn Simpson, 10 vols. (Berkeley: University of California Press, 1953–62), 7:389–90, 6:155; and 3:113 and 254–55; and 8:196.

3. Tillich, *System. Theol.*, 1:240.

4. As he states in the "Sydneyean Psalm Translations," ll. 8–9 and in "La Corona, Ascension," l. 13.

5. These words in apposition reflect Blake's use of them as synonymous; see William Blake, *The Complete Writings of William Blake, with Variant Readings*, ed. Geoffrey Keynes (London: Oxford University Press, 1966), Letter, to James

Blake, 30 Jan. 1803, K 822; "VLJ," K 613 and 604; J 77, K 716; and J 91:11, K 738.

6. Letter, to Dr. Trusler, 23 Aug. 1799, K 794.

7. See "Introduction," SE, K 210; M 24:71–76, K 370; and "VLJ," K 614.

8. See "On the Virginity of the Virgin Mary and Johanna Southcott," K 418; "VLJ," K 610; J 61:17–25, K 695; J 90:34, K 736; "On Cennini," K 779; and "EG," K 756; also "Ghost Abel," K 780.

9. See Northrop Frye, "Blake" in English Romantic Poets, ed. Carolyn and Laurence Houtchens (New York: New York University Press, 1957), p. 20 and n. 12 below.

10. From Henry Crabb Robinson, Remains in Blake, ed. Alfred Kazin (New York: Viking Press, 1949), p. 680.

11. See Blake's Job: William Blake's Illustrations to the Book of Job, ed. S. F. Damon (Providence, R. I.: Brown University Press, 1966), especially illustration XVII and J 55:30–35, K 686 and chap. 3, nn. 119 and 129.

12. See M 3:3–4, K 482; J 40:47, K 667; and J 70:19, K 709, for example. See also Rudolf Bultmann, Theology of the New Testament, trans. Kendrich Grobel, (New York: Charles Scribner's Sons, 1951 and 1955), 1:304–6.

13. See "VLJ," K 605–6, 613, and 617, for example.

14. See Ludwig Feuerbach, The Essence of Christianity, trans. George Eliot (New York: Harper and Row, 1957), pp. 25 ff; see also Karl Barth's "Introduction" to this edition, pp. xiv–xvi and xxv.

15. Yeats, for example, writes that "The Vision is my 'public philosophy.' My 'private philosophy' is the material dealing with the individual mind which came to me with that on which the mainly historical Vision is based." (The Letters of W. B. Yeats, ed. Alan Wade (London: Rupert Hart-Davis, 1954), Letter, to Ethel Mannin, 9 Oct. (?1938), p. 916).

16. This change was implicitly present in the dispute between taking the Eucharist literally, in which the actual body was immanent (as did Luther), or figuratively, as a commemoration in which the real body was no longer present (as did Zwingli), as discussed.

Bibliography

Adams, Hazard. "The Blakean Aesthetic," *JAAC* 13 (1954) : 233–48.

————. *William Blake: A Reading of the Shorter Poems.* Seattle: University of Washington Press, 1963.

————. *William Blake and W. B. Yeats: The Contrary Vision.* Ithaca, N.Y.: Cornell University Press, 1955.

Alspach, Russell. "Additions to Alan Wade's *Bibliography of W. B. Yeats.*" *Irish Book* 1 (Spring 1959).

Altizer, Thomas. "William Blake and the Role of Myth in the Radical Christian Vision," *CRAS* 9: 461–82.

————. *The New Apocalypse: The Radical Christian Vision of William Blake.* East Lansing, Mich.: Michigan State University Press, 1967.

Aquinas, St. Thomas. *On the Truth of the Catholic Faith: Summa Contra Gentiles, Book IV: Salvation.* Translated by Charles O'Neil. New York: Doubleday and Co., 1957.

————. *The Summa Theologica of St. Thomas Aquinas.* Literally translated by Fathers of the English Dominican Province. 20 vols. London: T. Baker Ltd., 1927.

Auerbach, Erich. *Mimesis.* Translated by Willard Trask. New York: Doubleday and Co., 1957.

————. *Scenes from the Drama of European Literature.* Translated by Ralph Manheim. New York: Meridian Books, 1959.

Augustine, Saint. *Basic Writings of S. Augustine.* Edited by Whitney Oates. 2 vols. New York: Random House, Inc., 1948.

————. *The City of God.* Translated by Marcus Dods. New York: 1950.

————. *The Enchiridion.* Translated by J. F. Shaw. Chicago: Henry Regnery Co., 1966.

————. *Sermons on the Liturgical Seasons.* Translated by Sister Mary Muldowney. New York: Fathers of the Church, 1959.

Bainton, R. H. *The Reformation of the Sixteenth Century.* Boston: Beacon Press, 1952.

Battenhouse, Roy, ed. *A Companion to the Study of St. Augustine.* New York: Oxford University Press, 1955.

Beer, John. *Blake's Humanism.* New York: Barnes and Noble, Inc., 1968.

Bentley, Gerald, ed. *Vala, or The Four Zoas, a Facsimile of the MS and a Transcript of the Poem and a Study of its Growth and Significance.* Oxford: Clarendon Press, 1963.

————, and Nurmi, Martin. *A Blake Bibliography.* Minneapolis: University of Minnesota Press, 1964.

————. *Blake Records.* Oxford: Oxford University Press, 1969.

Bettenson, Henry, ed. *Documents of the Christian Church.* 2nd ed. New York: 1963.

Boehme, Jacob. *The Works of Jacob Boehmen.* Edited by G. Ward and T. Langcake [Law's trans.] 4 vols. London: G. Robinson, 1764–81.

Blackstone, Bernard. *English Blake.* Cambridge: Cambridge University Press, 1949.

Blake, William. *The Complete Writings of William Blake, with Variant Readings.* Edited by Geoffrey Keynes. London: Oxford University Press, 1966.

————. *Blake's Grave.* Commentary by S. F. Damon. Providence: Brown University Press, 1963.

————. *Blake's Illustrations to the Bible.* Edited by Geoffrey Keynes. London: The Blake Trust, 1957.

————. *America.* Copy A. Pierpont Morgan Library, New York.

————. *America.* Copy C. Houghton Library, Harvard University, Cambridge, Mass.

————. *Catalogue of William Blake's Drawings and Paintings in the Huntington Library.* Edited by H. C. Baker; revised by R. R. Ward. San Marino, Calif.: Anderson, Ritchie and Simon, 1969.

————. *A Catalogue of the Works of William Blake in the Tate Gallery.* Edited by Martin Butlin, Anthony Blunt, and John Rotherstein. London: Heinemann, Ltd., 1957.

————. *A Descriptive Catalogue of an Exhibition of the Works of William Blake selected from Collections in the U.S.* Philadelphia: Philadelphia Museum of Art, 1939.

————. *Drawings of William Blake: 92 Pencil Studies.* Edited by Geoffrey Keynes. New York: Dover Press, 1970.

————. *Europe.* Copy C. Houghton Library, Harvard University, Cambridge, Mass.

————. *Jerusalem.* Facsimile Copy C. Edited by Geoffrey Keynes. London: The Blake Trust, 1952.

————. *Jerusalem.* Copy D. Houghton Library, Harvard University, Cambridge, Mass.

————. *Jerusalem.* Copy F. Pierpont Morgan Library, New York.

————. *Blake's Job: William Blake's Illustrations to the Book of Job.*

Edited by S. F. Damon. Providence: Brown University Press, 1966.

————. *The Marriage of Heaven and Hell*. Copy A. Houghton Library, Harvard University, Cambridge, Mass.

————. *The Marriage of Heaven and Hell*. Copy C. Pierpont Morgan Library, New York.

————. *The Marriage of Heaven and Hell*. Copy G. Houghton Library, Harvard University, Cambridge, Mass.

————. *The Marriage of Heaven and Hell*. Photographs of Facsimile Copy I. Edited by Clark Emery. Coral Gables: University of Miami Press, 1963.

————. *Milton*. Copy C. New York Public Library (Rare Book Room), New York.

————. *Milton*. Facsimile Copy D. London: The Blake Trust, 1967.

————. "Watercolour Illustrations to Milton's 'L'Allegro' and 'Il Penseroso' with Blake's Autograph Notes." Pierpont Morgan Library (Print Room), New York.

————. *William Blake: Poet, Painter, Prophet, A Study of the Illuminated Books*. Edited by Geoffrey Keynes. London: The Blake Trust, 1964.

————. *The Poetry and Prose of William Blake*. Edited by David Erdman and Harold Bloom. New York: Doubleday and Co., 1965.

————. *Songs of Innocence and Experience*. Facsimile Copy Z. Edited and with commentary by Geoffrey Keynes. London: The Blake Trust, 1967.

————. "There is No Natural Religion." [b] Copy D. Houghton Library, Harvard University, Cambridge, Mass.

————. "There is No Natural Religion." [b] Copy G*. Pierpont Morgan Library, New York.

————. "There is No Natural Religion." [b] Copy L. Pierpont Morgan Library, New York.

————. *Vala, or the Four Zoas, a Facsimile of the MS and a Transcript of the Poem and a Study of its Growth and Significance,* by Gerald Bentley. Oxford: Clarendon Press, 1963.

————. *The Art of William Blake. Bi-Centennial Exhibition at the National Gallery*. Washington, D.C.: Smithsonian Institute, 1957.

Blake Newsletter. Edited by Morton Paley. vol. 2, no. 4 (April 1969) through vol. 4, no. 2 (Fall 1970).

Blake Studies. Edited by Roger Easson and Kay Long. vol. 1, nos. 1 and 2 (Fall 1968 and Spring 1969); vol. 2, nos. 1 and 2 (Fall 1969 and Spring 1970).

Bloom, Harold. *Blake's Apocalypse*. New York: Doubleday and Co., 1963.

————, and Hilles, Frederick, eds. *From Sensibility to Romanticism*. New York: Oxford University Press, 1965.

————. *The Visionary Company.* New York: Doubleday and Co., 1963.

————. *Yeats.* New York: Oxford University Press, 1970.

Blunt, Anthony. *The Art of William Blake.* New York: Columbia University Press, 1959.

Bottrall, Margaret. *The Divine Image; a Study of Blake's Interpretation of Christianity.* Rome: Edizioni di Storia e Letteratura, 1950.

Bradford, Curtis. *Yeats at Work.* Carbondale, Ill.: Southern Illinois University Press, 1965.

Bronowski, Jacob. *William Blake and the Age of Revolution.* New York: Harper and Row, 1969.

————. *William Blake: 1757–1827: A Man without a Mask.* London: Secker and Warburg, 1943.

Brooke-Rose, Christine. *A Grammar of Metaphor.* London: Secker and Warburg, 1965.

Brown, N. O. *Life Against Death.* New York: Random House, 1959.

————. *Love's Body.* New York: Random House, 1968.

Buber, Martin. *Pointing the Way.* Translated by Maurice Friedman. New York: Harper and Row, 1963.

Bultmann, Rudolf. *Theology of the New Testament.* Translated by Kendrick Grobel. New York: Charles Scribner's Sons, 1955.

————. *History and Eschatology.* New York: Harper and Row, 1955.

Burke, Kenneth. *The Rhetoric of Religion: Studies in Logology.* Berkeley, Cal.: University of California Press, 1970.

Calvin, John. *Institutes of the Christian Religion.* Translated by John Allen. Philadelphia: Westminster Press, 1936.

————. *Theological Treatises.* Translated by J. K. Reid. Library of Christian Classics 22. Philadelphia: Westminster Press, 1954.

Carr, Rev. A. *The Gospel According to St. Matthew.* Cambridge: Cambridge University Press, 1888.

Case, Shirley J. *A Bibliographical Guide to the History of Christianity.* New York: P. Smith, 1951.

Catholic Encyclopedia, The. Edited by Charles Herberman "and numerous others." 15 vols. New York: Encyclopedia Press Inc., 1911.

Charles, Archdeacon R. H. *The Apocrypha and Pseudepigraphia of the Old Testament.* 2 vols. Oxford: Oxford University Press, 1963.

————. *A Critical and Exegetical Commentary on the Revelation of St. John.* 2 vols. New York: Charles Scribner's Sons, 1920.

————. *Eschatology.* New York: Schocken Books, 1963.

————. *Lectures on the Apocalypse.* Oxford: Oxford University Press, 1922.

Clark, Neville. *Interpreting the Resurrection.* Philadelphia: Westminster Press, 1967.

Clarke, John. *The God of Shelley and Blake.* London: J. M. Watkins, 1930.

Clements, Wolfgang. "Donne's Holy Sonnet 14." *MLN* 77 (1962):486–89.

Coffin, Charles. "Donne's Divinity." *Kenyon Rev.* 16 (1954): 292–98.

Cohn, Norman. *The Pursuit of the Millennium.* London: Secker and Warburg, 1962.

Cross, F. L., ed. *The Oxford Dictionary of the Christian Church.* London: Oxford University Press, 1958.

Damon, S. Foster. *A Blake Dictionary.* Providence: Brown University Press, 1965.

———. *William Blake: His Philosophy and Symbols.* Boston: Houghton Mifflin Co., 1924.

———. *A Note on the Discovery of a New Page of Poetry in William Blake's Milton.* Boston: Club of Odd Volumes, Merrymount Press, 1925.

Davies, J. G. *The Theology of William Blake.* Oxford: Oxford University Press, 1948.

Denzinger, Heinrich. *The Sources of Catholic Dogma.* Translated by Roy Deffarria. St. Louis: Herder, 1957.

Donne, John. *The Anniversaries.* Edited, with an introduction and commentary by Frank Manley. Baltimore: Johns Hopkin's University Press, 1963.

———. *Devotions on Emergent Occasions.* Edited by John Sparrow. Cambridge: Cambridge University Press, 1923.

———. *Devotions Upon Emergent Occasions.* Ann Arbor, Mich.: University of Michigan Press, 1965.

———. *Divine Poems.* Edited by Helen Gardner. Oxford: Clarendon Press, 1966.

———. *Elegies, Songs and Sonnets.* Edited by Helen Gardner. Oxford: Clarendon Press, 1966.

———. *Essays in Divinity.* Edited by Evelyn Simpson. Oxford: Oxford University Press, 1952.

———. *Sermons.* Edited by George Potter and Evelyn Simpson. 10 vols. Berkeley, Cal.: University of California Press, 1953–1962.

Donoghue, Denis, and Mulryne, J. R., eds. *An Honoured Guest: New Essays on W. B. Yeats.* New York: St. Martin's Press, 1966.

Early Christian Fathers. Translated and edited by Cyril Richardson, Eugene Fairweather, Edward Hardy, and Massey Shepherd. Library of Christian Classics, vol. 1. Philadelphia: Westminster Press, 1953.

Eliade, Mircea. *Cosmos and History.* Translated by Willard Trask. New York: Harper and Row, 1959.

————. *Myth and Reality*. Translated by Willard Trask. New York: Harper and Row, 1963.

————. *The Sacred and the Profane: The Nature of Religion*. Translated by Willard Trask. New York: Harcourt, Brace and World, 1959.

————. *The Two and the One*. Translated by J. M. Cohen. New York: Harper and Row, 1965.

Eliot, T. S. *The Complete Poems and Plays*. New York: Harcourt, Brace and World, 1952.

Ellmann, Richard. *Emminent Domain: Yeats Among Wilde, Joyce, Pound, Eliot and Auden*. New York: Oxford University Press, 1967.

————. *The Identity of Yeats*. New York: Oxford University Press, 1964.

————. *Yeats: The Man and the Masks*. New York: E. P. Dutton and Co., 1948.

Erdman, David. *A Concordance to the Writings of William Blake*. 2 vols. Ithaca, N.Y.: Cornell University Press, 1967.

————. "Dating Blake's Script: the 'g' hypothesis," *Blake Newsletter* 3, no. 1, (15 June 1969) : 8–13.

————. *William Blake: Prophet Against Empire*. Princeton, N.J.: Princeton University Press, 1954.

Eusebius. *The History of the Church from Christ to Constantine*. Translated by G. A. Williamson. Baltimore: Penguin Books, 1965.

Fackenheim, Emil. *The Religious Dimension in Hegel's Thought*. Boston: Beacon Press, 1970.

Farrell, Walter. *A Companion to the Summa Theologica*. 4 vols. New York: Sheed and Ward, 1951.

Ferrer, Austin. *A Rebirth of Images*. Boston: Beacon Press, 1963.

Feuerbach, Ludwig. *The Essence of Christianity*. Translated by George Eliot. New York: Harper and Row, 1957.

Fisher, Peter. *The Valley of Vision: Blake as Prophet and Revolutionary*. Edited by Northrop Frye. Toronto: University of Toronto Press, 1961.

Frye, Northrop. *Anatomy of Criticism*. Princeton, N.J.: Princeton University Press, 1957.

————. "Blake," *English Romantic Poets*. Edited by Carolyn and Laurence Houtchens. New York: New York University Press, 1957.

————, ed. *Blake: A Collection of Critical Essays*. Englewood Cliffs, N.J.: Prentice-Hall, 1966.

————. "Blake's 'Introduction to *Experience*.'" *HLQ* 21 (1957) : 57–67.

————. "Blake's Reading of the Book of Job." *William Blake: Essays for S. F. Ramon*. Edited by Alvin Rosenfeld. Providence, R.I.: Brown University Press, 1969, 221–34.

————. *Fables of Identity: Studies in Poetic Mythology.* New York: Harcourt, Brace and World, 1963.

————. *Fearful Symmetry.* Boston: Beacon Press, 1962.

————. "Notes for a Commentary on *Milton.*" *The Divine Vision.* Edited by Vivian de Sola Pinto. London: Gollencz, 1957. pp. 99–137.

————. *The Return of Eden.* Toronto: University of Toronto Press, 1965.

————, ed. *Romanticism Reconsidered.* New York: Columbia University Press, 1966.

————. *The Stubborn Structure.* London: Methuen, 1970.

————. "The Rising of the Moon: a Study of 'A Vision.'" *An Honoured Guest.* Edited by Denis Donoghue and J. R. Mulryne. New York: St. Martin's Press, 1966. pp. 8–33.

————. "The Top of the Tower." *Southern Rev.* 5, no. 3, n.s. (Summer 1969) : 850–71.

Gardner, Helen, ed. *John Donne: A Collection of Critical Essays.* Englewood Cliffs, N.J.: Prentice-Hall, 1962.

Gilchrist, Alexander. *Life of William Blake.* 2 vols. London: Macmillan, 1863.

Goodenough, Erwin. *By Light, Light: The Mystic Gospel of Hellenistic Judaism.* New Haven: Yale University Press, 1935.

Grant, John. *Discussions of William Blake.* Boston: D. C. Heath and Co., 1961.

Grossman, Allen. *Poetic Knowledge in the Early Yeats.* Charlottesville, Va.: University of Virginia Press, 1969.

Hagstrum, Jean. *William Blake: Poet and Painter.* Chicago: University of Chicago Press, 1964.

Hall, James, and Steinmann, Martin, eds. *The Permanence of Yeats.* New York: Collier Books, 1961.

Harnack, Adolf. *The History of Dogma.* Translated by Neil Buchanan. 7 vols. London: Williams and Norgate, 1894.

————. *Outlines of the History of Dogma.* Translated by E. K. Mitchell. Boston: Beacon Press, 1957.

Harper, George. *The Neo-Platonism of William Blake.* Chapel Hill, N.C.: University of North Carolina Press, 1961.

Hartman, Geoffrey. *Wordsworth's Poetry: 1787–1814.* New Haven: Yale University Press, 1964.

Hastings, James, ed. *Encyclopedia of Religion and Ethics.* 13 vols. New York: Charles Scribner's Sons, 1908–26.

Henn, Thomas. *The Lonely Tower.* London: Methuen, 1966.

Hirsch, Eric. *Innocence and Experience: An Introduction.* New Haven: Yale University Press, 1964.

Hirst, Désirée. *Hidden Riches: Traditional Symbolism from the Renaissance to Blake*. London: Eyre and Spottiswoode, 1964.

———. "On the Aesthetics of Prophetic Art." *British Journal of Aesthetics* 4 (1964) : 248–52.

Hone, Joseph. *W. B. Yeats: 1865–1939*. London: St. Martin's Press, 1962.

Hopkins, Gerard Manley. *A Hopkins Reader*. Edited by John Pick. New York: Doubleday and Co., 1966.

Houtchens, Carolyn, and Houtchens, Laurence. eds. *English Romantic Poets and Essayists*. New York: New York University Press, 1957.

Hughes, Richard. "The Woman in Donne's 'Anniversaries.'" *ELH* 34 (1967) : 307–26.

Irenaeus. *Five Books Against Heresies*. Translated by John Keble. London, 1872.

James, William. *Varieties of Religious Experience*. New York: New American Library, 1958.

Jeffares, A. Norman. *A Commentary on the Collected Poems of W. B. Yeats*. Stanford, Cal.: Stanford University Press, 1968.

———. *W. B. Yeats: Man and Poet*. New York: Barnes and Noble, 1949.

Jerusalem Bible. Edited by Alexander Jones. New York: Doubleday and Co., 1965.

Jesuit Fathers of St. Mary's College. *The Church Teaches*. St. Louis, Mo.: B. Herder, 1955.

Johnson, Ernest, ed. *Religious Symbolism*. New York, 1955.

Kazin. Alfred, ed. *Blake*. New York: Viking Press, 1940.

Kelly, J. N. D. *Early Christian Creeds*. New York: Longmans, Green, 1950.

Keast, William, ed. *Seventeenth Century English Poetry: Modern Essays in Criticism*. New York: Oxford University Press, 1962.

Kermode, Frank. *Romantic Image*. New York: Random House, 1964.

———. *The Sense of an Ending*. New York: Oxford University Press, 1967.

Keynes, Geoffrey. *A Bibliography of William Blake*. New York: Grolier Club of New York, 1921.

———, and Wolf, Edwin. *William Blake's Illuminated Books: A Census*. New York: Grolier Club of New York, 1953.

———. "Blake's Library," *TLS* (6 November 1959), p. 648.

———, ed. *John Milton: Poems in English with Illustrations by William Blake*. 2 vols. London: Nonesuch Press, 1926.

Kidd, B. J., ed. *Documents Illustrative of the Continental Reformation*. Oxford: Oxford University Press, 1911.

Leishman, J. B. *The Monarch of Wit.* New York: Harper and Row, 1966.

————. *Themes and Variations in Shakespeare's Sonnets.* New York: Harper and Row, 1966.

Lewis, R. W. B. *Trials of the Word.* New Haven: Yale University Press, 1965.

Lietzmann, Hans. *The Beginnings of the Christian Church.* Translated by Bertram Woolf. New York: Charles Scribner's Sons, 1949.

Lister, Raymond. *Beulah to Byzantium: A Study of Parallels in the Works of William Blake, W. B. Yeats, Samuel Palmer, and Edward Calvert.* No. II of the Dolmen Press Yeats' Centenary Papers. Dublin: Dolmen Press, 1965.

Luther, Martin. *A Compend of Luther's Theology.* Edited by Hugh Kerr. Philadelphia: United Lutheran Publication House, 1953.

————. *Luther's Works: Sermons.* Translated and edited by John Doberstein. Philadelphia: Muhlenberg Press, 1959.

————. *Works of Martin Luther.* Translated and edited by H. E. Jacobs. 6 vols. Philadelphia: A. J. Holman Co., 1915–32.

MacIntyre, Alasdair. *Secularization and Moral Change.* Oxford: Oxford University Press, 1967.

Margoliouth, Herschel. *William Blake.* Hamden, Conn.: Archer Books, 1967.

Martz, Louis. *The Poetry of Meditation.* New Haven: Yale University Press, 1962.

Marvell, Andrew. *Poems of Andrew Marvell.* Edited by Hugh MacDonald. Cambridge, Mass.: Harvard University Press, 1960.

Melchiori, Giorgio. *The Whole Mystery of Art: Pattern into Poetry in the Work of W. B. Yeats.* London: Rutledge, 1960.

Miller, J. Hillis. *Poets of Reality.* Cambridge, Mass.: Harvard University Press, 1965.

Milton, John. *Paradise Lost.* New York: Odyssey Press, 1937.

————. *Paradise Regained, Minor Poems, and Sampson Agonistes.* New York: Odyssey Press, 1937.

————. *Prose of John Milton.* Edited by Max Patrick. New York: Doubleday and Co., 1967.

Miner, Paul. "William Blake's 'Divine Analogy.'" *Criticism* 3, (Winter 1961): 46–61.

More, Paul, and Cross, Frank, eds. *Anglicianism.* Milwaukee, Wis.: Morehouse Publishing Co., 1935.

Morton, Arthur. *The Everlasting Gospel: A Study in the Sources of William Blake.* London: Laurence and Wishart, 1958.

New Catholic Encyclopedia. Prepared by Editorial Staff of the Catholic

University of America. 15 vols. New York: McGraw Hill, 1966.

Nock, Arthur D. *Early Gentile Christianity and its Hellenistic Background.* New York: Harper and Row, 1964.

———. *St. Paul.* New York: Harper and Row, 1963.

Nurmi, Martin. *Blake's Marriage of Heaven and Hell; a Critical Study.* Kent, Ohio: 1957.

Nygren, Anders. *Agape and Eros.* Translated by Philip Watson. London: S.P.C.K., 1953.

Otto, Rudolf. *The Idea of the Holy.* Translated by John Harvey. New York: Oxford University Press, 1958.

Panofsky, Erwin. *Tomb Sculpture: Four Lectures on Its Changing Aspects from Ancient Egypt to Bernini.* New York: H. N. Abrams, 1964.

Parkinson, Thomas. *W. B. Yeats: the Later Poetry.* Berkeley, Cal.: University of California Press, 1964.

Parrish, Stephen, and Painter, James, eds. *A Concordance to the Poems of W. B. Yeats.* Ithaca, N. Y.: Cornell University Press, 1966.

Percival, Milton. *William Blake's Circle of Destiny.* New York: Octagon Books, 1964.

Pinto, Vivian de Sola, ed. *The Divine Vision: Studies in the Poetry and Art of William Blake.* London: Gollancz, 1957.

Pope, Marvin, ed. *Anchor Job.* New York: Doubleday and Co., 1965.

Preston, Kerrison, ed. *The Blake Collection of W. Graham Robertson.* London: Faber, 1952.

Price, Martin. *To the Palace of Wisdom.* Carbondale, Ill.: University of Southern Illinois, 1964.

Raine, Kathleen. *Defending Ancient Springs.* New York: Oxford University Press, 1967.

———. *Blake and Tradition.* 2 vols. Princeton, N. J.: Princeton University Press, 1968.

———. *William Blake.* London: Thames and Hudson, 1970.

———. "Yeats' Debt to William Blake." *TQ* 8 (1965): iv, 165–81.

Rice, Eugene. *The Renaissance Idea of Wisdom.* Cambridge, Mass.: Harvard University Press, 1958.

Robinson, Henry Crabb. *Blake, Coleridge, Wordsworth, Lamb, etc. being Selections from the Remains of Henry Crabb Robinson.* Edited by Edith Morley. London: Manchester University Press, 1922.

Roe, Albert. *Blake's Illustrations to the Divine Comedy.* Princeton, N. J.: Princeton University Press, 1953.

Rose, Edward. "Mental Forms Creating: 'Fourfold Vision' and the Poet as Prophet in Blake's Design and Verse." *JAAC* 23 (1964): 173–83.

———. "The Structure of Blake's Jerusalem." *Bucknell Review* 11 (May 1963) : 35–54.

———. "The Symbolism of the Opened Center and Poetic Theory in Blake's Jerusalem." *Studies in English Literature* 5 (1965) : 587–606.

———. " 'Visionary Forms Dramatic': Grammatical and Iconographical Movement in Blake's Verse and Designs." *Criticism* 8 (1966) : 111–25.

Rosenfeld, Alvin, ed. *William Blake: Essays for S. Foster Damon.* Providence, R. I.: Brown University Press, 1969.

Rudd, Margaret. *Divided Image; a Study of William Blake and W. B. Yeats.* London: Routledge, 1953.

———. *Organiz'd Innocence; the Story of Blake's Prophetic Books.* London: Routledge, 1956.

Russell, Archibald. *The Engravings of William Blake.* London: J. Ritchards, Ltd., 1912.

Saul, George. *A Prolegomena to the Study of Yeats' Poems.* Philadelphia: Pennsylvania University Press, 1957.

Saurat, Denis. *Blake and Milton.* New York: Russell and Russell, 1965.

Scholem, Gershom. *Jewish Mysticism.* New York: Schocken Books, 1961.

———. *On the Kabbalah and its Symbolism.* New York: Schocken Books, 1969.

Schorer, Mark. *William Blake: The Politics of Vision.* New York: Random House, 1946.

Scott, Nathan. "Prolegomenon to a Christian Poetic." *Journal of Religion* 35 (October 1955) : 191–206.

Seeberg, Reinhold. *Textbook of the History of Doctrines.* Translated by Charles Haye. Grand Rapids, Mich.: Baker Book House, 1952.

Shakespeare, William. *Sonnets.* Edited by Douglas Bush. Baltimore: Penguin Books, 1961.

Singer, June. *The Unholy Bible: A Psychological Interpretation of William Blake.* New York: C. J. Jung Foundation, 1970.

Southern Review. W. B. Yeats' Memorial Issue, vol. 7, no. 3 (Winter 1941–42).

———. *W. B. Yeats: Critical Perspectives.* vol. 5 no. 3, (n.s.) (July 1969) : 831–935.

Stallworthy, Jon. *Between the Lines.* Oxford: Oxford University Press, 1963.

———. *Vision and Revision in Yeats's Last Poems.* Oxford: Oxford University Press, 1969.

Stendahl, Krister, ed. *Immortality and Resurrection.* New York: Macmillan, 1965.

Swedenborg, Emanuel. *Angelic Wisdom concerning the Divine Love and the Divine Wisdom.* New York: Swedenborg Foundation, 1941.

Swinburne, A. C. *William Blake.* New York: B. Bloom, 1967.

Tertullian. *De Resurrectione Carnis.* Translated and with Commentary by Ernest Evans. London: S.P.C.K., 1960.

Tillich, Paul. *Systematic Theology.* 3 vols. Chicago: University of Chicago Press, 1951–63.

———. *Theology of Culture.* New York: Oxford University Press, 1969.

Todd, Ruthven. *Tracks in the Snow.* London: Charles Scribner's Sons, 1946.

Unterecker, John, ed. *Yeats: a Collection of Critical Essays.* Englewood Cliffs, N. J.: Prentice-Hall, 1963.

Ure, Peter. *Towards a Mythology: Studies in the Poetry of W. B. Yeats.* London: Hodder and Stoughton, 1946.

Van Sinderin, Adrian. *William Blake: The Mystic Genius.* Syracuse, N. Y.: Syracuse University Press, 1949.

Vendler, Helen. *Yeats' Vision and the Later Plays.* Cambridge, Mass: Harvard University Press, 1963.

Verbeke, G. *L'évolution de la Doctrine du Pneuma.* Paris: Desclée de Brouwer, 1945.

Wade, Alan. *A. Bibliography of the Writings of W. B. Yeats.* London: Rupert Hart-Davis, 1958.

Whitaker, Thomas. *Swan and Shadow: Yeats' Dialogue with History.* Chapel Hill, N. C.: University of North Carolina Press, 1964.

Wicksteed, Joseph. *William Blake's Jerusalem: A Commentary.* London: The Blake Trust, 1954.

Wilder, Amos. *Theology and Modern Literature.* Cambridge, Mass.: Harvard University Press, 1958.

Williams, George. *The Radical Reformation.* Philadelphia: Westminster Press, 1962.

Williamson, George, "The Design of Donne's Anniversaries," *MP* 60 (1962): 183–91.

Willis, John, ed. *The Teachings of the Church Fathers.* New York: Herder and Herder, 1966.

Wilson, F. A. C. *Yeats' Iconography.* London: Gollancz, 1960.

———. *Yeats and Tradition.* London: Barnes and Noble, 1960.

Wilson, Mona. *The Life of William Blake.* London: Nonesuch, 1927.

Yeats, John B. *Letters to his Son W. B. Yeats and Others, 1899–1922.* Edited by Joseph Hone. London: Faber and Faber, 1945.

Yeats, William Butler. *Autobiography.* New York: Collier-Macmillan, 1965.

————. *The Collected Plays of W. B. Yeats.* New York: Macmillan, 1963.

————. *Essays and Introductions.* New York: Macmillan, 1961.

————. *Explorations.* New York: Macmillan, 1962.

————. *The Letters of W. B. Yeats.* Edited by Alan Wade. London: Rupert Hart-Davis, 1954.

————. *Letters on Poetry to Dorothy Wellesley.* New York: Oxford University Press, 1964.

———— and Moore, T. Sturge. *W. B. Yeats And T. S. Moore: Their Correspondence: 1901–1937.* Edited by Ursula Bridge. New York: Oxford University Press, 1953.

————. *Mythologies.* New York: Macmillan, 1959.

————, ed. *Poems of William Blake.* London: Muses' Library, 1910.

————. *Uncollected Prose of W. B. Yeats.* Edited by John Frayne. Vol. 1. New York: Columbia University Press, 1970.

————. *The Variorum Edition of the Poems of W. B. Yeats.* Edited by Peter Allt and Russell Alspach. New York: Macmillan, 1965.

————. *The Variorum Edition of the Plays of W. B. Yeats.* Edited by Russell Alspach. London: Macmillan, 1966.

————. *A Vision.* London: T. Werner Lourie, 1925.

————. *A Vision* (1938 ed.). New York: Macmillan, 1961.

————, and Ellis, Edwin, eds. *The Works of William Blake, Poetic, Symbolic, Critical.* 3 vols. London: Bernard Quaritch, 1893.

————, and Ruddock, Margot. *Ah, Sweet Dancer.* Edited by Roger McHugh. London: Macmillan, 1970.

Zwerdling, Alex. *Yeats and the Heroic Ideal.* New York: New York University Press, 1965.

Index